Thinking About Criminal Justice

Thinking About Criminal Justice

A Reader

First Edition

Edited by Dennis E. Hoffman
University of Nebraska, Omaha

cognella
SAN DIEGO

Bassim Hamadeh, CEO and Publisher
Jennifer Codner, Senior Field Acquisitions Editor
Anne Jones, Project Editor
Susana Christie, Senior Developmental Editor
Jeanine Rees, Production Editor
Asfa Arshi, Graphic Design Associate
Trey Soto , Licensing Specialist
Natalie Piccotti, Director of Marketing
Kassie Graves, Senior Vice President, Editorial
Jamie Giganti, Director of Academic Publishing

Printed in the United States of America.

cognella® | ACADEMIC PUBLISHING
3970 Sorrento Valley Blvd., Ste. 500, San Diego, CA 92121

Contents

Introduction

Do you get caught up in the high drama of criminal trials, like the trial of Derek Chauvin for the murder of George Floyd? Do you watch *Dateline* even though you know from watching previous episodes of this TV show that it's always the husband "whodunit"? Do you immerse yourself in portraits of the lives and the work of crime scene investigators on *CSI* because you can see yourself working in a crime lab? Do you feel a sense of injustice and outrage every time you watch a video of the police using deadly force against an unarmed person of color? Do you want to take your interest in criminal justice to the next level? The next level is beyond media stereotypes of cops, criminals, and victims. The next level is beyond "just the facts" about crime rates, incarceration rates, and racial disparities in criminal justice. The next level involves you in questioning long-standing criminal justice policies and sacred cows (i.e., ideas, customs, or practices assumed to be immune from criticism) of the criminal justice system.

A word of caution. The road to deeper understanding is paved by critical thinking. This road will be littered with roadblocks. You will be challenged. You will crash into barriers. Roadblocks will include:

- Egocentric thinking: viewing everything as "all about you" so that you can't empathize with others and can't step outside your own perspective to view things from another point of view.
- Groupthink: desiring harmony in a group or wanting to be popular in a group to the degree that you are inclined to conform to whatever a group thinks.
- Drone mentality: failing to pay attention to what is going on around you.

- Bias: showing prejudice in favor of or against one thing, person, or group, usually in a way considered to be unfair.
- Truthiness: assuming that a particular statement is true based on the intuition or perception of some individual or group, without regard to evidence, locale, or facts.

Think of these barriers as dragons in a videogame. By slaying the dragons, you can attain something more precious than gold—the capacity to think critically about criminal justice.

If you are new to critical thinking, here is a simple introduction to what it is and what it isn't.

Critical Thinking IS	Critical Thinking IS NOT
Skepticism	Memorizing
Questioning	Group thinking
Challenging reasoning	Blind faith
Making evidence-based judgments	Going on gut instincts and emotions
Uncovering biases	Stereotyping

In case you are wondering at this moment whether or not it is practical to center the study of criminal justice around critical thinking, just know that this is a good thing. It shows skepticism or doubt on your part. One of the traits of a critical thinker is skepticism. Nothing is more practical inside and outside criminal justice than critical thinking.

Much of a criminal justice professional's workday is spent asking questions. Questioning is at the heart of critical thinking. Examples of criminal justice professionals asking others for information include detectives interrogating suspects in criminal investigations; prosecutors and defense attorneys examining and cross-examining witnesses in criminal trials; and correctional counselors interviewing justice-involved people housed in jails and prisons to figure out what can be done to facilitate their reentry into society. Yet, it's a safe bet that few criminal justice professionals who have taken an introductory criminal justice course will report that taking such a course made them powerful critical thinkers. That's a missed opportunity.

What if you are not intending on becoming a criminal justice professional? What good is critical thinking for you?

Critical thinking spurs learning and the exchange of ideas. It fuels innovation and better performance. It allows you to take the perspective of others and gain a greater appreciation of the values of equity, inclusiveness, and diversity. And it can mitigate risk by uncovering unforeseen pitfalls and hazards. The development of critical-thinking skills is invaluable not only to criminal justice professionals but to everyone.

How to Do a Critical Thinking Scan (CTS)

IN MEDICINE, A COMPUTERIZED TOMOGRAPHY (CT) scan combines a series of X-ray images taken from different angles around your body and uses computer processing to create cross-sectional images (slices) of the bones, blood vessels, and soft tissues inside your body. CT scan images provide more detailed information than plain X-rays do. A CT scan has many uses, but it's particularly well-suited to quickly examine people who may have internal injuries from car accidents or other types of trauma. A CT scan can be used to visualize nearly all parts of the body and is used to diagnose disease or injury as well as to plan medical, surgical, or radiation treatment.

For criminal justice, the editors of this anthology use the terminology to refer to a multifaceted critical-thinking exercise that we invented. Ours is similar to a medical CT scan. Both involve perspective taking (i.e., looking at specimens or texts from various angles) and focusing internally (i.e., on logical fallacies inherent in a person's reasoning). We recommend that you use our CT scan, or CTS, for every reading in this anthology.

This is probably as good a time as any to throw our cards on the table. We want to be open and honest. In our experience, the major problems of the criminal justice system share a root cause: a lack of critical thinking. In our experience in the criminal justice system, reforming the system depends on citizens and policymakers having the capacity to think critically about alternative solutions. Too many criminal justice policymakers and decision makers do not reason through pressing issues and fail to take the time to evaluate policies and solutions from all sides.

Leaders often jump to conclusions or support a policy because it has a catchy name like "Three Strikes and You're Out." Even worse, legislators and other leaders in criminal justice support and provide funding to anticrime programs like DARE (Drug Abuse Resistance Education) despite evidence that the programs do not work. A lack of metacognition—or thinking about thinking—is also a major driver of problems in the criminal justice system.

Lack of thinking about thinking is especially evident in cases where criminal justice policymakers and decisionmakers choose to ignore evidence due to their overconfident attitude that they already know all the answers.

To help students get better at critical thinking, we created CTS. Based on our experience teaching students how to think critically about criminal justice, we have pulled together these five principals of critical thinking and wrapped them into a package we call CTS:

1. Ask questions.
2. Acknowledge bias.
3. Reason through logic.
4. Diversify thought.
5. Exhibit fair-mindedness.

Now, you might be thinking, "I already do these things." And maybe you do, but just not as deliberately and thoroughly as you could. Cultivating these five habits of mind go a long way in helping you become better at critical thinking.

1. Ask questions: Questioning is a uniquely powerful tool for thinking. It spurs learning and the exchange of ideas, it fuels innovation and performance, and it builds rapport and trust among team members. People do not ask enough questions. Why? People may be eager to impress others with their own ideas. Perhaps they aren't curious enough to ask. They may think they already know the answers. Or perhaps they worry that they will ask the wrong question and be viewed as stupid. Maybe the biggest inhibitor is that most people do not understand how beneficial good questioning can be. Of course, it's hard to question everything. Perhaps the most basic critical thinking question you need to ask when thinking critically about criminal justice is "How do you know you know what you think you know?" Philosophers call this "the epistemological question." *Epistemology* is the investigation of what distinguishes justified or warranted belief from mere opinion.
2. Acknowledge bias: A necessary step for a critical thinker is identifying their biases that might cloud or distort thinking. Bias is a tendency to believe that some people, ideas, and so on are better than others, which often results in treating some people unfairly. Explicit bias refers to attitudes and beliefs (positive or negative) that we consciously or deliberately hold and express about a person or group. Implicit bias includes attitudes and beliefs (positive or negative) about other people, ideas, issues, or institutions that occur outside of our conscious awareness and control, which affect our opinions and behavior. Everyone has implicit biases—even people who try to remain objective (e.g., judges and journalists). However, people can work to combat and change these biases. One type of bias we want you to be on the lookout for is confirmation bias. This is the subconscious tendency we all have to seek and interpret information and other evidence in ways that affirm our existing beliefs, ideas, expectations, or hypotheses. Often, confirmation bias involves "cherry-picking." *Cherry-picking* refers to taking or accepting only

those items or evidence that are consistent with our core ideas, beliefs, and values. At every level of our thinking, we need to pause and ask ourselves if we could be subject to any biases. This is not easy. It takes self-awareness. It requires us to reflect upon and evaluate what and how we are thinking. Similarly, institutions in the criminal justice system must be on the lookout for systemic bias. This is necessary to root out biased policies, such as drug laws and cash bail, that yield racial, gender, and class disparities and inequities in the criminal justice system. What is cash bail? On any given day, nearly half a million people languish in jail cells in the United States. They are waiting for their criminal cases to move forward even though they have not been convicted of a crime. People in pretrial detention now make up more than two thirds of America's jail population. They are presumed innocent, yet they suffer the harms of incarceration unless they have enough money to pay bail and buy their freedom.

3. Reason through logic: Years ago, one of the editors of this anthology, Dr. Hoffman, took on the task of trying to solve Nebraska's prison overcrowding problem. The state's prison population had been increasing for years. A common explanation attributed the rising prison population to more crime. Since there were few proven ways to reduce street crime, Hoffman was told that there wasn't much chance of reducing the prison population. It turned out that people had made the reasoning mistake of jumping to conclusions. That is, people had drawn a sweeping conclusion based on insufficient evidence. When Hoffman investigated alternative explanations for prison population growth, he discovered that criminal justice policies, not crime, were driving the rise in prison population. For the state of Nebraska, improving its reasoning helped policymakers improve the management of its prison population. Policies relating to admitting people to prison and releasing them from prison could be changed. So the moral of the story is to pay close attention to the chain of logic constructed by arguments that you read in this anthology. Is the argument supported by evidence? Is the evidence relevant to the argument? Being aware of common thinking fallacies can also allow you to think more logically. For instance, people often engage in what's known as post hoc thinking. In this fallacy, people believe that because Event Y followed Event X, Event Y must have been caused by Event X. But until that assumption is tested, there is no way to know if this is correct.
4. Seek diversity of thought: For many criminal justice professionals who want to understand the minds of justice-involved people, whether they be lawbreakers or victims, it makes sense to do some perspective-taking. That is, do your best to try to see things from the other person's point of view, imagining that you are in their shoes. Benefits of perspective-taking include increased altruism, decreased stereotyping, and a stronger connection with another person.
5. Exhibit fair-mindedness: *Fair-minded critical thinking* means an ability to reconstruct the strongest and most unprejudiced versions of points of view and frameworks of thought opposed to one's own perspective. It also requires you to reason honestly and impartially to determine when your own point of view is weaker and when an opposing point of view is stronger. Fair-mindedness entails a conscious effort to treat all viewpoints alike, without reference to one's

own feelings and self-interests or the feelings of others, such as a friend or organization. By including fair-mindedness in your approach to critical thinking, you automatically invoke a concern for justice. Fairness is an underlying element of the concept of justice.

Tips for using the CTS to analyze articles:

- Dig deep: An excellent CTS is much more than just "I liked the article," "I hated it," or "It bored me." Every reader brings different experiences and beliefs to the interactions with articles and other media. Pay attention to the emotions, observations, and questions you have as you read the articles in this anthology.
- Do a CTS for as many articles as possible: Why? Because critical thinking is a learned skill. By doing it, you learn it. It is like how you learn to ride a bike. You get on, fall off, and keep getting back on until you master it.
- Apply the CTS to other courses and other disciplines: The CTS allows you to take a deep dive into text and other material. It is much more than just snorkeling at the surface.
- Use the Template for Doing a CTS: When you write your CTS, the main headings should look like what follows, and what you write under each heading should address all the questions under each heading:

Your Name
Exact Word Count (Recommended Minimum=600 words; Okay to exceed 600 words)

Reading Number and Article Title

Personal Connection and Acknowledgment of Bias. How did you personally connect with the text of the article, and what biases do you bring with you? Complete this sentence fragment: "I can (or cannot) relate to this article because ..." What connection, if any, does this article have to your life and your personal history? What personal and/or political biases did you bring to the reading of this text? What feelings and emotions did you feel while reading the text?

My Thinking. What do you think of this article? Show your thinking. Pay attention to what goes through your mind as you read or observe. Think critically about your own reaction to the article. How did this article impact you? Did it teach you something? Confuse you? Challenge you? Reassure you? Move you? Make you angry? Specify details, quotes, or insights in the piece that made the biggest impression on you.

Reasons and Evidence. What reasons and evidence, if any, does the author supply in support of their main argument or arguments? What reasons and evidence, if any, did you supply to back up any claims you made in My Thinking?

Perspective-Taking. Did the author or authors of the article present a one-sided argument? A *one-sided argument* is an informal fallacy that occurs when only the reasons supporting a claim or argument are supplied while all reasons opposing it are omitted. What different perspectives, frames of reference, theories, and points of view did the authors use? What did you learn from the author's use of multiple perspectives that you would not have learned if the authors had made a one-sided argument? Do you have a perspective on this issue or problem that differs from the authors? If so, what is it?

My Textual Analysis. Pick out four passages in the reading that challenge your thinking and take you out of your comfort zone. Free write about each passage. Tell what you are thinking and feeling about each passage. When you write about each passage, **type the passage in bold so the passage stands out**.

Impact. How did doing the CTS change your mind, broaden your awareness, confirm what you already knew, or debunk your previous take on this subject? How would you rate your own job of asking questions throughout the CTS? What was the ratio of the number of claims you made to the number of questions you asked?

A Note on Grading, Grades, and Rubrics

How can you and your professor assess your work using the CTA? Would a rubric help? A *rubric* is a scoring tool that explicitly represents the performance expectations for an assignment. A rubric divides the assigned work into parts and describes the characteristics of the work associated with each part at varying levels of performance mastery. We supply a rubric so that either you can grade yourself or your professor can grade you.

We recommend the holistic grading of each CTS. *Holistic grading* is a method of evaluating a piece of work based on its overall quality. It is also known as single-impression scoring.

The criteria we recommend you use to grade each CTS include (a) accuracy of content; (b) comprehensiveness or completeness; and (c) clarity and readability. Full points means you met all the criteria, you answered all the questions associated with each of the five principals of critical thinking, you reached or exceeded the minimum word count, and you understand the material thoroughly. Half points means parts of the CTS are inaccurate, incomplete, and/or incomprehensible. Zero points means the CTS is unacceptable because it either does not meet the minimum word count, fails to meet my three grading criteria, or fails to address all the questions associated with each of the five principals of critical thinking.

Using a rubric makes assessing and grading fast and easy.

Why does it make grading and grades so easy?

Because thinking critically is like swinging a golf club. Both swinging a golf club and thinking critically about criminal justice are difficult. Supposedly, there are seven things to remember when swinging a golf club, including keeping your eye on the ball. Thinking critically about criminal justice is even more complicated. Our CTS streamlines the process by asking you to concentrate on doing five things.

Unit I

What Is Criminal Justice?

Introduction to Unit I

What do the words "criminal justice' mean to you? Criminal justice has different meanings. It can be defined as a system, a career, or as an academic discipline. In exploring meanings of criminal justice, context matters. *Context* refers to the environment or setting in which something (e.g., a word, an event, or a system) exists. When we contextualize something, we place it in an appropriate setting or set of circumstances, one in which it may be properly considered. Context matters.

Take, for example, the legal context of the murder of George Floyd. The signature event for recent criminal justice history has been the Minneapolis police killing of George Floyd, an unarmed African American man, on May 25, 2020. Ex-Minneapolis police officer Darren Chauvin was charged with Floyd's murder and accused of using too much deadly force to restrain Floyd. Part of Chauvin's defense was to blame the victim. Chauvin's defense attorneys tried to pin the cause of Floyd's death on Floyd's use of drugs. In Chauvin's trial, both the prosecution and defense introduced mountains of evidence to sway the jury. Ultimately, the jury found Chauvin guilty of murdering Floyd.

But what if we take the murder of George Floyd out of its legal context and see it in a broader historical context? Amy Frykholm's interview with legal scholar and social activist Michelle Alexander in the article "Criminal Injustice" contextualizes criminal justice. In Reading 1.2, Alexander explains how mass incarceration has been the lynchpin of American crime control policy over the past several decades. It has been the elephant in the room. By plugging you into the conversation between Frykholm and Alexander, we deepen your understanding of the defining civil rights problem of recent decades—mass incarceration.

The existence of different meanings of criminal justice is emphasized in Unit I. For example, both Dennis E. Hoffman's "Racialized Bias in Introductory Criminal Justice Textbooks" and Ruth Peterson's "Interrogating Race, Crime, and Justice" focus on criminal justice/criminology as a discipline. These readings afford students a chance to dive deep, to ask questions as to how the various social realities of criminal justice are constructed and to ask questions about how criminal justice advantages some groups while disadvantaging other groups.

So let's hit the pause button. What questions do you have at this point?

After reading the title of Hoffman's article, for instance, did you ask yourself, "Who cares? Why should I care if the textbook I am required to read for an introductory criminal justice textbook is biased?"

Americans place great faith in textbooks as a means of providing students with a basic understanding of a variety of subjects. To a significant extent, textbooks define and determine what is important and what is deemed worth of knowing. Yet textbooks do not deserve their reputation as impartial educational tools that simply teach students facts and skills.

Criminal justice textbooks as well as textbooks covering other subjects incorporate attitudes and ways of looking at the world. In making judgments about what should be included and what should be excluded, and how particular issues should be framed, textbook authors assign positive or negative interpretations to particular events, thereby asserting a set of values. The fact that these values are often not declared explicitly, but remain implicit, does not make them less powerful.

You should never consider criminal justice knowledge as something that is objectively out there in a value-free sort of way. Instead, think of criminal justice ideas and perspectives as reflecting specific values and interests that scholars and researchers bring to the social construction of knowledge. Different interests lead to the construction of different ways of knowing that influence our perceptions of criminal justice.

Let's explain it another way. Introductory criminal justice textbooks are more than collections and classifications of facts. As any good lawyer knows, it is possible to present biased arguments that can be dressed up to appear factual. By the careful choice of what facts to include or exclude, it is possible to construct arguments that can be wholly one-sided yet can be asserted to "fit the facts." Textbooks are influenced by the political, ideological, or moral beliefs of their authors. Usually, these beliefs support the status quo, dominant groups in society, and mainstream understandings about which criminal justice reforms are reasonable or feasible.

Hoffman's principal concern is with the presentation by introductory criminal justice textbooks of issues that are important to understanding the nexus between criminal justice and racism in the United States. In Reading 1.3, "Racialized Bias in Introductory Criminal

Justice Textbooks," Hoffman identifies racially biased themes in textbooks. He also presents proposals for reducing racial bias in criminal justice texts.

Like Hoffman's article, Ruth Peterson's "Interrogating Race, Crime, and Justice" zeroes in on the discipline. In Reading 1.4, Peterson picks up where Hoffman's article left off. She celebrates the contributions of scholars of color to the study of crime and criminal justice. She also emphasizes that African Americans are joined in their efforts by scholars of multiple other ethnicities.

Unlike Hoffman, Peterson goes beyond issues of race/ethnicity within criminal justice/criminology as an academic discipline to acknowledge the lethal violence between police and people of color that has typified unrest, racial tension, and political protest in U.S. society. Peterson seeks to make the discipline relevant, offering recommendations regarding how scholars might proceed with their research so as to inform debates about crime policy.

Let's pause. What questions do you have? What if you have no questions? Then what? Whenever you get to the point where you have no more questions, ask "What's missing?"

What's missing is a discussion of Reading 1.1, Paula Jones and Debbie Haydon's "Learning to Think Critically." Why do you think we are talking about the first selection last?

Could it be because we want you to benefit from the recency effect? The *recency effect* is a cognitive bias in which those items, ideas, or arguments that come last are remembered more clearly than those that came first. In jury psychology, for example, the more recently something is heard, the clearer something may exist in a juror's memory. As a result of the recency effect, the side delivering the final closing argument in a criminal trial—the defense—has an advantage.

What we want you to remember while reading this anthology are a few simple points:

- Critical thinking is an essential part of criminal justice.
- To improve as a critical thinker, you must practice, practice, practice.
- As you use CTS to practice, periodically flip back to the Introduction, How to Do a CTS, and Reading 1.1 to remind yourself what critical thinking is and how to do it.

Reading 1.1

Learning to Think Critically

Dr. Paula Jones and Dr. Debbie Haydon

Critical thinking involves questioning and reasoning skills. Educators strive to teach students how to ask good questions, analyze information, and advance their knowledge in the fields they are studying. Through technology, the amount of information available today is indeed massive and readily available for students to access. However, it is imperative for learners to become skilled at critically evaluating and analyzing this large pool of information. The ultimate goal in learning better critical thinking skills is to avoid becoming passive receptors of information. Students can benefit from learning proven methods that help them weed through the information and make sense of the facts and opinions presented on any given topic. Educators strive to help students learn how to make sound evaluations of information presented instead of passively accepting it as fact. Students need to have opportunities within lessons that permit them to develop reasoning skills. Opportunities within lessons may require students to sort through information, analyze information and resources, and make sound decisions. One challenge facing educators today is how to teach students to take information, reason through it, and use the information to solve problems and think critically.

Some say that students in higher educational institutions are *adrift*. In a recent book titled *Academically Adrift*, the authors report on a study that followed over 2,300 students at 24 different college institutions over a 4-year period (Arum & Roksa, 2011). The purpose of the study was to measure what students had learned after 2 and 4 years of college. The authors' research included survey responses, transcripts, and a standardized test administered in the students' first semester and then again at the end of their second year of college. Arum and Roksa (2011) reported that students who participated in this study had not learned the critical thinking, reasoning, and written communication skills expected of college graduates. In fact, the results showed that 45% of the students made no significant improvement in their critical thinking and reasoning skills during the first 2 years of college. In addition, after 4 years of college, 36% of students showed no significant gains in higher order thinking skills.

This is a significant finding with implications about how employable graduates might be in regard to the skills sought in the current workforce. Today's employers are asking for colleges and universities to do more in developing students' skills in using real-world problem-solving techniques. In fact, based on a study conducted in 2009, employers seek employees who can demonstrate they have the ability to solve problems, are resourceful, and can offer a richer skill set to their employers (Humphreys, 2010). In another study that surveyed 302 employers, Marklein (2010) reported that 81% of the employers expected higher education institutions to place more emphasis on developing student critical thinking skills. Based on these research studies, it is evident that educational institutions need to devote more time and resources to aid students in developing their problem solving, reasoning, and critical thinking skills.

What is Critical Thinking?

According to Elder (2007), "critical thinking is self-guided, self-disciplined thinking which attempts to reason at the highest level of quality in a fair minded way" (para. 7). To expand this definition, critical thinking is a manner of thinking about any topic or problem where the thinker attempts to improve the quality of his or her thinking. Nosich (2009) indicates that critical thinking is defined using four key areas. He states that critical thinking is reflective, involves standards in which thinking is evaluated, is authentic, and involves being reasonable. So, one could rationalize that critical thinking would involve *reflective thinking* or thinking about one's own thinking in order to justify decisions being made. Elder and Paul (2008) agree that critical thinking is where the thinker attempts to analyze their own thinking based on clear standards.

From the instructor's point of view, teaching students to think critically might include teaching students key standards used to evaluate their own thinking. Teachers may also want to provide opportunities for students to question their own answers. In other words, critical thinking skills include an intended focus placed on questioning used to evaluate the answers as opposed to just evaluating the answers to questions originally assigned.

Critical thinking does not focus on being critical or negative (Nosich, 2009). Instead, critical thinking depends on developing a combination of skills to think through and problem solve in a fair-minded way. Nosich (2009) writes that to learn to think critically is to learn to think things through and to think them through well. Critical thinking involves thinking about our thinking. Therefore, critical thought would include thinking accurately, clearly, sufficiently, and reasonably (2009).

Why Adopt a Model for Critical Thinking?

The ultimate goal for most educational settings is to better prepare students to reason, think analytically, and to communicate more effectively. One of the first challenges a school faces is how to achieve this goal. Usually, the "how" involves more than reading books, listening to instructions, or even working in groups. What educators need is a proven method or model that is used to develop thinking skills.

Selecting and implementing a critical thinking model is one way to provide successful implementation methods to develop students' thinking skills. This is an important first step that allows schools to plan and organize training and professional development opportunities for faculty and staff. Using a proven critical thinking model also encourages the use of a common language in methods used for developing critical thinking skills across a variety of disciplines. Having a common language is important from both the faculty and student perspectives. For example, when a student is introduced to a critical thinking model in one course, it is helpful for the student to see similar graphics of the model as well as to hear and read consistent language across other courses. Using consistent language and graphics to explain the critical thinking model permits students to understand and buy into the model as it applies to the specific course. Using the common language also prepares students to apply the model in other classes, especially when the other courses teach or demonstrate the same model. The students may begin to see that the method works. They may also begin to see that the model works in a variety of disciplines that helps make the model useful in developing skills of thinking and reasoning in real-life settings. Using a common language supports faculty, students, and staff in communicating about the model with others.

Using a critical thinking model provides a set of tools that could be used to support students in developing thinking skills. In addition, a model supports effective methods of developing critical thinking skills across various disciplines. The Paul and Elder model includes three components: (1) the Elements of Thought; (2) the Intellectual Standards to measure quality of thinking; and (3) the Intellectual Traits that set the goal of developing specific traits. Each component serves a different but equally important role in supporting the development of critical thinking and reasoning skills. Therefore, there is a need to take a moment to briefly define each component and the role it serves.

According to Paul and Elder (2009), thinking or thought can be broken into *elements*. Elements of thought include an examination of the components that allow one to reason. Using the Elements of Thought does not imply there is a starting place. In fact, that is why the model is displayed in a circle. The analysis of one's reasoning is an ongoing process and can begin at any of the elements displayed. To use the Elements of Thought, one must understand that all reasoning has the following elements in common:

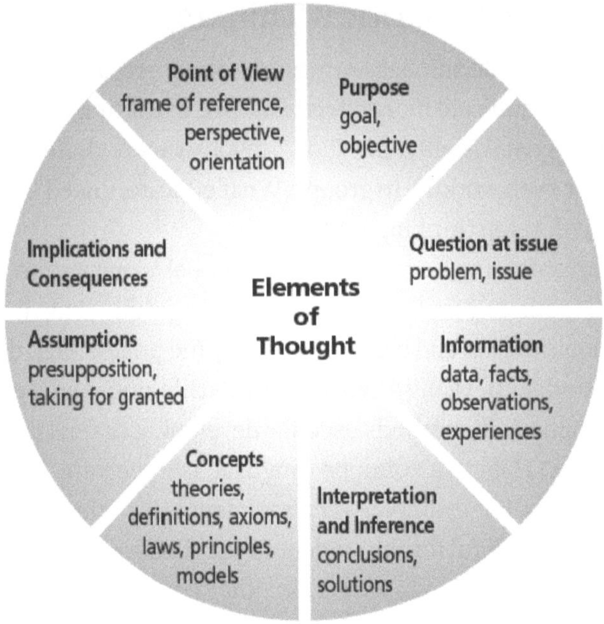

FIGURE 1.1.1 Elements of Thought.

- All reasoning or thought has a purpose.
- All reasoning has a primary question or problem at issue.
- All reasoning includes some form of information or data.
- All reasoning is subject to interpretation and inferences to form conclusions.
- All reasoning is influenced by concepts, theories, principles, or models.
- All reasoning is subject to assumptions.
- All reasoning leads to some type of implication or consequence.

The Elements of Thought have the potential to be a valuable tool for educators because the elements provide a scaffold of reasoning composed of eight components. These components can be used to allow a person to analyze their thinking or reasoning. In addition, these Elements of Thought are deeply connected and, if changed, will impact the other elements. For example, if the purpose of the thought is changed, then the question or problem being addressed must be changed. This would then imply that the information or data needed to answer the question must change as well. Therefore, by changing any one of the Elements of Thought, all of the other elements would be impacted.

Assessment of Thought

Thinking is generally evaluated by a set of standards. Depending on the person's perspective or experiences, the standards may vary. However, Paul and Elder (2009) suggest that when we analyze our thinking, we should strive to assess our thinking using a set of standards called the Intellectual Standards, as identified in Figure 1.1.2. The questions displayed alongside each standard are used as a guide for achieving that specific standard.

According to Paul and Elder (2009), using the Elements of Thought to break down and analyze thinking and using the Intellectual Standards to assess thinking should lead to the ultimate goal of developing Intellectual Traits associated with good thinking skills.

Paul and Elder (2009) believe that critical thinking is more than just a set of skills. Critical thinking also involves specific traits that should be supported and encouraged through

Clarity	Could you elaborate further? Could you give me an example? Could you illustrate what you mean?
Accuracy	How could we check on that? How could we find out if that is true? How could we verify or test that?
Precision	Could you be more specific? Could you give me more details? Could you be more exact?
Relevance	How does that relate to the problem? How does that bear on the question? How does that help us with the issue?
Depth	What factors make this a difficult problem? What are some of the complexities of this question? What are some of the difficulties we need to deal with?
Breadth	Do we need to look at this from another perspective? Do we need to consider another point of view? Do we need to look at this in other ways?
Logic	Does all this make sense together? Does your first paragraph fit in with your last? Does what you say follow from the evidence?
Significance	Is this the most important problem to consider? Is this the central idea to focus on? Which of these facts are most important?
Fairness	Do I have any vested interest in this issue? Am I sympathetically representing the viewpoints of others?

FIGURE 1.1.2 Intellectual Standards.

self-questioning techniques. These Intellectual Traits are associated directly with being able to critically analyze a situation or problem from different perspectives in a fair-minded way. Paul and Elder identify these Intellectual Traits as (1) intellectual humility, (2) intellectual courage, (3), intellectual empathy, (4) intellectual integrity, (5) intellectual perseverance, (6) faith in reason, and (7) fairmindedness (Figure 1.1.3).

Teaching students to think critically has benefits. A well-cultivated thinker raises vital questions. A strong problem solver comes to well-reasoned conclusions and solutions, testing them against relevant criteria and standards. A critical thinking student thinks open-mindedly and sees things from different perspectives—assessing their own assumptions as they work through information to solve a problem or find a solution. A critical thinker communicates effectively regarding the solutions identified and methods used to come to those conclusions or solutions.

[...] good thinking or problem solving cannot really be done in isolation. Therefore, educators need to establish and facilitate opportunities to communicate, self-reflect, and seek feedback from others during a course. The Paul and Elder model may prove to support the development of teamwork skills as well as critical thinking skills. As students think through and analyze their reasoning, they may benefit from the opportunity to talk through their

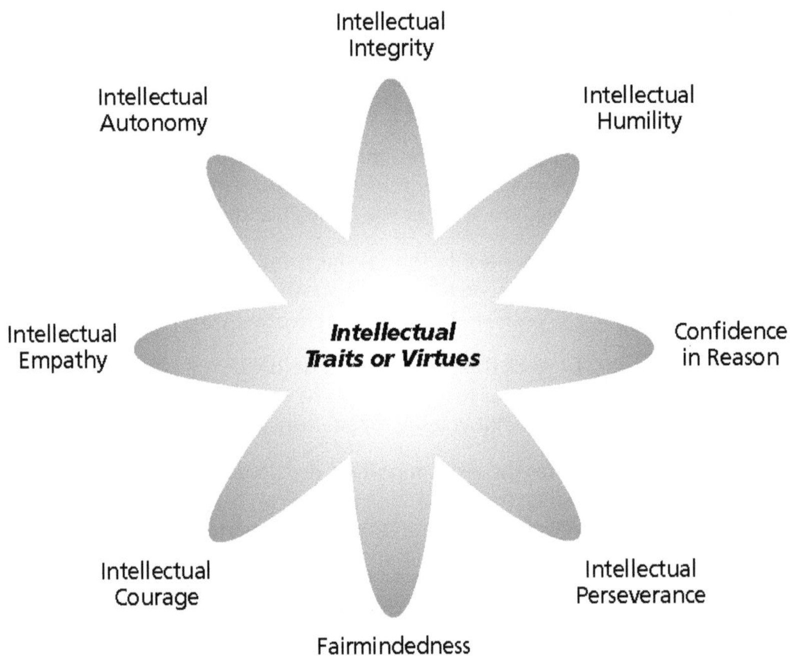

FIGURE 1.1.3 Intellectual Traits.

questions or their suggestions or ideas with others, just as professionals in a particular field of study would do.

References

Arum, R., & Roksa, J. (2011). *Academically adrift: Limited learning on college campuses*. University of Chicago Press.

Elder, L. (2007). Another brief conceptualization of critical thinking. Critical Thinking Community website, retrieved from http://www.criticalthinking.org/aboutCT/define_critical_thinking.cfm.

Elder, L., & Paul, R. (2008). *The thinker's guide to Intellectual Standards: The words that name them and the criteria that define them*. Foundation for Critical Thinking.

Elder, L., & Paul, R. (2009). *The aspiring thinker's guide to critical thinking*. Foundation for Critical Thinking.

Humphreys, M. (2010). Employers seek more college-educated workers with higher levels of learning and broader sets of skills, new survey reveals. Association of American Colleges and Universities website retrieved from http://www.aacu.org/press_room/press_releases/2010/employersurvey.cfm.

Marklein, M. (2010). Group urges improved value, breadth of college degrees. *USA Today*. Retrieved from http://www.usatoday.com/news/education/2010-01-21-collegelearning21_ST_N.htm.

Nosich, G. (2009). *Learning to think things through: A guide to critical thinking across the curriculum*. Pearson Education.

Reading 1.2

Criminal Injustice

Amy Frykholm

IN HER 2010 BOOK the new Jim Crow: Mass Incarceration in the Age of Colorblindness, *civil rights lawyer Michelle Alexander examines the practices and policies that have quintupled the U.S. prison population over the past 40 years. She argues that these policies have created a permanent underclass of disenfranchised convicted felons who are overwhelmingly black and Latino. Alexander has worked for the American Civil Liberties Union and was a clerk for Supreme Court Justice Harry Blackmun. She teaches at the Moritz College of Law at Ohio State University.*

How did you begin your research into the patterns of racial discrimination and social control that you call the "new Jim Crow"?

I was inspired by my experience working as director of the Racial Justice Project for the ACLU in California. I was representing victims of racial profiling and police brutality and investigating patterns of drug enforcement in poor communities of color. I was also working with people who were being released from prison to reenter a society that had never had much use for them. I awakened to the reality that our criminal justice system functions more as a system for racial control than as a system for crime prevention. I found out that what I thought I knew about the criminal justice system—and I thought I knew quite a bit; I was a lawyer, after all—was sheer myth.

I believed, for example, that the explosion in our prison population could be explained primarily by poverty, poor schools and broken homes—conventional explanations offered by the media and mainstream politicians. Back then I thought that blacks were more likely to use and sell illegal drugs than whites. I thought that the War on Drugs was aimed primarily at rooting out violent offenders and drug kingpins. I also believed that although life might be difficult for people after they are released from prison, those who worked hard and had self-discipline could make it.

Amy Frykholm, "Criminal Injustice," *The Christian Century*, vol. 129, no. 10, pp. 22–25.

I came to realize that the explosion in our prison population, especially the explosion in the number of blacks in prison, is not driven by crime or crime rates. People of all colors use and sell illegal drugs at the same rates. The War on Drugs does not root out violent offenders. On the contrary, the people who come into the criminal justice system through the drug war are not violent and arc arrested on relatively minor drug offenses—the same kinds of offenses that occur frequently in middle-class white communities and are largely ignored.

Those released from prison are trapped in a legal second-class status for life. Finding work is not just difficult after prison; it is downright impossible. Ex-offenders are locked out of the legal economy. They are denied access to public housing; they are denied food stamps. And to make matters worse, they are saddled with hundreds of thousands of dollars in fees, fines, court costs—and often the need to pay back child support. Paying all of these fees can be a condition of parole.

I came to see that we have, yet again, created a vast new legal system for racial and social control, a penal system unprecedented in world history—a system that locks the majority of black men in many urban areas into a permanent underclass status And yet we claim, as a nation, to be colorblind.

What made this system of social control possible?

The system of mass incarceration was born out of our nation's racially divisive politics. The War on Drugs was part of the Republican Party's "southern strategy." That strategy used racially coded "get tough" language on issues of crime and welfare to appeal to poor and working-class whites, especially in the South where whites were anxious about the gains made by African Americans in the civil rights movement. When President Ronald Reagan declared his War on Drugs, it was an effort to make good on campaign promises to get tough on crime. Subtly, the enemy in the war became racially defined.

The courts rallied to facilitate the War on Drugs by eviscerating Fourth Amendment protections against unwarranted searches and seizures and by dosing the courthouse doors to claims of racial bias at every stage in the criminal justice process, from searches to sentencing.

Legislators began to compete with each other over who could be tougher on crime. Democrats and Republicans alike began supporting harsh new mandatory minimum sentences for minor drug offenses, sentences even harsher than murderers receive in other Western democracies.

At its core, this system is supported by a deliberate indifference to people who are thought of as the other, people living in ghettoized communities, people who we consciously and perhaps even more often unconsciously imagine to be no good, not worthy of our care and concern, to be largely disposable, to be beyond redemption. Unconsciously willing to believe the worst possible things about "those people," we've been able to turn a blind eye as we've passed these laws and ushered people into a permanent underclass.

How is colorblindness a problem?

People typically think of colorblindness as a virtue; to say "I don't care if he is black" is considered a good thing. But it can also be a form of cruelty. It can be a way of being indifferent to the experiences of racial groups.

Colorblindness can be a way of dismissing an important dimension of a person's experience and the experience of a community. This blindness and indifference allow many of us to turn away from those who are desperately in need of our care, compassion and concern.

What role has the privatization of prisons played?

Mass incarceration was not the result of a profit motive. It was born out of our nation's racial divisions and anxieties. But once the race to increase incarceration began, it quickly became apparent to corporations and to a range of private interests that profits could be made from caging human beings. Private prison companies were born, and they are doing quite well on the New York Stock Exchange in a time of economic recession.

Some companies now use prison labor rather than send jobs overseas. They can use prison labor because even though the 13th Amendment abolishes slavery, it makes an exception for forced labor in prison. These companies can avoid minimum wage laws and the usual costs of labor.

There are corporate interests, like phone companies, that charge exorbitant costs for services to prisoners and their families. Private health-care companies do a great business through their contracts with prisons, though they usually provide substandard care to people behind bars. There are also the Taser gun manufacturers.

We also have to consider public organizations like prison guard unions. Those groups don't just lobby for higher wages and better working conditions; they lobby for harsh mandatory minimum sentences that provide job security. There are entire communities—mostly rural and white—whose economic growth and stability are based on prisons. Most new construction of prisons has been in these communities. Although prisons are often advertised as providing far more benefits to their communities than they actually deliver, the reality is that many of these communities now view prisons as essential to their economic health.

How do we make sense of the fact that it is cheaper to pay for four years of tuition to Princeton University than to incarcerate someone, and yet we are willing over and over again to pay this exorbitant social and financial cost?

It was not a rational policy debate that led to the decision that we would incarcerate 2.5 million Americans and place another 7 million under correctional control. It was a system developed by emotionally and racially charged politics that are misinformed. The system we have is a reflection of our divisions, our anxieties, our social impulses, our conscious and unconscious racial biases.

PHOTO 1.2.1 CONSCIOUS AND UNCONSCIOUS BIAS: Alexander's work has focused on racial disparity in the criminal justice system.
Photo Courtesy of Zocalo Public Square

We've known for decades that it is far cheaper to invest in education than incarceration. The billions of dollars for incarceration would be better spent on sending young people to good schools and colleges, rather than locking them up at early ages. Yet we continue to do it.

The New York police department just reported that in the year 2010, officers stopped and frisked 600,000 people; 90 percent of these people were African American and Latino, and less than 15 percent of these stops occurred in response to any sign of criminal activity.

Hundreds and thousands of people—mostly black and Latino young men—are being stopped, searched and frisked as a matter of routine. The data show a virtual police state in some communities that saddles young people with criminal records for having a little weed on them—all but guaranteeing that they will be locked out of the legal economy. Then we wonder why we have a recidivism rate of 70 percent. It is because we have constructed a system that is irrational and counterproductive.

Obviously changes in the legal system are needed, but you say they are woefully insufficient. Why is that?

Many people just focus on the size of the prison population when discussing the question of mass incarceration. For example, they say if we reduce prison sentences, then we can reduce the prison population by a third or a quarter or a half or whatever the target is.

But simply changing the length of prison sentences does not in any way dismantle this caste-like system. The system depends on the prison label, not just prison time. We could reduce the prison population in half by cutting sentence length, but if people, upon release, still face all of this legal discrimination, they will cycle back in and out of prison. They may stay for a shorter amount of time.

As long as we have a drug war raging, we are going to have people swept into the system at very young ages, usually before they are old enough to vote. They acquire criminal records that will follow them through their whole lives, relegating them to a second-class status by law.

To think about ending mass incarceration, we've got to think about much more than reducing the amount of prison time. In my view, that scale of change cannot be just about prison time or about saving state governments money. We've got to change an entire mind-set. We've got to learn to view poor folks of color, who have been so demonized in recent decades, with the same level of compassion that we extend to people we perceive to be "like us."

If we were just to return to the incarceration rates of the 1970s, before the War on Drugs and the get-tough movement began, we would have to release four out of five of the people in prison today. A million people employed by the criminal justice system would lose their jobs. To talk in a serious way about ending the system means grappling with its scale. It is going to require a new public consensus that the lives of poor kids in the 'hood are equally valuable as the lives of the kids populating our college campuses.

You've said that many strategies of the civil rights era are ineffective in the new regime. Why?

In recent decades, civil rights advocacy moved from the streets and churches to courtrooms and behind-the-scenes negotiations with legislators. We've delegated lawyers as spokespeople of the movement, as opposed to community members and faith leaders. This means that the movement is less connected to the communities it claims to represent and has lost its moral authority. For understandable reasons, civil rights lawyers became very invested in affirmative-action programs, which helped a relative few but exacerbated the divisions and tensions between poor and working class along racial lines. Those programs resulted in a sprinkling of people of color attending elite universities and created an illusion of progress. The colorblind rhetoric contributed to all of us being deluded that we are on the road to the Promised Land, when in fact we had already taken a U-turn.

How have people responded to your work?

The biggest surprise to me is that it has been embraced so well by many of the folks that I imagined would resist it. Civil rights organizations, which I criticize pointedly in my book, have embraced it. Maybe it is because I criticize myself as well and acknowledge that I too did not understand the impact of mass incarceration—I wasn't pointing a finger at others without pointing it at myself. I was as shocked as anyone to realize that there are more African-American people under correctional control today than were enslaved in 1850, that in some states 90 percent of the people sent to prison on drug charges are African American, even though they are no more likely to be guilty of drug-related crimes.

People don't realize the extent to which ex-felons are excluded from the legal economy. You can't even get a license to be a barber in my state of Ohio if you have a drug felony on your record. A whole web of laws has been independently justified on the basis of getting tough on crime, but it really does add up to a trap for people. I have been encouraged that when provided with the data and information, many are willing to say, "We do need to make this a higher priority."

I have also been pleased by the reception in faith communities. The deep irony is that the very folks who ought to be the most sensitive to the demonization of the "despised," the prisoners, have been complicit and silent.

In my research, I found that many people would say that church was the last place where they would go for help or support or understanding when they got out of prison. It was the place where they felt the most condemned and unwelcome. Pastors would be quick to wave a finger at black men for the way they dressed or for their conduct as fathers. Church was the place where they felt the most shame for their circumstances. As a result, I viewed faith leaders as an important audience for this book. I wanted those people to have a broader understanding of the system and to realize that it wasn't all about individual choices.

Some have criticized your book for overlooking the experiences of women within the criminal justice system. Is that criticism fair?

The book explicitly focuses on the experiences of black men in the criminal justice system—a system whose prison population is overwhelmingly made up of men. That being said, women are the fastest growing segment of the prison population, and their experiences are as important, and even more disconcerting, than those of men. Women are often the primary caretakers of children, for example. What does it mean for the future of families if more and more women are incarcerated?

But my work on this book was primarily inspired by investigating patterns of law enforcement directed at young black and Latino men. I find in the academic community that when scholars write books about the experience of women in the criminal justice system, no one says, "Well, why didn't you talk about men?" When you write a book that addresses the unique experience of black men, everyone says, "Well, why didn't you talk more about women?"

There is a lot more to say about the experiences of women and immigrant groups, a whole host of folks who have been negatively affected by this system. I intended to contribute one piece of the puzzle with the hope of inspiring others to add other pieces.

Do you see seeds of the social movement that you envision?

Absolutely. There are people who have been trying to approach this work from a movement-building perspective for a long time. I am particularly inspired by the Ella Baker Center for Human Rights, a group in Oakland that has conducted youth campaigns to close juvenile prisons in California. These are successful multiethnic, multiracial campaigns for education, not incarceration, with a human rights framework.

I see a potential paradigm shift in faith communities in prison ministries, from primarily viewing prison ministry as a way to save individual souls to viewing it as an opportunity to serve communities and populations in prison and to raise consciousness for collective liberation rather than only individual salvation. I've seen a shift in the approach to reentry from providing "job training and pep-talks" to beginning to organize "ban the box" campaigns to end the practice of preventing convicted felons from finding work. Faith groups are showing more of an interest in felon disenfranchisement, shifting away from viewing the problem of criminality as one involving an offender who can't get his life together to the bigger picture of a systemwide problem.

Many people are turning to the Occupy movement for new forms of political action. Do you see any connection between the kind of social movement you call for and Occupy?

I am so grateful that the Occupy movement burst onto the scene and forced into mainstream discussion the problem of economic inequality and the concentration of wealth and power. That is enormously important. But the 99 percent vs. the 1 percent framing obscures a lot. We are not all situated similarly within that 99 percent. Most of the 99 percent has been willing to turn a blind eye to the predicament of the demonized other. And many in the Occupy movement come from backgrounds in which it has been easy to be ignorant of and indifferent to those who are in ghetto communities or cycling in and out of prisons. That is not a swipe at them. It is a statement of how easy it has been to overlook this system of social control and how disparate our communities can be.

The old Jim Crow system had "Whites Only" signs. Black people were at the back of the bus. It was obvious and undeniable that a system of social control existed designed to deny some people access to resources and equality. But prisons are out of sight and out of mind. People in and out of prisons and enmeshed in poverty are physically separate from the rest of us, from places where there are jobs and a good education system. It is easy to be ignorant and in denial. Consciousness-raising is critically important at this stage.

If you could direct the energies of people who read your book and want to act, what would you urge them to do?

I think the better question might be: What do you feel most inspired to do? What is your sphere of influence? In your faith community, what can you do to raise awareness? You are more likely to get constructive answers that way than by asking. "What is most important to do?"

A great deal depends on what region of the country a group is in. What is the makeup of the group? Some are really fired up to end disenfranchisement laws. Others are outraged that people cannot get access to food. Some simply want to make sure that their particular faith community is really open and welcoming to people who are returning home from prison, setting a tone of welcome.

No matter what a group decides to do, what matters is the way you do it. The need for far-reaching compassion and for a serious understanding of the politics that gave rise to this system is high. We need to paint with a broad brush to get at the magnitude of the problem. We cannot shrink from the hard conversations about race. The way that we go about this work will transform our efforts from piecemeal ones into a larger movement, grounded by a shared commitment to the humanity of us all.

Reading 1.3

Racialized Bias in Introductory Criminal Justice Textbooks

A Content Analysis

Dennis E. Hoffman

"Anyone who thinks race does not skew the application of criminal justice in this country is just not paying close enough attention," Senator Rand Paul (2014) wrote for TIME, amid violence in Ferguson, Missouri, over the police shooting death of Michael Brown in August of 2014. Paul (2014) declared in the same essay that "Given the racial disparities in our criminal justice system, it is impossible for African-Americans not to feel like their government is particularly targeting them." Analyzing the racially-charged situation in Ferguson, *New York Times'* columnist Charles Blow (2014) argued that the peaceful protests, violence, and looting in Ferguson were about not only the perceived injustice of the police killing an unarmed African-American young man but also about systematic racial bias in America's educational, economic, and legal institutions. Blow emphasized that these biases do "material damage" and breed "a sense of disenfranchisement and despair" which in turn depresses aspirations and destroys motivation (Blow, 2014, p. 3). Is it possible that the kind of institutional racial bias that Blow wrote so passionately about exists at the heart of the academic discipline of criminal justice in the field's introductory criminal justice textbooks? Is it also possible that current introductory criminal justice textbooks fail to reflect what Paul and many ordinary citizens perceive as the unquestioned significance of race in criminal justice today?

If the past is any guide to the present, then the answer to both questions would seem to be "yes." In the one and only critical examination of the treatment of race and ethnicity in introductory criminal justice textbooks ever conducted in the 100-year history of the discipline of criminal justice, Sam Walker and Molly Brown (1995) observed that none of the 13 textbooks they sampled provided adequate coverage of race and ethnicity and that all exhibited "patterns of evasion" of racial issues. Although Walker and Brown (1995) laid blame for the defective textbooks on a systems orientation taken by each of the textbooks, Walker and Brown (1995) failed to provide a plausible reason why a systems approach would be incompatible with an appreciation of the central role of race. More importantly, they ignored a telling detail: all of the 17 male and 2 female authors of the 13 textbooks Walker and Brown surveyed appear to have been White. This "whiteout" raises the possibility that the results of Walker and Brown's (1995) study may be due to a particular way of framing race. Were White authors of the introductory textbooks in the 1994 sample almost exclusively viewing realities of race and justice through a White lens? If so, are the authors of today's introductory criminal justice textbooks making the same mistake?

Sociologist Joe Feagin (2013) defined the white racial frame as an overarching white worldview that includes "... racial stereotypes, prejudices, ideologies, images, interpretations and narratives, emotions, and reactions to language accents, as well as racialized inclinations to discriminate" (p. 3). Additionally, Feagin claimed that this white-centered framing is common in the perspectives of contemporary social scientists. According to him, it structures social scientists' thinking and shapes what they see or do not see. The trouble with the white racial frame, in Feagin's view, is its destructive impact. White framing encompasses both a strong favoritism toward whites and whiteness, and a strong disdain for racial "others." Even worse, it shapes the scripts whites and others act on, such as in acts of discrimination. In this way, the white racial frame re-creates and reinforces the racially stratified patterns and structures of society. In short, the white racial frame protects society's unequal resources and hierarchy of power (Feagin, 2013, p. 3).

Given the destructive power of the white racial frame, this researcher wanted to examine how today's introductory criminal justice texts frame race and explore whether or not this framing might be producing racialized textbook bias. Racialized textbook bias is defined as misinformation that promotes White majority interpretations of reality (Mitchell, 2013, p. 1). A premise underlying the concept of racialized bias is that textbooks are neither bias nor value free (Zeece, 1997; Romanowski, 1996). Because racialized textbook bias can feed myths about minority groups and reinforce institutional racism, biased misrepresentations of people of color in introductory criminal justice textbooks ought to be identified and rooted out. The purpose of this study was to answer three questions: (1) How is race framed in today's introductory criminal justice textbooks? (2) Does racialized textbook bias exist in these same books? (3) If racialized bias exists in these books, what forms does it take?

Literature Review

This study borrows from and builds upon the pioneering work of Sam Walker and Molly Brown (1995) as well as from the innovative theoretical and methodological approach to the study of racialized textbook bias devised by sociologist Michele E. Mitchell (2013).

Walker and Brown's (1995) Trailblazing Research

In response to critics charges that criminal justice scholars and criminologists were treating race as a taboo topic and tiptoeing around it in the early 1990s, Walker and Brown (1995) devised a research strategy for assessing the race and ethnicity content of a sample of 13 introductory criminal justice textbooks in print in 1994. One part of their research plan involved an examination of tables of contents and indices of all the textbooks to count references to race and ethnicity. Another part consisted of developing a survey instrument listing all possible topics in criminal justice in which race and ethnicity might be mentioned. Using this instrument as a guide, Walker and Brown then scanned each textbook to determine which subjects received coverage. In addition, Walker and Brown used this instrument to determine coverage of a shorter list of subjects. For example, they asked whether a textbook identified race and ethnicity as a core issue in criminal justice. Finally, researchers used the instrument to develop a list of six key public and scholarly issues. These issues related to critical decision points in the justice process (e.g. police use of physical force, police use of deadly force, and the death penalty).

Walker and Brown (1995) characterized the results as "disturbing" (p. 76). None of the textbooks identified race and ethnicity as a major issue in criminal justice and none covered all six key issues. Researchers identified several "patterns of evasion." These included a systems orientation, which researchers' blamed for the "general failure to cover race and ethnicity" (Walker and Brown, 1995, p. 71); the near-total neglect of Latinos and all other minority groups except African-Americans; and the sanitizing or whitewashing of racially-charged issues and cases through the removal of references to race and ethnicity.

Walker and Brown (1995) interpreted their results to mean that "students were being educated very poorly about one of the most important issues in the field." They accused textbook authors of shoddy scholarship because the authors had failed to incorporate readily available material on race and justice into their textbooks. They also indicted textbook reviewers for failing to hold textbook authors accountable for providing coverage of race and ethnicity. Nowhere did Walker and Brown (1995) use the term "bias."

If Walker and Brown (1995) had raised the issue of racial bias, they might have attempted to explore the hidden biases of the White authors of the textbooks they examined. To do this, Walker and Brown (1995) would have had to figure out a method for determining if the written words of these authors indicated that these authors held an inclination, temperament, or outlook to not only present or hold a partial perspective but also to refuse to consider alternative points of view. Such an investigation of bias in textbooks would differ significantly from the type of research done by Walker and Brown (1995).

Mitchell's (2013) Du Bosian Conceptualization of Racialized Textbook Bias

Perhaps if Michele Mitchell's (2013) methodology for analyzing racialized bias in Georgia's history textbooks had been available when Walker and Brown were examining introductory criminal justice textbooks, then Walker and Brown's (1995) study might have taken a different turn. The genius of Mitchell's scholarship is that she offers a new and different way to study the existence of race bias in textbooks by returning to a Dubosian perspective. Based on a DuBoisian theoretical perspective on race prejudice (Du Bois, 1889; 1920; 1935; 1940), she conceptualized race bias in textbooks as a symptom of racism and race prejudice in American society. Following Du Bois, she argued that racism shaped U.S. social institutions in the 20th century—and continues to impact American institutions of socialization today. However, Mitchell sees race prejudice today as qualitatively different from race prejudice during the time in which Du Bois conducted his scholarly work on reconstruction. It is this modern day "laissez faire racism" that her research on racialized textbook bias attempts to uncover as race prejudice in Georgia history textbooks. A key claim in her perspective is that public education systems "inadvertently promote the marginalization, compartmentalization, and omission of people of African descent through racialized textbook bias" (Mitchell, 2013, p. 8).

Mitchell (2013) defined marginalization as "the representation of White majority perceptions for people of African descent by relegating and limiting the visibility of this group in textbooks" (Mitchell, 2013, p. 7) to the point where the "smallest amount of information pertaining to Africans or African-Americans is included in textbooks" (Mitchell, 2013, p. 8). From Mitchell's (2013) perspective, compartmentalization consists of White majority perceptions of people of African descent that considers information valid only within specific categories, such as slavery, Civil Rights, crime, and sports. Omission is defined as White majority perceptions of people of African descent that excludes significant information about this group.

In a nutshell, Mitchell claimed that textbook authors frame race by a White lens. She regards this framing as both constructing distorted images of the history and culture of people of African descent and as having the consequences of devaluing African-American history and of promoting racial inequality (Mitchell, 2013, p. 61). By creating a conceptual framework, Mitchell (2013) laid the groundwork for identifying, categorizing, and coding representations of race bias in Georgia History textbooks.

Results from Mitchell's analysis showed the representation of people of African descent in Georgia history textbooks was compartmentalized. As Mitchell put it, "If the discussion was not one centered on slavery, racism, music, or sports, then Blacks were deemed insignificant to Georgia's history" (Mitchell, 2013, p. 62). Based on this finding, Mitchell declared that White majority perceptions of the significance of Black people to Georgia's history were continuing to "perpetuate race prejudice in the form of racialized textbook bias" (Mitchell, 2013, p. 62). As for omissions, Mitchell reported that the textbooks excluded the history and culture of Africa and its people, the Black perspective on slavery, and the voices of Black women. Evidence of marginalization was also found in the textbooks' legitimation of slavery and the depersonalization of stories about Blacks and Native Americans compared to the personalization of stories about Whites (Mitchell, 2013, p. 63).

Mitchell (2013) summarized the meaning of her results in these words: "The marginalization, compartmentalization, and omission of Black people in Georgia history textbooks ought not to be viewed simply as a distorted view of the past, we must understand that the racially prejudiced representation of Blacks in history textbooks also informs students about the present" (Mitchell, 2013, pp. 61–62).

Methods

The research design combined quantitative and qualitative methods for conducting a content analysis of a sample of 20 introductory criminal justice textbooks in print in 2014. (See Appendix A.) A mixed-method approach to the text analysis was adopted because the researcher sought to produce both a comprehensive and deep understanding of the problem of racialized textbook bias. Identifying bias in textbooks begins with an understanding that bias exists in two forms: blatant and unobtrusive (Zeece, 1997). Blatant bias is seen in textbooks presenting obvious stereotypes. Group characteristics are fixed with little attention to variation within groups. Unobtrusive bias is more difficult to detect. This kind of bias sometimes happens not because of the content of a textbook, but because of omission or one-sidedness. For example, students might be exposed to a single perspective, a single outlook—and usually the perspective is Euro-American (Zeece, 1997). To search for unobtrusive racial bias, this study used a four-step process.

Step one was the framing of race bias in introductory criminal justice textbooks. With a slight modification, Mitchell's (2013) Dubosian framework was applied. The only alteration consisted of an attempt to more clearly flesh out a framework for the conceptualization and analysis of racialized textbooks bias. In the magnificent final chapter of *Black Reconstruction in America, 1860–1880*, "The Propaganda of History," Dubois (1935) unfurled his approach to textbook bias. He began by stating three themes about Reconstruction in textbooks: (1) All Negroes were ignorant; (2) All Negroes were lazy, dishonest and extravagant; (3) and Negroes were responsible for bad government during Reconstruction (pp. 711–712). Next, DuBois supplied evidence to document each theme and interpreted the meaning of these themes for students reading accounts of Reconstruction. In his interpretation he brought to light omissions that he cleverly spun into the following counter-narrative: "White historians have ascribed the faults and failures of Reconstruction to Negro ignorance and corruption. But the Negro insists that it was Negro loyalty and the Negro vote alone that restored the South to the Union; established the new democracy, both for white and black, and instituted the public schools" (p. 713). Du Bois used this counter-narrative to deconstruct the master narrative of mainstream White historians and to offer an alternative to the dominant discourse. To eliminate racialized textbook bias, Du Bois recommended contrasting the pro-slavery narratives of White owners with the untold counter-narratives in slave biographies (p. 720) and recognizing African-American agency in the struggle against slavery and other forms of racial oppression (p. 716). Finally, Du Bois stressed that African-American scholars were not silent on Reconstruction, only unheard or dismissed by white academics.

The second step in the research plan for this study involved an objective, systematic, and quantitative description of the manifest race content of introductory criminal justice textbooks. Like Walker and Brown (1995), the present study relied upon thematic or topical analysis (Berg, 2004, p. 273) as a way of getting close to the data and developing a deep appreciation of the race content. The researcher was interested in looking for broader patterns in the data in order to then conduct a more fine-grained analysis. The researcher catalogued race content from introductory textbooks using Walker and Brown's (1995) baseline list of topics and adding a list of contemporary race-related topics. Topics added included racism and racial profiling. (See Appendix B.) Based on the researcher's reading of the all race content in the sample of textbooks, inductive topics derived bottom-up were added to create a comprehensive list of topics. Examples of inductive topics added include racial disparities, the War on Drugs as a contributor to racial disparities, *McCleskey v. Kemp* (1987), and mass incarceration. (See Appendix B.) With this step, the researcher minimally identified, described, and categorized all race content at a semantic level.

Step three involved immersion, crystallization (Borkan, 1999), and interpretation. A common complaint about quantitative analysis is that it fails to take context into account. For this reason, a qualitative approach to discovering marginalization, omission, and compartmentalization was employed. During this phase, the researcher first immersed himself in data relating to racial bias in the narrative of textbooks in the 2014 sample and examined it in detail. Periodically, the researcher suspended the process of reading and examining the racial bias data (immersion) in order to attempt to identify and articulate racialized themes, missing information, and one-sided interpretations noticed during the immersion process. The dual processes of immersion and crystallization continued until all the race content in the 2014 sample had been examined and patterns of racialized bias emerged from that data that were meaningful and could be articulated and substantiated.

Step four was the quantification and qualification of themes, patterns, and anomalies of race bias within the texts. The quantitative component sought to address the compartmentalization of people of color into specific sections and chapters within the texts. A simple coding scheme measured the existence of racialized textbook bias through the presence or absence of specific words and themes. The qualitative component included identifying themes, patterns, and anomalies within sentences, paragraphs, sentences, and chapters by way of compartmentalization, omission, and marginalization of information on race and ethnicity.

Since a major concern with the introductory criminal justice textbooks was the content—what was included and what was excluded—omission warrants special attention. Identifying omission began with a comparison of what was observed in the text to the topics and words listed on the comprehensive survey instrument. This data-driven approach began with the text, but the researcher supplemented it with a Dubosian theoretical frame of race prejudice to inform the analysis of what was excluded from textbooks. For example, some phenomena representing marginalization were identified using the survey instrument, while other phenomena representing omission were coded during data analysis. A text discussing the death penalty without citing *McCleskey v. Kemp* (1987) (which is a key case regarding the argument that the death penalty is racially discriminatory) constituted an omission. Another text which cites *McCleskey* but fails to criticize the intent requirement of *McCleskey* constituted marginalization of discrimination. Failure to criticize *McCleskey's* intent requirement creates the misguided impression that there can be no discrimination without intent. An intent-based definition of racial discrimination is not only illogical as sociologist Robert K. Merton (1947) pointed out 50 years ago, but also so narrows the definition of discrimination that discrimination as a legal claim and a theoretical construct is neutered and rendered irrelevant to discussions of race and ethnicity.

Results

As Table 1.3.1 shows, the 20 introductory criminal justice texts in the 2014 sample exhibit race and justice themes that some might term "anomalies" or distortions of the truth. Xs in Table 1.3.1 indicate the presence of a particular hidden theme. Each theme is embedded in narrative and was excavated through use of a DuBosian understanding of racialized textbook bias as omission, marginalization, and compartmentalization. All 37 male and 7 female authors of the 20 textbooks in the 2014 sample appear to be white.

Theme #1: Race and Ethnicity are NOT Central to Criminal Justice

In her 2011 Sutherland Award Address in honor of being named the President of the American Society of Criminology (ASC), criminologist Ruth Peterson (2012) called for placing race and ethnicity at the center of the study of crime and justice. She stated that her main reason for making this argument was because of the ubiquity of race-ethnic disparities in crime

TABLE 1.3.1. Themes in Introductory Criminal Justice Texts in Print 2014

			Lies			
Texts	**Race and Ethnicity are NOT Central to Criminal Justice**	**Racism Need NOT be Defined**	**Michelle Alexander's Concept of Mass Incarceration Is NOT Worth Knowing**	**The Drug War is NOT a Major Contributor to Racial Disparities**	**No Discrimination Without Intent**	**Anything But Racism Causes Racial Disparities**
Adler et al. (2012)	X	x	x		x	
Albanese (2013)	X	x	x	x		
Anderson and Slate (2011)	X	x	x	x	x	x
Bohm and Haley (2014)	X	x	x	x	x	
Cole et al. (2015)		x	x	x	x	
Cox and Mc-Camey (2008)	X	x	N.A.		x	
Fagin (2014)	X	x		x	x	
Fuller (2014)	X	x	x	x	x	
Gaines and Miller (2015)	X	x	x		x	x
Hendrix (2014)	X	x	x	x	x	
Lab et al. (2013)	X	x	x	x	x	x
Mentor (2013)	X	x	x	x	x	x
Owen et al. (2012)	X	x	x	x	x	x
Peak (2015)	X	x	x	x	x	
Schmalleger (2015)		x	x	x	x	x
Shelden et al. (2008)		x	N.A.			
Siegel and Worrall (2014)	X	x	x	x	x	
Travis (2012)	X	x	x		x	
Waldron et al. (2009)	X	x	N.A.		x	x
Wright (2012)	X	x	x	x	x	x

x = Theme in text; N.A. = Text published prior to Alexander (2010) and criminal justice (p. 306). Given that an outstanding scholar and former ASC president took such a strong position, it might come as surprise to discover that none of the 20 textbooks in the 2014 sample identified race and ethnicity as a major theme in criminal justice. Similarly, race/ethnicity never appears in any chapter titles of textbooks in the 2014 sample and only rarely appears in headings and subheadings within chapters. Two of the 20 texts (Schmalleger, 2015 and Cole et al., 2015) feature special sections on multiculturalism.

Schmalleger's (2015) section "Multiculturalism and Diversity in Criminal Justice" (pp. 24–26) downplays the significance of race and ethnicity as illustrated in the following statement: "Race and ethnicity are only buzzwords that people use when they talk about multiculturalism" (Schmalleger, 2015, p. 26). According to the *Merriam-Webster Dictionary* (2014), a buzzword is "an important-sounding, usually technical word or phrase often of little meaning used chiefly to impress laymen" (p. 1). Whereas Schmalleger (2015) makes no mention of either discrimination or racism in his discussion of multiculturalism and criminal justice, Cole et al. (2015) emphasize the prominence of inequality and discrimination in their discussion of crime and justice in a multicultural society (Cole et al., 2015, pp. 116–125). Then, too, Cole et al. stress that African Americans, Hispanics, and other minorities receive unequal treatment in the criminal justice system.

Insofar as putting race and ethnicity at the core of the study of criminal justice is concerned, one of the 20 textbooks in the 2014 sample (Shelden et al., 2008) makes a serious attempt to allow students to view concepts, issues, themes, and problems from several ethnic perspectives and points of view. The other textbooks feature a mainstream-centric perspective as the only perspective from which issues, problems, concepts can be viewed. In contrast to all the other texts, Shelden et al. (2008) acknowledge the power of counter-narratives to help us to understand the experiences of different groups from their own perspectives and give voice to individual, institutional, and societal oppression. "American history is viewed differently," Shelden et al. (2008) state, "by women and men, by African Americans and Mexican Americans and whites, by the rich and by the poor" (p. xxvi). Shelden et al. (2008) stress that criminal justice "... can be seen from different perspectives" (p. xviii) and they promise to present an "alternative interpretation" of criminal justice that reflects the authors' tendency to "side with the underdog poor and minority groups" (p. xviii). By infusing race/ethnicity content into four chapters (i.e. the chapters on police functions, sentencing, the modern prison system, and the juvenile justice system), Shelden et al. (2008) partially deliver on their promise. Overall, however, the book suffers from unevenness because the first six chapters contain relatively little race/ethnicity content.

The meaning of these findings is that current introductory criminal justice textbooks ignore race and ethnicity as central to understanding crime and justice. In her Sutherland Address, Ruth Peterson (2012) identified three consequences associated with the failure to recognize race and ethnicity as core concepts: (1) a preoccupation with "narrow explanations that beg many of the questions we seek to answer"; (2) a failure to treat Whites as a race, and consequently, an additional failure to explore how privilege associated with Whiteness affects the crimes we study, the processing of suspects and defendants, and the punishments we dispense; and (3) a continuing reliance on superficial anti-crime policies that that leave the structural roots of crime unaddressed and force racial and ethnic minorities to bear the heaviest burden for social and economic inequality (Peterson, 2012, p. 323).

Theme #2: Racism Need NOT be Defined or Explained Because Everyone Knows It When They See It

The phrase "I know it when I see it" is a colloquial expression by which a person attempts to categorize an observable fact or a happening, even though the category lacks clearly defined parameters. The phrase was infamously used in this sense by U.S. Supreme Court Justice Potter Stewart (1964) to describe his threshold test for obscenity in *Jacobellis v. Ohio*. The same rationale seems implicit in the omission of a definition of racism from all textbooks in the 2014 sample.

Many of the texts in the 2014 sample mention racism, but perhaps none mention it more frequently than Anderson and Slate (2011) which contains nine references to racism in its Index (p. 516). For example, Anderson and Slate (2011) claim that, "No history of the police can be useful in understanding the present state of American policing, nor help in objectively assessing the profession's future directions, without acknowledging its racist influences" (p. 105). Elsewhere this text states that, "The problems of police brutality and racism are powerful and lingering" (p. 191). Unfortunately, the impact of such strong statements on students is blunted by the failure to define racism.

Besides lacking definitions of racism, none of the textbooks explain any of the following major theories of racism: the institutional racism perspective, racial formation theory, systemic racism, and colorblind racism. All of these theories are in vogue today, and the failure to discuss and explain these theories reveals a blind spot in current introductory criminal justice texts. Relatedly, two texts (Siegel and Worrall, 2014; Gaines and Miller, 2015) discuss racial threat theory and another two (Owen et al., 2015; Fuller, 2014) discuss critical race theory. Fuller (2014) accurately portrays critical race theory as (a) holding that people of color are overrepresented at every decision point of the criminal justice system, (b) seeing race as a crucial variable for understanding the dynamics of criminal justice, and (c) asserting that the justice system "legitimizes white supremacy and oppresses people of color" (p. 102). In contrast to Fuller (2014), Owen et al. (2015) marginalize critical race theory by rejecting it on the flimsy grounds that it is "not mainstream," relies on qualitative methods, and fails to propose "workable reform" (p. 356). In fairness to Owen et al. (2015), it should be noted that they also concede that critical race has sensitized legal educators and others to social justice concerns.

The omission of definitions and theories of racism—combined with the marginalization of critical race theory—means that most of the current introductory criminal justice textbooks never give a fair hearing to the possibility that racism might be an important social force shaping crime and justice in America. Then, too, the lack of a definition of racism (or of different types of racism) makes it impossible for students to interpret research evidence bearing on an argument that is explored in Anderson and Slate (2011) and in most of the other textbooks in the 2014 sample—namely, the argument that the criminal justice system is (or is NOT) racist. It turns out that "The criminal justice system is racist" is a "definition argument" (ramage, Bean, and Johnson, 2012) in which there is much disagreement about the definition. The truth is that people don't know racism when they see it. Because they tend to define racism differently, Whites and people of color have difficulty having conversations about race and ethnicity. For most Whites, racism is prejudice. For most people of color, racism is systemic or institutionalized (Bonilla-Silva, 2010, p. 8).

Theme #3: Michelle Alexander's Concept of Mass Incarceration is NOT Worth Knowing

One text in the 2014 sample (Fagin, 2014) discusses and briefly explains Michelle Alexander's (2010a) idea of mass incarceration. Another text (Wright, 2012) cites Alexander (p. 67) and mentions the term mass incarceration twice (p. 178 and p. 196) but never defines the term or fleshes out the racialized aspects of mass incarceration. Eighteen of the 20 texts fail to mention Alexander's concept of mass incarceration. Taken together, the neglect of Alexander and mass incarceration seem remarkable within the context of American criminal justice in the 21st century.

Alexander was not the first or the last to expose the havoc wrought by mass incarceration, but she is by far the most famous. Alexander's (2010a) *The New Jim Crow* popularized the concept of mass incarceration and ignited a nationwide crusade to end mass incarceration. With the publication of the New York Times best seller *The New Jim Crow: Mass Incarceration in the Age of Colorblindness* in 2010, Alexander catapulted to fame as a public intellectual and social activist. In *The New Jim Crow,* Alexander (2010a) argued that systematic racial discrimination in the U.S. resumed following the Civil Rights Movement's progress and manifested itself in mass incarceration. In her conceptualization, mass incarceration is fueled by the War on Drugs and it functions as a system of racialized control similar to how Jim Crow operated.

For more than a decade, researchers from various disciplines have been documenting the social and economic damage caused by America's 40-year experiment of locking up huge numbers of citizens. Since race, poverty, and incarceration overlap so significantly, the weight of mass incarceration falls overwhelmingly on communities of color, and particularly on young Black men. As the *New York Times* (2014) editorialized in "End Mass Incarceration Now," "If there is any remaining disagreement about the destructiveness of this experiment, it mirrors the so-called debate over climate change."

Other scholars of color practically banished from pages of current introductory criminal justice texts include gang researchers Diego Vigil, Joan Moore, Elijah Anderson, Martin Sanchez-Jankowski, Ruth Horowitz; violence researcher Ramero Martinez; criminologist Ruth Peterson; and race expert and urban sociologist William Julius Wilson. With respect to Peterson and Wilson, a notable exception to the practice of excluding scholars of color from textbooks in the 2014 sample is Siegel and Worrall's (2014) multivalent explanation of the relationship between race and crime (pp. 72–74). Drawing upon the significant contributions of Peterson and Wilson, Siegel and Worrall weave an explanation that stresses system bias, cultural bias, and structural bias.

Overall, data on scholars of color cited in the 2014 sample indicate that the long-standing problem of excluding scholars of color in criminal justice and criminology (Young and Sulton, 1991; Free, 1999; Gabbidon and Taylor Greene, 2001; Taylor Greene, Gabbidon, and Ebsersole, 2001; Taylor Greene and Gabbidon, 2003; Gabbidon, Taylor Greene, and Wilder, 2004) persists in today's introductory criminal justice textbooks. But what does it mean? Few would deny the intellectual loss from having scholars with different perspectives and backgrounds excluded from contributing to the dialogue about race and justice in America. The exclusion of Michelle Alexander and mass incarceration, for example, might mean that a counter-narrative on mass incarceration is unavailable in most current introduction criminal justice textbooks. Owen et al. (2015) prove that this is not true in all cases of textbooks that ignore both Alexander and mass incarceration. By presenting the concept of "justice reinvestment" (which means that money spent on incarceration can be better spent on other initiatives), they offer a valuable counter-narrative.

Theme #4: The Drug War is NOT a Major Contributor to Racial Disparities in Criminal Justice

The truth about the War on Drugs and racial disparities has long been known. Researcher Michael Tonry (1995) noted that "anyone with knowledge of drug-trafficking patterns and police arrest policies and incentives could have foreseen that the enemy troops in the War on Drugs would consist largely of young, inner-city, minority males" (p. 4). In their seminal analysis of research on racial and ethnic disparities in crime and criminal justice, Robert J. Sampson and Janet L. Lauritsen (1997) stated that the drug war has caused black arrest rates to skyrocket (p. 364), the number of black males under correctional supervision to soar (p. 360), and racial discrimination in juvenile justice to worsen (p. 360). Similarly, the Human Rights Watch (2000) concluded that the War on Drugs has been waged disproportionately against Black Americans. Based on a critical examination of research and data relating to the War on Drugs, Kenneth B. Nunn (2002) stated that the War on Drugs has had a "devastating effect on African American communities nationwide" (p. 381). He stressed that throughout the drug war, African Americans have been disproportionately investigated, detained, searched, arrested, and charged with the use, possession and sale of illegal drugs. According to Nunn, vast numbers of African Americans have been jailed and imprisoned under tough drug trafficking laws. Several years after Nunn's article, sociologist Karen Rosich (2007) observed that "the War on Drugs" and other 'get tough' legislation enacted since the 1980s at the state and federal levels disadvantage African Americans" (p. 9). More recently, Murakawa and Beckett (2010) assessed the evidence on this question and declared that "... as is now well known, the War on Drugs is one of the most important causes of rising levels of racial inequality in arrests and prison admissions" (p. 707).

Six texts (Adler et al., 2012; Anderson and Slate, 2011; Fagin, 2014; Mentor, 2013; Siegel and Worrall, 2014; and Waldron et al., 2009) contain no references to the War on Drugs in their indices or their narratives and no explicit statements in the narratives declaring that the drug war is partly responsible for racial disparities in criminal justice. Seven texts (Albanese, 2013; Cole et al., 2015; Hendrix, 2014; Lab et al., 2013; Peak, 2015; Schmalleger, 2015; Wright, 2012) mention the drug war but fail to explicitly link it to racial disparities. The presence of three of the oldest and best-selling texts (Siegel and Worrall, 2014; Cole et al., 2015; and Schmalleger, 2015) in these two groups of textbooks that fail to implicate the drug war as being responsible for racial disparities is noteworthy.

Of the seven texts that told the truth (Bohm and Haley, 2014; Cox and McCamey, 2008; Fuller, 2014; Gaines and Miller, 2015; Owen et al., 2015; Shelden et al., 2008; and Travis, 2012), Shelden et al. (2008) stands out. This text repeatedly hammers home the theme of the drug war causing racial disparities. After stating "there is abundant evidence that the war on drugs has been essentially a war on African Americans" (p. 143), Shelden et al. (2008) explain the drug war's racialized impact on the following areas: the prison-industrial complex, selection of targets for drug enforcement; processing of juveniles; sentencing; law enforcement strategies; incarceration rates for people of color; and the incarceration rate for women of color. Shelden et al. (2008) characterize the impact of the drug war on communities of color as system-wide and massive.

What are we to make of the 13 current textbooks that fail to explicitly link the drug war to racial disparities? This omission suggests shoddy scholarship, denialism (i.e. denying reality to avoid an inconvenient truth), or both.

Theme #5: No Discrimination Without Intent

Few cases involving race, criminal law and criminal procedure have had the impact of *McCleskey v. Kemp* (1987). The Supreme Court's decision in McCleskey shielded criminal justice policies and practices from being challenged on the basis of racially disparate impact. Simply put, *McCleskey* is a major roadblock to eliminating racial disparities in the criminal justice system. The *McCleskey* case began with Warren McCleskey, an African-American being sentenced to death in 1978 for killing a White police officer. McCleskey appealed, arguing that the death penalty in Georgia was administered in a racially discriminatory—and therefore—unconstitutional manner. In support of his argument, McCleskey's lawyers introduced research showing that the race of the defendant and victim determined who was sentenced to death in Georgia. In a 5–4 decision, the U.S. Supreme Court ruled against McCleskey and found that unless he could provide evidence showing that a specific person in his case acted with a racially discriminatory purpose, then his death sentence would stand.

The impact of McCleskey has been far-reaching. Civil rights advocate and law professor Michelle Alexander (2010b) criticized the decision saying that *McCleskey* had "immunized the criminal justice system from judicial scrutiny for racial bias." According to Alexander, *McCleskey* made it impossible to challenge any aspect of the criminal justice process for racial bias because evidence of conscious intentional bias is almost impossible to come by in the absence of an admission (Alexander, 2010b). Adding to the criticism, criminologist Marjorie Zatz (2000) pointed out that the Supreme Court's intent standard fails to acknowledge the reality of institutional racism. Arguing that discrimination problems in criminal justice today stem more from "disparate impact" than from intent, Zatz declared that decisions like *McCleskey* reveal that the law is defined to be blind to discrimination as systemic and institutional. Put another way, the High Court's emphasis on intent is critical because it is based on the premise that racism is rooted in individual consciousness—in prejudice and bias—instead of institutions and systems. The Court's stance in *McCleskey* implies that once we transcend prejudicial individual consciousness about race, we will be left with neutral, rational, and objective criminal justice institutions.

Given the significance of *McCleskey* for the issue of racial discrimination in capital punishment in particular and racial disparities in general, it is surprising that 10 of the 20 textbooks in the 2014 sample (Anderson and Slate, 2011; Cox and McCamey, 2008; Fuller, 2014; Lab et al., 2013; Owen et al., 2015; Peak, 2015; Siegel and Worrall, 2014; Travis, 2012; Waldron et al., 2009; Wright, 2012) neglected to mention this key case. Equally disturbing, however, is the fact that of the 10 texts that mentioned *McCleskey* (Adler et al., 2012; Albanese, 2013; Bohm and Haley, 2014; Cole et al., 2015; Fagin, 2014; Gaines and Miller, 2015; Hendrix, 2014; Mentor, 2013; Schmalleger, 2015: Shelden et al., 2008) only two (Albanese, 2013 and Shelden et al., 2008) criticized the "intent" requirement in *McCleskey* (1987).

The meaning of these omissions is that there would seem to be a good chance that students–and even some of the authors of introductory criminal justice textbooks—might be left in the dark about discrimination. Schmalleger (2015) illustrates the confusion. "Contemporary research appears to disprove claims that today's American justice system is intentionally racist" (Schmalleger, 2015, p. 49). With this statement, Schmalleger seems to be saying, "It's the intent that counts." The implied logic of "It's the intent that counts" goes like this: You've just been accused of saying or doing something racist. As far as you're concerned, the fact that you didn't *intend* for your statement or action to be racist, somehow, makes what you said or did NOT racist.

An exception to the problems associated with ignoring *McCleskey* and the intent requirement is Cole et al.'s (2015) declaration about discrimination. Despite Cole et al.'s failure to criticize *McCleskey* (pp. 480–481), the authors define discrimination without making intent a requirement. According to them, discrimination occurs when groups are "differentially treated without regard to their behavior or qualifications. ..." (p. 117). They also come ridiculously close to accusing the criminal justice system of institutional racism when they charge that at each stage of the criminal justice process, "the system itself operates in ways that may put minority group members at a disadvantage" (p. 121), but stop short of labeling this structural pattern as institutional racism.

Reflecting back on the findings, 10 texts failed to mention *McCleskey* and 6 mentioned the case but failed to critique its intent requirement. If criminal justice education is to move beyond basic academics and equip students with the critical thinking skills necessary for them to flourish in a diverse, global world, such racialized omissions must be eliminated.

Theme # 6: Anything but Racism Causes Racial Disparities

Since the trailblazing research of W. E. B. Du Bois (1899) on race and crime more than a century ago, researchers have been on a quest to understand racial/ethnic disparities in criminal justice processing and to figure out the extent to which racism and discrimination are responsible for patterns of overrepresentation. Regarding the 20 introductory criminal justice textbooks in the 2014 sample, this prima facie case can be made: When most of the authors of the texts in the 2014 sample were writing their books, there was plenty of evidence available indicating that racial disparities at various stages of the criminal justice process were at least partly attributable to racism and discrimination. Exhibit A would be sociologist Karen Rosich's (2007) extensive review of the literature on racial disparities in criminal justice in which she concluded that racial discrimination existed at various points in the criminal justice system (p. 21). Exhibit B would be Samuel Walker, Cassia Spohn, and Miriam DeLone's (2011) *The Color of Justice* which identified disparities at various stages of criminal justice processing as "institutionalized discrimination" and "contextual discrimination."

One group of two texts (Lab et al. 2013; Anderson and Slate, 2011) ignores racial disparities in criminal justice. Perhaps not coincidentally, neither recognizes the War on Drugs as having a significant influence on criminal justice policy and practice. A second group consisting of one text (Schmalleger, 2015) acknowledges the existence of racial disparities but offers no explanations for some disparities and offers explanations attributing other disparities to anything except racism. Schmalleger (2015) concedes that "past evidence shows that blacks and other minorities in the U.S. have been disproportionately sentenced to death," but then maintains that "more recent evidence is not as clear" (p. 370). In support of this claim, Schmalleger cites research indicating no "intentional" racial or ethnic bias in how capital punishment is administered in federal cases; then, he refers to research stating that overrepresentation of underrepresented groups in those receiving the death penalty is due to being "arrested on facts that could support a capital charge, not because the justice system acts in a discriminatory fashion" (p. 370).

Finally, a third group of 17 texts (Adler, et al., 2012; Albanese, 2013; Bohm and Haley, 2014; Cole et al., 2015; Cox and McCamey, 2008; Fagin, 2014; Fuller, 2014; Gaines and Miller, 2014; Hendrix, 2013; Mentor, 2013; Owen et al., 2015; Peak, 2015; Shelden et al., 2008; Siegel and Worrall, 2014; Travis, 2012; Waldron, et al., 2009; Wright, 2012) take the position that either racism or racial discrimination at least partly account for racial disparities in criminal justice.

Support for this position varies.

At one extreme, Cox and McCamey (2008) assert that "Blacks in particular face discrimination in the system of criminal justice, beginning with arrest and continuing through incarceration" (p. 15). Other texts compartmentalize, segregating acknowledgment of the impact of race and racism to sections on the death penalty, drugs, or a few other topics. For example Fagin (2014) labels racially disproportionate minority confinement as "institutional racism" (p. 236) and federal cocaine laws as "discriminatory" (p. 198). Similarly, Gaines and Miller (2014) concede that racial disparities in arrests might be called "institutional racism" (p. 86) and that "... police bias is responsible for the disproportionate numbers of minorities in American prisons and jails...." (p. 197). At the lower end of a continuum of support, nine texts (Adler, et al., 2012; Peak, 2015; Albanese, 2013; Bohm and Haley, 2014; Fuller, 2014; Hendrix, 2013; Mentor, 2013; Waldron et al., 2009; Wright, 2012) see racism or discrimination as contributing to racial disparities in a single stage or aspect of the criminal justice process. Representative of this compartmentalizing is Hendrix's (2013) statement that "Analyses of social characteristics of death row inmates suggest that the death penalty continues to be employed in a selective and discriminatory manner" (p. 279).

There is a danger here of not seeing the forest for the trees. The forest is the fact that through a combination of omission, marginalization, and compartmentalization 12 of the

20 texts either ignore, explain away, or minimize racism/racial discrimination as a factor contributing to racial disparities in criminal justice.

Discussion

This study asked how race is framed in today's introductory criminal justice textbooks and it took a deep look at the discourse about race inside these textbooks. It examined a set of topics relating to racial justice and discovered a way of talking about race and justice that represents the shared knowledge or understanding of the textbook authors. This cultural discourse provides a conceptual model or frame of reference around which these authors map their perceptions of the social reality of race and criminal justice. This frame of reference has been revealed to consist of a largely unacknowledged set of beliefs, assumptions, and feelings that underlie, sustain, and inform the perceptions and thoughts of these textbook writers.

Skeptics of this approach to the study of racialized textbook bias might want to blame the anomalies and omissions in the introductory textbooks on a few "bad apples" and scapegoat individual textbook writers, but the systematic nature of the patterns observed in this study render such an interpretation untenable. The rather dramatic and surprising omissions of significant information about race and justice can be understood through a DuBosian lens that focuses on racialization in the forms of marginalization, omission, and compartmentalization.

In applying Mitchell's (2012) DuBoisian framework, this researcher stumbled onto what multicultural educator Yolanda Wattsjohnson (2003) called "White Silence." She argued that White academics' silence in the face of injustice "maintains the status quo, attributes power to those already in power, and marginalizes those who are not" (p. 14). Although White Silence exposed in a sample of introductory criminal justice textbooks in print in 2014 should be understood as a disciplinary problem and a publishing industry problem, individual publishers and textbook writers bear an ethical responsibility to address racialized textbook bias. Here are some modest proposals that can provide for different and decisive discourses about race and justice inside introductory criminal justice textbooks.

To Write Against Racism in Criminal Justice, Start with a Definition. What is noticeably missing from all of the texts in the 2014 sample is a definition of racism. The distinguished Black Studies professor Manning Marable (1992) defined racism as "a system of ignorance, exploitation, and power used to oppress African-Americans, Latinos, Asians, Pacific Americans, American Indians and other people on the basis of ethnicity, culture, mannerisms, and color" (p. 5). This definition moves the discussion of race and racism from a Black-White discourse to one that includes multiple voices and perspectives (Solozano and Yosso, 2002, p. 24).

Emphasize Intersections of Oppression. Highlight layers and inter-connections of subordination based on race, gender, class, immigration status, surname, phenotype, accent, and sexuality.

Distinguish Between Curriculum Infusion and Curriculum Transformation. When a curriculum is merely infused with ethnic and gender content, students view the experiences of cultural groups from the perspectives and conceptual frameworks of the dominant culture. Groups such as African Americans and Latinos are added to the curriculum, but their experiences are viewed from the perspective of mainstream criminal justice and criminology. When curriculum infusion occurs in this manner without transformation, people of color are added but are viewed only from mainstream perspectives. When real curriculum transformation occurs, according to multicultural educational expert James Banks (2014), textbook writers make paradigm shifts and view social reality from the perspectives of different racial, ethnic, cultural, and gender groups.

Change the Narrative by Offering Counter-Narratives. Whose perspectives are privileged in the introductory criminal justice texts in the 2014 sample and whose are silenced? The problem with making mainstream criminal justice/criminology the default or master narrative in an introductory criminal justice text, as this study illustrates, is that it silences the points of view, experiences, and research of people of color. To remedy this problem, textbook writers should use counter-narratives to highlight the voices and agency of people of color and to challenge mainstream narratives as well as to challenge the tendency to view the mainstream narrative as the norm and all others as aberrant (Bamberg and Andrews, 2004; Solorzano and Yosso, 2002).

Diversify the Authors, Consultants, and Reviewers. Instead of having only white authors write introductory textbooks, publishing companies should recruit multicultural teams to write textbooks and hire multicultural education specialists as consultants and reviewers.

Develop More Scholars of Color Who Might Write Their Own Textbooks. Ohio State University's Racial Democracy, Crime, and Justice Network offers a prototype. One of its goals is to support junior scholars of color in their efforts to publish, to gain promotion in the academy, and to overcome various barriers to success. Other avenues for achieving this goal include more scholarships and post-docs for students of color.

Take Heart: The White Racial Frame is NOT an Iron Cage. Last but not least, everyone associated with the enterprise of teaching introductory criminal justice—the publishers, textbook writers, teachers, and students—should take heart in the fact that the "white racial frame" is an ideal type, not an iron cage. All individual Whites do not make use of the white racial frame in the same way. Race does not predetermine outlook. Whites can hold African American or other racial/ethnic points of views, while African Americans can subscribe to Eurocentric perspectives (Barak, 1991). Most importantly, there have always been White scholars in criminal justice and criminology like Sam Walker who have fought against racism. Future White writers of introductory criminal justice textbooks can proudly identify with these scholars and join the tradition of struggling for social justice.

Appendix A

Introductory Criminal Justice Texts Included in This Study

Adler, F., Mueller, G. O. W., and Laufer, W.S. (2012). *Criminal justice.* McGraw Hill Publishing Company.

Albanese, J. S. (2013). *Criminal justice.* Pearson.

Anderson, P. R. and Slate, R. N. (2011). *The decision-making network: an introduction to criminal justice.* Carolina Academic Press.

Bohm, R. M. and Haley, K. N. (2014). *Introduction to criminal justice.* McGraw Hill.

Cole, G. F., Smith, C. E., and DeJong, C. (2015). *The American system of criminal justice,* 14th ed. Wadsworth/Cengage Learning.

Cox, S. M. and McCamey, W. P. (2008). *Introduction to criminal justice.* Carolina Academic Press.

Fagin, J. A. (2014). *CJ2014.* Pearson.

Fuller, J. R. (2014). *Criminal justice: mainstream and crosscurrents.* Oxford University Press.

Gaines, L. K. and Miller, R. L. (2015). *Criminal justice in action.* Cengage.

Hendrix, N. (2013). *Experience criminal justice.* McGraw-Hill.

Lab, S. P., Williams, M. R., Holcomb, J. E., Burek, M. W., King, W. R. King, and Buerger, M. E. (2013). *Criminal justice.* Oxford University Press.

Mentor, K. E. (2013). *Criminal justice.* Kendall Hunt.

Owen, S. S., Fradella, H. F., Burke, T. W., and Joplin, J. (2015). *Foundations of criminal justice,* 2nd Edition. Oxford University Press.

Peak, K. J. (2015). *Introduction to criminal justice.* Sage.

Schmalleger, F. (2015)· *Criminal justice today,* 13th ed. Pearson.

Shelden, R. G., Brown, W. B. Brown, Miller, K. S. Miller, and Fritzler, R. B. (2008). *Crime and criminal justice in American society.* Waveland Press, Inc.

Siegel, L. J. and Worrall, J. L. (2014). *Introduction to criminal justice.* Wadsworth/Cengage.

Travis, L. F. (2012). *Introduction to criminal justice,* 7th ed. Anderson Publishing.

Waldron, R. C., Quarles, C., McElreath, M., Waldron, M. and Milstein, D. (2009). *The criminal justice system.* K&M Publishers, Inc.
Wright, J. (2012). *Introduction to criminal justice.* Bridgeport Education, Inc.

Appendix B

Revised Topical Survey Instrument (Based on Walker and Brown, 1995)

Author(s):

Title:

Publisher:

Publication Date:

I. GENERAL INTRODUCTION

A. Race as central to study of criminal justice/race a major theme in text
B. Racial disparities as a major problem/causes of racial disparities
C. Race discrimination as a major problem in criminal justice
D. Multicultural education as a major theme in criminal justice
E. Race discrimination as a major problem in criminal justice
F. Drug war as major contributor to racial disparities
G. Racism in criminal justice system/racism defined
H. Racism in American society

II. CRIMINAL LAW AND PROCEDURE

A. O.J. Simpson Case and Trial
B. George Zimmerman Trial

III. CRIMINAL BEHAVIOR/OFFENDERS AND VICTIMS

A. People of color as crime victims
B. People of color as offenders
C. Racial disparities in victimization and criminal involvement
D. Race and drug crimes
E. Race and hate crimes

IV. THEORIES OF CRIME

A. Do any of the discussions of theory attempt to explain the overrepresentation of minorities in the criminal justice system?
B. Critical race theory

V. THE POLICE

A. Police Field Practices

1. Deadly force
2. Physical force
3. Arrest
4. Stop and frisk
5. Patrol deployment
6. Discretion, generally
7. Racial profiling
8. Immigration and law enforcement
9. Drug law enforcement

B. Police-community relations (PCR)

1. Community relations as a problem
2. PCR program
3. Training in race/human relations

C. Police employment practices

1. Recruitment of minorities
2. Affirmative action
3. Promotion and assignment
4. Discipline/handling of complaints

VI. THE COURTS

A. Pretrial release
B. Legal representation
C. Prosecution/charging/plea bargaining
D. Jury selection/composition
E. Minorities as judges
F. Sentencing (non-capital cases)
G. Crack cocaine disparity
H. The death penalty/*McCleskey v. Kemp*/intent requirement
I. Other

VII. CORRECTIONS

A. Prison population (racial composition)
B. Classification/work assignment, etc.
C. Inmate subculture/gangs
D. Community-based corrections

1. Probation
2. Parole
3. Work/education release/furlough
4. New intermediate sanctions

E. Minorities as correctional officials
F. Mass incarceration/Michelle Alexander
G. Incarcerated immigrants
H. Law of corrections
I. Race and prison gangs
J. Race and prison violence
K. Race and prison riots

VIII. JUVENILE JUSTICE

A. Overrepresentation of minorities in juvenile crime
B. Juvenile court procedures
C. Sentencing of juveniles
D. Racial disparities
E. Race and juvenile gangs
F. Cradle to prison pipeline

References

Alexander, M. (2010a). *The new jim crow.* The Free Press.

Alexander, M. (210b). Appearance with Bryan Stevenson and Bill Moyers (April 2). *Bill Moyers Journal* http://www.pbs.org/moyers/journal/04022010/watch.html Retrieved August 22, 2014.

Bamberg, M. and Andrews, M. (Eds.) (2004). *Considering counter-narratives: Narrating, resisting, making sense.* John Benjamins.

Banks, J. (2014). *An introduction to multicultural education.* Pearson Education, Inc.

Barak, G. (1991). Cultural literacy and a multicultural inquiry into the study of crime and justice. *Journal of Criminal Justice Education,* 2, 173–192.

Berg, B. L. (2004). *Qualitative research methods,* 5th Edition. Pearson.

Blow, C. M. (2014). Frustration in Ferguson. http: //www.nytimes.com/2014/08/18/opinion/Charles-m-blow-frustration-in-ferguson-html Retrieved August 22, 2014.

Bonilla-Silva, E. (2010). *Racism without racists.* The Rowman and Littlefield Publishing Group, Inc.

Borkan, J. (1999). Immersion/crystallization. In B. F. Crabtree and W. C. Miller (Eds.), *Doing qualitative research,* 2nd edition, Sage, 179–194.

Du Bois, W. E. B. (1935). *Black reconstruction: An essay toward a history of the part which Black folk played in the attempt to reconstruct democracy in America, 1860–1880.* Albert Saifer Publisher.

Du Bois, W. E. B. (1920). *Darkwater: Voices from within the veil.* Harcourt, Brace, & Howe.

Du Bois, W. E. B. (1899, 1967). *The Philadelphia negro: A social study. Noble Offset Printers, INC.*

Du Bois, W. E. B. (1940, 1986). *Dusk of dawn: An essay toward an autobiography of a race concept.* Library of America.

Feagin, J. R. (2013) *The white racial frame.* Routledge.

Free, M. (1999). Racial issues in contemporary criminology textbooks: the case of African Americans. *Contemporary justice review,* 1, 429–466.

Gabbidon, S. L., Taylor Greene, H., and Wilder, K. (2004). Still excluded? An update on the status of African American scholars in the discipline of criminology and criminal justice. *Journal of Criminal Justice Education,* 41, 384–406.

Gabbidon, S. L., and Taylor Greene, H. (2001). The presence of African American scholarship in early American criminology texts (1918–1960). *Journal of Criminal Justice Education,* 12, 301–310.

Human Rights Watch. (2000). United States: Stark race disparities in drug incarceration. http://www.org/news/2000/06/07/united-states-stark-race-disparities-drug-incarceration.

Marable, M. (1992). *Black America.* Open Media.

McCleskey v. Kemp. (1987). 481, US279.

Merriam-Webster Dictionary. (2014). http://www.merriam-webster.come/dictionary/buzzword. Accessed August 20, 2014.

Merton, R. K. (1947). Discrimination and the American creed. In R. M. MacIver (ed.) *Discrimination and National Welfare. Harper & Brothers,* 99–128.

Mitchell, M. D. (2013). The Color Line and Georgia History Textbooks: A Content Analysis. Thesis. Georgia State University.

Murakawa, N., and Beckett, K. (2010). The penology of racial innocence: the erasure of racism in the study and practice of punishment. *Law & Society Review,* 44, 695–730.

New York Times. (2014). End mass incarceration now. (May 25), SR 10.

Nunn, K. B. (2002). Race, crime, and the pool of surplus criminality: Or why the 'war on drugs' was a 'war on Blacks.' *The Journal of Gender, Race & Justice,* 6, 381–446.

Paul, R. (2014). Rand Paul: We must demilitarize the police. *TIME* http://time.com/3111474/rand-paul-ferguson-police/ Accessed August 14, 2014.

Peterson, R.D. (2012). The central place of race in crime and justice. *Criminology,* 50, 303–328.

Ramage, J. D. Bean, J. C., and Johnson, J. (2012). *Writing arguments.* Pearson Education, Inc.

Romanowski, M. H. (1996). Problems of bias in history textbooks. *Social Education,* 60, 170–173.

Rosich, K. J. (2007). *Race, ethnicity, and the criminal justice system.* American Sociological Association.

Sampson, R. J., and Lauritsen, J. L. (1997). Racial and ethnic disparities in crime and criminal justice in the United States. *Ethnicity, Crime, and Immigration,* 21, 311–374.

Solorzano, D. G. and Yosso, T. J. (2002). Critical race methodology: Counter-storytelling as an Analytical Framework for education research. *Qualitative Inquiry,* 8, 23–44.

Stewart, P. (1964). *Concurring opinion in Jacobellis v. Ohio, 378 U.S. 184, regarding possible obscenity in The Lovers.*

Taylor Greene, H. (2001). A multi-faceted analysis of the presence of African Americans in juvenile delinquency texts published between 1997 and 2000. *Journal of Criminal Justice Education,* 24, 87–101.

Taylor Greene, H., and Gabbidon, S. L. (2003). African American scholarship in criminological research published in the 1990s. *Journal of Criminal Justice Education,* 14, 1–15.

Tonry, R. (1995). *Malign neglect: Race, crime and punishment in America.* Oxford University Press.

Walker, S. (2011). *Sense and nonsense about crime, drugs, and communities* (7th edition.). Wadsworth.

Walker, S., Spohn, C., and DeLone, M. (2011). *The color of justice: Race, ethnicity, and crime in America.* Wadsworth.

Walker, S., and Brown, M. (1995). A pale reflection of reality: the neglect of racial and ethnic minorities in introductory criminal justice textbooks. *Journal of Criminal Justice Education,* 6, 61–83.

Wattsjohnson, Y. M. (2013). End white silence. *Multicultural Perspectives,* 5, 12–18.

Young, V., and Sulton, A. T. (1991). Excluded: the current status of African American scholars in the field of criminology and criminal justice. *Journal of Research in Crime and Delinquency,* 28, 101–116.

Zatz, M. S. (2000). The convergence of race, ethnicity, gender, and class on court decision making. *Criminal justice: The National Institute of Justice Journal,* 3, 503–552.

Zeece, P. D. (1997). Books, bias, and best practice. *Early Childhood Education Journal,* 24, 173–177.

Reading 1.4

2016 Presidential Address to the American Society of Criminology

Interrogating Race, Crime, and Justice in a Time of Unease and Racial Tension

Ruth D. Peterson, Department of Sociology, Ohio State University

This address has a twofold purpose. First, as the first African American to serve as president of the American Society of Criminology (ASC), I celebrate the contributions of scholars of color to the study of crime and criminal justice and to the ASC. I do so by pointing out the accomplishments of several African American scholars whose contributions are numerous and exemplary. I also emphasize that African Americans are joined in their efforts by scholars of multiple other colors, including, Latinos/as, Native Americans, and Asians. Second, in view of responses to apparent unrest and racial tension in U.S. society that is signaled by lethal violence between police and U.S. residents of color, I offer four recommendations regarding how we might proceed with our research, and report our findings, in ways that improve the likelihood of helping to inform societal debates and policy developments around crime and justice issues. In my conclusion, I encourage the ASC to 1) continue to grow the diversity of its membership and to integrate the research and findings of scholars of color into the mainstream of criminology; and 2) take further steps to conduct research and share findings with diverse audiences to ensure that post-truth does not become normative regarding crime and justice issues.

Thank you very much for that AMAZING ovation!!! Let me begin this address by thanking my friend Laurie Krivo for her warm introduction, for being my academic partner for nearly 25 years, and for serving with Katheryn Russell-Brown as program co-chairs for this very fine meeting. Laurie, Katheryn, and the great program committee that they put together are due full credit for the organization and success of the program that we have enjoyed at this conference. I am forever grateful to them. Along with the program committee, I must also sing the praises of Andrea Leverentz and Marianne Fisher Giorlando, who co-chaired the local arrangements

Ruth D. Peterson, "Interrogating Race, Crime, and Justice in a Time of Unease and Racial Tension," *Criminology*, vol. 55, no. 2, pp. 245–272.

committee, as well as of members Hollie Brehm, Xiaojin Chen, Kelly Frailing, and Volkan Topalli. They provided us with great information about, and suggestions for, enjoying New Orleans. I am also grateful to all of the committee chairs and members that worked on behalf of the Society during the past year. I wish that I could speak the name of every person who served, but our time is too limited. Still, I want to recognize them all for the work carried out under the auspices of my presidency; I can truly say that my most important contribution to the society this year was putting together very fine committees. They, in turn, undertook the work while I looked on assured that good decisions would be made.

Jody Owens II, thank you so very much for your work.[1] In the world of crime and criminal justice, little seems more important to me than efforts to assist young people in their plights to gain a little stake in this great society and, eventually, to become productive citizens. This means that we have to do all that we can to bring a measure of humanity even to those who are in trouble with the law. Thank you for doing your part in this respect and for setting an example that others can emulate. Also, thank you for sharing information about how and why you do the work that you do with this group. We can see from your comments the extent to which you are in the trenches. I commend you for your commitment, hard work, and jobs well done.

Finally, I want to thank all members of the ASC for providing me with this opportunity to serve as President of the Society. Being president of the ASC is an honor and rare privilege, one that I do not take for granted. I am also quite aware that the Society itself positioned me for this role by providing many opportunities that propelled me forward and helped to bring me to this moment.[2] There is a very long list of more senior (in career, that is) and peer scholars who have engaged with me, shared ideas, sponsored me in a variety of roles, supported my activities, or otherwise have made it possible for me to succeed. The group is so large that I have to forego any attempt to name them.

1. Jody E. Owens II is the 2016 recipient of the ASC "President's Award for Distinguished Contributions to Justice." This award was bestowed upon him for his work as the director and managing attorney of the Mississippi Office of the Southern Poverty Law Center. In this role, his contributions to justice are numerous and include addressing unconstitutional conditions of confinement of children and youth in for-profit and public detention facilities; efforts to reform Mississippi's juvenile justice, educational, and mental health systems; and litigating matters involving mass incarceration, private prisons, and the school to prison pipeline (see https://www.splcenter.org/about/staff/jody-owens-ii).

2. Participating in the ASC has helped to shape my career through knowledge and contacts that stemmed from being given the opportunity to serve as program chair for the 50th anniversary meeting; the collegiality and opportunities that come from participating in the Divisions on People of Color and Crime and on Women and Crime; being elected to the Executive Board for three different positions; being selected for several society and division awards (Fellow Status, the Sutherland Award, the Coramae Richey Mann Award, etc.); and having the graduate fellowships for race and ethnicity diversity named in my honor.

Thus, I hope that you all know who you are and know that I am grateful to each of you, individually and collectively, for being the village that helped to bring about this criminologist. I thank you all.

Progression of the Address

For the remainder of my time, I hope to make two general points related to the theme of this year's annual meeting: "The Many Colors of Crime and Justice." First, I seek to pay tribute to the contributions to criminology and criminal justice of people of color, particularly African Americans, but also other groups, for example, Latinos, Native Americans, underrepresented Asians, and the like.[3] Second, in light of recent real-world crime and justice events that signal a certain amount of unease and racial tension in contemporary society, I want to suggest a few directions that I believe would be fruitful for crime and justice researchers to take in their efforts to provide meaningful information that would help to inform ongoing discussions and policy directions. I see these two purposes of my talk as interrelated in ways that render it something of a hybrid of messages that are distinct in some ways but that cannot stand alone apart from one another.[4] Together, the two messages lend concrete meaning to the "Many Colors" theme. Thus, I hope that you gather from my talk how and why I see it as beneficial to democratize further both the study of crime and justice, broadly speaking, and the American Society of Criminology.

The Many Potential Colors of ASC Presidents

In her introduction, Laurie, and elsewhere Katheryn and Laurie, have drawn attention to the fact that I am both the first African American and the first African American woman to hold the office of ASC president (Krivo and Russell-Brown, 2016). They view this as a

3. Focusing on the contributions of people of color necessarily means that I am not giving due attention to the work of our White colleagues who have contributed to scholarship on race/ethnicity and crime/justice, and who have supported young scholars of every variety of color in their efforts to conduct research on issues related to this topic. I apologize for this important omission. Nevertheless, in the limited timeframe of this presentation and in the limited space for the resulting *Criminology* article, I feel that on this occasion, it is important to draw attention to some of the critical ways that scholars of color have contributed to criminology and to the Society. Still, I appreciate the contributions of colleagues of all colors in exploring the many colors of crime and justice and in fostering the success of young scholars from underrepresented groups.
4. The talk is also a hybrid in combining information based on 1) my professional knowledge of ongoing research and scholarly activities related to race/ethnicity and crime/justice and 2) my personal experiences with, and knowledge about, other scholars of color who have made, or are making, a mark on the field.

cause for celebration. I appreciate this point of view, and as noted, I am grateful to all of you for electing someone of my ilk to serve in this role. I also want to acknowledge that I am sharing this moment with Lorenzo Boyd who is in the middle of his term as the first African American male to serve as president of the Academy of Criminal Justice Sciences (ACJS).[5] Importantly, Lorenzo is not the first Black ACJS president. That honor goes to Janice Joseph.[6] Here, I want to set being the first African American president of the ASC in context, for the historical record as I have lived it as a member of the society, and by acknowledging the work of a few African American scholars on whose broad shoulders I have stood and continue to stand.

For starters, those of you who are familiar with my work know that for the past 20-plus years, it has been grounded in the thinking and prior work of two African American scholars who are not necessarily thought of as criminologists: Dr. William Edward Burghardt Du Bois and Dr. William Julius Wilson. In an effort to shed light on varying crime patterns across groups and neighborhoods of different colors, I have deliberately tried to bring research to bear on Du Bois' perspective on the positions of Blacks in urban America. As he noted:

> Crime is a difficult subject to study, more difficult to analyze into its sociological elements, and most difficult to cure or suppress. It is a phenomenon that stands not alone, but rather as a symptom of countless wrong social conditions (Du Bois, 1899 [1973]: 241–2).[7]

Besides attempting to demonstrate the contemporary applicability of Du Bois' claims, Laurie Krivo and I have been particularly interested in Wilson's arguments regarding how the industrial transformation of U.S. society has resulted in the "disproportionate concentration of the most disadvantaged segments of the urban black population" (Wilson, 1987: 58; see also Wilson, 1996), thereby creating a social milieu of concentrated disadvantage and

---

5. Lorenzo Boyd, whose scholarship focuses on policing, race, and crime, is an associate professor and chair of the Department of Criminal Justice at the University of Maryland—Eastern Shore. He is the 2016–2017 president of the ACJS.

6. Janice Joseph is Distinguished Professor of Criminal Justice at Stockton University. Her research focuses largely on delinquency and juvenile justice but also on gender issues. She was the 47th president of the ACJS during 2009–2010.

7. In his book, *The Philadelphia Negro*, W. E. B. Du Bois (1899 [1973]) sought to identify the *deeper social roots* of the overrepresentation of Philadelphia's "Negroes" in arrest, court, and prison statistics. As such, he provided a very early call for assessing and interpreting crime and justice statistics in the context of the times, as well as in relationship to the social circumstances of the lives of the groups under consideration.

social isolation for this group. This extreme disadvantage and social isolation is argued to lead to unusually high levels of crime (and other social dislocations) because of how it impedes the ability of communities to sustain basic institutional structures and various sources of social control. In several of my analyses with Laurie, we have examined the merits of Wilson's framework (e.g., Krivo and Peterson, 1996, Krivo, Peterson, and Kuhl, 2009; Peterson and Krivo, 1993).

We have also examined hypotheses drawn from Sampson and Wilson's perspective on the role of structural differentiation in accounting for crime across racially distinct communities, as suggested in the following claim (e.g., Krivo and Peterson, 1996; Peterson and Krivo, 2010):

> [T]he sources of crime [are] remarkably invariant across race and [are] rooted instead in the structural differences among communities, cities, and states in economic and family organization (Sampson and Wilson, 1995: 41).

Earlier today, it was a privilege for me to host a plenary featuring Bill Wilson along with Robert J. Sampson and María B. Vélez. In this session, they revisited the racial invariance hypothesis and the work attempting to test this theme, while posing a host of questions and issues for scholars to think about going forward. Although Bill has left the conference, I thank him for participating and for his work that has served as a catalyst for mine with Laurie, and in turn for María's, who is carrying forward her own brand of neighborhood crime research that also addresses issues raised by Wilson, Sampson and Wilson, Robert Bursik, and others (e.g., see Lyons, Vélez, and Santoro, 2013; Vélez, Lyons, and Boursaw, 2012; Vélez, Lyons, and Santoro, 2015).

Second, I dedicate this talk and this moment to the memory of Coramae Richey Mann and Laura T. Fishman, two strong and gifted African American women criminologists. Or as Gloria Naylor may have described them:

> [T]hey milled like determined spirits [within mainstream criminology].... They cursed, badgered, ... and shared their [wisdom].... They were hard-edged, soft centered, brutally demanding, and easily pleased [these pioneering women of criminology]. They came, they went, grew up, and grew old beyond their years. Like an ebony phoenix, each in her own time and with her own season had a story [of lasting import] (Naylor, 1983: 4–5).

Coramae's and Laura's entries into the field preceded mine by only a short time, and I have no doubt that had they lived longer, or had they been my exact contemporaries, one or both of them would have been elected to the office that I now hold. As it stands, they were "pioneers" whose legacies include three common characteristics: 1) a body of cutting edge scholarship on issues that continue to be significant; 2) a tradition of working hard to sponsor and bring young scholars along; and 3) active involvement in assisting community organizations in serving justice (or other troubled) populations and their families. Coramae was prolific, and her scholarship covered a variety of crime and justice concerns: criminal offending, unequal justice, female crime, how images of color shape images of crime and outcomes of justice, and so on (e.g., Mann, 1984, 1990, 1993, 1996; Mann and Zatz, 2002; see also Mars, 2002, for an assessment of Mann's contributions). She challenged us to take a comprehensive approach to understanding disparities by relying on broad societal theories and by bringing both quantitative and qualitative evidence to bear on the issues investigated. Coramae also emphasized that we should not ignore girls and women in examining issues of criminality or disparate treatment in criminal justice arenas.

Laura Fishman's early work was focused on an important collateral consequence of incarceration: family members "doing time on the outside." Research on this issue has surged in recent years as attention to what is termed "mass incarceration" and its consequences has taken hold (e.g., Braman, 2004; Christian, 2005; Comfort, 2003, 2007; Travis and Waul, 2003). But, Laura laid the groundwork for these more recent studies in her 1990 book titled, *Women at the Wall: A Study of Prisoners' Wives Doing Time on the Outside*, and related articles (e.g., Fishman, 1987, 1988, 1991). During the later part of her career, she took up the challenge of exploring issues related to prisoners and HIV/AIDS. These studies were focused on African American and Latino inmates, and she often examined issues related to their family and peer relations (e.g., Fishman, 2007).

Although I was not much younger in career than either Mann or Fishman, I personally benefitted from their advice and sponsorship. Moreover, I had the opportunity to witness how they worked one on one with younger scholars and with collective groups through building projects and fostering collaborations that enhance the productivity of all concerned. I have tried to follow in their footsteps in both regards, but I confess that I am probably better at building institutional structures to help foster the success of young scholars than I am in the one-on-one role, although I try. In either case, my success is in part their success, and I hope that my service as president of the American Society of Criminology honors them and gives voice to their legacies.

In thinking about pioneering criminologists of color, I would be remiss if I did not also offer shout-outs to Julius Debro and Darnell Hawkins who like Coramae and Laura preceded my entry into the field by only a brief period. Julius brought attention to drug use among minority populations, institutional racism in criminal justice, and education and training of criminology scholars (e.g., Bolek, Debro, and Trimble, 1992; Conley and Debro, 1997; Debro, 1976, 1981). He also taught many of us lessons about how to sponsor young scholars. In addition, Julius has been a model for how to build institutions and for how to give back to organizations that are instrumental in your success, including the ASC. In line with his efforts to contribute in these latter ways, the Division on People of Color and Crime (DPCC) recognized him by naming its service award in his honor. And I am proud to have been one of the recipients (with Laurie Krivo) of the Julius Debro Service Award for our efforts at institution building.[8]

Like Coramae Richey Mann, Darnell Hawkins has been a prolific contributor to the criminology and criminal justice literatures. It is impossible to itemize all the areas of research to which he has contributed but among them are attitudes toward police, family violence, homicide differentials, response bias in survey research, juvenile offending, juvenile justice, the courts, crime control and prevention, and so on (e.g., Baller et al., 2001; Hawkins, 1975, 1987, 2003, 2011; Schuck, Rosenbaum, and Hawkins, 2008). The breadth of Darnell's contributions means that his work overlaps with that of many in the field, including mine. Some of his analyses of racial disparities in criminal justice set the stage for work that I undertook on this topic, and I have benefitted considerably from his critiques of my work on legal decision-making and on the race and ethnic patterning of crime. Indeed, it is still difficult to conduct a study of racial disparities of any variety without having to wrestle with one or more of the methodological or theoretical critiques that Darnell offers as he continues to write and publish on race, crime, and justice. Even in retirement, he remains a critical voice warning us to think bigger, work harder, resharpen our reasoning, and capture more of the nuances of how race/ethnicity is related to crime/justice. In addition, our approaches to academic service and organizational involvement have meant that Darnell and I are often in the same rooms at the same time. As such, I have benefitted tremendously from his knowledge and his wisdom. Julius and Darnell, I am grateful to you for your pioneering efforts and for being there to assist all of us who followed you and now serve the field with you.

Robert Crutchfield and Vernetta Young are my African American criminology contemporaries. We came into the field around the same time, have stood together on many platforms, and share a commitment to helping to diversify both the organizations in which we participate (i.e., universities, research organizations, ASC, etc.) and perspectives on crime and justice. Bob's research has focused on inequality in crime and punishment with particular

8. In the early 2000s, Laurie and I helped to found the Racial Democracy, Crime and Justice Network (RDCJN), and served as co-principal investigators of this National Science Foundation–funded project to improve the quality of research on race/ethnicity and crime/justice and to support younger scholars from underrepresented groups in their efforts to succeed in academic careers.

attention to the role of labor markets, employment, and jobs at both individual and aggregate levels, as well as for both youth and adults (e.g., Crutchfield, 1989, 2014; Crutchfield, Matseuda, and Drakulich, 2006; Crutchfield and Pitchford, 1997; Crutchfield and Wadsworth, 2013). He has also focused attention on race/ethnicity and the criminal justice system (e.g., Crutchfield, Fernandes, and Martinez, 2010; Drakulich and Crutchfield, 2013). Vernetta took up the charge of gender, race, and criminal justice, especially with respect to incarceration and juvenile detention (e.g., Young, 1986, 1994; Young and Harrison, 2001; Young and Reviere, 2006; Young and Taylor Greene, 1995). She also gave systematic attention to the need and potential for incorporating African American perspectives into criminology research and curricula (e.g., Young and Sulton, 1991; Young and Taylor Greene, 1995). In light of her contributions, Adams-Fuller (2003) has written a biographical tribute to Vernetta.

Throughout my career, my work has overlapped with these scholars. For example, Bob and I share an interest in race/ethnic differences in neighborhood crime, and Vernetta and I have overlapping interests in addressing the role of women in crime and justice. In addition, all three of us (as individuals and collectively) have tried to address, in a practical way, some of the concerns raised by Vernetta and her colleagues pertaining to incorporating research and perspectives of African American and other underrepresented groups into the mainstream of criminology. In looking back, I can recall times that Bob, Vernetta, and I had cause to wonder aloud about surviving as African Americans in this very White criminological world. But we have survived and in the process have contributed some important findings, while working together à la Coramae Richey Mann, Laura Fishman, Julius Debro, and Darnell Hawkins to improve the environment and create infrastructures for the success of scholars of color that come after us. I am grateful to these kindred spirits for their contributions as individual scholars, as well as for being supportive colleagues for me, and others, along the way.[9]

Let me now return to Katheryn and Laurie's call for celebration; I say again that I am grateful to have my ASC presidency acknowledged as a mark of progress for the society and the discipline. At the same time, I believe that the ASC is a progressive organization. Therefore, I am certain that I will not be the last African American president and that I, and future African American presidents, will be joined by presidents of many colors, including Latinos, Asians, Native Americans, and the like. We shall not be "one and done."

---

9. Here, I have noted just six of my African American contemporaries who have made important contributions to the crime and justice literature and who have also been active in the ASC. Of course, there are many others, most of whom joined the field somewhat later than I (e.g., Shaun Gabbidon, Chinita Heard, Katheryn Russell-Brown, the late Becky Tatum, Helen Taylor Greene, etc.). All have made important substantive contributions to the field and have done their parts to enhance the quality of participation of other scholars of color.

Race/Ethnicity and Crime/Justice: Interrogating an Issue of Continuing Significance

During the ASC's 2011 annual meeting in Washington, DC, I had the privilege of giving the Edwin H. Sutherland Address (Peterson, 2012). I assumed that the address would be my swan song to the field.[10] Thus, I spoke to you about the direction that I believe studies of crime and criminal justice should take. I called for placing race and ethnicity at the center of crime and justice studies regardless of the particular focus and whether the goal is to understand disparate patterns across race and ethnic groups. Essentially, too, this call was a request for scholars to embed assessments of crime and justice within an understanding of broad-structured societal inequality and, as such, to recognize that race and ethnicity are organizing principles (i.e., structural conditions) within society that themselves condition the distribution of criminogenic conditions, the responses to crime, and the consequences that flow from these responses. I tried to illustrate the value of this structural approach with findings from a series of studies that Laurie and I have undertaken to account for disparities in neighborhood crime across communities of different colors (see, e.g., Krivo and Peterson, 1996; Krivo, Peterson, and Kuhl, 2009; Peterson and Krivo, 2010). This is also the approach that members of the Racial Democracy, Crime and Justice Network (RDCJN) and I recommended in our book on *The Many Colors of Crime,* where we laid out a specific research agenda for developing a broader and deeper understanding of the relationship between race/ethnicity and crime/justice (Peterson, Krivo, and Hagan, 2006).

Although I still consider my Sutherland address to be my most fundamental statement to the Society, a year later at the 2012 meeting in Atlanta, and following in the wake of the killing of Trayvon Martin by George Zimmerman and its aftermath, I shared the podium with Elijah Anderson to discuss the implications of this case for criminological research.[11] Referring to his article, "The Iconic Ghetto," Eli argued that events like the Martin–Zimmerman incident stem from the fear-inducing image of Blacks that come from the fact that many members of this group reside in the "Iconic Ghetto," i.e., disadvantaged urban areas that have come

---

10. During the summer of 2011, I retired from my faculty position at Ohio State University. Unlike Darnell Hawkins, I did not expect to continue to conduct research and write scholarly articles. Instead, I anticipated that any continuing academic contributions would be through my work with the RDCJN in facilitating the academic progress of younger scholars from underrepresented groups.

11. Elijah Anderson (urban ethnographer and sociologist at Yale University) is another scholar of color who has contributed important scholarship to the crime and justice area. Most notably, his writings on the role of culture, particularly the code of the street, provides a mainstay perspective on the relationship between structure and culture in contributing to crime in neighborhoods (Anderson 1994, 1999). As such, Anderson's conceptualization and research on this issue has laid the foundation for a host of investigations of how culture is linked to crime (e.g., Jones, 2009; Kirk and Papachristos, 2011; Matsueda, Drakulich, and Kubrin, 2006; Stewart and Simon, 2010).

to symbolize the impoverished, crime-prone, drug-infested, violent area of the inner city where, in the minds of many, "the Black people live" (Anderson, 2012; see also, Anderson, 2011, 2015). My comments were focused on what kinds of research and research approaches would be required to assess the merits of Eli's claims. In speaking to these issues, once again, I called for a structural race approach to the study of crime and justice.

Well, here we are 4 years later, and I am singing pretty much the same song. At this point, the Trayvon Martin case seems long ago, but in my mind, it also marks a starting point for numerous highly publicized cases of young Black males dying prematurely under circumstances that render a lot of us ill at ease about the state of race relations in this country, the state of criminal justice in this country, and the state of criminal justice knowledge in the world. Most of the highly publicized cases involve police officers killing Black males in contexts where they claim that their own lives are being threatened. By now, some cases are so familiar that simply reciting the names of those killed (Michael Brown, Eric Garner, Freddie Gray, Tamir Rice, Alton Sterling, etc.) brings up uneasy images of how they were killed and raises questions regarding the meaning of their deaths in the context of a society where a fundamental principle is "equality before the law." Highly publicized cases like the ones noted are only a part of the story. According to "The Counted" database assembled by *The Guardian*, as of November 8, 2016, 903 people had been killed by police in the United States, with non-Whites (i.e., Blacks and Latinos) making up a disproportionate share (nearly 41 percent) of those killed. The respective figure for 2015 was 1,146 individuals killed by police. Similarly, *The Washington Post* data on "Fatal Force" report figures of 807 killed by police to date in 2016 and 991 in 2015.[12] Included in the mixture are killings of women and girls of color by police, which receive little coverage by the media and largely go unnoticed by the public (Crenshaw, 2016; see also, African American Policy Forum, 2015; Khaleeli, 2016).[13] Additional sources (e.g., Officer Down Memorial Page [ODMP] and Law Enforcement Officers Killed or Assaulted [LEOKA] data) report an elevation in killings of police officers by citizens that some say show racial motivations in reverse.[14]

---

12. By year's end 2016, "The Counted" database showed that the number killed had grown to 1,092 (The Guardian, n.d.); the corresponding figure for "Fatal Force" was 963 (The Washington Post, n.d.).
13. Based on the aforementioned databases, girls and women are approximately 4 to 5 percent of citizens killed by police. Crenshaw (2016) and others have drawn attention to the fact that the names and stories of the deaths of female victims go unrecognized in contexts where the names of many male victims are immediately recognized and their stories are known.
14. Based on ODMP data, in 2016, 142 police officers were killed in the line of duty, 79 by gunfire or other form of assault; other deaths were a result of accidents or certain illnesses (see http://www.odmp.org/search/year?year=2016). LEOKA data indicate that in 2015 (the latest year for which data are available), 41 officers were feloniously killed. Among known offenders ($N = 37$), 18 were non-White and 16 were White (see https://ucr.fbi.gov/leoka/2015).

Given their volume, and helped by the considerable media attention that some incidents have received, killings of non-Whites by law enforcement officers are having an influence in everyday society. Notably, the impact of publicized cases of killings of people of color by police, and vice versa, are multifold, including 1) the aforementioned assembly of databases by *The Guardian* and *The Washington Post* to track the numbers and circumstances of such killings; 2) a growing body of literature comprising assessments of the patterns, meaning, and consequences of such killings (e.g., Boyles, 2015; Durán, 2016; Hutto and Green, 2016; Johnson, Warren, and Farrell, 2015); 3) discussions on the right and left for changes in laws and legal procedures; 4) protest demonstrations and nascent social movements and counter movements (e.g., Black Lives Matter; Say Her Name; and the Yarn Mission); and dare I say, 5) growing recognition that it may be time to put race and ethnicity at the forefront of the study of crime and justice. In recognition of concerns about these types of killing and their implications for unrest and racial tension, in this final statement to the Society, I want to identify several specific ways in which I believe criminologists can work to contribute scholarship that would be timely and that would help to inform ongoing discussions and policy decisions.

Take Stock of How Race/Ethnicity and Crime/Justice Are Related

Race and ethnic disparities in crime and justice are long-standing. This is true regardless of the topic under consideration, for example, killings, sentencing, trust in criminal justice authorities, and the like. Such patterns raise the question of where we are in understanding how race/ethnic disparities come to be and function in society. Do the recurring observations mean that scholars have made little progress in explaining them or that society has made little progress in addressing them? Do the disparities observed in the twenty-first century reflect the same causes and have the same consequences as disparities observed in the nineteenth or the twentieth century? I do not know the answers to these questions, but I am certain that neither the distribution of crime or justice patterns, nor the research on these topics, is static. Thus, a timely and important step for scholars would be to take stock of what is known and not known about the linkages among race/ethnicity and crime/justice at this historical point, with an eye to how things have changed over time and what the patterns imply about the links between criminal justice outcomes and inequality in society (e.g., individuals' life chances, groups' democratic participation, and social engagement). I have in mind work similar to that undertaken by the National Academies of Sciences, Engineering, and Medicine (NASEM) on incarceration, which set in context the knowledge base and the meaning that should be attached to high rates of incarceration in the United States (Travis, Western, and Redburn, 2014).

A couple of illustrations may help to make clear why I see taking stock as important. First, perspectives on what appear to be racialized processes in criminal justice outcomes (police killings, arrests, sentences, etc.) have evolved over time. One contemporary viewpoint is that such outcomes are no longer the product of racial animus manifest in constant antagonism based on skin color and racial heritage. In earlier periods, events such as police killings of suspects of color that cause concern and controversy today would likely have been "inscribed in law, justified in public policy, and enforced through violence that was condoned and tolerated by White society" (Provine and Peterson, 2015: 325). In contrast, today's racial bias is argued to be implicit, more about the reactive side of individual minds than about conscious racial animus. This is the same type of explanation that Anderson offered in his 2012 talk in contrasting the death of Trayvon Martin at the hands of George Zimmerman in 2012 with that of Emmett Till in 1955.[15] It is also a theme that comes across in Johnson, Warren, and Farrell's (2015) recent volume, *Deadly Injustice*, that flowed from the Martin–Zimmerman incident. Several papers in *Deadly Injustice* describe the core of contemporary racism in terms of racial aversion and latent bias operating primarily at the unconscious level (e.g., Banks, Eberhardt, and Ross, 2006; Drakulich and Siller, 2015; Gau and Jordan, 2015; Kang et al., 2011; Like, Sexton, and Porter, 2015; Russell-Brown, 2015; Sykes et al., 2015). These studies add to a growing body of literature in which researchers assess the role of implicit bias in policing and other aspects of criminal justice (e.g., Greenwald, Oakes, and Hoffman, 2003; James, Klinger, and Vila, 2014; Lee, 2013; Rachlinski et al., 2008; Rattan et al., 2012).

One difficulty in considering the role of implicit bias in race/ethnic disparities in crime and justice is the fact that, apparently, we all hold implicit biases about people of color, and particularly about Blacks (Greenwald and Banaji, 1995; but see Shepherd, 2011; Shepherd, in press). If implicit bias is a "constant" (in statistical terms) in an inequitable society like the United States, then it must play a role in supporting inequality through the way that criminal justice officials organize their work and treat individuals with whom they come in contact. But the question for criminologists is how unconscious processes in the mind are turned into behaviors on the ground. In particular, we need to know when, where, and under what circumstances implicit biases are activated and turned into biased behaviors, speech, and discriminatory actions. Answering this question means going beyond individual studies to consider whole bodies of evidence on racial disparities. We need to know what conclusions can be drawn from collective sets of studies about the extent to which implicit bias operates to produce disparities on its own or in conjunction with the social circumstances surrounding crime and criminal justice. This type of taking stock will provide needed information

15. Emmett Till was a 14-year-old African American youth who was killed by Roy Bryant and his half-brother because these men were disturbed by Till's reported flirtation with Bryant's wife. The murder was grisly, and although they later admitted their guilt, the two men were acquitted during the original Mississippi trial.

on how implicit bias as a factor in disparities in criminal justice relates to legal culpability for disparate treatment (does it generally render disparate treatment as legally excusable); whether implicit bias becomes explicit difference in action in the same manner across various agencies/components of the criminal justice system, for different populations (as workers or targets), in public versus private spaces, when others are present or not, or in all types of settings (suburban, more urban, rural, well maintained, deteriorating, etc.); and how to address resulting inequalities if implicit bias is not a source of legal culpability but provides a broad base of support for disparities in crime and criminal justice. Assessing this last issue would include examining knowledge about how well strategies (educating publics, officials, etc.) for reducing the impact of implicit bias work, which ones would likely have the greatest benefits, and in what contexts. In brief, taking stock will permit criminologists to draw conclusions about what is known already about the role of implicit bias in crime and justice, its underlying causes and consequences, and what issues need further attention.

Understanding the links among immigration, crime, and justice is another area that would benefit from taking stock of the existing knowledge base. Notably, perspectives and research on the relationship between immigration and crime (at both individual and aggregate levels) have evolved over time. Media accounts and some earlier perspectives suggested that, through a variety of mechanisms, immigrant status contributes to greater participation in crime at the individual level and to higher crime rates in the aggregate (e.g., Wortley, 2009). Yet, the results of most recent research demonstrate that the link between immigration and crime is negative rather than positive (e.g., Ferraro, 2016; Green, 2016; Hagan, Levi, and Dinovitzer, 2008; Kubrin, Hipp, and Kim, 2016; Martinez, 2014; Martinez and Valenzuela, 2006; Ramey, 2013; Sampson, 2008; Stowell et al., 2013; Tonry, 1997; Wadsworth, 2010), and that "increasing immigration tracks with the broad reductions in crime the United States has witnessed since the 1990s" (Sampson, 2008: 2). Indeed, the findings from individual-level studies show that across generations, for the children of immigrants and then their children, crime and other problem behaviors are more rather than less prevalent, suggesting that U.S. nativity rather than immigrant status is more likely to be a prologue to participation in crime. Similarly, aggregate-level studies tend to provide evidence that rates of crime are lower in communities and areas with higher percentages of immigrants.

Interestingly, public and political perspectives have not necessarily kept pace with academic work (Sampson, 2008). For example, in the current political climate, it is not unusual to see news stories suggesting, or polling data showing, that many U.S. residents view immigration and crime as closely related (Calamur, 2016; Gallup, 2017; Pew Research Center, 2015; Rasmussen Reports, 2015; Somin, 2015). This discrepancy between researcher and public views is one reason that it is important to take stock of what we know and do not know about immigration and crime, as well as to share what we find with the public and policymakers. In this area, stock-taking endeavors could address how confident we should be in the findings and conclusions of scholarship showing negative (or positive) effects. By evaluating the literature as a whole, we can address questions such as the following: What factors are likely responsible for persistent or changing outcomes? How do changes over time in the contexts of immigration affect the relationship between immigration and crime? To what extent does the impact of immigration depend on which immigrant group is being considered (i.e., those who can eventually "become White" versus those whose color or other characteristics are associated with "minority" status) or whether an area is an established immigrant destination that has resources for integrating groups into the community? What are the effects of changes in immigration policies such as local police enforcement of federal immigration law, or laws that define immigrant status itself as a crime?

Overall, I am suggesting that in the current context where racial tensions seem to loom large, and where the public and policymakers are having conversations that might affect the extent of race/ethnic disparities in crime and justice going forward (in either direction), it is important for scholars 1) to take stock of what is known and not known on contemporary crime and justice issues; and 2) to share the findings from such assessments with concerned publics and officials in ways that help inform ongoing discussions, while pointing out additional research that is needed. For one example of how to impart scientific theories and research in a manner that would be accessible to lay and political publics, please visit the societypages.org (https://thesocietypages.org/pubcrim/). I recognize that concerns about race and ethnic patterns and disparities in criminal justice are ubiquitous. Thus, taking stock would be a big undertaking, and we might have to do so in stages. Still, the goal would be to assess what it is that we know with any degree of certainty, and what additional research is needed to advance our knowledge base and enhance the quality of decisions made in policy contexts. Having taken stock should also increase the likelihood that future work is aimed at investigating issues that need greater attention and that might be more informative for ongoing and future debates and policy efforts.

Undertake Directed Research to Answer Looming General Questions

After taking stock, we should use the knowledge gained from this process to undertake directed research aimed at answering looming general questions and shedding light on two related issues: 1) the processes through which race/ethnic disparities are achieved; and 2) the extent to which disparities reflect an *über* system of discrimination, making it more difficult for those subject to this system to overcome obstacles to achievement and social mobility. The importance of such assessments has been articulated by sociologist Barbara Reskin in two separate discussions about racial and gender disparities in stratification broadly speaking, not exclusively with respect to crime and justice (see Reskin, 2003, 2012). In her 2002 Presidential Address to the American Sociological Association, she argued that *explanation* of racial and gender disparities requires scholars to move beyond questions of how disparate are the patterns to examine the mechanisms or intervening variables that link ascribed characteristics to outcomes of varying desirability. It is fair to say that crime and justice scholars have increasingly attempted to examine causal mechanisms in their studies of race and ethnic disparities (e.g., Bishop, 2005; Bridges and Steen, 1998; Matsueda and Heimer, 1987; Ousey and Lee, 2008). Nonetheless, the relevant processes linking race/ethnic status to different crime and justice outcomes are not well understood for most areas of research undertaken by criminologists. Nor is it clear that we have addressed mechanisms at all levels of analysis that Reskin sees as important (i.e., interpersonal, societal, and organizational). Moreover, as we go forward in trying to understand such issues as how implicit bias contributes to race/ethnic disparities in crime and justice, it will be important to explore fully the mechanisms by which such bias is linked to disparate outcomes across race and ethnicity.

More recently, Reskin (2012) provided a system analysis of why racial disparities persist across multiple domains (e.g., residential location, schooling, employment, health, housing, credit, and justice) and with what consequences. She argues that these apparently separate domains are reciprocally related and comprise an integrated system:

> Pervasive disparities across major institutional spheres comprise a race discrimination system, [with] emergent effects that can affect their components.... [T]he emergent effect of pervasive racial disparities is *über* discrimination, a meta phenomenon that maintains or exacerbates black-white disparities (Reskin 2012: 18).

Thus, current attempts to advance racial justice in response to a given concern (e.g., disparities in sentences) likely do not work because researchers fail to take this system into account. As such, Reskin contends that we need to move away from developing ad hoc policy responses that focus on a given domain without attention to identifying and intervening at leverage points; implementing interventions that operate simultaneously across subsystems; isolating subsystems from the larger discrimination system; and directly challenging the processes through which emergent discrimination strengthens within-subsystem disparities.

Criminology and criminal justice scholars recognize the potential interrelatedness of subsystems (e.g., policing, prosecution, courts, and probation) of criminal justice. And some scholars attempt to capture the links between one component of that system and another through reciprocal feedback or other processes, or by highlighting how disparities in one entity build on and further disparities in another (e.g., Guevara, Herz, and Spohn, 2006; Rodriguez, 2010; Stolzenberg, D'Allesio, and Eitle, 2013; Wooldredge et al., 2015). However, to my knowledge, we do not have an overarching theory of how linkages work across multiple justice organizations. Furthermore, many studies of linkages between justice entities have focused on just two at a time.

Other studies aim to link criminal justice processes and outcomes to disparities in other social subsystems (e.g., employment, family context, health, housing, residential location, schooling, voting, and the like). Witness, for example, the growing body of literature on collateral consequences of criminal punishment (e.g., Foster and Hagan, 2009; Harris, 2016; Manza and Uggen, 2006; Pager, 2003, 2007; Pattillo, Weiman, and Western, 2004; Schnittker et al., 2015; Tewksbury and Mustaine, 2007; Western, 2006). Yet, here too our approach is piecemeal, focused on some areas of justice and societal components more than on others, considering just one entity each from the justice and society arenas, and not necessarily addressing reciprocity between the systems examined. In brief, then, criminologists should begin to conceptualize and examine empirically whether there is a system or systems of *über* discrimination within the criminal justice arena and, if so, how such is manifest in various contexts of location and time. Importantly, too, assessing *über* discrimination in the crime and justice context requires that we focus on and demonstrate the links within and across two levels: one pertaining to the interface between various agencies of crime and justice and another pertaining to the interface of criminal justice agencies and other institutional contexts. Indeed, it may be *essential* to address the latter issue as it pertains to the larger structural context of crime and justice. It is also important to have this information to tell the story of how crime and justice outcomes affect individuals' life chances and have consequences for democratic and full participation of groups in the United States and elsewhere.

Attend to Data Limitations by Collecting Data and Encouraging Data Collection

An additional concern in efforts to explain how and why race/ethnicity and crime/justice are associated is a lack of appropriate data for addressing some issues. For example, those who examine neighborhood crime have had to wrestle with data issues as no national database exists that includes crime counts for areas below the police department level. We have worked around this problem mainly by gathering address-based data from local departments (e.g., Krivo and Peterson, 1996; Kubrin et al., 2011; McNulty, 2001). But this has often meant examining neighborhood crime for a single or small number of places, thereby making it difficult to make comparisons across racially/ethnically distinct but economically similar neighborhoods, and to draw firm conclusions about broader areas of the United States or about the broad set of race/ethnic neighborhoods as some areas have much larger proportions of some groups than of others (but see Baumer, Wolff, and Arnio, 2012; Hipp, 2007; Peterson and Krivo, 2010).

As another example, there is a paucity of recent research on lethal encounters between citizens and police, in part due to a lack of data for situations in which police officers kill citizens. Earlier, I referenced *The Guardian* and *The Washington Post* as making available databases ("The Counted" and "Fatal Force," respectively) with information on lethal encounters in which police officers kill citizens. I am grateful to these news organizations for stepping in to track incidents and for keeping these records. Their availability allows us to provide estimates about who is involved in these incidents, which seems far better than guessing based on cases that gain extensive media attention. They also give us a perspective from the point of view of witnesses, as opposed to of police officers. At the same time, it is unfortunate that we do not have official law enforcement records about these events for a variety of reasons: for purposes of continuity in maintaining data that give us a picture of incidents over time as a public good (we do not know for how long news organizations will gather or keep data); for purposes of accountability in knowing how our public institutions behave; and to avoid suspicion that police and police departments are covering up (contrary to an implicit bias perspective) inappropriate or unlawful behavior by not reporting such incidents, thereby adding to mistrust of law enforcement.

These are just two examples of why I am concerned about the availability of data to investigate some issues. In both cases, efforts are being made to provide data of these types (e.g., Lauritsen and Cork, 2016). This gives me some hope, but there are many other areas where quality data are needed, such as observed for Canada (Millar and Owusu-Bempah, 2011; Owusu-Bempah and Millar, 2010). Also, there are efforts to curtail data-gathering and access to race-based data within the United States. For example, there is currently a bill (S. 103) proposed in the U.S. Senate to "disallow the use of federal funds ... to design, build, maintain, utilize, or provide access to a Federal database of geospatial information on community racial disparities or disparities in access to affordable housing" (https://www.congress.gov/115/bills/s103/BILLS-115s103is.pdf). This type of curtailment of data collection may have serious consequences for scholars interested in crime and justice. My point here is that when we are trying to find answers to sensitive questions that reflect on race/ethnic disparities as they pertain to crime and justice, it is important to have relevant data to answer questions. Thus, as we go forward with our work, we should be mindful of where the data limitations are, collect primary data when necessary and possible, speak up in requesting important types of data when opportunities arise, and make our voices heard against the curtailment of data such as proposed in S. 103. Otherwise, we will make limited progress in improving our knowledge base on some important issues.

Be Inclusive: Bring the Full Array of Diverse Perspectives, Approaches, and Colors of Scholars into the Mainstream of Criminology

My final recommendation brings us back to thinking about the contributions of scholars of color. Recently, Bob Crutchfield and I had occasion to comment on how much more colorful the membership of the ASC seems compared with when we first started attending these meetings. Back then, among the African American portion, we all knew one another and could call each other by name. This is no longer the case. There has definitely been growth in the number of scholars of color participating in the ASC, and not just scholars of the color Black. The growth in Latino scholars and scholarship may be even more pronounced. Nonetheless, scholars of color are still underrepresented in our fields. In addition, their research questions, approaches, and interpretations of patterns of crime and justice are underrepresented in the mainstream of crime and justice literature.

It is difficult to know with any certainty the true proportion (within the ASC or otherwise) of criminologists of color. Yet, recently, Miller and Brunson (2011) relied on race–ethnic identification of the ASC's membership to try to provide a count. They reported that among those who provided this information (approximately 61 percent of members), collectively non-Whites make up only an estimated 19.0 percent of our association's members, with 5.6 percent being Black, 5.1 percent Latino/a, 5.8 percent Asian, 1.0 percent Native American, and 1.4 percent identifying as "Other." Also, the results of research undertaken by the American Sociological Association (ASA), a field that historically has produced a large share of crime and justice scholars, indicates that scholars of color are a small proportion of participants in graduate sociology departments (Spalter-Roth and Erskine, 2007). Furthermore, the evidence from both criminology and sociology reveals that the relative representation of scholars of color decreases moving through career stages from PhD to full professor.[16] Miller

16. Data for sociology show that for the year 2000, assistant professors in sociology were distributed across racial groups approximately as follows: 77 percent White, 10 percent Black, 7 percent Asian or Pacific Islander, 4 percent Hispanic, 1 percent Native American, and less than 1 percent Other. Moreover, the already small representation of people of color is reduced as you proceed through the faculty ranks so that, by the full professor level, all persons of color make up only 10 percent of faculty, with the groups distributed as

and Brunson (2011) perceived this pattern to be suggestive of groups' relative status and ability to impact important norms, policies, and decisions within programs and within the field.

Others concur, pointing out that the problem of underrepresentation is not limited to the composition of the field. Notably and unfortunately, the research contributions of scholars of color tend not to work their way into the mainstream of the discipline. As Gabbidon, Taylor Greene, and Wilder (2004) note regarding the status of African Americans in criminology and criminal justice, Black scholars do not receive due recognition for their work. Their research is less likely to be published in prestigious mainstream journals, cited in other published works, discussed in textbooks, or taken into account by policy makers and the mainstream media. These scholars argue that the devaluing of African American scholarship coupled with Blacks' scarcity in doctoral granting institutions, on editorial boards, and in leadership positions within predominantly White universities have detrimental consequences for, among other things, understanding crime and justice and addressing problems related to crime and criminal justice treatment that are disproportionately borne by Blacks and other underrepresented populations (see also Kim and Hawkins, 2013; Turner and Myers, 2000). We have less research on patterns for other groups of color, but what is true for African Americans is likely true, at least in part, for Latinos and Native Americans.

Collectively, these types of underrepresentation may be consequential for understanding the relationship between race/ethnicity and crime/criminal justice. We need to account for the thinking and research findings of scholars of all colors in the interpretations and conclusions that we draw about the meaning and importance of crime and justice patterns. Notably, scholars of color are often familiar with the populations/communities being studied in a different way than our White colleagues. This means that by excluding scholars from underrepresented groups, and their work, we may be excluding different and valuable insights about, perspectives on, and approaches to investigating patterns of crime and justice. Indeed, we know from research on differential perceptions that people of different colors have different interpretations of crime and justice events, and often offer different kinds of explanations of participation in crime as offenders or victims (see Gabbidon, Taylor Greene, and Young, 2002, and Taylor Greene and Gabbidon, 2012, for a variety of African American perspectives on crime and justice). It is important to air alternative explanations, as well as to measure and analyze them as competing explanations alongside other perspectives. Also,

follows: Blacks = 4 percent, Asian or Pacific Islander = 4 percent; Hispanic = 2 percent; Native American = .3 percent, and Other = .4 percent. Nelson, Brammer, and Rhoads (2007) found similar patterns for several social science disciplines (economics, political science, psychology, sociology) that train scholars who study crime and justice (http://faculty-staff.ou.edu/N/Donna.J.Nelson-1/diversity/Faculty˙Tables˙FY07/07Report.pdf; see also, Curtis, 2015, at http://www.asanet.org/research-and-publications/research-sociology/research-briefs/faculty-pipeline-sociology-and-other-stem-disciplines).

excluded researchers may be asking fundamental questions that grow out of their specific experiences that could lead to basic, and crucial, findings. In my own case, I would not say that I have homegrown experience with crime in urban communities of color,[17] but most of the questions on which my career is based have been almost embarrassingly fundamental. Nonetheless, they were being overlooked in the mainstream. I could not overlook them because I had difficulty buying into the conclusions from other work; they often seemed oddly unrecognizable to me.

When I consider the research being undertaken by younger scholars of color today, I am impressed by the kinds of unique information that they are adding to our literature. Who else would give attention to explicating the role of Black Child Savers in the early juvenile court movement (Ward, 2012); violence and other offending among girls of color (Jones, 2009); race and deviance in online communities (Gray, 2012, 2014); the views and roles of officers of color in how minority communities are policed (Brunson and Gau, 2015; Owusu-Bempah, 2015); the consequences for minority youths of policing the paths to school (Rios, 2011; Shedd, 2015); how the racial divide operates in the context of local jails (Walker, 2016); guilt by association of law-abiding youth (Durán, 2013; Rios, 2011); racial/ethnic politics and consequences of enforcing immigration policies (Macias-Rojas, 2016; Zatz and Rodriguez, 2015); guilt by association of documented immigrants and U.S. Latino citizens (Armenta, 2017); and the like.

Upon seeing this list, some will complain that the work of some of the scholars noted is not "rigorous" enough for mainstream criminology, signaling that it is not quantitative. However, it behooves us to keep in mind that many varieties of evidence may be important in shedding light on a given subject. For example, although results from on-the-ground observational studies cannot answer the question of the extent to which policing strategies in non-White communities across the United States are exercised in a discriminatory manner, they can lend substance to related issues regarding trust, perceptions that residents hold about their experiences with police in various contexts, the sources of their concerns, the balance that residents would want to see struck between solving crime and use of particular targeted strategies like saturation policing in areas, or stop and frisk. For the sake of gaining such insights, I say, consider all types of evidence in trying to shed light on important issues, and build on what is offered in studies of all kinds.

17. I grew up in the rural South (southern Georgia) during the Jim Crow era and moved to Ohio after high school. Except for a few years in inner city Cleveland, during most of my time in the North, I have resided in college towns (Madison, Wisconsin; Iowa City, Iowa; Columbus, Ohio) and in predominantly White and middle-class areas of these locales.

Conclusion

Let me now summarize a few points and draw a few brief conclusions. First, I hope that you have gleaned from my talk a couple of themes regarding criminologists of color. Scholars of color have long contributed to the ASC and to the fields of criminology and criminal justice. Furthermore, the Society and the field have grown in their color composition over the past several decades. This is gratifying, but scholars of color are still underrepresented proportionately and in the degree to which their work is given credit and attention. Thus, we need to do more to increase the numbers and to make sure that the voices of all contributing scholars are heard, and that their work is not arbitrarily excluded from consideration in the mainstream literature, or in assessing the state of knowledge on issues of race, crime, and justice.

Second, the contemporary period of unrest and racial tension brings attention to the need for research that better accounts for race and ethnic disparities in crime and criminal justice outcomes. An important starting point is to take stock of what we know, do not know, and need to know, including what data we need access to and why.

Third, following from the proposed assessment, researchers should proceed to address questions that need attention but with an eye to shedding light on the mechanisms that link race/ethnicity with crime and justice at multiple levels, as well as on potential systems of *über* discrimination, including what consequences flow from them.

We have a long way to go, but the attention to these issues should have positive payoffs in the following ways. To begin, a diverse and integrated ASC is better positioned to offer a richer and deeper understanding of racial disparities. Therefore, by taking steps to enhance the participation of scholars of different colors in the field, as well as to enhance the extent to which their work is taken seriously, we will add value and offer a criminology in the future that is better able to make meaningful contributions to discussions about how and why racial and ethnic differences in social life, including with respect to crime and the criminal justice system, persist and change.

Additionally, by proceeding substantively in the manner that I have suggested, particularly with regard to *über* discrimination, we should make progress that is not possible when we confine ourselves to studying each part of the criminal justice system independently, and crime and justice processes as separate from a range of other institutions that together have powerful effects on people's lives in ways that may be more inequitable than any particular "net effect." Together, these steps will help us move beyond simple notions of individual discrimination that supposedly is more unconscious than explicit to much more complex and nuanced understandings. This should also mean a lesser likelihood of developing policies that are themselves discriminatory or add to existing disparities. For example, we would not end up decreasing stop and frisk because of its differential impact on race/ethnic groups only to shift to other types of surveillance with similar risks because we missed the real story about the social institutional bases for how groups are treated. In the process, value will be added to the progress that I have claimed by bringing in the perspectives of scholars of color and of others from distinct backgrounds.

Overall, then, we should use this time of social unrest and racial tension to think about where we are and where we go from here, as well as to begin the process of building an even more useful criminology, one that answers more fully questions, such as the following: What direction are racial and ethnic disparities taking? What do they mean in the twenty-first century racial/ethnic context? Under what circumstances do criminal justice activities harm individuals/communities in particular ways? What types of changes are needed in light of improved understanding of the problem? Furthermore, I hope that we will communicate our findings in such a way that groups and communities of all varieties will be able to understand them, identify themselves in our literature, and thereby, learn from and rely upon our work.

On a final note, in light of the outcome of the United States's recent presidential election, and the worry about what lies ahead for the most marginalized groups, I have been concerned about the relevance of giving an address that encourages people to keep doing research on inequality in crime and criminal justice. Throughout the writing process, I was nagged by the question of whether in the current social and political context undertaking research is the best way for criminologists to contribute to the well-being of our society, and especially to serve underserved and disadvantaged populations. But, while here in New Orleans, I learned that the *Oxford Dictionaries* chose the term *post-truth* as its word of the year. Post-truth is an adjective describing situations where facts are disregarded in the face of emotional appeals. This brought me to the realization that it is probably more important than ever to keep up our work to uncover the true patterns, causes, and consequences that are reflected in the diverse and too often oppressive realities faced by people in the United States and around the world in relation to crime and justice. Further, I was gratified to find this realization being underscored during the course of the conference as the justice reform activists, civil rights attorneys, and local justice officials who spoke during our plenaries one by one implored us to bring the data, and to provide the research results that allow them to tell the stories and make their cases for what Janai Nelson termed the "humanity of law" and the "order of justice."[18] I take their messages to heart and believe that criminologists serve society well to the extent that we undertake quality research and share important findings with diverse audiences, thereby ensuring that with respect to crime and justice, *post-truth* does not rule the day.

18. Janai Nelson is associate director-counsel of the NAACP's Legal Defense and Educational Fund, Inc. During the 2016 annual meeting of the ASC, she served as a panelist and gave a presentation during the "Civil Rights and Criminal Justice" Plenary Session.

References

Adams-Fuller, Terrie Marie. 2003. Living up to her convictions: A view into the life of Vernetta D. Young. *Women and Criminal Justice* 15:19–31.

African American Policy Forum. 2015. *Say Her Name: Resisting Police Brutality Against Black Women.* New York: Center for Intersectionality and Policy Studies. http://static1.squarespace.com/static/53f20d90e4b0b80451158d8c/t/560c068ee4b0af26f72741df/1443628686535/AAPF_SMN_Brief_Full_singles-min.pdf.

Anderson, Elijah. 1994. The code of the streets. *The Atlantic Monthly* 273:81–94.

Anderson, Elijah. 1999. *Code of the Street: Decency, Violence, and the Moral Life of the Inner City*. Norton.

Anderson, Elijah. 2011. *The Cosmopolitan Canopy: Race and Civility in Everyday Life*. Norton.

Anderson, Elijah. 2012. The iconic ghetto. *The ANNALS of the American Academy of Political and Social Science* 642:8–24.

Anderson, Elijah. 2015. The white space. *Sociology of Race and Ethnicity* 1:10–21.

Armenta, Amada. 2017. Racializing crimmigration: Local law enforcement agencies and the institutional production of immigrant criminality. *Sociology of Race and Ethnicity* 3:82–95.

Baller, Robert D., Luc Anselin, Steven F. Messner, Glenn Deane, and Darnell F. Hawkins. 2001. Structural covariates of U.S. county homicide rates: Incorporating spatial effects. *Criminology* 39:561–88.

Banks, R. Richard, Jennifer L. Eberhardt, and Lee Ross. 2006. Discrimination and implicit bias in a racially unequal society. *California Law Review* 94:1169–90.

Baumer, Eric P., Kevin T. Wolff, and Ashley N. Arnio. 2012. A multicity neighborhood analysis of foreclosure and crime. *Social Science Quarterly* 93:577–601.

Bishop, Donna M. 2005. The role of race and ethnicity in juvenile justice processing. In *Our Children, Their Children: Confronting Racial and Ethnic Differences in American Juvenile Justice*, eds. Darnell F. Hawkins and Kimberly Kempf-Leonard, University of Chicago Press.

Bolek, Catherine S., Julius Debro, and Joseph E. Trimble. 1992. Overview of selected federal efforts to encourage minority drug abuse research and researchers. *Drugs & Society* 6:345–75.

Boyles, Andrea S. 2015. *Race, Place, and Suburban Policing: Too Close for Comfort.* University of California Press.

Braman, Donald. 2004. *Doing Time on the Outside: Incarceration and Family Life in Urban America.* University of Michigan Press.

Bridges, George S., and Sara Steen. 1998. Racial disparities in official assessments of juvenile offenders: Attributional stereotypes as mediating mechanisms. *American Sociological Review* 63:554–70.

Brunson, Rod K., and Jacinta Gau. 2015. Officer race vs. macrolevel context: A test of competing hypotheses about Black citizens' experiences with and perceptions of Black police officers. *Crime & Delinquency* 61:213–42.

Calamur, Krishnadev. 2016. Are immigrants prone to crime and terrorism? *The Atlantic*. https://www.theatlantic.com/news/archive/2016/06/immigrants-and-crime/486884/.

Christian, Johnna. 2005. Riding the bus: Barriers to prison visitation and family management strategies. *Journal of Contemporary Criminal Justice* 21:31–48.

Comfort, Megan. 2003. In the tube at San Quentin: The "secondary prisonization" of women visiting inmates. *Journal of Contemporary Ethnography* 32:77–107.

Comfort, Megan. 2007. *Doing Time Together: Love and Family in the Shadow of the Prison*. University of Chicago Press.

Conley, Darlene J., and Julius Debro. 1997. School and community politics: Issues, concerns, and implications when conducting research in African-American communities. *Substance Use & Misuse* 32:1973–8.

Crenshaw, Kimberlé. 2016. Presentation during plenary session on Protesting racism: Dynamics of "Black Lives Matter" as a social movement. Presented at the annual meeting of the American Sociological Association, Seattle, WA, August.

Crutchfield, Robert D. 1989. Labor stratification and violent crime. *Social Forces* 68:489–512.

Crutchfield, Robert D. 2014. *Get a Job: Labor Markets, Economic Opportunity and Crime*. New York University Press.

Crutchfield, Robert D., April Fernandes, and Jorge Martinez. 2010. Racial disparity in the criminal justice system: How much is too much? *Journal of Criminal Law and Criminology* 100:903–32.

Crutchfield, Robert D., Ross Matsueda, and Kevin Drakulich. 2006. Race, labor markets and neighborhood violence. In *The Many Colors of Crime: Inequalities of Race, Ethnicity, and Crime in America*, eds. Ruth D. Peterson, Lauren J. Krivo, and John Hagan. New York University Press.

Crutchfield, Robert D., and Susan R. Pitchford. 1997. Work and crime: The effects of labor stratification. *Social Forces* 76:93–118.

Crutchfield, Robert D., and Tim Wadsworth. 2013. Aggravated inequality: Neighborhoods, school, and juvenile delinquency. In *Macro Economic Effects on Youth Violence*, ed. Richard Rosenfeld. New York University Press.

Curtis, John W. 2015. The faculty pipeline in sociology and other STEM disciplines. *American Sociological Association*. http://www.asanet.org/research-and-publications/research-sociology/research-briefs/faculty-pipeline-sociology-and-other-stem-disciplines.

Debro, Julius. 1976. The Black offender as victim. In *Afro-Americans: A Social Science Perspective*, eds. Rutledge M. Dennis and Charles Jarmon. University Press of America.

Debro, Julius. 1981. Criminology and criminal justice education in historically black colleges and universities. In *Race, Crime, and Criminal Justice*, eds. R. L. McNeely and Carl Pope. Sage.

Drakulich, Kevin M. and Robert D. Crutchfield. 2013. The role of perceptions of the police in informal social control: Implications for the racial stratification of crime and control. *Social Problems* 60:383–407.

Drakulich, Kevin M., and Laura Siller. 2015. Presumed danger: Race, bias, stigma, and perceptions of crime and criminals. In *Deadly Injustice: Trayvon Martin, Race and the Criminal Justice System*, eds. Devon Johnson, Patricia Y. Warren, and Amy Farrell. New York University Press.

Du Bois, W. E. B. 1899 [1973]. *The Philadelphia Negro: A Social Study*. University of Pennsylvania Press.

Durán Robert J. 2013. *Gang Life in Two Cities: An Insider's Journey*. Columbia University Press.

Durán, Robert J. 2016. No justice, no peace. *Du Bois Review: Social Science Research on Race* 13:61–83.

Ferraro, Vincent. 2016. Immigration and crime in the new destinations, 2000–2007: A test of the disorganizing effect of migration. *Journal of Quantitative Criminology* 32: 1–23.

Fishman, Laura T. 1987. Patterns of accommodation among wives of criminals. *Journal of Contemporary Ethnography* 16:176–204.

Fishman, Laura T. 1988. Stigmatization and prisoners' wives' feelings of shame. *Deviant Behavior* 9:169–92.

Fishman, Laura T. 1990. *Women at the Wall: A Study of Prisoners' Wives Doing Time on the Outside*. State University of New York Press.

Fishman, Laura T. 1991. Treacherous trysts, tender trade: Prisoners' wives as contacts and contraband carriers. *Women and Criminal Justice* 2:45–70.

Fishman, Laura T. 2007. Resistance, redemption, and transformation: African American and Latino prisoners living with the HIV/AIDS virus. In *Racializing Justice, Disenfranchising Lives: The Racism, Criminal Justice, and Law Reader*, eds. Manning Marable, Keesha Middlemass, and Ian Steinberg. Palgrave MacMillan.

Foster, Holly, and John Hagan. 2009. The mass incarceration of parents in America: Issues of race/ethnicity, collateral damage to children, and prisoner reentry. *The ANNALS of the American Academy of Political and Social Science* 623:179–94.

Gabbidon, Shaun L., Helen Taylor Greene, and Vernetta D. Young. 2002. *African American Classics in Criminology and Criminal Justice*. Sage.

Gabbidon, Shaun L., Helen Taylor Greene, and Kideste Wilder. 2004. Still excluded? An update on the status of African American scholars in the discipline of criminology and criminal justice. *Journal of Research in Crime and Delinquency* 41:384–406.

Gallup. 2017. Immigration. http://www.gallup.com/poll/1660/Immigration.aspx.

Gau, Jacinta M., and Kareem L. Jordan. 2015. Profiling Trayvon: Young Black males, suspicion, and surveillance. In *Racializing Justice, Disenfranchising Lives: The Racism, Criminal Justice, and Law Reader*, eds. Manning Marable, Keesha Middlemass, and Ian Steinberg. Palgrave MacMillan.

Gray, Kishonna L. 2012. Deviant bodies, stigmatized identities, and racist acts: Examining the experiences of African-American gamers in Xbox Live. *New Review of Hypermedia and Multimedia* 18:261–76.

Gray, Kishonna L. 2014. *Race, Gender, and Deviance in Xbox Live: Theoretical Perspectives from the Virtual Margins*. Routledge.

Green, David. 2016. The Trump hypothesis: Testing immigrant populations as a determinant of violent and drug-related crime in the United States. *Social Science Quarterly* 97:506–24.

Greenwald, Anthony G., and Mahzarin R. Banaji. 1995. Implicit social cognition: Attitudes, self-esteem, and stereotypes. *Psychological Review* 102:4–27.

Greenwald, Anthony G., Mark A. Oakes, and Hunter G. Hoffman. 2003. Targets of discrimination: Effects of race on responses to weapons holders. *Journal of Experimental Social Psychology* 39:399–405.

The Guardian. n.d. The Counted: People killed by the police in the US, recorded by the Guardian—with your help. https://www.theguardian.com/us-news/series/counted-us-police-killings.

Guevara, Lori, Denise Herz, and Cassia Spohn. 2006. Gender and juvenile justice decision making: What role does race play? *Feminist Criminology* 1:258–82.

Hagan, John, Ron Levi, and Ronit Dinovitzer. 2008. The symbolic violence of the crime-immigration nexus: Migrant mythologies in the Americas. *Criminology & Public Policy* 7:95–112.

Harris, Alexes. 2016. *A Pound of Flesh: Monetary Sanctions as Punishment for the Poor* (American Sociological Association's Rose Series). Russell Sage Foundation.

Hawkins, Darnell F. 1975. Estimation of nonresponse bias. *Sociological Methods and Research* 3:461–88.

Hawkins, Darnell F. 1987. Beyond anomalies: Rethinking the conflict perspective on race and criminal punishment. *Social Forces* 65:719–45.

Hawkins, Darnell F. 2003. On the horns of a dilemma: Criminal wrongs, civil rights, and the administration of justice in African-American communities. *Contributions in Criminology and Penology* 55:431–58.

Hawkins, Darnell F. 2011. Things fall apart: Revisiting race and ethnic differences in criminal violence amidst a crime drop. *Race and Justice* 1:3–48.

Hipp, John R. 2007. Income inequality, race, and place: Does the distribution of race and class within neighborhoods affect crime rates? *Criminology* 45:665–97.

Hutto, Jonathan W. Sr., and Rodney D. Green. 2016. Social movements against racist police brutality and department of justice intervention in Prince George's County, Maryland. *Journal of Urban Health: Bulletin of the New York Academy of Medicine* 93:S89–121.

James, Lois, David Klinger, and Bryan Vila. 2014. Racial and ethnic bias in decisions to shoot seen through a stronger lens: Experimental results from high-fidelity laboratory simulations. *Journal of Experimental Criminology* 10:323–40.

Johnson, Devon, Patricia Y. Warren, and Amy Farrell. 2015. *Deadly Injustice: Trayvon Martin, Race, and the Criminal Justice System*. New York University Press.

Jones, Nikki. 2009. *Between Good and Ghetto: African American Girls and Inner-City Violence* (Rutgers Series in Childhood Studies). Rutgers University Press.

Kang, Jerry, Mark Bennett, Devon Carbado, Pam Casey, Nilanjana Dasgupta, David Faigman, Rachel Godsil, Anthony G. Greenwald, Justin Levinson, and Jennifer Mnookin. 2011. Implicit bias in the courtroom. *University of California Los Angeles Law Review* 59:1124.

Khaleeli, Homa. 2016. #SayHerName: Why Kimberlé Crenshaw is fighting for forgotten women. *The Guardian*. May 30. https://www.theguardian.com/lifeandstyle/2016/may/30/sayhername-why-kimberle-crenshaw-is-fighting-for-forgotten-women.

Kim, Bitna, and Paul M. Hawkins. 2013. Who's getting cited: Representation of women and non-white scholars in major American criminology and criminal justice journals between 1986–2005. *International Journal of Criminology and Sociology* 2:306–21.

Kirk, David S., and Andrew V. Papachristos. 2011. Cultural mechanisms and the persistence of neighborhood violence. *American Journal of Sociology* 116:1190–233.

Krivo, Lauren J., and Ruth D. Peterson. 1996. Extremely disadvantaged neighborhoods and urban crime. *Social Forces* 75:619–48.

Krivo, Lauren J., Ruth D. Peterson, and Danielle P. Kuhl. 2009. Segregation, racial structure, and neighborhood violent crime. *American Journal of Sociology* 114:1765–1802.

Krivo, Lauren J., and Katheryn Russell-Brown. 2016. ASC in New Orleans: The many colors of crime and justice. *The Criminologist* 41:1–4.

Kubrin, Charis E., John R. Hipp, and Young-An Kim. 2016. Different than the sum of its parts: Examining the unique impacts of immigrant groups on neighborhood crime rates. *Journal of Quantitative Criminology*. Epub ahead of print. doi:10.1007/s10940-016-9320-y.

Kubrin, Charis E., Gregory D. Squires, Steven M. Graves, and Graham C. Ousey. 2011. Does fringe banking exacerbate neighborhood crime rates? *Criminology & Public Policy* 10:437–66.

Lauritsen, Janet L., and Daniel L. Cork, eds. 2016. *Modernizing Crime Statistics—Report 1: Defining and Classifying Crime* (Panel on Modernizing the Nation's Crime Statistics, Committee on National Statistics and Committee on Law and Justice). The National Academies Press. http://www.nap.edu/c.

Lee, Cynthia. 2013. Making race salient: Trayvon Martin and implicit bias in a not yet post-racial society. *North Carolina Law Review* 91:1556–612.

Like, Toya, Lori Sexton, and Savannah Porter. 2015. Threat, danger and vulnerability: Trayvon Martin and Gwen Araujo. In *Racializing Justice, Disenfranchising Lives: The Racism, Criminal Justice, and Law Reader*, eds. Manning Marable, Keesha Middlemass, and Ian Steinberg. Palgrave MacMillan.

Lyons, Christopher J., María B. Vélez, and Wayne A. Santoro. 2013. Neighborhood immigration, violence, and city-level immigrant political opportunities. *American Sociological Review* 78:604–32.

Macias-Rojas, Patrisia. 2016. *From Deportation to Prison: The Politics of Immigration Enforcement in Post-Civil Rights America*. New York University Press.

Mann, Coramae Richey. 1984. *Female Crime and Delinquency*. University of Alabama Press.

Mann, Coramae Richey. 1990. Black female homicide in the United States. *Journal of Interpersonal Violence* 5:176–201.

Mann, Coramae Richey. 1993. *Unequal Justice: A Question of Color*. Indiana University Press.

Mann, Coramae Richey. 1996. *When Women Kill*. State University of New York Press.

Mann, Coramae Richey, and Marjorie Sue Zatz (eds.). 2002. *Images of Color, Images of Crime: Readings*. Roxbury.

Manza, Jeff, and Christopher Uggen. 2006. *Locked Out: Felon Disenfranchisement and American Democracy*. Oxford University Press.

Mars, Joan Rosemary. 2002. Coramae Richey Mann on women, crime and the color of American justice. *Women and Criminal Justice* 13:1–25.

Martinez, Ramiro, Jr. 2014. *Latino Homicide: Immigration, Violence, and Community*. Routledge.

Martinez, Ramiro, and Abel Valenzuela Jr. (eds.). 2006. *Immigration and Crime: Race, Ethnicity, and Violence*. New York University Press.

Matsueda, Ross L., Kevin Drakulich, and Charis E. Kubrin. 2006. Race and neighborhood codes of violence. In *The Many Colors of Crime: Inequalities of Race, Ethnicity, and Crime in America*, eds. Ruth D. Peterson, Lauren J. Krivo, and John Hagan. New York University Press.

Matsueda, Ross L., and Karen Heimer. 1987. Race, family structure, and delinquency: A test of differential association and social control theories. *American Sociological Review* 52:826–40.

McNulty, Thomas L. 2001. Assessing the race-violence relationship at the macro level: The assumption of racial invariance and the problem of restricted distributions. *Criminology* 39:467–90.

Millar, Paul, and Akwasi Owusu-Bempah. 2011. Whitewashing criminal justice in Canada: Preventing research through data suppression. *Canadian Journal of Law and Society* 26:653–61.

Miller, Jody, and Rod K. Brunson. 2011. Minority candidates are highly encouraged to apply: Making diversity matter in criminology and criminal justice. *The Criminologist* 36:17.

Naylor, Gloria. 1983. *The Women of Brewster Place: A Novel in Seven Stories*. New York: Penguin Books.

Nelson, Donna J., Christopher N. Brammer, and Heather Rhoads. 2007. A National Analysis of Minorities in Science and Engineering Faculties at Research Universities. http://faculty-staff.ou.edu/N/Donna.J.Nelson-1/diversity/Faculty_Tables_FY07/07Report.pdf.

Ousey, Graham C., and Matthew R. Lee. 2008. Racial disparity in formal social control: An investigation of alternative explanations of arrest rate inequality. *Journal of Research in Crime and Delinquency* 45:322–55.

Owusu-Bempah, Akwasi. 2015. Black police officers' perspectives on crime control and police legitimacy in Toronto, Canada. Presented at the annual meeting of the Racial Democracy, Crime and Justice Network. Columbus, OH, July.

Owusu-Bempah, Akwasi, and Paul Millar. 2010. Research note: Revisiting the collection of "Justice Statistics by Race" in Canada. *Canadian Journal of Law and Society* 25:97–104.

Pager, Devah. 2003. The mark of a criminal record. *American Journal of Sociology* 108:937–75.

Pager, Devah. 2007. *Marked: Race, Crime, and Finding Work in an Era of Mass Incarceration*. University of Chicago Press.

Pattillo, Mary E., David Weiman, and Bruce Western (eds.). 2004. *Imprisoning America: The Social Effects of Mass Incarceration*. Russell Sage Foundation.

Peterson, Ruth D. 2012. The central place of race in crime and justice—The American Society of Criminology's 2011 Sutherland address. *Criminology* 50:303–28.

Peterson, Ruth D., and Lauren J. Krivo. 1993. Racial segregation and black urban homicide. *Social Forces* 71:1001–26.

Peterson, Ruth D., and Lauren J. Krivo. 2010. *Divergent Social Worlds: Neighborhood Crime and the Racial-Spatial Divide*. Russell Sage Foundation.

Peterson, Ruth D., Lauren J. Krivo, and John Hagan. 2006. *The Many Colors of Crime: Inequalities of Race, Ethnicity, and Crime in America*. New York University Press.

Pew Research Center. 2015. Half say immigrants in the U.S. are making crime and economy worse. September 23. http://www.pewhispanic.org/2015/09/28/modern-immigration-wave-brings-59-million-to-u-s-driving-population-growth-and-change-through-2065/ph_2015-09-28_immigration-through-2065-44/.

Provine, Doris Marie, and Ruth D. Peterson. 2015. Afterword: Reducing racialized violence and deracializing justice. In *Deadly Injustice: Trayvon Martin, Race, and the Criminal Justice System*, eds. Devon Johnson, Patricia Y. Warren, and Amy Farrell. New York University Press.

Rachlinski, Jeffrey J., Sheri Lynn Johnson, Andrew J. Wistrich, and Chris Guthrie. 2008. Does unconscious racial bias affect trial judges. *Notre Dame Law Review* 84:1195.

Ramey, David. 2013. Immigrant revitalization and neighborhood violent crime in established and new destination cities. *Social Forces* 92:597–629.

Rasmussen Reports. 2015. Most agree with Trump that illegal immigration increases crime. July 8. http://www.rasmussenreports.com/public_content/politics/current_events/immigration/july_2015/most_agree_with_trump_that_illegal_immigration_increases crime.

Rattan, Aneeta, Cynthia S. Levine, Carol S. Dweck, and Jennifer L. Eberhardt. 2012. Race and the fragility of the legal distinction between juveniles and adults. *PLoS one* 7:e36680. doi:10.1371/journal.pone.0036680.

Reskin, Barbara F. 2003. Modeling ascriptive inequality: From motives to mechanisms. *American Sociological Review* 68:1–21.

Reskin, Barbara F. 2012. The race discrimination system. *Annual Review of Sociology* 38:17–35.

Rios, Victor M. 2011. *Punished: Policing the Lives of Black and Latino Boys*. New York University Press.

Rodriguez, Nancy. 2010. The cumulative effect of race and ethnicity in juvenile court outcomes and why preadjudication detention matters. *Journal of Research in Crime and Delinquency* 47:391–413.

Russell-Brown, Katheryn. 2015. Go ahead and shoot—the law might have your back: History, Race, implicit bias, and justice in Florida's stand your ground law. In *Racializing Justice, Disenfranchising Lives: The Racism, Criminal Justice, and Law Reader*, eds. Manning Marable, Keesha Middlemass, and Ian Steinberg. Palgrave MacMillan.

Sampson, Robert J. 2008. Rethinking crime and immigration. *Contexts* 7:28–33.

Sampson, Robert J., and William J. Wilson. 1995. Toward a theory of race, crime, and urban inequality. In *Crime and Inequality*, eds. John Hagan and Ruth D. Peterson. Stanford University Press.

Schnittker, Jason, Christopher Uggen, Sarah K.S. Shannon, and Suzy McElrath. 2015. The institutional effects of incarceration: Spillovers from criminal justice to health care. *Milbank Quarterly* 93:516–60.

Schuck, Amie M., Dennis P. Rosenbaum, and Darnell F. Hawkins. 2008. The influence of race/ethnicity, social class, and neighborhood context on residents' attitudes toward the police. *Police Quarterly* 11:496–519.

Shedd, Carla. 2015. *Unequal City: Race, Schools, and Perceptions of Injustice*. Russell Sage Foundation.

Shepherd, Hana. 2011. The cultural context of cognition: What the implicit association test tells us about how culture works. *Sociological Forum* 26:121–43.

Shepherd, Hana. In press. Methods for studying the contextual nature of implicit cognition. In *Oxford Handbook of Cognitive Sociology*, eds. Wayne Brekhus and Gabriel Ignatow. Oxford University Press.

Somin, Ilya. 2015. The Volokh conspiracy: Immigration and crime. *The Washington Post*. https://www.washingtonpost.com/news/volokh-conspiracy/wp/2015/07/14/immigration-and-crime/?utm_term=.8d3c4141e0e1.

Spalter-Roth, Roberta, and William Erskine. 2007. Race and ethnicity in the sociology pipeline (ASA Research Brief). American Sociological Association Research and Development Department. http://www.asanet.org/research-and-publications/research-sociology/research-briefs/race-and-ethnicity-sociology-pipeline.

Stewart, Eric A., and Ronald L. Simons. 2010. Race, code of the street, and violent delinquency: A multilevel investigation of neighborhood street culture and individual norms of violence. *Criminology* 48:569–605.

Stolzenberg, Lisa, Stewart J. D'Alessio, and David Eitle. 2013. Race and cumulative discrimination in the prosecution of criminal defendants. *Race and Justice* 3:275–99.

Stowell, Jacob I., Steven F. Messner, Michael S. Barton, and Lawrence E. Raffalovich. 2013. Addition by subtraction? A longitudinal analysis of the impact of deportation efforts on violent crime. *Law & Society Review* 47:909–42.

Sykes, L. Bryan, Alex R. Piquero, Jason Gioviano, and Nicolas Pittman. 2015. Up to no good: The context of adolescent discrimination in neighborhoods. In *Racializing Justice, Disenfranchising Lives: The Racism, Criminal Justice, and Law Reader*, eds. Manning Marable, Keesha Middlemass, and Ian Steinberg. Palgrave MacMillan.

Taylor Greene, Helen, and Shaun L. Gabbidon. 2012. *African American Criminological Thought.* SUNY Press.

Tewksbury, Richard, and Elizabeth Ehrhardt Mustaine. 2007. Collateral consequences and community re-entry for registered sex offenders with child victims: Are the challenges even greater? *Journal of Offender Rehabilitation* 46:113–31.

Tonry, Michael. 1997. Ethnicity, crime, and immigration. In *Crime and Justice: A Review of Research*, vol. 21, ed. Michael Tonry. University of Chicago Press.

Travis, Jeremy, and Michelle Waul. 2003. *Prisoners Once Removed: The Impact of Incarceration and Reentry on Children, Families, and Communities*. The Urban Institute.

Travis, Jeremy, Bruce Western, and Stephens Redburn (eds.). 2014. *The Growth in Incarceration Rates in the United States: Exploring Causes and Consequences* (Committee on Law and Justice, Division of Behavioral and Social Sciences and Education). The National Academies Press.

Turner, Caroline Sotello Viernes, and Samuel L. Myers. 2000. *Faculty of Color in Academe: Bittersweet Success.* Allyn & Bacon.

Vélez, María B., Christopher J. Lyons, and Blake Boursaw. 2012. Assessing the relationship between mortgage lending and crime: An analysis of Seattle neighborhoods (1981–2007). *Criminology* 50:1025–56.

Vélez, María B., Christopher J. Lyons, and Wayne A. Santoro. 2015. The political context of the percent Black-neighborhood violence link: A multilevel analysis. *Social Problems* 62:93–119.

Wadsworth, Tim. 2010. Is immigration responsible for the crime drop? An assessment of the influence of immigration on changes in violent crime between 1990 and 2000. *Social Science Quarterly* 91:531–53.

Walker, Michael L. 2016. Race making in a penal institution. *American Journal of Sociology* 121:1051–78.

Ward, Geoff K. 2012. *The Black Child-Savers: Racial Democracy and Juvenile Justice.* University of Chicago Press.

The Washington Post. n.d. Fatal Force. https://www.washingtonpost.com/graphics/national/police-shootings-2016/.

Western, Bruce. 2006. *Punishment and Inequality in America.* Russell Sage Foundation.

Wilson, William Julius. 1987. *The Truly Disadvantaged: The Inner City, the Underclass, and Public Policy.* The University of Chicago Press.

Wilson, William Julius. 1996. *When Work Disappears: The World of the New Urban Poor.* Knopf.

Wooldredge, John, James Frank, Natalie Goulette, and Lawrence Travis. 2015. Is the impact of cumulative disadvantage on sentencing greater for Black defendants? *Criminology & Public Policy* 14:187–223.

Wortley, Scot. 2009. Introduction. The immigration-crime connection: Competing theoretical perspectives. *Journal of International Migration and Integration* 10:349.

Young, Vernetta D. 1986. Gender expectations and their impact on black female offenders and victims. *Justice Quarterly* 3:305–27.

Young, Vernetta D. 1994. Race and gender in the establishment of juvenile institutions: The case of the South. *The Prison Journal* 74:244–65.

Young, Vernetta D., and Roderick Harrison. 2001. Race/ethnic differences in the sequences of drugs used by women. *Journal of Drug Issues*: 31:293–324.

Young, Vernetta D., and Rebecca Reviere. 2006. *Women Behind Bars: Gender and Race in US Prisons*. Lynne Rienner.

Young, Vernetta D., and Anne Thomas Sulton. 1991. Excluded: The current status of African-American scholars in the field of criminology and criminal justice. *Journal of Research in Crime and Delinquency* 28:101–16.

Young, Vernetta D., and Helen Taylor Greene. 1995. Pedagogical reconstruction: Incorporating African-American perspectives into the curriculum. *Journal of Criminal Justice Education* 6:85–105.

Zatz, Marjorie S., and Nancy Rodriguez. 2015. *Dreams and Nightmares: Immigration Policy, Youth, and Families*. University of California Press.

Comprehension Questions for Unit I

Questions for Reading 1.1

1. What skills does critical thinking involve?
2. What is the ultimate goal of learning better critical-thinking skills?
3. According to Elder, what is critical thinking?
4. Why is it important to adopt a model for critical thinking?
5. What are the three components of the Paul and Elder critical-thinking model?

Questions for Reading 1.2

1. What inspired Michell Alexander to start her research into the pattern of racial discrimination and social control that Alexander calls "the new Jim Crow"?
2. According to Alexander, why is colorblindness a problem?
3. What role has the privatization of prisons played in mass incarceration?
4. What made mass incarceration possible?
5. Why doesn't Alexander think that simply reducing prison sentences will solve the mass incarceration problem?

Questions for Reading 1.3

1. Define "racialized textbook bias."
2. What were the main findings from Walker and Brown's (1995) study, and how did they interpret the results?
3. What did Michele Mitchell identify as the three components of racialized textbook bias?
4. What methodological approach did Hoffman use to do his research?
5. What were Hoffman's major findings?

Questions for Reading 1.4

1. What are the two purposes of Ruth Peterson's presidential address to the American Society of Criminology?
2. What four recommendations does she make regarding how we should proceed with our research in ways that will better inform debates over criminal justice policy?
3. What two conclusions does she draw?

Unit II

Which Type of Crime Is Most Serious?

Introduction to Unit II

Modern democracies base their crime control and criminal justice policies upon knowledge about crime. In the United States, there are three major sources of public knowledge about crime: governmental statistics, the media, and scientific research. Unfortunately, these information sources limit the public's ability to fully understand the kinds of crime that it should consider serious. By focusing on particular types of serious crime and ignoring the possibility that other types of crime also might be serious, crime information sources give Americans a myopic view of the crime problem in the United States.

A synonym for "seriousness" is "gravity." Assumptions are made about the gravity of crimes whenever legislators create criminal laws, government law enforcement agencies prioritize certain types of crimes, or prosecutors decide not to prosecute certain types of crime, because the crimes do not seem serious enough to warrant the expenditure of resources. Despite the fact that gravity is not a commonly used concept in the United States criminal justice system, it operates just below the surface in policy decisions. The usual way we rank the seriousness of crimes is by comparing either the statutory maximum sentences available for those crimes (where there is a relatively definite sentencing guidelines system) or comparing the likely guidelines sentences. So we might assume that felonies—usually but not always defined as crimes punishable by more than a year in jail—are usually more serious than misdemeanors.

In reality, however, the line between felonies and misdemeanors is blurry. For example, under some state laws, it is a felony to injure a racehorse, but failing to report the death of a minor is a misdemeanor. In essence, criminal penalties—cobbled together through new laws and repealed laws over the course of generations—can be a garbled mess.

When you look behind the scenes and peek into the decision-making process involved in defining crimes and punishment, you can understand why this is so. For lawmakers sitting in judiciary committee meetings considering changes in criminal law, typical conversations lack the gravity and consideration one might expect: "What does this crime sound like to you? A 1-year, 3-year, or 5-year penalty?" In the end, lawmaking can be a discretion-filled, bias-laden, emotion-driven, and politically motivated exercise of governmental power.

The readings in Unit II remind us to question the reasoning behind the designation of certain crimes as more serious than other types of crime. Such designations are only as good as the assumptions on which they rest. In particular, the readings in this unit encourage students to ask:

- What assumptions are you making about the seriousness of certain types of crime?
- Are the assumptions justified?
- How are your assumptions shaping your point of view?
- Which of your assumptions might reasonably be questioned?

In Reading 2.1, Paul Leighton and Jeffrey Reimer zoom in on the importance of social class for criminal justice. While concentrating on how social class shapes the criminal justice system's reaction to street crime and white-collar crime, they decry how ideology hides inconvenient truths from the public. Their identification of inequality as the root cause of both street and white-collar crime leads them to embrace the radical solution of income and wealth redistribution.

Pete Simi makes a pitch for more research on White supremacist terror (WST) in Reading 2.2. He argues that this type of crime poses a clear and neglected threat to our democratic society. It is noteworthy that Simi issued his prescient wake-up call about the danger of WST at a time when the government, the media, and even terrorism experts were downplaying the threat of WST and ignoring social networks involving extremists and terrorists.

Reading 2.3 features what some experts consider the most dangerous crime of the 21st century: cybercrime. In this reading, Tom Marchetti assumes that the threat of cybercrime is omnipresent and provides advice on how the average everyday person can minimize risk of victimization. At the end, Marchetti claims that an insurance broker can help citizens understand evolving risks and options to address exposure. While an insurance broker might be someone to consult about your individual risk protection, the Federal Bureau of Investigation (FBI) takes a broader view. The FBI stresses that malicious cyber activity threatens the public's safety and our national and economic security. The FBI's cyber strategy is to impose risk and consequences on cyber adversaries. The FBI's goal is to change the behavior of criminals and nation-states who believe they can compromise U.S. networks, steal financial and intellectual property, and put critical infrastructure at risk without facing risk themselves. Learn more about what you can do to protect yourself from cyber criminals, how you can report cybercrime, and the FBI's efforts to combat cybercrime at their website (https://www.fbi.gov/investigate/cyber).

In Reading 2.4, Ed Morales unveils the real voter fraud that is taking place in U.S. elections. U.S. politicians have repeatedly, and falsely, claimed the 2016, 2018, and 2020 elections were "rigged" by large numbers of people voting illegally. Yet research reveals that fraud is very rare in U.S. elections. (If you are interested in taking a look at some of this research, go to https://www.brennancenter.org/our-work/research-reports/debunking-voter-fraud-myth.) Voter impersonation is practically nonexistent. Many instances of alleged fraud are actually mistakes by voters or by election administrators. Although it is important to protect the integrity of our elections, we must be careful not to undermine free and fair access to voting in the name of preventing a problem that does not exist. If voter fraud in the United States is not real, then what is the real voter fraud? Is it possible that the real voter fraud constitutes a bigger threat to our democratic society than phantom voter fraud that politicians have been "crying wolf" about in recent years?

Reading 2.1

A Suitable Amount of Street Crime and a Suitable Amount of White-collar Crime

Inconvenient Truths about Inequality, Crime and Criminal Justice

Paul Leighton and Jeffrey Reiman

CHRISTIE'S BOOK, *A SUITABLE AMOUNT OF Crime*, notes that "crime does not exist as a stable entity":

> It is like a sponge. The term can absorb a lot of acts—and people—when external circumstances make that useful. But it can also be brought to reduce its content, whenever suitable for those with a hand on the sponge.
>
> (2004: ix–x)

Acts that can be potentially criminalized are "an unlimited natural resource," although Christie believes that many crimes are genuinely harmful acts that are rightfully defined as crimes (ibid.: 10). The context thus is not moral relativism, but an interest in the volume of acts that become criminalized: "what is the suitable number of officially stigmatized sinners?" And, "is it possible to establish upper, and eventually lower, limits to the amount of punishment that ought to be applied in a modern society?" (ibid.: 101).

The criminalization of drug use is one of many concerns raised in this regard. Oxford's *Crime and Public Policy* notes that there is not moral consensus about whether recreational drug use should be a crime, so "the creation and enforcement of drug laws are seen more as policy decisions rather than as imperatives" (Lynch and Pridemore 2010: 38). The United States chose not just to criminalize recreational drug use but to launch a "war on drugs," which is a substantial source of its prison population. Christie notes that Swedish plans during the 1970s to lower their prison population from 4,000 to 500 were sidetracked when severe punishments became tools in the Swedish war on drugs (2004: 38). Russia seemed to be embracing a drug war as well, so "the lost war against drugs in the West is now dangerously close to being repeated in the East, with predictable results" (ibid.: 110).

Paul Leighton and Jeffrey Reimer, "A Suitable Amount of Street Crime and a Suitable Amount of White-Collar Crime: Inconvenient Truths about Inequality, Crime and Criminal Justice," *The Routledge Handbook of International Crime and Justice Studies*, ed. Bruce A. Arrigo and Heather Y. Bersot, pp. 302–324.

The drug wars, in part because of their failure, keep the criminal justice systems of many nations busy with street criminals. Indeed, beyond the drug war, Christie observes that "if I had the urge to construct a situation for the promotion of crime, then I would have shaped our societies in a form very close to what we find in a great number of modern states" (ibid.: 51). Social and economic policies "encourage unwanted forms of behavior" (ibid.) and again keep the criminal justice systems of many nations busy with lower-class street criminals. The poor, whose behavior has been defined as criminal, become the raw materials of the criminal justice industry (Christie 2000). An increasing number of countries have a prison- or criminal justice-industrial complex, reminiscent of the military-industrial complex that former US President Eisenhower warned about. It is composed of politicians, government bureaucrats, and all the companies who see criminal justice as a lucrative market rather than a burden on taxpayers (Selman and Leighton 2010). With the advent of private prisons—for-profit companies building and/or managing prisons for government—criminals are increasingly "bodies destined for profitable punishment" (quoted in Leighton and Selman 2012).

Thus, we might say that the poor are the object of conspicuous consumption by the criminal justice system. But the wealthy are not consumed. For example, even in the midst of a full-blown drug war in the USA, wealthy college drug dealers are the "anti-targets" of criminal justice agents; they are repelled from entering the system even when they seem to be "deliberately trying to draw attention to themselves or test[ing] social and legal boundaries" (Mohamed and Fritsvold 2010: 11–12). This is not just the "get-out-of-jail-free" card familiar to players of the *Monopoly*™ board game, but a "never-go-to-jail-in-the-first-place" card (ibid.: 132). Further, while those with their hand on the criminal justice sponge suck up shoplifters and vandals, they have decided not to pursue those responsible for the global financial crisis of 2008:

> *Nobody goes to jail.* This is the mantra of the financial-crisis era, one that saw virtually every major bank and financial company on Wall Street embroiled in obscene criminal scandals that impoverished millions and collectively destroyed hundreds of billions, in fact, trillions of dollars of the world's wealth—and nobody went to jail.
>
> (Taibbi 2011, emphasis in original)

While the poor are conspicuously consumed by the criminal justice system, one might be tempted to say the wealthy are conspicuously not consumed because it is well known that prisons are full of poor people. But the class bias in consumption is hidden when the criminal law does not translate the many harms done by the wealthy and by corporations into crimes. And, criminal justice data neither captures information on class (to help assess bias when rich and poor commit the same crime), nor does it report on the prevalence and cost of white-collar crime (even based on the current inadequate level of criminalization of these harms).

The question about a suitable amount of crime, criminalization and penal control, thus needs to be answered not in the aggregate for a society, but asked separately: what is a suitable amount of crime in the street, and what is a suitable amount of crime in the suites? Such an analysis is consistent with Christie's criminological consciousness, and he explicitly notes that class is relevant to an evaluation of criminal justice systems. He believes that "penal systems carry deep meanings" (2004: 101) and a clue to read their meaning is

> the question of *the nature of the receivers* of the intended pain, particularly how representative they are of the population in general with regard to age, gender, race, class, etc. An extremely biased prison population might indicate severe defects somewhere in that system.
>
> (2004: 102, emphasis in original)

Christie's concerns warrant further analysis, especially as applied to neglected issues about economic class, which is among the most important sociological variables. So, our project in this [reading] is to start an analysis of the overconsumption of poor people by the criminal justice system, the under-consumption of the rich, and the defects of systems that exhibit such bias. This inquiry is important not just because of the relative neglect of class analysis in criminal justice, but also because many nations have high degrees of economic inequality and "the simple fact is that a criminal justice system cannot be any more just than the society it protects" (Reiman 2001: 17). Further, as Braithwaite (1992: 83) notes, inequality is linked to both the crimes of the poor (by creating unfulfilled needs, either absolute or based on "advertising and dramatization of bourgeois lifestyles") and crimes of the rich (by making them unaccountable and undermining their respect for the dominion (self-determination) of others.

But Christie raises another concern that is not frequently examined: that society is structured to promote street crime—a point Currie also notes in describing America's "pro-crime" policies (1985: 226)—which adds to the consumption of the poor by the criminal justice system. Critical theory and conflict theory generally argue that the function of criminal justice is to control the "dangerous classes," but fail to consider ideological benefits from "crime" being associated with the poor.

Further, while Christie appreciates the role of harm in selecting appropriate conduct of the poor to criminalize, he fails to apply the same analysis to acts of the wealthy, where death, injury and fraud cause real harm but are not criminalized. This largely mirrors the dominant criminological discussion about whether behavior such as drug use and prostitution are "victimless" crimes and thus should be decriminalized, but does not consider that acts of the wealthy also have victims and should be criminalized. Even if the current reality is a global deregulatory race to the bottom, the criminal justice system still should protect people from the worst threats to their lives, health and property, and do so regardless of whether those threats are from the rich or poor. On another level, reflection on harmful conduct and the prohibitions of criminal law is important because crime is defined by a political system. Thus, philosophical reflection on the concept of crime is necessary for criminology to establish its "intellectual independence of the state, which to my mind is equivalent to declaring its status as a social science rather than an agency of social control, as critical rather than servile, as illumination rather than propaganda" (Reiman 2013: 243).

In the first section that follows, "Class, ideology and the failures of criminal justice," we discuss the foundation for this analysis, *The Rich Get Richer and the Poor Get Prison: Ideology, Class and Criminal Justice*, now in its tenth edition (Reiman and Leighton 2013). While the book is a critique of the American criminal justice system, the concerns it raises apply, to varying degrees, to many developed nations. We argue that the criminal justice system was responsible for only a modest amount of the decline in crime in the USA, and question why anti-crime policy does not target a number of sources of crime (like inequality) as well as better fund research-based crime prevention programs. The book also argues that many harmful acts of businesses and corporations should be criminalized because they are done knowingly, recklessly or negligently. Further, it argues that there is class bias in the system when rich and poor commit the same crime. Finally, the book tries to explore how a criminal justice system that neither protects society nor achieves justice is allowed to continue.

The second section, "No wealth of data ... ," provides a brief overview of data about inequality, including how corporate "persons" factor in. It also critiques the state of criminal justice data about both the class of criminal offenders and white-collar crime. The third section, "Research directions that give justice more class," highlights several strategies to highlight inequality and class that do not depend on changing government policy about data collection. The fourth section, "Policy implications of the inconvenient truths about wealth," reviews recommendations about better criminal justice data before elaborating on the link between inequality and crime. That higher levels of crimes in the suites and crimes on the streets are both linked to higher levels of inequality means that redistribution can reduce all types of crime. The conclusion considers the ideological benefits that accrue to the wealthy and powerful from a system that fails to remedy sources of crime, fails to criminalize harmful acts of the wealthy and that fails to track both class bias and crimes of the wealthy.

Class, Ideology and the Failures of Criminal Justice

The Rich Get Richer (Reiman and Leighton 2013) invites the reader to entertain the idea that the goal of the criminal justice system is not to eliminate crime or to achieve justice, but to project to the American public a credible image of the threat of crime as a threat from the poor. To accomplish this, the justice system must engage in a publicly visible struggle against a sizable population of poor criminals. To do that, it must fail to significantly reduce the level of crimes that poor people commit. Crime may, of course, occasionally decline—but largely because of factors other than criminal justice policies, and never to such an extent that street crime ceases to be a spectacle in the public's consciousness.

This upside-down idea of criminal justice originated 40 years ago in one of Reiman's seminars. The class discussed many systemic problems of the system: arbitrariness in sentencing and treatment in prison; deprivation of dignity, physical violence, and the lack of meaningful rehabilitation or vocational training within prison; the inescapability of the "ex-con" stigma, and the lack of legitimate opportunities for the ex-prisoner. The class kept confronting

> [the] irrationality of a society that builds prisons to prevent crime knowing full well that they do not, and one that does not seriously try to rid its prisons and post-release practices of those features that guarantee a high rate of recidivism, the return to crime by prison alumni.
>
> (Reiman and Leighton 2013: 2–3)

Near the end of the semester, Reiman asked students to design a criminal justice system that would maintain a stable and visible "class" of criminals. He describes the response as "electrifying": "when asked to design a system that would maintain and encourage the existence of a stable and visible 'class of criminals,' the students 'constructed' the American criminal justice system!" (ibid.: 3). Obviously crime is a complex social practice, so there will be areas of improvement and occasional effective programs, but they will be the exceptions and not the beginning of a trend. Indeed, four decades after this seminar, the problem is still recognizable to American students, to Christie, and probably to people in many nations.

The Rich Get Richer notes that the criminal justice system was the cause of *some* of America's dramatic decline in crime. A nation that locks up enough people, and grants police greater power to interfere with liberty and privacy, will prevent some crime. But the cost of criminal justice intervention compared to its effect makes it inefficient at best. For all the hundreds of billions of dollars the USA put into incarceration over the last decades, Zimring suggests that a "best guess of the impact" of incarceration on crime rates "would range from 10% of the decline at the low end to 27% of the decline at the high end" (2007: 131, 55). The effect is modest because prisons have criminogenic (crime-producing) qualities that offset the effects of incarceration. Prisons brutalize the individuals in them rather than rehabilitate and reintegrate them; they also harm the community by undermining the formation of families, having negative effects on the children of incarcerated parents, and eroding informal community social control systems.

To the extent that prisons are criminogenic, they are *sources* of crime that society chooses not to fix. This is part of the first failure of criminal justice, which is the failure to fight crime in ways that can meaningfully reduce it. Other sources of crime—like the easy availability of guns—are unique to the USA. But many nations criminalize drugs and favor incarceration over treatment. And, as is most relevant here, many nations have high levels of inequality and social exclusion that are part of the normal operations of society, not a temporary or abnormal feature (Mooney 2008).

Because policy does not seek to change sources of crime and allows criminogenic environments and practices to persist, it is appropriate to ask readers to look at criminal justice "through the looking glass." This means reversing expectations about criminal justice and inquiring about the benefits of the current system. We call this way of looking at criminal justice policy the *Pyrrhic defeat* theory. A "Pyrrhic victory" is a military victory purchased at such a cost in troops and treasure that it amounts to a defeat. The Pyrrhic defeat theory argues that the failure of the criminal justice system yields such benefits to those in positions of power that it amounts to a victory.

The Pyrrhic defeat theory draws on Erikson's (1966) *Wayward Puritans*, which builds on Durkheim, who "suggested that crime (and by extension other forms of deviation) may actually perform a needed service to society by drawing people together in a common posture of anger and indignation" (quoted in Reiman and Leighton 2013: 43). If deviance and crime promote social solidarity, Erikson wondered whether

> [we can] then assume that [social institutions] are organized in such a way as to promote this resource? Can we assume, in other words, that forces operate in the social structure to recruit offenders and to commit them to long periods of service in the deviant ranks?
>
> (ibid.)

He answers in the affirmative and notes that

> prisons have done a conspicuously poor job of reforming the convicts placed in their custody; but the very consistency of this failure may have a peculiar logic of its own. Perhaps we find it difficult to change the worst of our penal

> practices because we expect the prison to harden the inmate's commitment to deviant forms of behavior and draw him more deeply into the deviant ranks. (ibid.)

Both Durkheim and Erikson endorse the general proposition that the failure to eliminate deviance promotes social solidarity, and then jump to a specific conclusion: that the form this failure takes in a particular society is explained by the contribution it makes to promoting consensus on shared beliefs and thus feelings of social solidarity. This jump leaves out the important question of how a society forms its particular consensus around one set of shared beliefs (say, fraud by financial institutions) rather than another (say, drug use). Durkheim and Erikson imply that a consensus already exists and social institutions reflect beliefs already in people's heads. But consensus is created, not just reflected, by social institutions—and the failure to stamp out deviance creates a very particular value-laden consensus. The Pyrrhic defeat theory reveals how the failure of criminal justice works to create and reinforce a specific set of beliefs

> about what is dangerous and what is not, and about who is a threat and who is not. This does not merely shore up general feelings of social solidarity; it allows those feelings to be attached to a social order characterized by striking disparities of wealth, power, and privilege, and by considerable injustice. (Reiman and Leighton 2013: 49)

This analysis has some similarities with Foucault's work, who also suggests that the failure of prisons serves a function for society. *Discipline and Punish* notes that complaints about the failure of prisons to prevent crime and their tendency to promote recidivism have accompanied the prison throughout its history—so much so that Foucault asks, "Is not the supposed failure part of the functioning of the prison?" (1977: 271). The prison "has succeeded extremely well ... in producing delinquents, in an apparently marginal, but in fact centrally supervised milieu; in producing the delinquent as a pathologized subject" (ibid.: 277). That is, lawbreakers are transformed into a delinquent in need of correction and treatment, which in turn licenses a permanent policing of the poor "dangerous class." Foucault suggests that the new prison regime was a response to a "new threat" posed by peasants and workers against the "new system of the legal exploitation of labour" (ibid.: 274), by which he means capitalism. This is a class-based explanation of the new prison regime, in which criminality gets identified "almost exclusively" with "the bottom rank of the social order" (ibid.: 275).

In the next section, we note how social theory has become "de-classed," and this phenomenon applies to Foucault's larger theory of modern society—how prison spreads out into a "carceral archipelago" and becomes a whole system of institutions and practices (including disciplines such as psychology and medicine) aimed at "normalization" (ibid.: 296–297). Power in the form of surveillance and self-discipline is everywhere, exercised by everyone on him or herself and on everyone else. But the class-based analysis of power about the origins of the prison system vanishes and Foucault mystifies the exercise of power because "rather than operating along a class axis that might be eliminated, and to serve interests that might be identified and critiqued, power now seems its own goal, a universal fact of modern life" (Reiman and Leighton 2013: 50). Also absent from Foucault's analysis is attention to the difference between those forms of discipline that are necessary for the freedom of each to coexist peacefully with the freedom of the rest and those forms of discipline that simply serve the interests of the rich and powerful.

The second failure of the criminal justice system discussed in *The Rich Get Richer* is to adequately criminalize harms done by the wealthy and thus protect people from serious threats to their lives, health and property. This failure to protect people from the harmful acts of the rich also helps to shape the ideological message that it is (only) the poor who commit crimes and thus should be the focus of criminal justice control. As Quinney argues, crime has a "social reality" rather than an objective reality because crime is "created" by decisions of lawmakers, police, prosecutors, judges and juries. But as Christie notes, rape and murder are acts appropriately called crimes, so the question is whether the label of crime is applied appropriately. We argue that

> the label is applied appropriately when it is used to identify all, or at least the worst, acts that are harmful to society. The label is applied inappropriately when it is attached to harmless acts or when it is not attached to seriously harmful intentional acts.
>
> (Reiman and Leighton 2013: 74)

Calling crime created points to human actors rather than objective dangers as determining the shape that the reality of crime takes in our society. If the label "crime" is applied consistently to the most dangerous or harmful acts, then it is misleading to highlight the role of human decision-makers in creating reality because "crime" mirrors a reality that already exists. On the other hand, if the label is not applied appropriately, then criminal law is more like a carnival mirror that throws back a distorted image. The image cast back is false because

> large becomes small, and small large; grave becomes minor, and minor grave. Like a carnival mirror, although nothing is reflected that does not exist in the

> world, the image is more a creation of the mirror [i.e., the legislators and criminal justice system] than a picture of the world.
>
> (ibid.: 72)

Because our normal intuition about which acts should be crimes is itself shaped by the criminal law,

> criminology must look at crime while staying open to the idea that the legal definitions and, just as crucially, all the righteous beliefs that normally surround the legal enterprise are less than the whole truth, and perhaps even misleading or ideological.
>
> (Reiman 2013: 247)

Rather than having its central concept—crime—defined by the state, criminology must "seek its own understanding of what crime is" (ibid.) through philosophical reflection about harm and "a moral theory about what human beings owe to their fellows in the way of conduct" (ibid.: 248).

The Rich Get Richer follows up this concern by imagining a conversation with a Defender of the Present Legal Order about the limitations of what is currently defined as crime and the model of interpersonal victimization behind it. While a full review of that argument is beyond the scope of this [reading], we should emphasize that the failure to properly criminalize the harmful acts of the wealthy and corporations do not just make "crime" look like the activity of the poor. More importantly, the failure to criminalize knowing, reckless and negligent acts of corporations means that the criminal justice system fails to protect people from certain losses of life and property, as well as violations of their bodily autonomy. The regulatory system has an important role in trying to prevent these harms, but the criminal law and criminal justice system are necessary to punish and deter serious harm.

The third failure discussed by *The Rich Get Richer* is the failure to remedy class bias in the processing of those who violate the existing criminal law. At each step, from arresting to sentencing, the likelihood of being ignored, released or treated lightly by the system is greater for the wealthy than poor. The US government does not collect data that would verify this claim, and over successive editions of *The Rich Get Richer* the number of studies on class has declined markedly. Nor does the government publish data about the cost and prevalence of white-collar and corporate crime. As we show below, the crime reports of other developed countries do not do this either, with a few minor and woefully incomplete exceptions. First, though, we review the distributions of wealth in several developed nations to remind readers of the significant amount of inequality and the significance of class, which highlights how "the general marginalization of class in much of the social sciences literature is astonishing" (Mooney 2008: 68).

No Wealth of Data ...

Mooney notes that while "class remains a primary determinant of social life," most public "discourses about modern society have been largely de-classed" (2008: 68). The neglect of class occurs in a context where "the scale of this inequality is almost beyond comprehension, perhaps not surprisingly as much of it remains hidden from view" (ibid.: 64). In contrast, this section provides an overview of the key concepts used to examine inequality, which usually exclude corporations. The second part of this section reviews the deplorable state of government-published data on class related to criminal offending.

No Wealth of Data about Wealth

Class is less frequently analyzed than race or gender, but it provides an important view of economic inequality and thus social justice. While class can be conceptualized in different ways (Barak *et al.* 2010: 73), we believe primary attention should be placed on income and wealth, because they allow a clear view of inequality in the distribution of economic power and resources. Income is the most straightforward indicator of class. It represents sources of individual revenue such as salary, interest, and the type of items that should be reported on income tax forms. By contrast, wealth is about assets like bank accounts, retirement accounts, houses, cars, and the ownership of stocks, bonds, and businesses; it also takes into account debts such as car loans, student loans, mortgages, and credit card balances. Wealth is what we accumulate over our lives and is about economic security and power. While income is unequally distributed, wealth is more unequal and this inequality is more important.

In the USA, data about household wealth comes from the Survey of Consumer Finances that is completed every three years. The results are reported by staff of the Federal Reserve, the semi-independent US central bank. The latest survey is from 2010 and the main report does not include data about the share of wealth held by certain percentile groups (Bricker *et al.* 2012)—the data that provide direct insight into inequality by revealing the share of wealth controlled by the richest 1 percent, 10 percent, etc. At this point in 2012, the latest available official data is from a 2007 working paper, which reveals that the bottom 50 percent in the USA owned 2.5 percent of the wealth while the top 1 percent owned 33.8 percent of the wealth (Kennickell 2009: 35). Such data is not available in a readily accessible form from the government, such as on the Department of Census website or in the widely used *Statistical Abstract of the United States.*

The United Kingdom publishes statistics on wealth on the website of Her Majesty's Revenue and Customs, which has a page for the "Distribution of Personal Wealth." The data are based on certain identified estates—those requiring a grant of representation to appoint an executor or transfer the estate to probate—and subjected to statistical procedures to make them more representative (see generally HMRC 2011). The data is reported in terms of ownership by decile, in contrast to the USA, where the poor have so little wealth that the ownership of the bottom five deciles is reported in aggregate, and where the rich have so much that the top decile is broken down into three categories (90th–95th percentile, 95th–99th and 99th–100th). Combining data for each country into common categories produces the results in Table 2.1.1.

TABLE 2.1.1 Share of net wealth owned by percentile groups in the USA and the UK, 2007

USA (share owned by percentile group)	Percentile group	UK (share owned by percentile group)
2.5	Bottom 50	13
26.0	50 to 90	42
71.5	Top 10	44

Source: Calculated from Kennickell (2009: 35) and HMRC (2011: Table 13.8). UK numbers are based on data from 2005 to 2007.

The USA exhibits the highest degree inequality among the developed nations, a situation made worse by the lack of national health care and some of the social supports that exist in European and the Scandinavian countries. Two economists from the US Federal Reserve note that the lowest levels of inequality "are found in, among others, Australia, Italy, Japan, and Sweden, and intermediate values in Canada, France, and the United Kingdom" (Cagetti and De Nardi 2008: 291). Table 2.1.2 provides data for (low inequality) Australia and (intermediate inequality) Canada. The report on wealth in Australia is notable for being relatively easy to read, with a section for definitions and the data on share of wealth by percentile group presented early in the report (Australian Bureau of Statistics 2011).

TABLE 2.1.2 Share of net worth by quintile, Canada and Australia

Australia 2009–10		Canada 2005
0.9	Lowest quintile (bottom 20%)	0.1
5.4	Second quintile	2.3
11.9	Third quintile	8.4
20.0	Fourth quintile	20.2
61.8	Highest quintile (top 20%)	69.2

Source: Statistics Canada (2005: 9) and Australian Bureau of Statistics (2011: 31)

Whether or not law engages in the legal fiction that corporations are "persons," corporations are key players in people's lives as employers, community members, and providers of necessary goods and services. Corporations need to be included in the analysis of economic resources in order to have a full understanding of how inequality relates to crime, justice and equality under a rule of law. The intense concentration of wealth in corporations generates considerable political power, makes accountability increasingly difficult, and increases inequality in a way that is largely invisible to criminological theory.

Using available data on corporate assets and liabilities results in numbers that are not comparable to household wealth, the best comparison is between household income and corporate revenue. In 2010, in the USA, the median *household* income was $49,445 (DeNavas-Walt *et al.* 2011: 5). The smallest company in the Fortune 500 (Seaboard) in 2010 had revenue of $4.3 billion (*Fortune* 2011). If the median household income is represented by the median height in the US, 5'7", then Seaboard would be more than 90 miles tall. The biggest company in the Fortune 500 (Wal-Mart) has revenue of $421.8 billion—which would be over 9,000 miles tall.

Another way to problematize the size of corporate personhood is to compare the revenue of a corporation against the gross domestic product (GDP) of a country. (GDP is a measure of the value of all goods and services produced by a country.) This process results in a list of the largest economies in the world and is presented in Table 2.1.3. That 34 corporations are in the top 100 largest economies highlights some of the problems that governments can have holding big corporations accountable. Corporations can effectively dominate the social control apparatus of many nations—including many developed nations (Alvesalo *et al.* 2006). Given that corporations hold massive economic resources, it would be surprising if there were no class-based dynamic to Foucault's analysis of surveillance and disciplinary power.

No Wealth of Data about Class and Criminal Justice

Official government data is important in shaping the perception of the "crime problem" by news media, the public, and policy-makers, not to mention criminology books and academic research. To the extent that government data about crime is "de-classed," then readers of that data will not develop a consciousness about the relationships between class, criminal behavior and social control. Our aim, then, is to explore two issues related to class and criminal justice data. First, to what extent do nations provide data on class, income or wealth, as they do with gender and race? Government data on gender and race do not answer all questions about bias in criminal justice processing, but their existence reminds people that the variables are important and facilitates accountability by allowing researchers to start probing problematic decision points to help uncover injustice. Second, nations have one or

TABLE 2.1.3 World's largest economies GDP and Fortune 500 revenue, 2010

Overall rank	Country rank	Company rank	Country/Company	GDP/Revenue (in billions of US$)
1	1		United States	15,064.8
2	2		China	6,988.5
3	3		Japan	5,855.4
7	7		United Kingdom	2,481.0
11	11		Canada	1,758.7
15	15		Australia	1,507.4
21	21		Saudi Arabia	560.3
29	29		South Africa	422.0
30		1	Wal-Mart Stores	421.8
31	30		United Arab Emirates	358.1
32		2	Exxon Mobil	354.6
50	48		Pakistan	204.1
51		3	Chevron	196.3
52	49		Romania	185.3
53		4	ConocoPhillips	184.9
57	53		Kuwait	171.1
61		5	Fannie Mae	153.8
62		6	General Electric	151.6
63	57		Hungary	147.9
64		7	Berkshire Hathaway	136.1
65		8	General Motors	135.6
66		9	Bank of America Corp.	134.2
67		10	Ford Motor	128.9
68		11	Hewlett-Packard	126.0
69		12	AT&T	124.6
70	58		Vietnam	121.6
71		13	J.P. Morgan Chase & Co.	115.5
72	59		Bangladesh	115.0
73		14	Citigroup	111.1
75	60		Iraq	108.6
76		16	Verizon Communications	106.5
77		17	AIG	104.4
78	61		Morocco	101.8

(Continued)

Table 2.1.3 (*Continued*)

Overall rank	Country rank	Company rank	Country/Company	GDP/Revenue (in billions of US$)
79		18	IBM	99.8
82		20	Freddie Mac	98.4
83	63		Slovak Republic	97.2
84		21	CVS Caremark	96.4
85		22	United Health Group	94.2
86		23	Wells Fargo	93.2
89		26	Procter & Gamble	79.7
91		28	Costco Wholesale	77.9
92	64		Azerbaijan	68.5
93		29	Marathon Oil	68.4
94		30	Home Depot	68.0
95		31	Pfizer	67.8
96		32	Walgreen	67.4
97		33	Target	67.4
100	66		Ecuador	65.3
101		35	Apple	65.2

Source: Fortune 500 from http://money.cnn.com/magazines/fortune/fortune500/2011/full_list International Monetary Fund, World Economic Outlook Database, September 2011. Gross domestic product is expressed in current (2011) US dollars. http://www.imf.org/external/pubs/ft/weo/2011/02/weodata/index.aspx.

two regular seminal reports on crime and victimization, and to what extent do those contain reporting on white-collar and corporate crime?

Developed nations share a commitment to a rule of law that includes equality before the law, so similar cases should not have different outcomes merely because one defendant is poor and another is rich. While nations that (rightly or wrongly) believe themselves to be homogeneous may not publish criminal justice statistics about race or ethnicity, developed nations have significant levels of inequality (as reviewed earlier). To ensure that the criminal justice system does not reflect and recreate excessive levels of inequality, governments should publish data about the class of criminal offenders and their movement through—or their removal from—the criminal justice system. Without data, accountability for class bias becomes substantially more challenging and there is a risk that criminal justice becomes "de-classed" at a time when it is providing law and order for a morally unjust economic system.

Developed nations have a victimization survey, but it is not well suited to identifying the income or wealth level of perpetrators, so our focus will be on publications reporting crimes known to the police. We do note, however, that some developed countries are willing to ask victims about their level of income, suggesting an awareness that class is important to understanding and responding to victimization. But even those nations do not ask offenders the same question.

Because the USA has the highest crime rates of any developed nation, it has more detailed reporting of crime than other developed nations. Both the National Crime Victimization Survey (NCVS) and reports on crimes known to the police (Federal Bureau of Investigation 2011) do include important information on gender and race/ethnicity, but the NCVS has only one table about the income of victims. Until 2004, the victimization survey reported on violent and property victimizations by income, but only the data on property crime victimization remains (Barak *et al.* 2010: 161–162). The most likely reason for the disappearance of this data is budget cuts that have reduced the sample size and thus made estimates of violent crime unstable because they occur less frequently than property crime. Still, officials made a conscious decision that retaining this limited data about class was not important enough to justify the expense. Developed nations have the resources, but choose not to collect data about the inconvenient truth of class bias, which leads to larger discussions about the inconvenient truth of inequality.

Australia reports on adult detainees' education level (Australian Institute of Criminology 2012a: 85) and *source of income* (full- or part-time job, welfare, friends/family, savings, sex work, drug dealing, shoplifting, other crime) (ibid.: 86–7). But there is no data about actual income or assets. The sections on criminal courts and corrections also contain nothing about income or wealth, in contrast with the numerous figures about age and gender. (Indigenous status is occasionally reported in this publication.) Given the detailed, thoughtful and systematic presentation of wealth data in Australia (Australian Bureau of Statistics 2011), it is disappointing that criminal justice data on class is absent.

British crime and victimization data are based on both the Crime Survey for England and Wales (CSEW) and crimes known to the police, neither of which contains data about class, race or gender. The survey reports on the number of offenses, but not the characteristics of victims or offenders, with the exception of a section on crime experienced by children aged 10–15 (Office for National Statistics 2012a). For some offenses, especially fraud, data is supplemented with other reports, but still do not cover the victim's or offender's race, citizenship, class or gender. The report on crimes known to the police focuses on whether a known crime is "detected" or "cleared-up" by the identification of a suspect, and whether there is a sanction (which can range from a warning to being charged) (Home Office 2012). The tables break down the percentage of outcomes for various crimes and the changes over time. But the data do not allow for an analysis of, say, whether class influences the decisions about which drug offenders get a warning and which are charged.

In Canada, the report on crimes known to police mostly breaks down the level of known offenses by geography (province/territory and city) and by year, with a few tables on the "characteristics of accused persons" containing gender and age (Statistics Canada 2012a). Data from the General Social Survey reports only limited information on the income levels of those experiencing property and violent victimization (Statistics Canada 2010: 22–3, 26), without a similar interest in the income of the offender. The publication *Adult Criminal Court Statistics in Canada* describes the volume of different crimes, age, sex, geography, outcome, and time-to-disposition of the case—but does not provide information on wealth or income (Statistics Canada 2012b).

The second important issue is whether the main reports on crime include crime in the suites as well as crime on the streets. A national report supposedly summarizing "crime" that does not include white-collar and corporate crime sends the message that street crime is "real" crime; it trivializes the serious harm done by the wealthy even as it presents great detail on even the minor wrongdoing of the lower classes. The point is not to have a report on "crime" and a separate one on white-collar and corporate crime, but to integrate the violations of law by rich and poor into a report that is a useful tool because it presents comprehensive information about criminal harms and the threats citizens face.

The NCVS in the USA does not have any questions about white-collar crime, even though the National White Collar Crime Center completed large-scale surveys in 1999 and 2005—and found that half of the households were aware of experiencing a white-collar victimization (Friedrichs 2010: 47). The Federal Bureau of Investigation (FBI) publishes data about offenses known to local police departments, which do not tend to be involved with white-collar crimes. The section on property crime includes the offenses of burglary, larceny-theft, motor vehicle theft, and arson. Larceny-theft excludes embezzlement, con games and fraud. The FBI does note that in 2010 there were about 78,000 arrests for forgery and counterfeiting, 188,000 for fraud, and almost 17,000 for embezzlement (Federal Bureau of Investigation 2011: Table 29). While many of these arrests are for small-scale scams and cons that are not central to the study of white-collar crime, the exclusion of these categories from the main body of a report on crime removes white-collar crimes from the public consciousness. As a result, during the collapse of Enron and other companies in 2001—when accounting fraud cost investors 70–90 percent of their money and top officials of those companies "were getting immensely, extraordinarily, obscenely wealthy" (in Reiman and Leighton 2013: 146)—the Department of Justice reported that "property crimes had continued their downward trend and fallen to an all-time low" (cited in Barak 2012: 73).

Following the corporate scandals that began with Enron (Reiman and Leighton 2013: 146), then-President Bush launched the Corporate Fraud Task Force. They issued reports on corporate fraud in 2003 and 2004, but they were lists of cases and settlements, with no effort to summarize data, discuss larger problems, make policy recommendations, etc. After 2004, the task force did not issue another report until early 2008, which included a substantial number of cases from the 2003 and 2004 reports. Although this report was issued right before the financial crisis, it did not detect or note any patterns that forewarned an imminent global crisis. There were no reports after the financial crisis and the website address for the task force contains the word "archive" (Corporate Fraud Task Force [no date]), implying—in the face of massive evidence to the contrary (Barak 2012)—that the time for a focus on corporate fraud has passed.

The Australian Capital Territory passed an industrial manslaughter act in 2003 to facilitate the prosecution of corporate bodies responsible for employee deaths, but the rest of the country follows the *Criminal Code Act* of 1995 that clarified how the overall criminal code applies to corporations. Australian crime statistics (Australian Institute of Criminology 2012a) do not indicate how frequently these provisions are applied, if ever. A detailed look at homicide does not address whether "employer" could be a victim–offender relationship or whether "workplace" contains any health and safety crimes (Australian Institute of Criminology 2008).

Australian reports on fraud do include fraudulent trade practices, in addition to the expected acts of forgery, counterfeiting, credit card fraud and other deceptive practices (Australian Institute of Criminology 2012a: 36). They also present minimal information on cybercrime, including malware (malicious software), compromised web sites, and scams (ibid.: 58), many of which are considered white-collar crime. The victimization survey does not ask about fraud, however, the Australasian Consumer Fraud Task Force conducts a yearly consumer fraud survey to assess the prevalence of consumer scams, which they define as attempts "designed to obtain someone's personal information or money or otherwise to obtain a financial benefit by deceptive means" (Australian Institute of Criminology 2012b: 1). Although this definition could include acts by businesses and financial institutions, reporting is limited to scams involving notices about advance fee scams, alleged lottery winnings, inheritance, financial advice, work from home, phishing (attempts to get personal information for activities like identity theft), dating, etc. The median 2010 loss was $700, and respondents also reported emotional trauma, loss of confidence in people and/or marital or relationship problems because of the victimization. Thus, these incidents are more serious than a range of acts frequently reported in regular crime statistics, like petty theft and most vandalism.

The British victimization survey (CSEW) contains information on offense types like "wounding"—and changes have increased the reporting of violent crimes without injuries (Office for National Statistics 2012a)—but wounding by defective consumer products or criminal health and safety violations are not asked about. Theft includes "bicycle theft and shoplifting" and "pick-pocketing" among the common forms of the offense (ibid.: 4, 42) as well as "opportunistic" incidents like the "theft of garden furniture" outside the house (ibid.: 43). But it neglects more serious crimes because "unauthorized taking" offenses do not apply to the behavior of financial institutions or business that try to impose inappropriate fees, penalties or charges to people's accounts.

According to the report, fraud is "often targeted at organisations rather than individuals" (ibid.: 56), but fraud targeted at individuals by institutions is not mentioned. Fraud data is supplemented by "non-National Statistics" from the National Fraud Intelligence Bureau about some white-collar crimes and scams involving charities, corporate employees, computer misuse, investment, insurance-related, advance fee, corporate procurement, telecommunications industry, banking/payment, and business trading (ibid.: 58). However, business trading is only about ("illegitimate") businesses set up to commit scams, not the scams of "legitimate" businesses. Telecommunications industry fraud refers to mobile phone fraud by individuals directed at telecom companies, not the behavior of the companies or telemarketing firms. The banking and payment fraud largely involves check/cheque fraud and (credit and debit) "plastic card" fraud, which means unauthorized purchases rather than financial institutions' wrongdoing. The corporate employee fraud refers to "an employee making a fraudulent claim for travel or subsistence" (Office for National Statistics 2012b: 35) rather than the behavior of executives perpetrating frauds on their employees, shareholders, customers, or the government. In these cases, police work with powerful institutions (e.g., the UK Cards Association) to prevent losses perpetrated by individuals, with no effort even to recognize that individuals are victimized by institutions. The British are starting a survey about the victimization of business establishments that will be incorporated into future releases of the regular CSEW survey reports (Office for National Statistics 2012a: 79), but there is no consideration of expanding the survey to include more victimizations of consumers, employees and communities by business establishments.

The British report on crimes known to the police helpfully includes under the "theft" category: "fraud by a company director" (207 offenses in 2010/11 and 45 in 2011/12), false accounting (108 offenses in 2010/11 and 75 in 2011/12) and fraud by abuse of position (1,033 offenses in 2010/11 and 1,170 in 2011/12) (Home Office 2012: 19). Further, homicide does include acts charged under the Corporate Manslaughter and Corporate Homicide Act 2007, under which an organization is guilty "if the way in which its activities are managed or organised causes a death and amounts to a gross breach of a relevant duty of care to the deceased" (Ministry of Justice 2008). The detailed table for violent crime reports that, in 2010/11, there was one such offense with no sanctions, and in 2011/12, there were two offenses and two sanctions (Home Office 2012: 16). Observers can then ask whether that level is too high, too low or seems consistent with the prevalence of the harm.

Every five years in Canada the General Social Survey collects information on a limited range of criminal offenses: "sexual assault, robbery, physical assault, break and enter, motor vehicle/parts theft, theft of household property, vandalism and theft of personal property" (Statistics Canada 2010: 6). Theft does not include consumer fraud, scams or white-collar financial fraud—harms that are typically more serious than vandalism. Violent victimization also excludes consumer products and workplace safety issues. The perceptions of personal safety asks about acts like walking alone or using public transportation after dark (ibid.: 18, 30), but not the behavior of corporations.

The section on property crimes known to Canadian police is part of a write-up on non-violent crime that is two pages long, mostly about breaking and entering and motor vehicle theft (Statistics Canada 2012a: 17–18). It provides no detail about fraud, which occurs at a similar rate to auto theft. Property crime does include fraud and identity theft, but it seems not to include frauds by financial institutions, especially those preying on the general public (ibid.: 30–31). Consumer fraud and fraudulent trade practices also are not considered.

In 2004, Bill C-45 modernized Canada's criminal code to clarify how it applied to increasingly complex organizations (Department of Justice (Canada) 2012). However, any crime reported under this law is not counted in a way that would allow the reader to see how frequently it is applied. Indeed, the first time criminal negligence was applied to a corporation was after four workers died from falling 13 stories when scaffolding collapsed on Christmas Eve in 2009. Thus, charges are unusual, but it is unclear if even these figures are reflected in the homicide reports, which include manslaughter (Statistics Canada 2011: 17) and thus ought to cover negligence. But data breakdowns on method (number of "other" offenses) (ibid.: 27) and relationship ("business relationship (legal)") (ibid.: 31) do not seem to include these four deaths for either 2009 or 2010.

Research Directions That Give Justice More Class

We suggest two avenues to help "re-class" data: one about general inequality in developed nations, and the other about white-collar and corporate crime. (The collection of data about an offender's income is important, but that is a policy issue requiring government action rather than being an existing research strategy.) The first avenue collects people's beliefs about the ideal distribution of wealth and their knowledge of current actual distributions. The results can start a conversation about the injustice of current distributions and provide insight into the effects of ideology. The second avenue works around omission of white-collar and corporate crime in official data by advocating that researchers use additional existing data sources to compile alternative or shadow statistics that paint a more realistic picture of crime. But data is still scarce where corporations victimize—sometimes on a mass scale—workers, consumers or communities, and this category of wrongdoing especially needs more original research on behalf of the public interest.

In his classic theory of justice, Rawls suggests evaluating society based on the preferences people would have if choosing from behind a veil of ignorance: decide what society should look like without knowledge of race, sex, class, religion, disability, etc. Norton and Ariely (2011) tried a simplified version of this by asking 5,500 adults to choose from three distributions, which, unknown to the subject, represented the distribution in Sweden, the USA and an equal distribution. Americans overwhelmingly chose Sweden, with very low levels of inequality.

In Rawls' writing, the veil of ignorance exercise includes specified information and thus constraints on what can be rationally agreed to. This yields the principle that justice requires the least inequality necessary to maximize the share of the worst off. We believe that inequality in the USA clearly is far greater than what would be necessary to increase the well-being of those at the bottom of the spectrum (Reiman and Leighton 2013: 205, n. 60). Subjects in Norton and Ariely's (2011) survey did not have the full information available in Rawls' exercise, but chose distributions of wealth far more equal than what exists in reality. The researchers did not just compare this "ideal" to the actual distribution of wealth, but they asked people what they believed the distribution of wealth to be. The full results are available in Table 2.1.4, which indicates that Americans believed the top 20 percent owned 59 percent of the wealth, when it was really 84 percent and people believe it should be 32 percent. This has profound implications for the amount of wealth distributed at the bottom: the ideal distribution for the poorest 60 percent would involve them owning about 45 percent of the wealth, compared to a perceived ownership of 20 percent of the wealth and an actual ownership of less than 5 percent.

TABLE 2.1.4 Actual, perceived, and ideal distributions of wealth in the United States

Wealth of poorest 60% as a percentage		**Wealth of richest 20% as a percentage**
5	Actual amount of wealth	84
20	Perceived amount of wealth	59
45	Ideal amount of wealth	32

Source: Calculated from Norton and Ariely (2011).

People collectively underestimate inequality by a substantial amount, and mistakes about economic facts support the unequal status quo. When ideas—whether intentionally or not—"distort reality in a way that justifies the prevailing distribution of power and wealth, hides society's injustices, and thus secures uncritical allegiance to the existing social order, we have what Marx called ideology" (Reiman and Leighton 2013: 195). Those with little far outnumber the top few percentage who have plenty. Thus, "the have-nots and the have-littles could have more if they decided to take it from the have-plenties. This, in turn, means that the have-plenties need the cooperation of the have-nots and the have-littles" (ibid.: 196). This cooperation must be voluntary, and so "the have-nots and the have-littles must believe it would not be right or reasonable to take away what the have-plenties have" (ibid.)—that the system is legitimate.

Replicating Norton and Ariely's work (2011) in other developed nations would help develop data on questions about social justice and ideology. Evidence that the existing society violates citizens' expectations for fairness is a powerful tool to motivate deeper investigation about what social arrangements should look like—and how to advocate for change. Also, the discrepancy between the actual distribution of wealth and what people believe it to be is important data for the study of ideology. Random error would be evenly distributed in a way that was equally likely to over- and under-estimate inequality, with the average being close to the correct value. But error that consistently underestimates inequality is the result of systematic forces and constitutes evidence of the effect of ideology, which refers to what is necessarily deceptive. Some writers use ideology to refer to a "belief system" or "world-view." But this "moral neutralization of the concept of 'ideology' dulls an instrument that thinkers such as Marx and others have sharpened into an effective tool for cutting through the illusions that dog our political life" (Reiman and Leighton 2013: 196).

"Systematic forces" does not mean that ideology is conscious deception. Marx wrote that "the ideas of the ruling class are in every epoch the ruling ideas ... The class which has the means of material production at its disposal, has control at the same time over the means of mental production" (in Reiman and Leighton 2013: 194). Those who have economic power own newspapers, endow universities, finance the publication of books and journals, and control television, radio and other electronic media. The controllers of the "means of mental production" broadcast a picture of reality that they believe to be accurate, and which will be largely the picture of reality that fills the heads of the readers and viewers of the mass media. What people take to be "common sense" or conventional wisdom is nevertheless based on a distorted consensus. And an important question this research helps us understand is how distorted people's pictures of reality are, and whether nations with higher levels of inequality have more distortion.

The second research direction involves putting class back into data about crime so it includes white-collar and corporate crime. Even though the existing law needs to further criminalize white-collar and corporate crime to mirror the harmful acts, crime reports should reflect all the threats to people's lives, health and property as currently defined by law, not merely compile data on the wrongdoing of the poor. Broader inclusion of data on white-collar and corporate crime in government reports requires policy changes, but researchers can still compile data from alternative sources to create de-classed crime reports (e.g. ibid.: 95). The goal would be to include fraud by a company director and corporate manslaughter (as the British do) or fraudulent trade practices (as Australia does). These alternative, or shadow, government statistics are explicit about their methodology, assumptions, and data sources—just like any transparent and useful data source.

However, this strategy has some important limitations because data increasingly comes from industries that study their own losses and victimization, usually by the poor and middle class. But there's little data—and little money to study—victimization perpetrated by corporations and industries. The discussion above noted that Britain worked with the trade association for credit and debit cards to gather more information on fraud—fraud against financial institutions, which pay for charges on lost and stolen cards. To the extent that abuses of consumers by card issuers are criminalized, no one collects data on the types of crimes, their frequency or aggregate cost to the public. A publication by the British National Fraud Authority (NFA)—an executive agency within the Home Office—has estimates of fraud *against* insurance companies and mortgage lenders (National Fraud Authority 2012: 17), but not corresponding estimates of fraud done *by* these industries against the public to boost profits. For example, in the USA—and most likely Britain too—"paying out less to victims of catastrophes has helped produce record profits," according to Bloomberg News (Dietz and Preston 2007). The investigative report did not put a total dollar amount on such losses, but noted:

> The insurance companies routinely refuse to pay market prices for homes and replacement contents, they use computer programs to cut payouts, they change policy coverage with no clear explanation, they ignore or alter engineering reports, and they sometimes ask their adjusters to lie to customers, court records and interviews with former employees and state regulators show.

Discussions of problems like fraud contain language that obscures the very existence of crimes by financial institutions. The NFA's discussion of fraud against individuals included "mass marketing fraud," which means unsolicited communications for money (National Fraud Authority 2012: 8–9) rather than false advertising or deceptive trade practices. "Insider-enabled fraud" is "staff fraud" and "employee fraud" (ibid.: 24), but not control fraud, which is perpetrated by executive-level insiders. Executives who control a company create fictitious profits to turn corporate assets into personal assets (through stock bonuses, etc.) and ultimately defraud a variety of people, like shareholders. Businesses "report sensational profits, followed by catastrophic failure" (in Barak 2012: 73)—a pattern that should be immediately recognizable to the British and citizens of every developed nation. Yet an Australian government report on fraud noted:

> Fraud affects all sectors of the community, extending from individuals who have responded to online offers to make 'quick money', to large companies and government departments that have suffered fraud at the hands of their employees or members of the public.
>
> (Australian Institute of Criminology 2012c: ix)

Certainly businesses and corporations in Australia have enough of a history of perpetrating fraud that they should be included as part of the basic description of the fraud problem.

In general, the missing data are about the crimes of the powerful that protect and advance the accumulation of capital (Barak *et al.* 2010: 11). Crime reports can retain data on minor theft, but they also need to recognize that

> the most consequential white-collar crimes—in terms of their scope, impact and cost in dollars—appear to require for their commission, that their perpetrators operate in an environment that provides access to both money and the organization through which money moves.
>
> (Braithwaite 1992: 86)

Financial and corporate interests make sure that acquisitive activities they perpetrate against people are not criminalized, and if criminalized, not prosecuted, counted or conceived of as "real" crime. Instead, wealthy industries produce data about their own victimization, including white-collar crimes like fraud by middle managers and card fraud. But the key to future research is to examine the direction of the victimization and explore the areas where the wealthiest and most powerful are the perpetrators, because those are the uncounted harms—and if left uncounted, the harms they represent will disappear from consciousness.

Policy Implications of the Inconvenient Truths about Wealth

The problem of inequality is the primary policy implication, but several smaller policy issues are worth noting briefly. First, the development of better data is necessary where a criminal justice system produces minimal data on class and is thus not accountable for bias. In the USA, for-profit probation companies are growing rapidly—with a debt collection business model and "onerous 'user fees'" (Bronner 2012)—so collection of data about income and wealth needs to be done in a way that does not lead to criminal justice becoming (more) complicit in legal extortion for private gain.

Second, policies need to promote the systematic collection and regular dissemination of data about white-collar and corporate harm, preferably in existing reports on the nation's crime problem. The inclusiveness of German crime data makes it a possible model in terms of what should be presented. For example, it includes economic crime, which captures criminal violations of the patent, trademark and copyright acts; the Act Against Unfair Competition, Act on the Financial Statements of Certain Enterprises and Groups, Insurance Industry Supervision Act, Securities Trading Act, and Economic Offenses Act of 1954; and, among others, criminal offenses according to the Wine Act and food products legislation (Bundeskriminalamt 2011: 8).

Third, existing laws regulating the conduct of the poor need to be applied equally to corporations or repealed for all. For example, the British crime data reports 2.7 million Antisocial Behavior Orders (ASBOs) (Office for National Statistics 2012a: 70). An ASBO is recorded using three simplified categories. As relevant here, *nuisance* includes "where an act, condition, thing or person causes trouble, annoyance, irritation, inconvenience, offence or suffering to the local community in general rather than to individual victims." And, *environmental* "captures incidents where individuals and groups have an impact on their surroundings, including natural, built and social environments" (ibid.: 71). ASBOs are described over a number of pages in the crime report that details noisy neighbors, drunk or rowdy behavior, litter, drug use/dealing, teenagers loitering, vandalism/graffiti, and abandoned/burnt-out cars (ibid.). But neither the law nor the concept applies to corporations, even though economic theory and legal structures drive it to focus narrowly on self-interest, thus maximizing the likelihood of inconsiderate behavior that damages others. Corporate behavior may not fit this law as it was written, but the question remains why nuisance behaviors of individuals are worth sanctioning and counting (and studying), but the nuisance behaviors of corporations are not. If the ASBO has merit—a debatable proposition (Prior 2009)—then it should also apply to "nuisance" and "environmental" impacts of corporate behavior that pollutes communities, economically exploits workers, cuts corners with workers' health and safety, commits unfair trade practices, produces dangerous products, defrauds consumers, etc. Some of these behaviors are already against the law, but an ASBO could fill in where the behavior is a nuisance that needs to be officially recognized but other systems do not have the resources for a full investigation and prosecution.

Attending to the recommendations above and other concerns raised by this [reading] requires policies to combat inequality. Braithwaite nicely summarizes the problem by explaining that inequality "worsens both crimes of poverty motivated by *need* for goods for use and crimes of wealth motivated by *greed* enabled by goods for exchange" (1992: 81). For Braithwaite, "need" is culturally constructed and based on community norms, expectations and advertising. In general, then, "the more unequal the class structure, the more scarce national wealth is devoted to gratifying greed among people whose needs are satisfied, the less is devoted to satisfying unmet needs" (ibid.: 83). As suggested by opportunity theory, where legitimate means to achieving such needs are blocked, illegitimate and criminal means for satisfying needs become more likely.

Even when the rich have their needs met, additional dollars still have value to them and they pursue additional wealth "to signify their worth by conspicuous consumption, to prove success to themselves, to build an empire, to leave an inheritance" (ibid.: 84). If legitimate means are blocked, the rich can pursue existing illegitimate means—or create new types of illegitimate means. The limitation on traditional opportunity theory is that it is not applied to the wealthy, and, notes Braithwaite, "if they are powerful enough, criminals can actively constitute illegitimate opportunities" (ibid.: 86). Further, these novel illegitimate strategies "excel because they cannot be contemplated by those who are not wealthy" (ibid.: 88), and at times they cannot be contemplated even by regulatory agencies.

One of the greatest advantages of the wealthy and corporations is to prevent their actions from becoming criminal in the first place. They can also use their resources to frustrate regulation and thus remain unaccountable for their wrongdoing and the harm they have caused to others. Braithwaite notes: "power corrupts and unaccountable power corrupts with impunity" (ibid.: 89). This analysis dovetails with Christie's concern about weak states, which is supported by a quote from Bauman: "weak, quasi-states can be easily reduced to the (useful) role of legal police precincts, securing a modicum of order required for the conduct of business, but need not be feared as effective brakes on the global companies' freedom" (Christie 2004: 36). Even though the USA is the largest global economy, Ritholtz—the CEO of a financial research firm and author of *Bailout Nation*—believes that the Securities and Exchange Commission is "defective by design" (in Reiman and Leighton 2013: 159). Meanwhile, the "janitors of the suitably weakened states" need to prove their worth, so fighting street crime "becomes indispensable in creating legitimacy" (Christie 2004: 37).

Inequality thus extends crime through the power of the wealthy and undermines the effectiveness of guardians who should protect the vulnerable from motivated offenders (Alvesalo *et al.* 2006). Braithwaite further argues that inequality reduces the respect the powerful have for the dominion of others, especially the poorest.

> [Dominion] includes the sphere of control citizens properly enjoy over their persons, their property and the province. To enjoy dominion, a citizen must

> live in a social world where other citizens respect his or her liberty and where mutual respect is socially assured and generally recognized.
>
> (Braithwaite 1992: 80)

The idea that greater levels of inequality lead to crime via contempt for the citizenship rights of the weak is an important complement to concerns that inequality and social exclusion lead the poor to commit crimes because they have little respect for the law (Reiman and Leighton 2013: 33, 186).

Further, inequality plays a role in violent crime as well. Braithwaite draws on Katz and others who have developed theories about the role of humiliation, which can turn into righteous rage and violent acts. While Katz focused on the immediate transformation of emotions and denied the relevance of background and material factors, Braithwaite integrates it:

> *[I]negalitarian societies are structurally humiliating.* When parents cannot supply the most basic needs to their children, when they are assailed by the ostentatious consumption of the affluent, this is structurally humiliating for the poor. Where inequality is great, the rich humiliate the poor through conspicuous consumption and the poor are humiliated as failures for being poor. Both sides of this equation are important. The propensity to feel powerless and exploited among the poor and the propensity of the rich to see exploiting as legitimate, both ... enable crime.
>
> (1992: 94, emphasis in original)

Currie's analysis is similar and emphasizes not just poverty or "the simple absence of material goods, but rather the deeper attitudes of hopelessness and alienation produced by inequalities that are unjust" (1985: 162). Simply put, "violence results 'not so much from lack of advantages as from being taken advantage of'" (ibid.).

Redressing inequality—and especially the alienation, exclusion and hopelessness—is important for social justice and crime prevention. This conclusion is not new, although it is an(other) inconvenient truth about inequality. As Braithwaite summarizes:

> If crime in the suites arises from the fact that certain people have great wealth and power, and if crime in the streets arises from the fact certain other people have very little wealth or power, then policies to redistribute wealth and power may simultaneously relieve both types of crime problems.
>
> (1992: 90)

Currie fills out this prescription by adding that "we must build a society that is less unequal, less depriving, less insecure, less disruptive of family and community ties, less corrosive of cooperative values" (1985: 225).

Conclusion

An issue raised in this [reading]'s Introduction was Christie's observation that prison populations biased in terms of the identity of the receivers of the intended pain can "indicate severe defects somewhere in that system" (2004: 102). In our view, there is bias, with the poor being (conspicuously) over-consumed by the criminal justice system and the rich being (inconspicuously) under-consumed. Based on *The Rich Get Richer and the Poor Get Prison*, we suggest that three separate defects contribute to this phenomenon. First, society does not deal with root causes of crime—especially inequality—and may enact policies that promote criminogenic conditions for the poor. Second, legislatures do not adequately criminalize real harms of business that create real victims of workers, consumers, investors and communities. Third, the criminal justice system operates with class bias, although it is hidden by both not collecting income data on criminal offenders and not including white-collar crimes in annual government reports on "crime."

This analysis has important implications because the moral legitimacy of a legal system hinges on whether coercion is being used in the interests of all equally, or whether it promotes some people's interests at the expense of others. Criminals and occupying troops use force to subject some people to the interests of others, while legal systems claim moral superiority because they are supposed to use force to protect equally the interests and rights of all and to punish equally all who endanger these interests or who violate these rights. This adds up to something that should be obvious but is not: A criminal justice system is criminal to the extent that it is not truly a system of justice (Reiman and Leighton 2013: 207).

Because the system protects certain interests does not mean that it is the result of a conspiracy. The focus on one-on-one (rather than corporate) harm reflects the main ways in which people harmed each other in the days before large-scale industrialization. The Pyrrhic defeat theory suggests that current failed criminal justice policies persist because they fail in a way that does not give rise to an effective demand for change. First, this failing system provides benefits for those with the power to make changes, while it imposes costs on those without such power. The wealthy experience low rates of victimization from street crime, generally profit from the opportunity to expose workers or consumers to extra risk, and benefit from class bias in processing offenders. Second, because the criminal justice system shapes the public's conception of what is dangerous, it creates the impression that the harms it is fighting are the real threats to society. Thus, even when people continue to experience "fear of crime," they only demand a continuation or escalation of the same policies: more police, more prisons, longer prison sentences, and so on.

Consider first the benefits that the system provides for those with wealth and power. The failure of criminal justice policy diverts attention from the harmful noncriminal acts of the well-off and focuses people's attention on a real threat of theft and violence on the street, and a large and visible population of poor criminals in the courts and prisons. This conveys a vivid image—supported by the crime reports that lack white-collar and corporate crime data—that the real threat to people's lives and limbs is from the poor. The media, criminal justice textbooks and public policy reports amplify this message by reproducing the statistics and dramatizing the interpersonal acts in the crime reports. This image of crime provides benefits to the rich and powerful through an ideological message that the threat to law-abiding Middle America comes from below them on the economic ladder, not above them. It creates (or reinforces) fear of, and hostility toward, the poor. It leads people to ignore the ways in which they are injured and robbed by the acts of the affluent, and thus it points toward a *conservative* defense of society's disparities of wealth, power, and opportunity—and leads them away from a *progressive* demand for equality and a more equitable distribution of wealth and power (Reiman and Leighton 2013: 180).

Discussion Questions

1. If you live in one of the countries whose distribution of wealth ownership appeared in this [reading], were you surprised at the level of inequality? Why or why not? If you live in another country, how do you think the distribution of wealth ownership would look—and can you find data about it?
2. What are three of the most important ways that inequality and class are linked to crime or criminal justice?
3. Do you think there is a suitable amount of street crime and white-collar crime in your country? On what basis could you argue that the amount of crime is "suitable"?
4. What happens when there is not a suitable amount of crime—that too much behavior is criminalized, or too little? Please answer this question with respect to both street and white-collar crime.
5. What is ideology? Why is it important when examining wealth as well as the criminal justice system?

Websites

Companion website for *The Rich Get Richer*: http://www.paulsjusticepage.com/reiman.htm.
Crime Talk: http://www.crimetalk.org.uk/.

Critical Criminology: http://critcrim.org/.

Matt Taibbi's Taibblog: http://www.rollingstone.com/politics/blogs/taibblog.

Tombs and Whyte, "A crisis of enforcement: The decriminalization of death and injury at work": http://www.crimeandjustice.org.uk/opus685/crisisenforcementweb.pdf.

References

Alvesalo, A., Tombs, S., Virta, E., and Whyte, D. (2006) "Re-Imagining Crime Prevention: Controlling Corporate Crime?" *Crime, Law and Social Change*, 45: 1–25.

Australian Bureau of Statistics (2011) *Household Wealth and Wealth Distribution, 2009–10*, Canberra: Australian Bureau of Statistics, available at: http://www.ausstats.abs.gov.au/Ausstats/subscriber.nsf/0/51342DFD54324472CA257928001107B4/$File/65540_2009-10.pdf (accessed 27 August 2012).

Australian Institute of Criminology (2008) *Homicide in Australia: 2006–07 National Homicide Monitoring Program Annual Report*, Canberra: Australian Institute of Criminology, available at: http://www.aic.gov.au/documents/F/F/B/%7BFFB9E49F-160F-43FC-B98D-6BC510DC2AFD%7Dmr01.pdf (accessed 27 August 2012).

Australian Institute of Criminology (2012a) *Australian Crime: Facts and Figures 2011*, Canberra: Australian Institute of Criminology, available at: http://www.aic.gov.au/documents/0/B/6/%7B0B619F44-B18B-47B4-9B59-F87BA643CBAA%7Dfacts11.pdf (accessed 27 August 2012).

Australian Institute of Criminology (2012b) *Australasian Consumer Fraud Taskforce: Results of the 2010 and 2011 Online Consumer Fraud Surveys*, Canberra: Australian Institute of Criminology, available at: http://www.aic.gov.au/documents/7/C/F/%7B7CF8C691-F02E-41EA-8DB4-74922AEED-DAF%7Dtbp50.pdf (accessed 27 August 2012).

Australian Institute of Criminology (2012c) *Fraud against the Commonwealth 2009–10 Annual Report to Government*, Canberra: Australian Institute of Criminology, available at: http://www.aic.gov.au/documents/B/5/1/%7BB514C8BC-4578-4D7F-A9C8-475FF1269004%7DMR18.pdf (accessed 27 August 2012).

Barak, G. (2012) *Theft of a Nation: Wall Street Looting and Federal Regulatory Colluding*, Rowman and Littlefield.

Barak, G., Leighton, P. and Flavin, J. (2010) *Class, Race, Gender and Crime*, 3rd edn, Rowman and Littlefield.

Braithwaite, J. (1992) "Poverty, Power, and White-Collar Crime," in K. Schlegel and D. Weisburd (eds.) *White-Collar Crime Reconsidered*, Northeastern University Press.

Bricker, J., Kennickell, A., Moore, K., and Sabelhaus, J. (2012) "Changes in U.S. Family Finances from 2007 to 2010: Evidence from the Survey of Consumer Finances," *Federal Reserve Bulletin*, 98(2): 1–80, available at: http://www.federalreserve.gov/pubs/bulletin/2012/pdf/scf12.pdf (accessed 27 August 2012).

Bronner, E. (2012) "Poor Land in Jail as Companies Add Huge Fees for Probation," *New York Times*, 2 July, available at: http://www.nytimes.com/2012/07/03/us/probation-fees-multiply-as-companies-profit.html (accessed 27 August 2012).

Bucks, B., Kennickell, A., Mach, T., and Moore, K. (2009) "Changes in U.S. Family Finances from 2004 to 2007: Evidence from the Survey of Consumer Finances," *Federal Reserve Bulletin*, 95: A1–A55, available at: http://www.federalreserve.gov/econresdata/scf/files/2007_scf09.pdf (accessed 27 August 2012).

Bundeskriminalamt (2011) *Police Crime Statistics, 2010*, Wiesbaden: Federal Criminal Police Office, available at: http://www.bka.de/nn_194552/EN/Publications/PoliceCrimeStatistics/policeCrimeStatistics_node.html?_nnn=true (accessed 27 August 2012).

Cagetti, M., and De Nardi, M. (2008) "Wealth Inequality: Data and Models," *Macroeconomic Dynamics*, 12 (Supplement 2): 285–313.

Christie, N. (2000) *Crime Control as Industry*, 3rd edn, Routledge.

Christie, N. (2004) *A Suitable Amount of Crime*, Routledge.

Corporate Fraud Task Force (n.d.) "The President's Corporate Fraud Task Force," Washington, DC: Department of Justice, available at: http://www.justice.gov/archive/dag/cftf/ (accessed 27 August 2012).

Currie, E. (1985) *Confronting Crime*, Pantheon.

DeNavas-Walt, C., Proctor, B., and Smith, J. (2011) *Income, Poverty, and Health Insurance Coverage in the United States: 2010*, U.S. Census Bureau, Current Population Reports, P60–239. U.S. Washington, DC: Government Printing Office, available at: http://www.census.gov/prod/2011pubs/p60-239.pdf (accessed 27 August 2012).

Department of Justice (Canada) (2012) *A Plain Language Guide Bill C-45—Amendments to the Criminal Code Affecting the Criminal Liability of Organizations*, Ottawa: Department of Justice, available at: http://www.justice.gc.ca/eng/dept-min/pub/c45/p02.html#sec2 (accessed 27 August 2012).

Dietz, D., and Preston, D. (2007) "Home Insurers' Secret Tactics Cheat Fire Victims, Hike Profits," *Bloomberg News*, August 3, available at: http://www.bloomberg.com/apps/news?pid=newsarchive&sid=aIOpZROwhvNI.

Erikson, K. (1966) *Wayward Puritans*, Macmillan.

Federal Bureau of Investigation (2011) *Crime in the U.S., 2010*, available at: http://www.fbi.gov/about-us/cjis/ucr/crime-in-the-u.s/2010/crime-in-the-u.s.-2010 (accessed 27 August 2012).

Foucault, M. (1977) *Discipline and Punish: The Birth of the Prison*, trans. A. Sheridan, Allen Lane.

Friedrichs, D. (2010) *Trusted Criminals*, Wadsworth/Cengage.

HMRC (Her Majesty's Revenue and Customs) (2011) "Table 13.8 Identified personal wealth," *Personal Wealth Statistics, 2001 to 03 and 2005 to 07*, available at: http://www.hmrc.gov.uk/stats/personal_wealth/intro-personal-wealth.pdf (accessed 27 August 2012).

Home Office (2012) *Crimes Detected in England and Wales 2011/12*, London: Home Office, available at: http://www.homeoffice.gov.uk/publications/science-research-statistics/research-statistics/crime-research/hosb0812/hosb0812?view=Binary (accessed 27 August 2012).

Kennickell, A. (2009) "Ponds and Streams: Wealth and Income in the U.S., 1989 to 2007," Federal Reserve Board, available at: http://www.federalreserve.gov/pubs/feds/2009/200913/200913pap.pdf (accessed 27 August 2012).

Leighton, P., and Selman, D. (2012) "Private Prisons, the Criminal Justice-Industrial Complex and Bodies Destined for Profitable Punishment," in W. DeKeserdy and M. Dragiewicz (eds) *Routledge Handbook of Critical Criminology*, Routledge.

Lynch, J., and Pridemore, W. (2010) "Crime in International Perspective," in J. Q. Wilson and J. Petersilia (eds.) *Crime and Public Policy*, Oxford University Press.

Ministry of Justice (2008) "Corporate Manslaughter and Corporate Homicide Act 2007," available at: http://www.justice.gov.uk/downloads/legislation/bills-acts/circulars/moj/corporate-manslaughter-act-2007-circular-9-feb-08.pdf (accessed 27 August 2012).

Mohamed, A. R., and Fritsvold, E. (2010) *Dorm Room Dealers*, Lynne Rienner.

Mooney, G. (2008) "Explaining Poverty, Social Exclusion and Inequality," in T. Ridge and S. Wright (eds.) *Understanding Inequality, Poverty and Wealth*, Policy Press.

National Fraud Authority (2012) *Annual Fraud Indicator*, London: Home Office, available at: http://www.homeoffice.gov.uk/publications/agencies-public-bodies/nfa/annual-fraud-indicator/annual-fraud-indicator-2012?view=Binary (accessed 27 August 2012).

Norton, M., and Ariely, D. (2011) "Building a Better America—One Wealth Quintile at a Time," *Perspectives on Psychological Science*, 6(1): 9–12.

Office for National Statistics (2012a) *Crime in England and Wales, Quarterly First Release to March 2012*, Office of National Statistics, available at: http://www.ons.gov.uk/ons/dcp171778_273169.pdf (accessed 27 August 2012).

Office for National Statistics (2012b) *User Guide to Crime Statistics for England and Wales*, Office of National Statistics, available at: http://www.ons.gov.uk/ons/guide-method/method-quality/specific/crime-statistics-methodology/user-guide-to-crime-statistics.pdf (accessed 27 August 2012).

Prior, D. (2009) "The 'Problem' Of Anti-Social Behaviour And The Policy Knowledge Base," *Critical Social Policy* 29(1): 5–23.

Reiman, J. (2001) "Criminal Justice Ethics," in P. Leighton and J. Reiman (eds.) *Criminal Justice Ethics*, Prentice Hall.

Reiman, J. (2013) Appendix II: "Between Philosophy and Criminology," in J. Reiman and P. Leighton *The Rich Get Richer and the Poor Get Prison*, 10th edn, Allyn & Bacon/Pearson.

Reiman, J., and Leighton, P. (2013) *The Rich Get Richer and the Poor Get Prison*, 10th edn, Allyn & Bacon/Pearson.

Selman, D., and Leighton, P. (2010) *Punishment for Sale*, Rowman and Littlefield.
Statistics Canada (2005) *The Wealth of Canadians*, Statistics Canada, available at: http://www.statcan.gc.ca/pub/13f0026m/13f0026m2006001-eng.pdf (accessed 27 August 2012).
Statistics Canada (2010) *Criminal Victimization in Canada, 2009*, Statistics Canada, available at: http://www.statcan.gc.ca/pub/85-002-x/2010002/article/11340-eng.pdf (accessed 27 August 2012).
Statistics Canada (2011) *Homicide in Canada, 2010*, Statistics Canada, available at: http://www.statcan.gc.ca/pub/85-002-x/2011001/article/11561-eng.pdf (accessed 27 August 2012).
Statistics Canada (2012a) *Police-Reported Crime Statistics in Canada, 2011*, Statistics Canada, available at: http://www.statcan.gc.ca/pub/85-002-x/2012001/article/11692-eng.pdf (accessed 27 August 2012).
Statistics Canada (2012b) *Adult Criminal Court Statistics in Canada, 2010/2011*, Statistics Canada, available at: http://www.statcan.gc.ca/pub/85-002-x/2012001/article/11646-eng.pdf (accessed 27 August 2012).
Taibbi, M. (2011) "Why Isn't Wall Street in jail?" *Rolling Stone*, 3 March, available at: http://www.rollingstone.com/politics/news/why-isnt-wall-street-in-jail-20110216 (accessed 27 August 2012).
Zimring, F. (2007) *The Great American Crime Decline*, Oxford University Press.

Reading 2.2

Why Study White Supremacist Terror? A Research Note

Pete Simi, University of Nebraska-Omaha, Omaha, Nebraska, USA

THIS [READING] DISCUSSES HOW THE CURRENT neglect of white supremacist violence impedes the development of terrorism scholarship. The decentralized organization of contemporary white supremacists is often confused with disorganization that has led some observers to claim that white supremacist terror (WST) poses a relatively benign threat and is essentially irrelevant. In contrast, I argue that white supremacist violence is part of a broader social movement strategy. Lastly, I discuss how four hot-button issues may contribute to a new large-scale wave of WST.

Introduction

The study of terrorism is growing faster than any other field in the social sciences (Schmid and Jongman 1988). Yet, observers have long noted the overall inadequacy of terrorism research stemming in part from superficial methodological designs, incomplete data, and unfettered value judgments regarding the motivations and tactics of terrorists (Silke 2003; Merari 1991; Schmid and Jongman 1988). Since 9/11, studies of terrorism have almost exclusively focused on radical Islamic fundamentalism, neglecting other types of terror groups thus creating another significant limitation to the field of terrorism research.

In this [reading], I discuss how neglecting white supremacist violence impedes the development of terrorism scholarship. Violence associated with white supremacist groups in the United States represents the most sustained form of terrorism in this country (Blee 2005a). Yet there is a tendency among contemporary observers to presume that white supremacist terror (WST) is relatively infrequent, which leads to an underestimation of the actual occurrence of this type of violence (e.g., see Hoffman 2006; Freiden 2005; Gardell 2003). Despite claims that WST poses a relatively benign threat and is essentially irrelevant, I argue that white supremacist violence is part of a "cycle of contention" that refers to a cyclical rise and fall of social movement activity (Tarrow 1989). The extent to which U.S. white supremacist violence is connected to a broader strategy has been largely ignored by terrorism scholars, in part, because contemporary white supremacists participate in a decentralized network that is often confused with disorganization. Lastly, I discuss how four hot-button issues present different types of threat that may contribute to another large-scale wave of WST.

The neglect of WST has several important implications. First, comprehensive understandings of terrorism require a broad range of empirical studies. Constructing explanations of terrorism based on only certain types of terrorism undermines theoretical development. Second, ignoring WST implicitly encourages the biased, but increasingly pervasive, view that terrorism is a "foreign" problem and thus the "cause" of terrorism resides in a Middle Eastern population of "exotic others" (Said 1978). Third, the academic neglect of WST reinforces a "conventional wisdom" (Galbraith 1958; Warner 1838) that WST is relatively infrequent and therefore does not warrant serious attention. Together these tendencies are part of what I refer to as a "consensus of irrelevance" which involves ignoring and/or trivializing WST.

Researching the U.S. White Supremacist Movement (WSM)

The United States has a long history of WST (Berlet and Lyons 2000; Jenkins 2003; Lipset and Raab 1970). WST is the violent expression of a complex set of doctrines produced and communicated by white supremacist groups. These groups are part of the larger WSM, which has been described as "... sharing common ideologies and goals and an overriding commitment to maintaining white supremacy. There are ongoing debates among the groups, but also sustained efforts to forge shared objectives ..." (Ferber 1998:49). Foremost is the commitment to white power and defending the "white race" from "genocide." The future world they envision is racially exclusive, where "non-whites" are vanquished, segregated, or at least subordinated to white authority.

The movement's four major branches include: the Ku Klux Klan, Christian Identity sects, neo-Nazis, and racist skinheads. These groups utilize a variety of legal tactics including forming political parties, organizing public marches and rallies, creating and distributing extremist literature, developing separatist communities and illegal activities such as bombing abortion clinics, violent attacks on "out-group" members, bank robbery, drug distribution, identity theft, counterfeiting, and tax evasion (see Berlet and Lyons 2000; Blazak 2001; Diamond 1995; Freilich and Chermak 2009; Freilich et al. 2001; Hamm 2002; Kaplan 1995; McCurrie 1998; Simi et al. 2008; Smith 1994; Sprinzak 1995; Weinberg 1998).

Various studies offer important insights about their organization and membership. First, scholars typically describe the WSM as loosely connected branches, each distinctive in their origins, ideological tenets, and activities (Aho 1990; Arena and Arrigo 2000; Barkun 1994; Berlet and Lyons 2000; Bjorgo and Kaplan 1998; Blazak 2001; Blee 2002; Burris et al. 2000; Dobratz and Shanks-Meile 2000; Ezekiel 1995; Ferber 1998; Futrell and Simi 2004; Kaplan and Weinberg 1998; Smith 1994).

Second, although a long history of research discounts extremists as distinctively pathological and psychologically deficient (Adorno et al. 1950; Hofstadter 1965; Lipset and Raab 1970), recent scholarship suggests that network connections and conventional political socialization explains how extremists typically become involved (Aho 1990; Blazak 2001; Blee 2002; Ezekiel 1995; Hamm 1993) and that members are drawn from a wide range of social class backgrounds and are not social isolates (Aho 1990; Blee 2002; Simi and Futrell 2009).

With a few exceptions, however, the literature examining the contemporary WSM has not explicitly analyzed the link between mobilization and terrorism (Blee 2005a). At the same time, much of the research that specifically examines this link, while insightful, is now dated (e.g., Bjorgo 1995; Kaplan 1995; Smith 1994; Sprinzak 1995). More recent treatments of U.S. WST provide evidence supporting the view that a substantial portion of white supremacist violence meets many standard definitions of terrorism (Blee 2005b; Blazak 2001; Hamm 2002). In this [reading], I examine the tendency to discount the threat of WST that stems, in part, from characterizing white supremacist violence as isolated incidents and failing to understand the relation between these incidents and a larger political strategy. As an alternative, I propose a framework to understand WST that combines the cycle of contention concept from the social movement literature (della Porta 1995; Tarrow 1989) as well as insight gleaned from the network sciences (Barabasi 2003; Buchanan 2003; Stohl and Stohl 2007; Watts and Strogatz 1998).

Theorizing the Neglect of WST

Dramatic events like 9/11 help generate "moral panics" (Cohen 1972), which refers to the intense feelings that are directed toward a group who are perceived as a significant threat. But not all potentially threatening groups are equally likely to generate moral panics (Cohen 1972; Hall et al. 1978). Government officials, the media, and scholarly researchers in the United States are far more likely to refer to violent incidents linked to "international" groups as terrorist than violent incidents linked to domestic radicals (Turk 2004). In terms of Middle Eastern terrorists, there is strong consensus about the danger they pose (Turk 2004), which is an important component of generating and sustaining a moral panic. Although white supremacists are highly stigmatized (Blee 2002; Kaplan 1995; Simi and Futrell 2009), they are not necessarily viewed as a significant terrorist threat (Frieden 2005). Instead the consensus regarding white supremacists typically involves characterizing them as "buffoons," "incompetent," and "disorganized" (e.g., Balch 2006; Hoffman 2006; Kaplan 1995). In addition, high levels of movement decentralization result in the appearance that the vast majority of bias-motivated violence is unrelated to hate groups (McDevitt et al. 2002). The perception that white supremacist groups are in disarray and that most hate crime is unrelated to hate groups discourages a more serious consideration of the threat of WST. In short, scholars, law enforcement, and the media do not pay much attention to the threat of WST because white supremacists are not perceived as "authentic" terrorists (Jenkins 2003).

Conceptual Links Between Terror, Extremism, and Hate Crime

Terrorism scholars continue to disagree about how to define the phenomenon (Schmid and Jongman 1988). In this [reading], I define terrorism as acts or threats of violence intended to generate fear beyond the immediate victim(s) and acts that are, at least somewhat, motivated by politics (Schmid and Jongman 1988; Blee 2005a). Terrorism by definition involves action or what people do. By default all terrorists are also extremists. Most extremists, however, do not explicitly plan or participate in acts of terrorism; therefore most extremists are not terrorists (Bjorgo 1995; Sprinzak 1995). Extremism, on the other hand, can be defined more in terms of adherents' beliefs and involves a broader range of behavior than terrorism. Individuals and groups who commit acts of WST are, in varying degrees and in varying ways, connected to a network where the circulation of extremist beliefs such as, anti-government, racist, anti-Semitic, homophobic, anti-abortion, and anti-immigrant, are prominent (Blee 2002; Hamm 2002; Kaplan 1995).

One notable characteristic about definitions of terrorism, including the one I use, is that various crimes that are typically subsumed under other conceptual categories may also fit. For example, an "organized crime" group may kill someone in order to generate fear beyond the immediate target and as part of their desire to attain or sustain power which one could argue involves politics. More germane to the discussion of WST, hate crime incidents are typically distinguished from "normal crime" (Sudnow 1965), in part, because the selection of the victim symbolically represents a larger community that the offender(s) wishes to harm (Jenness and Broad 1997; Levin 1999; Jacobs and Potter 1998).

According to previous research, most hate crime offenders are not affiliated with hate groups (McDevitt et al. 2002); this finding does not necessarily mean that hate groups do not either directly or indirectly exert influence on the incidence of hate crime (Beck 2000; Hamm 1993). Much of the social psychological literature suggests that changes in self concept and identification usually occur gradually from interaction and exposure to alternative styles and narratives (Kiecolt 2000:117). To the extent that hate crimes are closely connected to identity (both the offender's and the victim's), then it is reasonable to suggest the propaganda produced and distributed by white supremacist groups which now includes websites, music, YouTube videos, and a range of diffuse cultural material exerts influence well beyond those individuals most identifiable as hate group members (Simi and Futrell 2006). In addition, the very nature of the WSM's organization reflects a high degree of decentralization or what network analysts refer to as "distributed networks" (Watts and Strogatz 1998). Segmented and polycentric forms of organization (Gerlach 1971/1983; also, Gerlach and Hine 1970, 1973) leave clear-cut boundaries of membership ambiguous. Thus, the finding that most hate crimes are not committed by hate group members is questionable, in part, because it assumes traditional notions of membership that are largely inapplicable.

Because of the diffuse influence of the WSM and its decentralized network style of organization, I consider WST to include individual hate crime incidents initiated by members of the dominant racial group targeting individuals who represent minority out groups perceived, for varying reasons, to be threats (see also Blee 2005b; Hamm 1993). These incidents may be impersonal and well organized such as the Oklahoma City bombing or interpersonal and spontaneous such as the two perpetrators who stabbed an African American on their way to a neo-Nazi rally (retrieved from adl.org, May 1, 2008). Although the Oklahoma City bombing was relatively well organized, the perpetrators were not affiliated with a specific organization but instead were linked to a larger network of supremacists. In the second example, although the perpetrators responsible for the stabbing were affiliated with a specific extremist organization, the incident was relatively spontaneous. In both cases, however, the violence is appropriately viewed as terrorism as both incidents are part of a larger strategy of violence employed by the WSM.

Cycle of Contention, Social Movement Activism, and Terrorism

Political violence, including terrorism, is nested in social movements (della Porta 1995; Sageman 2004; Tilly 2004). A thorough understanding of terrorism thus requires analyses of the relationship between terror events and how the terror produced by an individual or group is, in turn, related to a larger social movement (Tilly 2004; Borum and Gelles 2005). Doing so helps answer questions about the extent to which a movement encourages adherents to express grievances through the use of violent tactics including terrorism. Tarrow's (1989; see also della Porta 1995) "cycle of contention" is an especially useful analytic tool for understanding the ebb and flow of movement-related violence. Cycle of contention refers to the rise and fall of social movement protest activity including violent and nonviolent political activity. Tarrow (1989) and della Porta's (1995) research in Italy shows that political violence including terrorism is present from the beginning of a protest cycle but varies in relation to the level of mass mobilization. Cycles of contentious politics influence a movement's "repertoire" of political tactics including decisions among some movement groups/members to use terror violence (Tilly 1995; Gamson 1975).

Viewing white supremacist violence as part of a cycle of contention provides a framework for understanding how seemingly disparate acts of extremist violence are part of a larger movement. WST is not a completely unified or coordinated effort and includes a diverse constellation of adherents (Sprinzak 1995). Research on other types of terror find similarly high levels of diversity within and among groups and that terror incidents are often organized from "the ground up" (Sageman 2004) lacking centralized coordination. Stohl and Stohl (2007) discuss how the metaphor of centralized, hierarchical networks to describe al-Qaeda's supposed organizational structure is misleading and often used for politicized reasons rather than analytic ones. The absence, however, of a centralized command structure is not the same as a completely disconnected and disorganized set of incidents. White supremacist violence is often related to a larger but decentralized network structure and that network structure, in turn, indirectly influences violent incidents. Despite significant decentralization among white supremacists, examining cycles of contention is still useful for assessing the different factors that may help produce an ebb or flow of WST.

Trivialization and a Growing Consensus of Irrelevance

Although the WSM has a long history characterized, at times, by wide political influence (Lipset and Raab 1970; Trelease 1971), many scholars and journalists contend that in recent years the movement has fragmented into a disorganized subculture (e.g., see Hoffman 2006; Gardell 2003). According to this perspective, WSM members resemble "outlandish and irrational buffoons" as opposed to the organized, well trained, and calculating adherents assumed to occupy terrorist groups. These observers also suggest that, in terms of terrorism, the U.S. extreme right is relatively unorganized, lacks mobilization potential, and has not produced much terrorist activity. This characterization is misguided and stems, in part, from notable incidents of domestic terrorism like the Oklahoma City and the Olympic Park bombings being divorced from the extremist ideology and relational links that helped produce these acts of violence (Chermak 2002; Wright 2006). Although both incidents received substantial media coverage (Chermak and Gruenewald 2006), neither was connected to a larger campaign of white supremacist terror. In fact, as Chermak (2002) shows, the Oklahoma City bombing and Timothy McVeigh were erroneously connected to the Militia Movement while McVeigh's links to white supremacy were largely ignored.

Although McVeigh's act of terrorism was officially characterized as an isolated act of three conspirators, there is evidence suggesting a much larger network of white supremacist activists were involved (Wright 2006; Hamm 2002). More specifically, there is evidence that links McVeigh to Elohim City, a white separatist community, members of the Aryan Republican Army (ARA), and White Aryan Resistance (WAR) (Arena and Arrigo 2000; Hamm 2002; Wright 2006). In terms of beliefs, McVeigh was inspired by neo-Nazi-leader William Pierce's (now deceased) *The Turner Diaries* (1978), which he sold at gun shows across the country and reportedly used the book as a blueprint for the bombing (Arena and Arrigo 2000; Hamm 2002; Wright 2006).

Eric Rudolph's violence, which killed 2 and injured 119 people, included setting off bombs at the 1996 Olympic games in Atlanta, abortion clinics in Atlanta and Birmingham, Alabama, and a lesbian nightclub in Atlanta and is another example of how WST is disconnected from the WSM. Rudolph is vehemently anti-abortion, anti-gay, anti-feminist, anti-Semitic, and feels that American culture is rapidly deteriorating (e.g., see Rudolph's writing on ArmyofGod.com). Rudolph's beliefs reflect his adherence to Christian Identity theology (one of the four major branches of the White Supremacy Movement), which preaches that Jews are the literal descendents of Satan and nonwhites are subhuman (Barkun 1994). In addition to his beliefs, Rudolph has a history of associations with Christian Identity adherents. For example, when Rudolph was eighteen he lived for six months at Pastor Dan Gayman's Christian Identity community, the Church of Israel, in Schell City, Missouri. While Rudolph lived there, Gayman served as his mentor and considered Rudolph as a potential spouse for one of his daughters (Vollers 2006). Despite Rudolph's clear ideological and associational ties to the WSM, his activity is often described as "single-issue, anti-abortion" terrorism or he is more generically referred to as a "radical Christian."

Part of the failure to connect incidents like the Oklahoma City bombing to a larger strategy of white supremacist violence is related to the decentralized nature of white supremacist networks. For instance, Buford Furrow's "lone wolf" shooting spree in a Jewish community center in 1999 was not simply an individual, interpersonal act of violence and hatred but represented the ideological tenets of the white supremacist group Aryan Nations that Furrow was affiliated with prior to the killings. In addition, Furrow considered himself a front line warrior in the WSM that he was helping galvanize. According to Furrow, he intended to ignite a "race war" by providing "... a wake-up call to America to kill Jews" (Gibney 1999). Likewise, in 1999, former World Church of the Creator (WCOTC) member Ben Smith launched a three-day, one-man ethnic-cleansing campaign that killed two people and wounded seven. Smith's actions were lauded by Matt Hale, the WCOTC's leader at the time, "Maybe he lost his life to make us a household name.... I have nothing but good things to say about Ben Smith ..." (retrieved www.g21.net, no date).

Incidents like Furrow or Smith's shooting spree should be viewed as part of a larger strategy of violence employed by the WSM not as random acts of isolated violence by deranged gunmen. Turk (2004) claims that domestic extremists have shifted from organizational to individual terrorism. While his point about the role of informal and decentralized networks is accurate, the use of the term "individual" is highly misleading. Turk's example of the Oklahoma City bombing as an individual act of terrorism is a case in point. Because white supremacist violence is often attributed to isolated individuals, specific incidents of white supremacist violence are not seen as part of a larger campaign. Some observers may counter that these incidents were not coordinated and thus lumping them together distorts the nature of white supremacist violence. My point, however, is that terror violence does not need to be completely coordinated to be part of a larger campaign and that the decentralized nature of white supremacist influence creates a "camouflage" of sorts that leads some astute observers to mistake decentralization for disorganization and thus irrelevance (e.g., see Hoffman 2006; Gardell 2003).

Hot-button Issues and the Mobilization of Threat

Although U.S. white supremacists have been increasingly marginalized from institutional politics since the 1960s, adherents sustain a robust culture of racial hatred and anti-government activism (Blee 2002; Dobratz and Shanks-Meile 1997; Futrell and Simi 2004; Futrell et al. 2006; Simi and Futrell 2006). The Southern Poverty Law Center reports that, in the decade following the Oklahoma City bombing, more than 60 terrorist plots were planned or carried out by right-wing extremists, 23 of which occurred between 2000 and 2005 (Blejwas et al. 2005, http://www.splcenter.org/intel/intelreport/article.jsp?aid 628). The list includes

> plans to bomb or burn government buildings, banks, refineries, utilities, clinics, synagogues, mosques, memorials and bridges; to assassinate police officers, judges, politicians, civil rights figures and others; to rob banks, armored cars and other criminals; and to amass illegal machine guns, missiles, explosives, and biological and chemical weapons. (p. 1)

If six terror plots a year is the baseline, are there reasons to believe that current issues exist today that may spark an increase in WST? Within the field of social movements, there is a long-standing debate regarding the role that grievances exert on adherents to either join organizations or participate in contentious action (Jenkins and Perrow 1977; McCarthy and Zald 1977; Snow et al. 1980). Much of the social movement literature demonstrates the influence often attributed to grievances is overstated (Snow et al. 1980; McAdam 1988).

A number of questions regarding the influence of grievances, however, remain unanswered. One issue that is particularly important is whether the emergence of high intensity issues that involve "moral shocks" (Jasper 1998; see also Wright 2006) exerts greater influence in generating mobilization than grievances within the normal range of intensity. Clearly, movement activists frequently use diagnostic techniques to frame social issues (Snow and Benford 1992; Snow et al. 1986) as a means to push for broad-scale change, garner organizational resources (e.g., fundraising), and recruit new members. But the identification of new "hot-button" issues may also affect adherents and "sympathetic bystanders" at a social-psychological and psychological level as well (Opp 1988). Individuals and groups may experience these new problems as "strains" (Smelser 1962) by developing heightened perceptions of imbalance, deprivation, power loss, conflict, and ambiguity; all potential catalysts for political mobilization (Smelser 1962; Useem 1997). These strains, in turn, may lead individual activists or groups of activists to reach a threshold or tipping point (Granovetter 1978). When this occurs activists may find existing tactics unsuitable for these "new" problems.

Previous research demonstrates that terror as a strategy of political violence does not remain constant but ebbs and flows in relation to larger dynamics of political action (Tarrow 1989; della Porta 1995). The ebb and flow of terror is part of a political movement's cycle of contention. New waves of terror are produced by a complex interplay of internal movement dynamics and external social forces. In particular, right-wing extremists may be especially responsive to a sense of threat as these catalysts seem to play a significant role in generating WST (Sprinzak 1995; Wright 2006). I argue that four relatively "new" problems have become increasingly salient at relatively the same time and their cumulative impact is likely to generate a new wave of WST (see also Jenkins 2008). Each of these issues in varying degrees evokes a sense of mortality among white supremacists and thus is especially likely to generate a heightened level of violence (Greenberg et al. 1997).

Changing Demographics

The WSM is mobilizing in opposition to a perceived "invasion" of immigrants from Mexico and the rest of Latin America. More specifically, white supremacists perceive undocumented migrants as part of a "plot" to "destroy the white race." Recent reports indicate that the number of U.S. hate groups have increased by more than 50 percent between 2000 and 2008 (Holthouse 2009). The increase has been attributed, in part, to fears regarding rising immigration levels (Holthouse 2009). The National Socialist Movement (NSM), for example, has focused extensively on the immigration issue and has been holding rallies across the country to galvanize opposition against immigration and recruit new members. Some white supremacists have become so impassioned about this issue that they have literally called for violent attacks on immigrants during nationally televised interviews. Veteran

Aryan extremist, Martin Cox, recently stated, "It's time to start killing these people ... that's the only way!" (National Geographic Channel, October 17, 2007).

The threat generated by demographic change can be explained by the concept "defended neighborhoods" (Suttles 1972; see also DeSena 1990; Meyer 2000; Rieder 1985). Defended neighborhoods are racially and ethnically homogenous communities where residents organize to prevent the settlement of racial and ethnic minorities. In relation to defended neighborhoods, empirical studies find that hate crime is most frequent in predominantly white areas experiencing a recent influx of minority populations (Grattet 2009; Green et al. 1998) and that white supremacist protest activity is greater in counties with increasing Hispanic populations (Beck 2000). White supremacists perceive areas like California and Arizona as defended neighborhoods as well as other areas farther removed from the border that are experiencing increases in the Latino immigrant population (e.g., eastern Iowa).

Economic Distress

Several scholars trace increased levels of hate violence to deteriorating economic conditions (Beck and Tolnay 1990; Hepworth and West 1988; Hovland and Sears 1940). The argument is that during times of economic hardship "the number of frustrated individuals increases, resulting in a host of aggressive behaviors directed against historically defined scapegoats or sources of economic competition" (Green and Rich 1998:275). Other studies, however, fail to detect a connection between unemployment rates and contemporary hate crime (Blee 2005b; Green et al. 1998; Krueger and Pischke 1997). While the role of economic forces may not be clear, what is clear is that the United States is facing the most serious threat to its economic system since the Depression of the 1930s (Elliott 2008). Some white supremacists clearly see poor economic conditions as a strain likely to improve recruiting efforts. For example, Jeff Schoep of the National Socialist Movement recently explained that his group's recent move to Michigan would help with recruitment because, "Detroit's a big city and the economy is not real good.... Anywhere the economy is bad, people are looking for answers. And I think we provide some" (Swickard 2008:np).

International Conflict

Since 2003 when the United States invaded Iraq, America's presence in the Middle East has generated controversy. National polls suggest high levels of dissatisfaction among Americans with the war in Iraq (CNN Opinion Research Corporation Poll 2010). White supremacists typically view foreign policy as Jewish-controlled and thus, the Iraq War was "orchestrated" to protect "Jewish interests." White supremacist Web forums are filled with discussions of this issue (Simi and Futrell 2006). Military involvement provides white supremacists with an "opportunity structure" (McAdam 1999; Tarrow 1994) in terms of recruitment, training, and enacting "violent fantasies" in "nonwhite" places (Simi and Futrell 2009). Participants in the wave of WSM terrorism that occurred during the 1980s and 1990s beginning with the "War in '84" and culminating in the Oklahoma City Bombing in 1995 were disproportionately likely to have military experience (Simi 2008).

Two recent reports confirm that white supremacists are increasing their efforts to infiltrate the military and are also targeting military personnel as part of their recruitment efforts (Holthouse 2006). In one of the reports a Department of Defense gang investigator discusses an internal investigation that uncovered 320 Aryan extremists at Fort Lewis, WA alone. Investigators also uncovered an online network of 57 Aryans on active duty at five different Army and Marine installations (Holthouse 2006). This corresponds with an "infiltration" strategy now popular within the movement (Simi and Futrell 2009; Blee 2002; Dobratz and Shanks-Meile 2000). In addition, these figures do not reflect the number of white supremacists who have served in private security firms where the standards regarding background checks are even lower. If a massive deployment is ordered, the withdrawal of troops will likely engender perceptions that the government "betrayed" its armed forces similar to the Vietnam War (Gibson 1994). This type of rhetoric will be a potential recruitment tool and impassion those already committed to the white supremacist cause.

Political and Cultural Change

The 2008 Democratic presidential victory means that a political transition that has historically been related to a resurgence of far right terrorism is currently taking place (Jenkins 2008). This victory, however, also means the country's first African-American president. It is hard to imagine something more alarming or infuriating for white supremacists than an African-American president. White supremacists already perceive an infusion of new "nonwhite" cultural and political elements as threats to the norms and values of "traditional American culture" (Green et al. 1999). As Sprinzak (1995:22) discusses, "... that the government has literally been taken over by the hated minority group.... It should therefore be destroyed with the same intensity as the original target group ..." For white supremacists an Obama administration confirms how far America has "fallen" and solidifies white supremacists' worst fears regarding their own cultural and political dispossession.

Even before Obama's election hundreds of death threats resulted in unprecedented Secret Service protection and at least two members of a network of neo-Nazis were planning to assassinate Obama after waging a killing spree targeting random blacks. Although this particular plot was relatively "far-fetched," as the Obama administration continues, it is plausible that more serious threats will emerge from small bands of white supremacists or a "lone-wolf" with the capacity necessary to effectively orchestrate an assassination plot.

Each of these hot-button issues on their own is helping mobilize white supremacists and thus is helping sustain lower levels of white supremacist violence that characterizes recent American history. Some observers have even referred to such violence as a "low-level race war" (Davis 1999). The cumulative impact of these issues, however, has a strong potential to generate a new wave of large-scale acts of domestic terrorism. This is the "perfect storm" that some observers are beginning to discuss. Within this constellation of factors, an Obama administration is the "tipping point," but the other factors galvanizing white supremacists are also critical. The absence of any one of these factors might be enough to prevent a new cycle of WST from emerging. Although this may sound alarmist, it is meant to be taken as a cautionary note to remind us that sometimes the gravest threat comes from those closest to home.

Conclusion

Peter Berger (1963) once suggested that sometimes things are more apparent than real. The idea that there has been little sustained violence in terms of WST and that relatively speaking WST poses little threat is a good example of Berger's axiom. In recent years white supremacists have developed a sophisticated presence in cyberspace (Simi and Futrell 2006), rejuvenated an international white power music industry (Futrell et al. 2006), and are actively recruiting in neighborhoods, schools, and prisons (Blazak 2001; Simi et al. 2008). Some white supremacist gangs are closely linked to profit-oriented criminal enterprises and have experienced substantial growth in the last decade (Simi et al. 2008).

Yet, media, scholars, governmental officials, and the general public often fail to acknowledge that white supremacist groups are little more than disorganized, dysfunctional, and "boisterous loudmouths." Crafting overly general characterizations aimed at simply dismissing white supremacists as irrelevant is psychologically comforting and an effective avoidance strategy (e.g., see Buchanan and Holthouse 2004; for similar arguments, Blee 2002; Kaplan 1995; Aho 1990). The implication, however, is that seriously considering the WSM and its potential for violence is unnecessary.

In contrast, I have argued that WST incidents are part of a larger cycle of contention. The cycle of contention is a useful concept for analyzing the continuity and discontinuity that may exist in a movement's use of violent strategies such as terrorism. Future research is needed that utilizes an events-data approach (Tilly 1995) to examine the relationship between violent and nonviolent white supremacist protest. This type of study should be especially sensitive to collecting data regarding network links and relations that will provide systematic analyses of this phenomenon.

If WST should be studied in relation to a larger movement context and cycle of contention then this is also true for other types of terrorism as well. For example, eco- and religious terrorism are both typically connected to a broader social movement and cycle of contention that helps explain their ebb and flow of violence. Yet, social movements and terrorism research occupy divergent paths that prevent a more robust understanding of terrorist violence. Although defining terrorism remains problematic, one of the most agreed-on dimensions of terrorism is the political nature of this behavior (Schmid and Jongman 1988). In this respect terrorism is, if nothing else, a political strategy and thus the conceptual and analytic tools that have been developed in the field of social movements should be at the center of the study of terrorism (Oberschall 2004; Tilly 2004; della Porta 1995).

References

Adorno, T. W., E. Frenkel-Brunswik, D. J. Levinson, and R. N. Sanford. 1950. *The Authoritarian Personality*. Harper & Row.

Aho, James A. 1990. *The Politics of Righteousness: Idaho Christian Patriotism*. University of Washington Press.

Arena, Michael, and Bruce Arrigo. 2000. "White Supremacist Behavior: Toward an Integrated Social Psychological Model." *Deviant Behavior* 21(3):213–244.

Balch, Robert. 2006. "Rise and Fall of Aryan Nations: A Resource Mobilization Perspective." *Journal of Political and Military Sociology*, Summer, 81–113.

Barabasi, Albert-Laszlo. 2003. *Linked: How Everything is Connected to Everything Else and What it Means for Business, Science, and Everyday Life*. Penguin Books.

Barkun, Michael. 1994. *Religion and the Racist Right: The Origins of the Christian Identity Movement*. University of North Carolina Press.

Beck, E. M. 2000. "Guess Who's Coming to Town: White Supremacy, Ethnic Competition, and Social Change." *Sociological Focus* 33(2):153–174.

Beck, E. M., and Stewart Tolnay. 1990. "The Killing Fields of the Deep South: The Market for Cotton and the Lynching of Blacks, 1882–1930." *American Sociological Review* 55(4):526–539.

Berger, Peter. 1963. *Invitation to Sociology: A Humanistic Perspective*. Doubleday.

Berlet, Chip and Mathew Lyons. 2000. *Right-wing Populism in America: Too Close for Comfort*. Guilford Press.

Bjorgo, Tore, ed. 1995. *Terror from the Extreme Right*. Frank Cass.

Bjorgo, Tore, and Jeffrey Kaplan. 1998. *Nation and Race: The Developing Euro-American Racist Subculture*. Northeastern University.

Blazak, Randy. 2001. "White Boys to Terrorist Men: Target Recruitment of Nazi Skinheads." *The American Behavioral Scientist* 44(6): 982–1000.
Blee, Kathleen. 2005a. "Racial Violence in the United States." *Ethnic and Racial Studies* 28:599–619.
———. 2005b. "Women and Organized Racial Terrorism in the United States." *Studies in Conflict and Terrorism* 28:421–433.
———. 2002. *Inside Organized Racism: Women in the Hate Movement.* University of California Press.
Blejwas, Andrew, Anthony Griggs, and Mark Potok. 2005. "Terror from the Right." *Southern Poverty Law Center Intelligence Report.* Number 118, summer.
Borum, Randy, and Michael Gelles. 2005. "Al-Qaeda's Operational Evolution: Behavioral and Organizational Perspectives." *Behavioral Sciences and the Law* 23:467–483.
Buchanan, Mark. 2002. *Nexus: The Groundbreaking Science of Networks.* W.W. Norton.
Buchanan, Susy and David Holthouse. 2004. "Barbecue Nations." *Phoenix New Times.* Retrieved February 19, 2004 from www.phoenixnewtimes.com
Burris, Val, Emory Smith, and Ann Strahm. 2000. "White Supremacist Networks on the Internet." *Sociological Focus* 33(2):215–235.
Chermak, Steven. 2002. *Searching for a Demon: The Media Construction of the Militia Movement.* Northeastern University Press.
Chermak, Steven, and Jeff Gruenewald. 2006. "The Media's Coverage of Domestic Terrorism." *Justice Quarterly* 23:428–461.
CNN Opinion Research Corporation Poll. 2010. Retrieved February 5, 2010 from http://www.pollingreport.com/iraq.htm
Cohen, S. 1972. *Folk Devils and Moral Panics.* Macgibbon and Kee.
Davis, Mike. 1999. *Ecology of Fear.* Random House.
della Porta, Donatella. 1995. *Social Movements, Political Violence, and the State: A Comparative Analysis of Italy and Germany.* Cambridge University Press.
DeSena, J. 1990. *Protecting One's Turf: Social Strategies for Maintaining Urban Neighborhoods.* University Press of America.
Diamond, Sara. 1995. *Roads to Dominion: Right-Wing Movements and Political Power in the United States.* Guilford Press.
Dobratz, Betty, and Stephanie Shanks-Meile. 2000. *White Power! White Pride!: The White Separatist Movement in the United States.* The Johns Hopkins University Press.
Elliott, Larry. 2008. "A Financial Crisis Unmatched Since the Great Depression." *Guardian* March 18.
Ezekiel, Raphael S. 1995. *The Racist Mind: Portraits of American Neo-Nazis and Klansmen.* Viking.
Ferber, Abby L. 1998. *White Man Falling: Race, Gender, and White Supremacy.* Rowman & Littlefield.
Freilich, Joshua and Steven Chermak. 2009. "Preventing Deadly Encounters Between Law Enforcement and American Far-Rightists." *Crime Prevention Studies* 25:141–172.

Freilich, Joshua D., Jeremy A. Pienik, and Gregory J. Howard. 2001. "Toward Comparative Studies of the U.S. Militia Movement." *International Journal of Comparative Sociology* 42:163–210.

Frieden, Terry. 2005. "FBI, ATF Address Domestic Terrorism." Available at http://cnn.com/US/05

Futrell, Robert, and Pete Simi. 2004. "Free Spaces, Collective Identity, and the Persistence of U.S. White Power Activism." *Social Problems* 51(1):16–42.

Futrell, Robert, Pete Simi, and Simon Gottschalk. 2006. "Understanding Music in Movements: The U.S. White Power Music Scene." *The Sociological Quarterly* 47:275–304.

Galbraith, John Kenneth. 1958. *The Affluent Society*. Houghton Mifflin.

Gamson, William. 1975. *The Strategy of Social Protest*. Dorsey Press.

Gardell, Mattias. 2003. *Gods of the Blood: The Pagan Revival and White Separatism*. Duke University Press.

Gerlach, Luther P. 1971. "Movements of Revolutionary Changeand Some Structural Characteristics." *American Behavioral Scientist* 14:812 836. Abridged version in Jo Freeman, ed. 1983. *Social Movements of the Sixties and Seventies*. Longman.

Gerlach, Luther P., and Virginia H. Hine. 1973. *Lifeway Leap: The Dynamics of Change in America*. University of Minnesota Press.

———. 1970. *People, Power, Change: Movements of Social Transformation*. Bobbs-Merrill.

Gibney, Frank Jr. 1999. "The Kids Got in the Way." *Time Magazine* 154(8). http://www.time.com/time/magazine/article/0,9171,991784,00.html

Gibson, William. 1994. *Warrior Dreams: Violence and Manhood in Post-Vietnam America*. Hill & Wang Publisher.

Granovetter, Mark. 1978. "Threshold Models of Collective Behavior." *American Journal of Sociology* 83:1420–1443.

Grattet, Ryan. 2009. "The Urban Ecology of Bias Crime: A Study of Disorganized and Defended Neighborhoods." *Social Problems* 56:132–150.

Green, Donald, and Andrew Rich. 1998. "White Supremacist Activity and Crossburnings in North Carolina." *Journal of Quantitative Criminology* 14(3):263–282.

Green, Donald, R. P. Abelson, and M. Garnett. 1999. "The Distinctive Views of Hate-crime Perpetrators and White Supremacists." Pp. 429–464. In *Cultural Divides: Understanding and Overcoming Group Conflict*, edited by D. A. Prentice and D. T. Miller. Russell Sage Foundation.

Green, Donald, J. Glaser, and A. Rich. 1998. "From Lynching to Gay Bashing: The Elusive Connection Between Economic Conditions and Hate Crime." *Journal of Personality and Social Psychology* 75(1):82–92.

Green, Donald P., Dara Z. Strolovitch, and Janelle S. Wong. 1998. "Defended Neighborhoods, Integration, and Racially-Motivated Crime." *American Journal of Sociology* 104:372–403.

Greenberg, J., S. Solomon, and T. Pyszczynski. 1997. "Terror Management Theory of Self-Esteem and Cultural Worldviews: Empirical Assessments." *Advances in Experimental Social Psychology* 29:139.

Hall, S., C. Critcher, T. Jefferson, J. Clarke, and B. Roberts. 1978. *Policing the Crisis*. Macmillan.

Hamm, Mark S. 2002. *In Bad Company: America's Terrorist Underground*. Northeastern University Press.

———. 1993. *American Skinheads*. Northeastern University Press.

Hepworth, J. T., and S. G. West. 1988. "Lynchings and the Economy: A Time Reanalysis of the Hovland and Sears (1940)." *Journal of Personality and Social Psychology* 55(2):239–247.

Hoffman, Bruce. 2006. *Inside Terrorism*. Revised and Expanded Edition. Columbia University Press.

Hofstadter, Richard. 1965. *The Paranoid Style in American Politics, and Other Essays*. Knopf.

Holthouse, David. 2009. "The Year in Hate." *SPLC Intelligence Report*. Available at http://www.splcenter.org/intel/intelreport/article.jsp?aid=1027 (accessed March 6, 2009).

———. 2006. "A Few Bad Men." *SPLC Intelligence Report*. 122 (Summer) Available at http://www.splcenter.org/intel/news/item.jsp?aid=66 (accessed September 9, 2009).

Hovland, C. I., and R. R. Sears. 1940. "Minor Studies of Aggression: VI. Correlation of Lynchings with Economic Indices." *Journal of Psychology* 9:301–310.

Jacobs, James and Kimberly Potter. 1998. *Hate Crime: Criminal Law and Identity Politics*. Oxford University Press.

Jasper, James M. 1998. "The Emotions of Protest: Affective and Reactive Emotions In and Around Social Movements." *Sociological Forum* 13:397–424.

Jenkins, Philip. 2003. *Images of Terror: What We Can and Can't Know About Terrorism*. Aldine Transaction.

Jenkins, Craig, and Charles Perrow. 1977. "Insurgency of the Powerless: Farm Worker Movements (1946–1972)." *American Sociological Review* 42:249–268.

Jenness, Valerie, and Kendall Broad. 1997. *Hate Crimes: New Social Movements and the Politics of Violence*. Aldine de Gruyter.

Kaplan, Jeffrey. 1995. "Right-Wing Violence in North America." Pp. 44–95. In *Terror from the Extreme Right*, edited by Tore Bjorgo. Frank Cass.

Kaplan, Jeffrey, and Leonard Weinberg. 1998. *The Emergence of a Euro-American Radical Right*. Rutgers University Press.

Kiecolt, K. Jill. 2000. "Self-Change in Social Movements." Pp. 110–131. In *Self, Identity, and Social Movements*, edited by Sheldon Stryker, Timothy J. Owens, and Robert W. White. University of Minnesota Press.

Krueger, A. B., and J. Pischke. 1997. "A Statistical Analysis of Crime Against Foreigners in Germany." *Journal of Human Resources* 32:182–209.

Levin, Brian. 1999. "Hate Crimes: Worse by Definition?" *Journal of Contemporary Criminal Justice* 15:6–21.

Lipset, Seymour Martin, and Earl Raab. 1970. *The Politics of Unreason: Right Wing Extremism in America, 1790–1977*. University of Chicago Press.

McAdam, D. 1999 [1982]. *Political Process and the Development of Black Insurgency*. University of Chicago Press.

———. 1988. *Freedom Summer*. University of Chicago Press.

McCarthy, John, and Meyer Zald. 1977. "Resource Mobilization: A Partial Theory." *American Journal of Sociology* 82:1212–1241.

McCurrie, Thomas. 1998. "White Racist Extremist Gang Members: A Behavioral Profile." *Journal of Gang Research* 5:51–60.

McDevitt, Jack, Jack Levin, and Susan Bennett. 2002. "Hate Crime Offenders: An Expanded Typology." *The Journal of Social Issues* 58:303–317.

Merari, A. 1991. "Academic Research and Government Policy on Terrorism." *Terrorism and Political Violence* 3(1):88–102.

Meyer, S. G. 2000. *As Long as They Don't Move Next Door: Segregation and Racial Conflict in American Neighborhoods*. Rowman & Littlefield.

Oberschall, Anthony. 2004. "Explaining Terrorism: The Contribution of Collective Action Theory." *Sociological Theory* 22:26–37.

Opp, Karl-Dieter. 1988. "Grievances and Participation in Social Movements." *American Sociological Review* 53:853–864.

Pierce, Wiliam [Andrew McDonald]. 1978. *The Turner Diaries*. National Vanguard Books.

Rieder, J. 1985. *Canarsie: The Jews and Italians of Brooklyn against Liberalism*. Harvard University Press.

Sageman, Marc. 2004. *Understanding Terror Networks*. University of Pennsylvania Press.

Said, Edward. 1978. *Orientalism*. Pantheon.

Schmid, Alex, and Albert Jongman. 1988. *Political Terrorism: A New Guide to Actors, Authors, Concepts, Data Bases, Theories, and Literature*. Transaction Books.

Silke, Andrew. 2003. *Terrorists, Victims, and Society: Psychological Perspectives on Terrorism and its Consequences*. Wiley.

Simi, Pete. 2008. "Recruitment among Right-Wing Terrorist Groups." National Institute of Justice. Final Report (2006-IJ-CX-0027).

Simi, Pete, and Robert Futrell. 2009. "Negotiating White Power Activist Stigma." *Social Problems* 56:89–110.

———. 2006. "Cyberculture and the Endurance of Radical Racist Activism." *The Journal of Political and Military Sociology* 34(1):115–142.

Simi, Pete, Lowell Smith, and Ann Reeser Stacey. 2008. "From Punk Kids to Public Enemy Number One." *Deviant behavior* 29:753–774.

Smelser, Neil J. 1962. *Theory of Collective Behavior*. Free Press of Glencoe.

Smith, Brent. 1994. *Terrorism in America: Pipe Bombs and Pipe Dreams*. New York University Press.

Snow, David, Burke Rochford, Steven Worden, and Robert Benford. 1986. "Frame Alignment Processes, Micromobilization, and Movement Participation." *American Sociological Review* 51:464–481.

Snow, David, Louis Zurcher Jr., and Sheldon Ekland-Olson. 1980. "Social Networks and Social Movements: A Microstructural Approach to Differential Recruitment." *American Sociological Review* 45: 787–801.

Snow, David, and Robert Benford. 1992. "Master Frames and Cycles of Protest." Pp. 133–155. In *Frontiers of Social Movement Theory*, edited by Aldon D. Morris and Carol McClurg Mueller. Yale University Press.

Sprinzak, Ehud. 1995. "Right-Wing Terrorism in a Comparative Perspective: The Case of Split Delegitimation." Pp. 1–43. In *Terror from the Extreme Right*, edited by Tore Bjorgo. London: Frank Cass.

Stohl, Cynthia, and Michael Stohl. 2007. "Networks of Terror: Theoretical Assumptions and Pragmatic Consequences." *Communication Theory* 17:93–124.

Sudnow, David. 1965. "Normal Crimes: Sociological Features of the Penal Code in a Public Defender Office." *Social Problems* 12:255–276.

Suttles, G. 1972. *The Social Construction of Communities*. University of Chicago Press.

Swickard, Joe. 2008. "Neo-Nazis Looking for You: Diversity, Economy Can Aid in Recruiting." *Detroit Free Press*, Retrieved May 12, 2008, from http://michiganunited.blogspot.com/2008 05 01 archive.html

Tarrow, Sidney. 1994. *Power in Movement: Social Movements and Contentious Politics*. Cambridge University Press.

———. 1989. *Democracy and Disorder: Protest and Politics in Italy 1965–1975*. Clarendon Press.

Tilly, Charles. 2004. "Terror, Terrorism, Terrorists." *Sociological Theory* 22(1):5–13.

———. 1995. *Popular Contention in Great Britain, 1758–1834*. Harvard University Press.

Trelease, Allen W. 1971. *White Terror: The Ku Klux Klan Conspiracy & Southern Reconstruction*. HarperCollins.

Turk, Austin. 2004. "Sociology of Terrorism." *Annual Review of Sociology* 30:271–286.

Useem, Bert. 1997. "Disorganization and the New Mexico Prison Riot of 1980." *American Sociological Review* 50:667–688.

Vollers, Maryanne. 2006. *Lone Wolf*. HarperCollins.

Warner, H. W. 1838. *An Inquiry into the Moral and Religious Character of the American Government*. Wiley and Putnam.

Watts, Duncan, and S. H. Strogatz. 1998. "Collective Dynamics of 'small-world' Networks." *Nature* 393:440–442.

Weinberg, Leonard. 1998. "An Overview of Right-Wing Extremism in the Western World: A Study of Convergence, Linkage, and Identity." Pp. 3–33. In *Nation and Race: The Developing Euro-American Racist Subculture*, edited by Jeffrey Kaplan and Tore Bjorgo. Northeastern University.

Wright, Stuart. 2006. *Patriots, Politics, and the Oklahoma City Bombing*. Cambridge University Press.

Reading 2.3

Avoid Catastrophe by Addressing Cyber Risk

You Could Fall Victim to a Cyber Attack or Breach at Any Time. Keep Disaster at Bay With These Guidelines.

Tom Marchetti

CYBERCRIME IS ON THE RISE AND represents devastating dangers. Understanding and guarding against these threats are now critical elements of governance.

Cyber risks include malicious assaults on people's credit cards or bank accounts. Risks also include the unintentional release of confidential employee, client, and donor information.

Besides revenue loss, cyber events can lead to costly litigation and damage to your reputation. Specific cyber risks that can affect your organization include:

- **Web site shut-down** or damage
- **Theft or damage** to intellectual property
- **Compromise of e-mails** with clients, vendors, collaborators, and service providers
- **Physical damage** to software and hardware
- **Transmission of computer viruses**, leading to destruction of systems.

To guard against these and other potential losses, follow these three steps:

Step 1: Assess Your Risks

To gauge your organization's vulnerability, start with the following questions:

Have you identified which information is sensitive and which is non-sensitive? Is sensitive information handled differently? Is it well protected?

Who has access to your computer systems? If you outsource IT, do you know and understand how information is backed up and stored?

How effective and up to date are your anti-virus and other protective programs?

Does your employee handbook include policies and procedures for data security?

Is access to private information (such as social security numbers, credit card numbers, expense reports, and copies of paychecks) limited to a few specific employees? Is this information password protected?

Does the organization have defined steps, including security measures, for transferring funds to a vendor or financial institution?

What are the procedures when employees upgrade mobile phones, laptops, tablets, and smartphones? Do you take steps to erase information from the old equipment?

Who are your outside providers? In what ways do you interface with them via technology? Do you require them to comply with your security standards?

Has your organization made any recent changes to the way it uses technology, such as uploading critical information to the cloud or installing new systems for communications and collaboration?

In addition, because many cybercrimes are carried out by employees, examine your hiring procedures. Be sure to conduct extensive background checks on candidates who will have access to financial, banking, and related resources.

Step 2: Manage Your Risks

Managing cyber exposure is the responsibility of everyone with computer access. Your IT professionals can help you establish security protocols, including protected password access, Web site restrictions, and e-mail encryption policies. But you and everyone else in the organization must understand the limitations of these fundamental measures and remain vigilant. Here are a few important precautions to take:

- **Have employees lock or shut down their computers** whenever they leave their work spaces.

- **Make certain that people close their Web browsers** when not in use.
- **Control access** to computers logged on to your network.
- **Be sure employees—especially those who work remotely—understand and follow** all security protocols.

Step 3: Evaluate Your Insurance Coverage

You may be covered for cyber loss through insurance policies you already have. Several types of policies—either in their general forms or through cyber-specific enhancements—cover losses related to technology breaches. These policies include:

- **business owner's** policy (BOP)
- **property** insurance
- **crime**
- **errors** and omissions
- **directors and officers** (D & O) liability insurance.

Some coverages that may be available under your existing policies include the following:

Targeted Hacker Attack/Electronic Vandalism covers costs related to the willful corruption, distortion, deletion, damage, or destruction of electronic data caused by a targeted hacker attack. Some policies extend coverage to loss from a computer virus caused by cyber vandalism. Typically, coverage only applies when these acts involve someone other than employees.

Interruption of Computer Operations provides extended "Business Income Interruption" insurance for loss of income if you're unable to operate due to damage to electronic data processing equipment.

Employee Dishonesty/Computer Fraud covers loss or damage resulting from theft by an employee, including fraudulent funds transfer.

Unfortunately, each of these coverage enhancements is typically limited at $10,000 to $100,000, which isn't much, given the potential magnitude of the exposures. Thus, you may want to consider standalone cyber-risk policies. A growing number of insurance companies now offer such policies. With increasing market competition, pricing has come down, making these policies more affordable. The policies often have multiple insuring agreements, or "modules," including:

Privacy Injury Liability protects your organization from the cost of judgments, settlements, and associated defense costs resulting from any unauthorized access to confidential information.

Network Security Liability covers security breaches in your computer network that give rise to:

- disruption or degradation of the network
- unauthorized use or disclosure of information
- any unplanned inability of an authorized party to gain access to the network.

Privacy Regulation Proceeding Coverage will reimburse costs associated with a civil, administrative, or regulatory proceeding by a governmental authority alleging any violation of a Security Breach Notice Law.

Privacy Event Expense Reimbursement covers expenses incurred to comply with Security Breach Notice Laws or related regulations and to retain crisis management resources (such as a defense counsel or public relations firm).

Extortion Demand Reimbursement covers expenses incurred when there is imminent danger of a loss or damage to the network, loss of confidential information, or defacement of the Web site.

First Party Network Interruption & Extra Expense Coverage covers lost income related to a network shutdown caused by unauthorized access, electronic virus, or denial of service attack.

Several of these coverage modules may not be available from all insurers; others may be limited or require additional premiums. Liability coverages may overlap with coverage under an errors & omissions policy. Alternatively, it may be appropriate to add broader cyber/network security coverage to your errors & omissions policy. This approach can help avoid coverage gaps and is cost-effective.

Both stand-alone policies and add-on coverages are subject to exclusions and conditions, which may create unexpected gaps. Some forms exclude claims for bodily injury or property damage. "Proprietary rights injury" exclusions encompass injury arising out of plagiarism, piracy, infringement, or misappropriation of copyright or trademark. Limits of $1 million to $10 million are common, but limits up to $50 million or more are available.

Stay Vigilant Concerning Cyber Risk

Remember that the cyber threat environment is dynamic: While security experts are improving protection and insurance companies are expanding their offerings, cybercriminals are becoming increasingly sophisticated. So cyber risk management must be an ongoing process. An experienced and knowledgeable insurance broker can help you understand the evolving risks, your current coverage, and options to address your exposure.

Reading 2.4

The Real Voter Fraud

Ed Morales

Nashville students staged a silent protest of Tennessee's new voter ID law at the statehouse last spring. States that enacted these laws, including Tennessee, saw a steep drop in voter turnout in 2014.

PHOTO 2.4.1

Republicans have found the ultimate weapon for winning elections: denying people the vote.

Last year, twenty-two states enforced tough new restrictions on voting, making it significantly harder for people of color, in particular, to cast ballots in the 2014 midterm elections.

TAKE THE CASE OF ANITA BUCK, a nurse in Carteret County, whose struggle to vote was documented by the South Carolina Coalition for Social Justice. Buck moved to Cumberland County to help at a local hospital for a nine-month stint. While she was living there, she updated her driver's license. When she moved back to her home in Carteret County, she tried to vote.

Only when she reached her polling place did she realize that her voter registration had been changed. She was told her name was no longer on the rolls, and since there was no same-day registration, she was out of luck. She voted with a provisional ballot, but the ballot did not count, since the law prohibits voting in the "wrong" county.

Millions of voters without a government-issued photo ID in the sixteen states that require it were disenfranchised in 2014. In addition, there are four states that now require documented proof of citizenship. The good news is that the rush of voter ID laws has had the unintended effect of broadening the voting rights coalition.

"The people without state IDs include the elderly, an increasing number of young people who aren't getting driver's licenses because they're not driving as much as generations before, people with disabilities, and tens of millions of women who are challenged because 90 percent of women change their names upon marriage," says Kathleen Unger of Vote Riders.

Besides laws that restrict voting or discriminate against voters by requiring voter IDs, there is an increasingly contentious battle being fought over felon disenfranchisement.

Florida New Majority shared the story of Francine Madera, a formerly incarcerated woman whose rights were restored. Madera says a poll worker told her that "I could only vote through a provisional ballot, and it wouldn't count anyway" since the records were not updated to show that her voting rights had been restored.

"Florida is one of three states left in the United States that does not restore your right to vote" if you are a felon who has served your time, you are off probation or parole, and you have paid all fines, says Sandra Benton of the Florida Coalition on Black Civic Participation. "To get your rights restored in Florida you have to petition the Clemency Board, which only meets four times a year. The process can take eight years or more, which is why over 1.5 million voters are disenfranchised in Florida."

Another major issue for the voting rights movement is vote dilution, accomplished through the blatant gerrymandering of districts. Joanna Cuevas Ingram of Latino Justice calls voter dilution a "very insidious, more complex form of voter discrimination."

"In our state they are explicitly drawing districts to attack black voters and weaken progressive and black alliances," says Anita Earls of North Carolina's Southern Coalition for Social Justice.

Helen Butler of the Georgia Coalition for the People's Agenda is helping to build a state campaign to mark the fiftieth anniversary of the Voting Rights Act in August 2015 with a series of tow n hall meetings, billboards, and a social media push.

Earls has been working with a coalition called SOLVE, Southern Leadership for Voter Engagement.

"A student group was very upset about the Appalachian State early voting site being closed," says Earls. "So we helped get a lawsuit filed that helped them force open that site again."

Earls also emphasizes the importance of building strong leaders.

"Leadership at the local level can impact voter turnout even when you're fighting against voter suppression," she said. "In Wake County, which had been Republican-leaning, Democrat and progressive voters turned out in large numbers and elected a seventy-member county commission that's all Democrats. If turnout in Fayetteville and Charlotte had done the same, it would have changed the outcome of the Senate race."

While activists are fighting local battles on the ground, there is one big idea that could give voting rights a boost nationwide: a Voters' Rights Amendment, which could start as individual pieces of state legislation and eventually become a Constitutional amendment.

Cuevas Ingram says the history of the Voting Rights Act and the civil rights movement points the way forward.

"We need to start thinking about how we respond as a nation to clarify the law and make sure the courts uphold equal protection and voting rights," she says. "Many people forget that when Dr. King and the civil rights movement pushed for the Voting Rights Act, it was a compromise. Many people would have liked to have seen it go further."

"I'm upset that I wasn't allowed to vote," said Dale Hicks, a thirty-eight-year-old veteran of the U.S. Marine Corps, who sought help from the South Carolina Social Justice Coalition after both same-day registration and online registration were eliminated, preventing him from updating his registration in time for Election Day after he moved to a new county. "A lot of people died so I could vote. I honored the call of duty by serving my country, and I want to honor the call of duty by voting."

Comprehension Questions for Unit II

Questions for Reading 2.1

1. Who decides what is a suitable amount of street crime and a suitable amount of white-collar crime?
2. What does the criminalization of drugs keep the criminal justice system busy with?
3. Why is the class bias of the criminal justice system hidden?
4. What are identified as inconvenient truths?
5. Explain how the image of crime in the media provides benefits to the rich and powerful through a conservative message.

Questions for Reading 2.2

1. What are the important implications of the neglect of White supremacist terrorism (WST)?
2. WST groups are part of the larger White supremacist movement, which has been described as sharing common ideologies and goals and an overriding commitment to maintaining ________.
3. Individuals and groups who commit acts of WST are, in varying degrees and in varying ways, connected to a network that circulates extremist beliefs such as ____________.
4. What "new" problems did Simi forecast would generate a new wave of WST?
5. Although defining terrorism remains problematic, one of the most agreed-upon dimensions of terrorism is the ________nature of this behavior.

Questions for Reading 2.3

1. What are five cyber risks that can affect your organization?
2. What three steps can you take to guard against the cyber risks?

Questions for Reading 2.4

1. What is the *real* voter fraud?
2. What is being done to deny people the right to vote?
3. On which groups is this "voter fraud" having a disproportionate impact?

Unit III

How Does Criminal Justice Intersect with Racism and Sexism?

Introduction to Unit III

Students come to criminal justice classrooms with a preconceived "Alice in Wonderland" notion of how the system works. By "Alice in Wonderland," we mean suitable to a world of fantasy or illusion—unreal. Some students want to praise the justice system, hold fast to the notion that justice is colorblind, and believe that the criminal justice system dispenses equal justice. For this reason, professors can face resistance when they ask students to examine how race, gender, class, and sexual orientation influence outcomes in the criminal justice process.

Each of these topics—gender, race, class, and sexual orientation—is difficult on its own. In criminal justice/criminology, however, professors have the additional responsibility of explaining how social locations in space intersect. *Intersectionality* is an analytical framework for understanding how aspects of a person's social and political identities combine to create different modes of discrimination and privilege. Needless to say, intersectionality adds complexity to the study of criminal justice. At the same time, intersectionality allows students to gain a more nuanced understanding of how privilege and disadvantage play out in the criminal justice system.

In Reading 3.1, Paul Butler lays out a picture of racial reality in criminal justice that many students will be able to relate to. The "celebration of triumph" narrative that Butler describes highlights progress in racial justice. By contrast, students might find the critical race perspectives that Katharine Tellis, Nancy Rodriguez, and Cassia Spohn espouse in Reading 3.2 to be discomforting.

Criminologist Meda Chesney-Lind approaches intersectionality from a feminist perspective in Reading 3.3. Given the backlash against feminism in recent years, some students might have to break down walls of resistance to the "dirty" word of "feminism" that have been wired into their heads by right-wing politicians and media.

Yet another way of looking at intersectionality is explored in Reading 3.4. Victor Rios, a former gang member turned criminologist, explains how his own intersecting identities—Latino, male, highly educated, heterosexual—influence his ability to tell the stories of young Black and Latino men who have become ensnared in a punitive social control system.

Reading 3.1

One Hundred Years of Race and Crime

*Paul Butler**

I. Introduction

This [reading] considers the evolution of thinking about criminal justice and racial justice over the last one hundred years.

If I were writing about race and crime in 1910, the year the *Journal of Criminal Law and Criminology* was founded,[1] the problem that I would have focused on would be lynchings, which were sometimes an extra-legal response to African-American criminal suspects (and sometimes just random mob violence). The National Association for the Advancement of Colored People (NAACP) was created the year before the *Journal*.[2] The NAACP began as a response to the domestic terrorism of rampant lynchings, which were mainly in the South but all over the country.[3] Most of the victims were African-American but there were Latino, Jewish, and immigrant victims as well.[4] Thus the main race and crime problem, as identified by the first significant civil rights organization, was black victimization by white criminals.

* Carville Dickinson Benson Research Professor of Law and Associate Dean for Faculty Development, George Washington University Law School. I thank the other participants in the symposium for helpful comments. Aaron J. Sussman provided exemplary research assistance. An early draft of this [reading] was presented at a faculty workshop at DePaul College of Law. Special thanks to Sumi Cho, Song Richardson, Terry Smith, and Deborah Tuerkheimer.

1. Jennifer Devroye, *The Rise and Fall of the Institute of Criminal Law and Criminology*. 100 J. Crim. L. & Criminology 7 (2010). The Institute established the *Journal of Criminal Law and Criminology* the following year. *Id.* at 8.
2. Gilbert Jonas, Freedom's Sword: The NAACP and the Struggle against Racism in America. 1909–1969 11 (2005).
3. *Id.* at 111 ("During its first two decades ... the NAACP's solitary political focus ... was the campaign to outlaw lynching nationally.").
4. W. Fitzhugh Brundage, Lynching in the New South: Georgia and Virginia, 1880–1930, 91, 100 (1993).

Other race and crime problems I would have focused on in 1910 include de jure discrimination against African Americans, including their exclusion from juries.[5] I would have been concerned about wrongful convictions, especially in death penalty cases when there was a black suspect and a white victim.[6] I probably would have mentioned the related concern of lack of effective assistance of counsel.[7] I would have complained about the way that the police enforced vagrancy laws.[8] If punishment came up outside of the death penalty context, there might be some discussion of chain-gangs or conditions in segregated "colored only" prisons.[9] I would have been concerned about quasi-scientific responses to criminality like eugenics and forced sterilization,[10] and worried about their application to African Americans.[11]

---

5. As a result of the decision in *Plessy v. Ferguson,* 163 U.S. 537 (1896), de jure segregation was still considered constitutionally valid. Even de jure racial segregation in housing had been upheld by stale courts until invalidated in *Buchanan v. Warley,* 245 U.S. 60 (1917). Of course, the doctrine of "separate but equal" was not struck down completely until *Brown v. Board of Education,* 347 U.S. 483 (1954). *See also* Michael J. Klarman, From Jim Crow to Civil Rights: The Supreme Court and the Struggle for Racial Equality 39–43 (2004) (explaining that, despite the holding in *Strauder v. West Virginia,* 100 U.S 303 (1880), which prohibited de jure exclusion of African-American jurors, subsequent decisions that rejected challenges to disenfranchisement allowed jurisdictions to exclude African-American jurors by selecting jurors through voter lists, since few blacks were registered to vote).
6. *See, e.g.,* Edwin M. Borchard, Convicting the Innocent: Sixty-Five Actual Errors of Criminal Justice 22–27 (1932) (detailing the story of Payne Boyd, an African-American man who, as a result of mistaken identity, was wrongly arrested and convicted for a white man's murder, even though thirty-one witnesses testified that the defendant was not Cleveland Boyd, the black man whom both parties admitted did commit the crime); *see also* Stuart Banner, The Death Penalty: An American History 137–43 (2002) (explaining that in some southern slates, the death penalty could be used to punish some crimes such as arson, murder, and robbery, but only if the defendant was black, and, in the case of rape and kidnapping, only if the victim was white).
7. The Sixth Amendment, which today guarantees indigent defendants the right to effective counsel, had not yet been incorporated; thus, not only was effective assistance of counsel not constitutionally guaranteed, but, in state prosecutions, indigent defendants practically had no right to counsel whatsoever. *See* Betts v. Brady, 316 U.S. 455, 461–62 (1942).
8. *See also* William O. Douglas, *Vagrancy and Arrest on Suspicion,* 70 Yale L.J. L. 13 (1960). *See generally* Jennifer Roback, *Southern Labor Law in the Jim Crow Era: Exploitative or Competitive?,* 51 U. Chi. L. Rev. 1161 (1984).
9. *See* David M. Oshinsky, "Worse than Slavery": Parchman Farm and the Ordeal of Jim Crow Justice 57–62 (1996) (describing the use of incarcerated African Americans as cheap labor); Nancy A. Ozimek, Note, *Reinstitution of the Chain Gang: A Historical and Constitutional Analysis,* 6 B.U. Pub. Int'l L.J. 753, 758–63 (1997) (describing the history of chain gangs and their disproportionate impact on African Americans).
10. *See. e.g.,* Buck v. Bell. 274 U.S. 200 (1927) (upholding forced sterilization of Carrie Buck, an alleged "feeble minded" woman).
11. Edward J. Larson, Sex, Race, and Science: Eugenics in the Deep South 165–69 (1995) (describing popularity of eugenics movements in the Deep South).

A few years down the road from 1910, as formal police departments spread about the country, I certainly would have written about the problem of police brutality, and the widespread antipathy that blacks and police—two very distinct groups—had for each other.[12]

If I had spoken to a conference of progressives, say the members of the NAACP, which from its inception included many whites,[13] I would also have mentioned the need for more black police officers. The suggestion that there needed to be more African-American prosecutors and judges would have been seen as so pie-in-the-sky as to be almost silly. In 1910 my great-grandfather cleaned outhouses for a living and, about twenty years later, my grandfather had one of the best jobs a black man could have he was a Pullman porter.

That was then, this is now. I am a law professor. The President of the United States is an African-American man. And there are almost one million African-American people in prison.[14] The major race and crime problems of our time are the mass incarceration of African Americans and the extraordinary disparities between blacks and whites in the criminal justice system.

The fundamental paradox is that, in 2010, while evidence of racial progress is everywhere, racial disparities in criminal justice have never been greater. Nearly one in three young black men has a criminal case: he's either locked up, on probation or parole, or awaiting trial.[15] If we look at black-white racial disparities in education,[16] housing,[17] health care,[18] employment,[19] the ratio is usually 2:1 or 3:1. So, for example, the black unemployment rate is often

---

12. Marilynn S. Johnson, Street Justice: A History of Police Violence in New York City 57–86 (2003) (describing race riots and police brutality in New York City's increasingly black "Tenderloin" district).
13. Jonas, *supra* note 2, at 11.
14. Bureau of Justice Statistics, U.S. Dep't of Justice, Prison Inmates at Midyear 2009—Statistical Tables 19 tbl.16 (2010), *available at* http://bjs.ojp.usdoj.gov/content/pub/pdf/pim09st.pdf.
15. Marc Mauer & Tracy Huling, Young Black Americans and the Criminal Justice System: Five Years Later 1–5 (1995). *available at* http://www.sentencingproject.org/doc/publications/rd_youngblack_5yrslater.pdf.
16. In 2007, the dropout rate for white students was 6.1%; for African Americans, it was 11.5%. Nat'l Center for Educ. Statistics, U.S. Dep't of Educ., The Condition of Education 2009 182 tbl.A-20-1 (2009), *available at* http://nees.ed.gov.pubsearch/pubsinfo.asp?pubid=2009081.
17. Though African Americans constitute less than one-sixth of the total population, they make up one half of the homeless population. *See* Daniel White & Charles Crawford, *African American Males and Homelessness: Voices from the Shelter, in* 1 Homelessness in America 189–92 (Robert Hartmann McNamara ed., 2008).
18. African Americans are more than twice as likely as white Americans to die of diabetes, and in their first year of life. 108.14% more African-American infants die than do white infants. *See* Vernellia R. Randall, *Racist Health Care: Reforming an Unjust Health Care System to Meet the Needs of African-Americans,* 3 Health Matrix 127, 140–43 (1993).
19. Bureau of Labor Statistics, Labor Force Characteristics by Race and Ethnicity, 2008 3–5 (2009), *available at* http://www.bls.gov/cps/cpsrace2008.pdf.

twice the white unemployment rate.[20] Those disparities have either remained constant over the last one hundred years, or have gotten better.[21] Right now the black-white incarceration disparity is 7:1.[22] Over the last several decades, as African Americans presumably have had more and more opportunities, have been freed of de jure discrimination, and as overt racial prejudice has become socially stigmatized, the black-white disparity in incarceration has risen.[23] How can this be explained?

II. The New Jim Crow

There are two competing narratives about race and criminal justice over the last one hundred years (or, more accurately, the last one hundred and fifty years, since the end of slavery). One narrative is that mass incarceration is the "New Jim Crow."[24] Under this analysis, slavery, de jure segregation, and now mass incarceration serve many of the same functions and have many of the same effects.[25] There are more blacks in the criminal justice system now

---

20. In 2008, the unemployment rate for African Americans was 10.1%. The unemployment rate for whites was 5.2%. *Id.* at 5 tbl.1.
21. *See, e.g.,* Nat'l Center for Educ. Statistics, *supra* note 16, at 183 tbl.A-20-2 (showing that the dropout rate for black students has dropped from 19.1% in 1980 to 8.4% in 2007).
22. In 2008, about 846,000 of the approximately 38 million African Americans were in jail or prison. In contrast, about 712,500 of the approximately 228 million white Americans were similarly incarcerated. That's one in forty-five blacks, and about one in three hundred and twenty whites. Bureau of Justice Statistics, Prison Inmates at Midyear 2008—Statistical Tables 17 tbl.16 (2009). *available at* http://bjs.ojp.usdoj.gov/content/pub/pdf/pim08st.pdf; U.S. Census Bureau, 2008 American Community Survey 1-Year Estimates, *available at* http://factfinder.census.gov/servlet/ADPTable?_bm=y&-geo_id=01000US&-qr_name=ACS_2008_1YR_G00_DP5.
23. In 1950, the incarceration rate (number incarcerated per every 100,000 persons) was 86 for whites and 406 for blacks; blacks were almost five times more likely to be locked up than whites. *See* Margaret Werner Cahalan, Historical Corrections Statistics in the United States, 1850–1984 65 tbl.3-31 (1986); U.S. Census Bureau, Statistical Abstract of the United States 1951 8 (1951), *available at* http://www2.census.gov/prod2/statcomp/documents/l95l-02.pdf. However, in 2008, the incarceration rate was 360 for whites and 2.461 for blacks; blacks are now almost seven times more likely to be locked up than whites: *see* Heather C. West, & William J. Sabol, Prison Inmates at Midyear 2008—Statistical Tables. 17 (2009); U.S. Census Bureau, 2008 American Community Survey, tbl.B02001, *available at* http://factfinder.census.gov/servlet/DTTable?_bm=y&-geo_id=01000US&-ds_name=ACS_2008_3YR_G00_&-mt_name=ACS_2008_3YR_G2000_B02001. Therefore, since 1950, the incarceration rate for whites has quadrupled, but the rate for blacks has more than sextupled.
24. *See, e.g.,* Michelle Alexander, The New Jim Crow: Mass Incarceration in the Age of Colorblindness (2010).
25. *Id.* at 185–95: *see also* Dead Prez, *Behind Enemy Lines, on* Let's Get Free (Loud Records 2000) ("Behind enemy lines, my niggas is cellmates./ Most of the youth never escape the jail fate./ Super maximum camps will advance their game plan/ to keep us in the hands of the man. Locked up.").

(incarcerated, on probation or parole, awaiting trial) than were slaves in 1850.[26] In 2006, one in nine young black men were in prison, and black men were eight times more likely to be in jail or prison than white men.[27] More black men are barred from voting than when the Fifteenth Amendment was ratified.[28]

Michelle Alexander's book, *The New Jim Crow,* advances the theory that, in today's "colorblind[]" era, police, prosecutors, judges, and legislators use criminal history as a proxy for race, thereby establishing (or maintaining) a racial caste system.[29] During the Jim Crow era, blacks were discriminated against, disenfranchised, excluded from juries, prevented from bringing legal challenges, and denied other civil, political, and legal rights.[30] The same can be said today about felons, a disproportionate number of whom are African-American.[31] Alexander asserts that in the era of mass incarceration, a newly freed felon has "scarcely more rights, and arguably less respect, than a freed slave or a black person living 'free' in Mississippi at the height of Jim Crow."[32]

According to Alexander, the war on drugs is the primary tool in creating today's caste system. Since the war on drugs began approximately thirty years ago, the U.S. penal population has almost sextupled, growing from around 300,000 to two million; more than half of these incarcerations were drug convictions.[33] Today, about half of a million people are in jail or prison for a drug offense; this is more than a ten-fold increase from 1980.[34] As a result, the United States has the highest incarceration rate in the world by far; we incarcerate 750 adults per 100,000, while Germany, for example, incarcerates 93 per 100,000.[35] The incarceration rate has skyrocketed despite the fact that the rate of violent crimes is historically low.[36]

The discriminatory results of the drug war are clear. Three-fourths of those imprisoned for drug offenses are black or Latino.[37] In seven states, 80% to 90% of imprisoned drug

---

26. Alexander, *supra* note 24, at 271 n.7 (citing Pew Center on the States, One in 31: The Long Reach of American Corrections (2009): U.S. Census Bureau, The Seventh Census of the United States: 1850 ix tbl. I (1853)).
27. Alexander, *supra* note 24, at 98.
28. *Id.* at 175.
29. *Id.* at 2.
30. *Id.* at 185–95.
31. *Id.* at 97, 185–95.
32. *Id.* at 138.
33. *Id.* at 6.
34. *Id.* at 59.
35. *Id.* at 6.
36. *Id.* at 99.
37. *Id.* at 96–97.

offenders are black.[38] Such disparities cannot be explained by disproportionate use of drugs by African Americans; blacks don't use drugs more than any other group, and some studies have even found that they use them less.[39]

Instead of a formally discriminatory legal regime under Jim Crow, the caste system of mass incarceration relies on the unchecked discretion of police officers and prosecutors. Though all races use illegal drugs at similar rates, law enforcement officers target inner-city minorities; one study in Seattle showed that officers more frequently surveilled open-air drug markets even though most citizen complaints regarded suspected drug use in residences, that officers targeted a downtown drug market even though the frequency of transactions was higher in an outdoor drug market in a white neighborhood, that officers arrested black dealers far more often than white dealers even though white dealers were plainly visible, and that officers overwhelmingly focused on crack cocaine, preferred by the African-American community, even though more overdose deaths were the result of heroin use.[40] The Supreme Court has contributed to this highly differential system. Between 1982 and 1991, 90% of Supreme Court decisions regarding the Fourth Amendment as applied to narcotics were reversals in favor of the government.[41] Frustrated, Justice Thurgood Marshall had to remind his colleagues that there is "no drug exception" to the Bill of Rights.[42]

Similar statistics reveal racial disparities in police officers use of traffic stops; on the New Jersey Turnpike, where 15% of drivers are black, 42% of stops, and 73% of arrests were of black motorists, even though whites were more likely to be found carrying illegal drugs in their vehicles.[43]

Even though America's laws must be formally colorblind, the Supreme Court has approved the practice of using race as a factor to determine whether an individual is sufficiently suspicious to investigate, at least in the context of immigration.[44] Moreover, the Court has made it difficult to challenge discrimination other than in its extreme forms. For example, the Court refused to grant relief to a death row inmate convicted in Georgia, where prosecutors sought the death penalty in 70% of cases involving blacks accused of killing whites

---

38. *Id.* at 96.

39. *Id.* at 97 (citing Nat'l Inst. on Drug Abuse, U.S. Dep't of Health & Human Serv., Monitoring the Future: I National Survey Results on Drug Use, 1975–1999: Secondary School Students (2000)).

40. *Id.* at 120–22, 124–25.

41. *Id.* at 61 (citing California v. Acevedo, 500 U.S. 565, 600 (1991) (Stevens, J. dissenting)).

42. *Id.* at 60 (citing Skinner v. Ry Lahor Executive's Ass'n. 489 U.S. 602, 641 (1989) (Marshall, J., dissenting)).

43. *Id.* at 131.

44. *Id.* at 128–30 (citing United States v. Brignoni-Ponce, 422 U.S. 873 (1975)).

but only 19% of cases involving whites accused of killing blacks.[45] The Court held that an undeniable pattern of discrimination was not sufficient and that the Equal Protection Clause would be implicated only if a defendant could prove that the prosecutor, judge, or jury consciously discriminated against the defendant in his own particular case.[46] Relying on this precedent, a subsequent Georgia Supreme Court decision upheld a statute allowing a judge to impose life imprisonment for a second drug offense, even though Georgia's prosecutors requested that the policy be applied against blacks sixteen times more often than against whites; 98.4% of persons discretionarily sentenced under the law were black.[47] The Court has also made it practically impossible to ensure a fair jury of one's peers; though the Court requires prosecutors to have a non-racially discriminatory justification for using a peremptory challenge,[48] the Court has accepted clearly pretextual justifications, such as having "the longest hair of anybody on the panel by far," or having a "mustache and goatee type beard," which according to the prosecutor in question, "look[ed] suspicious" and made the person "appear[] not to be a good juror for that fact. ..."[49] The Court has even closed the door to a plaintiff's fact-finding. When the federal public defenders in Los Angeles noticed that all of their crack defendants in the previous year were either black or Hispanic, they alleged selective enforcement and sought to acquire information regarding the prosecutors' charging decisions; the Court refused to grant discovery, requiring the defenders to show solid proof of selective prosecution before being allowed to investigate for solid proof of selective prosecution.[50]

Professor Alexander is not the first to compare the modern struggles of blacks to the Jim Crow era; similar rhetoric has consistently been used to criticize American criminal law, especially the war on drugs. In 1999, former executive director of the ACLU Ira Glasser compared the drug laws not only to Jim Crow but also to the internment of Japanese-Americans during World War II.[51] Like Alexander, Glasser blamed the drug war for discriminatory police tactics, such as racial profiling in the use of traffic stops and *Terry* stop-and-frisks.[52] In 2001, the Temple Political and Civil Rights Law Review hosted an entire symposium titled "U.S.

45. *Id.* at 106–09 (citing McCleskey v. Kemp, 481 U.S. 279 (1987)).

46. *Id.*

47. *Id.* at 111–12 (referring to Stephens v. State, 456 S.E.2d 560 (Ga. 1995)).

48. Batson v. Kentucky, 476 U.S. 79 (1986).

49. *Id.* at 120 (quoting Purkett v. Elm, 514. U.S. 765, 789 (1995)).

50. *Id.* at 113–15 (citing United States v. Armstrong, 517 U.S. 456 (1996)).

51. Ira Glasser, *American Drug Laws; The New Jim Crow,* 63 Alb. L. Rev. 703, 703–04 (2000).

52. *Id.* at 709–11.

Drug Laws: The New Jim Crow?"[53] In a 2002 article, Graham Boyd,[54] the founder of the ACLU's Drug Policy Litigation Project, voiced a number of the same concerns addressed in Alexander's book; he cites felon disenfranchisement,[55] disparities in enforcement,[56] prison labor,[57] revocation of government aid,[58] and child custody revocation proceedings for mothers who show signs of drug use[59] as signs that the drug war is the New Jim Crow.

In the New Jim Crow analogy, police and prosecutors are the modern overseers.[60] It is easy to caricature this narrative, and its exponents are quick to acknowledge that there are

---

53. Beverly Xaviera Watkins and Mindy Thompson Fullilove noted how, despite the recognition of the health dangers of the use of crack, particularly the spread of AIDS, the government failed to allocate resources or provide a sufficient government response. Beverly Xaviera Watkins & Mindy Thompson Fullilove, *The Crack Epidemic and the Failure of Epidemic Response,* 10 Temp. Pol. & Civ. Rts. L. Rev. 371, 377–83 (2001). Professor Diana Gordon examined change to drug laws, concluding that today's war on drugs is just another example of "a rear-guard action against full equality for racial minorities." Diana R. Gordon, *Drug Policy and the Dangerous Classes: A Historical Overview,* 10 Temp. Pol. & Civ. Rts. L. Rev. 315, 320 (2001). Professor Susan Frietsche examined policies highlighted in *Ferguson v. City of Charleston,* 532 U.S. 67 (2001), that required hospitals to perform a drug test on mothers of newborns; if the mother tested positive for drug use, they would be charged with distribution of drugs to a minor. Susan Frietsche, *Policing Drug Use During Pregnancy,* 10 Temp. Pol. & Civ. Rts. L. Rev. 411 (2001). Amy Kirsch addressed how welfare reform strips poor, uneducated, and often homeless women of necessary welfare benefits. Amy E. Hirsch, *Bringing Back Shame: Women. Welfare Reform, and Criminal Justice,* 10 Temp. Pol. & Civ. Rts. L. Rev. 417, 419–27 (2001). Eric E. Sterling, President of The Criminal Justice Policy Foundation, discussed the political background of the war on drugs, including politicians' exploitation of the death of college basketball sensation Len Bias to strengthen cocaine sentences. Eric E. Sterling, *Drug Laws and Thought Crime,* 10 Temp. Pol. & Civ. Rts. L. Rev. 327, 329–31 (2001). William H. Buckman and John Lamberth explained how police departments' drug courier profiles enable racial profiling in traffic stops. William H. Buckman & John Lamberth, *Challenging Racial Profiles: Attacking Jim Crow on the Interstate,* 10 Temp. Pol. & Civ. Rts. L. Rev. 387, 390–94 (2001). J. Whyatt Mondesire compared felon disenfranchisement to Jim Crow era poll taxes. J. Whyatt Mondesire, *Felon Disenfranchisement: The Modern Day Poll Tax,* 10 Temp. Pol. & Civ. Rts. L. Rev. 435 (2001). Marc Mauer, Assistant Director of the Sentencing Project, highlighted the abuses in police and prosecutor discretion. Marc Mauer, *Race, Drugs Laws, & Criminal Justice,* 10 Temp. Pol. & Civ. Rts. L. Rev. 321, 321–23 (2001). Kurt Schmoke, former Mayor of Baltimore and current Dean of Howard Law School, discussed his strategy for ending the drug war and the crime problem at the same time: shifting publicly allocated funds from criminal justice to public health. Kurt Schmoke, *Forging a New Consensus in the War on Drugs: Is It Possible?,* 10 Temp. Pol. & Civ. Rts. L. Rev. 351, 356 (2001).
54. Graham Boyd, *Collateral Damage in the War on Drugs,* 47 Vill. L. Rev. 839 (2002).
55. *Id.* at 843–45.
56. *Id.* at 845–46.
57. *Id.* at 848.
58. *Id.* at 848–49.
59. *Id.* at 847–48.
60. KRS-One, *Sound of da Police, on* Return of the Boom Bap (Jive Records 1993) ("The overseer rode around the plantation;/ the [police] officer is off patrolling all the nation,/ The overseer could stop you what you're

important differences between slaves, victims of legal segregation, and inmates.[61] The "New Jim Crow" analysis, however, focuses on the striking similarities. Both slavery and imprisonment, the argument goes, are caste defining and integral in the production of race.[62] Both are institutions that are inextricable from white supremacy.

III. The Celebratory Tradition

The competing narrative about race and crime is more optimistic. The "celebratory tradition" was originally described by Professor Randall Kennedy as a form of racial apologetics.[63] Here, I use the term in a non-pejorative sense. It is a way of identifying the concept that racial justice has been advanced in the last millennium and that the law has played an important role in this advancement. Professor Kennedy was critical of some constitutional scholars who he believed justified or ignored the Supreme Court's failures in race cases.[64] This inclination, Kennedy claims, arises from the pressure on legal scholars to provide "nationalistic self-congratulation" in order to bestow upon the Court the appearance of legitimacy.[65] In critiquing the celebratory tradition, Kennedy targeted the constitutional scholarship of Professor Benno Schmidt, particularly his work addressing the Court's jurisprudence during the Progressive era.[66]

---

doing;/ the officer will pull you over just when he's pursuing./ The overseer had the right to get ill,/ and if you fought back, the overseer had the right to kill;/ the officer has the right to arrest,/ and if you fight back they put a hole in your chest."); Immortal Technique, *You Never Know, on* Revolutionary Vol. 2 (Viper Records 2003) ("[I] [e]nded up locked up like an animal for a year,/ where the C.O.'s [correction officers] talk to you like they were the overseer.").

61. *See* Alexander, *supra* note 24, at 195–208.
62. *Id.* at 182–95.
63. Randall Kennedy, *Race Relations Law and the Tradition of Celebration: The Case of Professor Schmidt,* 86 Colum. L. Rev. 1622, 1629(1986).
64. *Id.* at 1622–27.
65. *Id.* at 1659.
66. *Id.* at 1628. Kennedy's critique highlights a number of Schmidt's writings. *See id.* at 1268 n.26 (citing Alexander M Bickel & Benno C. Schmidt. Jr., The Judiciary and Responsible Government: 1910–1921 (9 Oliver Wendell Holmes Devise, History of the Supreme Court of the United States 1984)); Benno C. Schmidt. Jr., *A Postscript for Charles Black: The Supreme Court and Race in the Progressive Era.* 95 Yale L.J. 1681 (1986); Benno C. Schmidt. Jr., *Juries, Jurisdiction, and Race Discrimination: The Lost Promise of* Strauder v. West Virginia, 61 Tex. L. Rev. 1401 (1983); Benno C. Schmidt. Jr., *Principle and Prejudice: The Supreme Court and Race in the Progressive Era. Part 1: The Heyday of Jim Crow,* 82 Colum. L. Rev. 444 (1982); Benno C. Schmidt, Jr., *Principle and Prejudice: The Supreme Court and Race in the Progressive Era. Part 2: The Peonage Cases,* 82 Colum. L. Rev. 646 (1982); Benno C. Schmidt. Jr., *Principle and Prejudice: The Supreme Court and Race in the Progressive Era. Part 3: Black Disfranchisement from the KKK to the Grandfather Clause,* 82 Colum. L. Rev. 835 (1982)).

Schmidt claimed, for example, that the Supreme Court's peonage decisions, which invalidated statutes forcing persons who breached employment contracts to become indentured servants,[67] effectively dismantled southern peonage and became "the most lasting of the White Court's contributions to justice for black people, and among its greatest achievements."[68] Kennedy accused Schmidt of a gross exaggeration; the Court's declarations plainly failed to end peonage, as many state officials defied the decisions and continued to apply the criminal law to acquire forced labor.[69] Therefore, Kennedy argues, the White Court, which Schmidt claims was distinctly more progressive than other Courts and other branches of government at the time, "did not challenge the prevailing ideology in the Age of Segregation, but fit quite readily within it"; the Court continually upheld segregation, and the few progressive decisions issued by the Court were quickly and easily evaded through legislative subterfuge.[70]

Ironically, given his critique of Schmidt, Kennedy himself is the leading practitioner of the celebratory tradition in criminal law scholarship. His book, *Race, Crime, and the Law,* revels in the progress that he believes the United States has made on race and crime issues.[71] In "(Color) Blind Faith: The Tragedy of *Race, Crime, and the Law,*" a critique of Kennedy's book, I noted that the book minimizes the law's failures and exaggerates its achievements.[72] Kennedy does not believe that racism remains a significant concern in American criminal justice.

A celebrant like Kennedy, revisiting the list of problems that I would have focused on in 1910, would note that many of those problems have, to a significant degree, been solved. Lynching is no longer a significant concern.[73] Formal legal impediments, like the exclusion of African Americans from juries, have been removed.[74] Thanks to the Supreme Court, accused people have many more rights, importantly including the right to a lawyer.[75] The Court has also declared unconstitutional some laws, like some anti-loitering statutes,

67. *See* United States v. Reynolds, 235 U.S. 133 (1914); Bailey v. Alabama, 219 U.S. 219 (1911).

68. Bickel & Schmidt, *supra* note 66, at 820.

69. Kennedy, *supra* note 64, at 1646–48.

70. *Id.* at 1648–52.

71. Randall Kennedy, Race, Crime, and the Law (1997).

72. Paul Butler, *(Color) Blind Faith: The Tragedy of* Race, Crime, and the Law, 111 Harv. L. Rev. 1270 (1998) (book review).

73. Carol S. Steiker, *Second Thoughts About First Principles,* 107 Harv. L. Rev. 820, 840 (1994).

74. Batson v. Kentucky, 476 U.S. 79 (1986) (declaring unconstitutional a prosecutor's use of race-based peremptory challenges).

75. Gideon v. Wainwright, 372 U.S. 335 (1963) (declaring that the Sixth Amendment requires states to provide counsel to indigent criminal defendants).

that allowed police to abuse their discretion.[76] And in addition to being a law professor, I am a former prosecutor.[77] There are many minority actors in the criminal justice system, including police officers, prosecutors, defense attorneys, jurors, judges, and significantly, lawmakers.[78]

How does the celebratory tradition deal with the higher rate of incarceration of African Americans and with other racial disparities in criminal justice? Here, in an odd way, it remains celebratory.

The celebratory tradition identifies the principle race and crime problem as under-enforcement.[79] The victims who merited the attention of criminal justice in the bad old days were almost exclusively white. Police and prosecutors were largely unconcerned about black-on-black or white-on-black crime.[80] Thus, the fact that there are so many black people in prison is, strangely enough, good news; all this law enforcement focus on the African-American community is reparation for the days when crimes against blacks went unanswered. Randall Kennedy argues that "the principal injury suffered by African-Americans in relation to criminal matters is not overenforcement but underenforcement of the law."[81]

Law enforcement, in this story, is a public good. For a group to complain about having too much of it would be like complaining it had too many schools or too many parks.

This narrative is also easy to caricature. In the academy, I've explored it in two contexts—first, in the aforementioned review of Randall Kennedy's *Race, Crime, and the Law*.[82] More recently, in promoting my own book, *Let's Get Free*,[83] I've had a series of debates with elected

---

76. City of Chicago v. Morales, 527 U.S. 41, 58 (1999) (invalidating Chicago's gang loitering law that prohibited "remain[ing] in any one place with no apparent purpose"); Kolender v. Lawson, 461 U.S. 352, 353 n.l (1983) (striking California's loitering statute requiring individuals who "wander[] ... from place to place without apparent reason or business" to explain their presence to police); Papachristou v. Jacksonville, 405 U.S. 156, 162 (1972) (invalidating Florida's loitering law "because it encourages arbitrary and erratic arrests and convictions"); Shuttlesworth v. City of Birmingham, 382 U.S. 87, 90 (1965) (reversing defendant's conviction under a statute, literally interpreted by the trial judge, that prohibited "stand[ing] or loiter[ing] upon any street or sidewalk ... after having been requested by any police officer to move on").

77. *See* Paul Butler, Let's Get Free: A Hip-Hop Theory of Justice I (2009).

78. *See* Nathaniel R. Jones, *For Black Males and American Society—The Unbalanced Scales of Justice: A Costly Disconnect*, 23 Cap. U.L. Rev. 1, 8–12 (1994) (describing progress in increased appointment of black judges and hiring of black police officers).

79. *See* Kennedy, *supra* note 71, at 19.

80. *Id.* at 60–75.

81. *Id.* at 19.

82. Butler, *supra* note 72.

83. Butler, *supra* note 77.

prosecutors across the country.[84] We have discussed whether the work that prosecutors do is consistent with social and racial justice. The prosecutors I've debated, many of whom are African-American, all claimed that their work is in the best interest of black people, even when that work includes locking up many blacks. These prosecutors have identified a different main race problem than mass incarceration. They, like Kennedy, believe that the principle problem remains the under-protection of law and, specifically, the disproportionate number of victims of violent crime, especially homicide, who are African-American.[85]

IV. Symbolic Versus Material Progress

My purpose here is to set out these competing narratives rather than to choose between them. We should note, however, that they seem impossible to reconcile. They cannot both be true. It the "New Jim Crow" theorists are correct, and the mass incarceration of blacks is simply the latest manifestation of racial subordination, conditions are worse than (or at least equally as bad as) they have ever been. The depressing statistics about the number of African Americans who are locked up and other extreme racial disparities seem to bear this out.

On the other hand, most people probably would say that an African American has a better chance of receiving a fair trial in 2010 than he or she would have had in 1910. It seems undeniable that the racial climate has improved over the last one hundred years.

Can racial justice in criminal law be better and worse at the same time? In her widely cited article, "Race, Reform, and Retrenchment," Professor Kimberlé Crenshaw provides a useful and nuanced way of thinking about two kinds of racial progress: symbolic and material.[86] Though Crenshaw wrote about constitutional law rather than criminal law, her analysis provides a helpful template for assessing the evolution of race, crime, and the law.

Crenshaw argues that the Supreme Court's civil rights cases benefit African Americans but, at the same, time make further material gains more difficult to obtain. She explains that during the Jim Crow era. blacks were faced with two types of oppression: "symbolic subordination" and "material subordination."[87] Symbolic subordination includes the states' respective efforts to reinforce a racist ideology of black inferiority by formally refusing to

---

84. *See, e.g., Butler and Barkow Discuss the Rote of Prosecutors in Social and Racial Justice,* NYU Law (Nov. 2, 2009), http://www.law.nyu.edu/news/forum_paul_butler (discussion with Anthony Barkow, who was a federal prosecutor for twelve years).

85. Kennedy, *supra* note 79, at 19.

86. Kimberlé Williams Crenshaw, *Race, Reform, and Retrenchment: Transformation and Legitimation in Antidiscrimination Law,* 101 Harv. L. Rev. 1331 (1988).

87. *Id.* at 1376–79.

provide social and political equality to blacks.[88] Material subordination is the actual economic subordination created by discriminatory policies and by the hegemonic racial hierarchy supported by the status quo.[89] Crenshaw argues that the Supreme Court has been highly effective in ending symbolic subordination, but has had only limited success in ending material subordination.[90]

With regard to race and crime, symbolic victories have been few and far between. This is not because the Supreme Court approves of race-based criminal laws but rather because most criminal statutes have been facially race-neutral for generations. Racial disparities have not been caused by discriminatory statutes; instead, such results have been achieved through the racialized exercise of discretion, including selective enforcement by police departments, selective prosecution, and selective sentencing by judges.

For example, the men convicted in *Moore v. Dempsey,*[91] *Powell v. Alabama,*[92] and *Brown v. Mississippi*[93]—outrageous examples of Jim Crow justice—were all charged under racially neutral criminal laws. Likewise, the anti-loitering laws, which were abusively applied to African Americans as described in *Shuttlesworth v. City of Birmingham,* were facially race-neutral.[94]

As I noted earlier, the Supreme Court has been reluctant to disturb this broad discretion, even when it is demonstrated to have racially skewed results. Black criminal defendants do obtain some of the normative benefits cited by Crenshaw. Minorities gained when the Court overturned those criminal laws that were facially discriminatory, such as the laws criminalizing anti-miscegenation invalidated in *McLaughlin v. Florida*[95] and *Loving v. Virginia.*[96] Moreover, African-American defendants have benefited from the stigma against racism that the Supreme Court's civil rights cases have helped to create.

---

88. *Id.* at 1377.

89. *Id.*

90. *Id.* at 1378–79.

91. 261 U.S. 86, 87 (1923) (involving black defendants charged with murder and convicted at the culmination of a lynch mob riot); *see also* Michael J. Klarman, *The Racial Origins of Modern Criminal Procedure,* 99 Mich. L. Rev. 48, 51–52 (2000) (explaining that the mob went on to kill up to 250 other African-Americans, and that "[s]eventy-nine blacks (and no whites) were prosecuted as a result of the riot").

92. 287 U.S. 45, 50, 53 (1932) (involving black defendants convicted of rape and sentenced to death after a trial, where counsel was not appointed until the morning of trial).

93. 297 U.S. 278, 281–82 (1936) (involving black defendants convicted of murder after police coerced a confession from them by hanging and beating them).

94. 382 U.S. 87, 88 (1965).

95. 379 U.S. 184, 184 (1964).

96. 388 U.S. 1, 2–3(1967).

Yet material progress—the reduction, say, of racial disparities—has not been the result. In a way, the success of the civil rights litigation in the Supreme Court may be partly to blame. Crenshaw notes that formal neutrality has hindered the civil rights movement's ability to make further advances.[97] The abolition of most facially discriminatory policies gives credence to the theory (more aspirational than actualized) that America is essentially a meritocratic society.[98]

Because race matters less in the law, it is thought by many to matter less in everyday life. Thus, factors other than the law are looked for to explain sub-standard black achievement—factors like culture or even genetics. This narrative harms African-American suspects because it diminishes the significance of race and racism. Pointing to facially discriminatory policies was an effective way for blacks to prove that the system was inherently oppressive; now that the "Whites Only" signs have been taken down, it is more difficult for African Americans to explain their experience, therefore making claims of racial subordination less credible to people who accept these dominant narratives.

V. Acknowledging the Continuing Significance of Race

In this Symposium, Professor Ronald Allen spoke about the political trend, during the 1970s, of running against the Court.[99] Now, the Court, rather than the politics, has changed. We have witnessed the decline of the optimism of the Great Society, and its criminal justice correlate, the rehabilitative ideal.

Thus, for the problem of mass incarceration, relief from the Supreme Court will come unexpectedly, like the results in *Booker*[100] and *Apprendi*,[101] rather than as the product of public interest litigation designed to bring the Court around. Groups like the NAACP and ACLU came late to recognizing mass incarceration as a race problem and a human rights problem, and thus missed the days of a more receptive Supreme Court. I consult on litigation strategy with some civil rights organizations, and their basic strategy is not to bring litigation, especially in federal court. No one, for example, thinks this is a good time to ask

---

97. Crenshaw, *supra* note 86, at 1378–84.

98. *Id.* at 1380.

99. *See* Ronald J. Allen, *Opening Remarks*, 100 J. Crim. L & Criminology 633 (2010).

100. United States v. Booker, 543 U.S. 220 (2005); *see also* Marc L. Miller. *A Map of Sentencing and a Compass for Judges: Sentencing Information Systems, Transparency, and the Next Generation of Reform*, 105 Colum. L. Rev. 1351, 1395 (2005) (calling the *Booker* opinion "dramatic and surprising").

101. Apprendi v. New Jersey, 530 U.S. 466 (2000); *see* Linda Greenhouse, *The Supreme Court: Trial by Jury: New Jersey Hate Crime Law Struck Down*, N.Y. Times, June, 27, 2000, at A19 ("Rarely has any case had such an immediate and dramatic impact on the practice of law.").

the Court to declare racial profiling unconstitutional. Even if the composition of the Court becomes more liberal, the weight of the precedent of the Burger, Rehnquist, and Roberts Courts is so daunting that it is difficult to imagine a welcoming climate in the foreseeable future. One exception might be the death penalty, where the Court is arguably more receptive to concerns about fairness.[102]

Charles Ogletree, among other scholars, has observed that the Warren Court, in its famed criminal procedure cases, was making advances in racial justice as much as criminal procedure.[103] Many of the litigants in these cases, including Mr. Miranda[104] and Mr. Terry,[105] were African-American or Latino. Significantly, however, the Court rarely discussed race in its criminal procedure opinions. Its racial justice work was covert and formally color-blind. Now even these "down low" kinds of interventions seem absent from the Court's criminal jurisprudence.

The central race and crime problem in the next one hundred years will be the efficacy of dealing with race and crime problems through color-blind law and policy. In the post-racial era, is it even possible to fix problems that are inextricably linked to racial subordination? The increase in racial disparities in incarceration can be attributed mainly to selective enforcement of the drug laws. Again, this enforcement is "discriminatory" in the sense that there is no evidence that African Americans disproportionately commit drug offenses.[106] The Court's equal protection jurisprudence, which requires a discriminatory intent, and its criminal procedure jurisprudence, which reifies law enforcement discretion, make this race and crime problem exceedingly difficult to address through civil rights litigation.

---

102. *See* Furman v. Georgia, 408 U.S. 238 (1972) (invalidating Georgia's death penalty system, citing ethnic disparities and basic fairness concerns). *But see* McCleskey v. Kemp, 481 U.S. 279, 353 (1986) (upholding Georgia's death penalty program despite study showing that "[w]hite-victim cases are nearly 11 times more likely to yield a death sentence than are black-victim cases"); Gregg v. Georgia, 428 U.S. 153 (1976) (holding that imposing the death penalty is not inherently unconstitutional, approving Georgia's new capital sentencing scheme).

103. Tracey L. Meares, *Everything Old is New Again: Fundamental Fairness and the Legitimacy of Criminal Justice,* 3 Ohio St. J. Crim. L. 105, 106 n. 4 (2005) (citing Professor Charles Ogletree. Lecture at the American Association of Law Schools Annual Meeting (Jan. 1990)).

104. Miranda v Arizona, 384 U.S. 436 (1966) (requiring exclusion of custodial interrogations by criminal defendants unless the defendant had been informed of his right to silence and right to counsel).

105. Terry v. Ohio, 392 U.S. I (1968) (allowing government officers to execute "pat and frisk" searches of suspects only if the officer has reasonable suspicion that the suspect is participating in illegal behavior).

106. Marc Mauer, The Changing Racial Dynamics of the War on Drugs 4 (2009), *available at* http://www.sentencingproject.org/doc/dp_raceanddrugs.pdf (noting that African Americans composed 12% of the total state prison population, but 45% of those incarcerated for a drug offense).

There are, in addition, some crimes that blacks do commit disproportionately.[107] For these crimes, the issue of whether race should be considered in assessing responsibility and punishment remains fraught. Blacks do not commit crimes because they are black. Their overrepresentation among some classes of offenders is attributable to social and environmental conditions such as poverty,[108] miserable schools,[109] broken families,[110] lack of access to health care,[111] and even lead poisoning.[112] All of these factors are in turn linked to racial subordination. If the law does not recognize this fundamental truth, if its remedies are all color-blind, then the symptoms are treated, but the disease remains. For a painful disease, a patient might be satisfied with treatment of symptoms; she might feel better, even if she has not been cured. Maybe this "improvement" is what the celebratory narrative celebrates.

Yet the disease remains. It metastasizes. This is the racial subordination that the "New Jim Crow" storytellers focus on. The disease cannot be cured unless it is diagnosed and treated. This would mean race-conscious remedies in criminal justice. We have such remedies in other areas of the law, for example employment and education, because we understand that color-blind solutions will perpetuate the status quo. Their legal status, however, is relentlessly contested, and they are politically unpopular. They do not seem to be the wave of the future. President Obama, criticized about the high rate of African-American unemployment, said. "I can't pass laws that say 'I'm just helping black folks.'"[113] He asserted that his overall fixes to the economy would benefit all, including African Americans.[114] The "rising tide will lift all boats" remedy also seems to be the prevailing view on race and crime:

---

107. *See* Uniform Crime Reporting Program, Fed. Bureau of Investigation, Age-Specific Arrest Rates and Race-Specific Arrest Rates for Selected Offenses, 1993–2001 59–69 (2003), *available at* http://www.fbi.gov/ucr/adducr/age_race_specific.pdf.

108. Ching-Chi Hsieh & M. D. Pugh, *Poverty, Income Inequality, and Violent Crime: A Meta-Analysis of Recent Aggregate Data Studies,* 18 Crim. Just. Rev. 182, 198 (1993).

109. Lance Lochner & Enrico Moretti, *The Effect of Education on Crime: Evidence from Prison Inmates. Arrests, and Self-Reports,* 94 Amer. Econ. Rev. 155, 183 (2004).

110. Cynthia C. Harper & Sara S. McLanahan, *Father Absence and Youth Incarceration,* 14 J. Res. on Adolescence 369, 380–86 (2004).

111. Rachel E. Barkow & David B. Edwards, *Commentary: How Health Care Can Reduce Crime,* Forbes.com. June 22, 2010. http://www.forbes.com/2010/06/22/health-care-crime-drugs-opinions-contributors-rachel-barkow-david-edwards.html.

112. Shankar Vedantam, *Research Links Lead Exposure, Criminal Activity,* Wash. Post, July 8, 2007, at A02, *available at* http://www.washingtonpost.com/wp-dyn/content/article/2007/07/07/AR2007070701073.html.

113. April D. Ryan, *Interview with President Barack Obama,* AprilDRyan.com, Dec. 21, 2009, http://aprildryan.com/2009/12/21/interview-with-president-barack-obama/.

114. *Id.*

improved access to health care, more jobs, improved education, elimination of "mandatory minimum sentences," and other means of restoring discretion to judges—all these will make things better for people of color in the criminal justice system. If the "New Jim Crow" school is correct, however, race will continue to confound criminal justice for the next one hundred years, or however long it takes to achieve explicit racial justice interventions in criminal justice.

On the bicentennial of the United States Constitution, Justice Thurgood Marshall reflected on the legal progress that the civil rights movement helped to achieve. Justice Marshall explained that, looking back, he saw victories, but looking forward, he saw more challenges:

> What is striking is the role legal principles have played throughout America's history in determining the condition of Negroes. They were enslaved by law, emancipated by law, disenfranchised and segregated by law; and, finally, they have begun to win equality by law.... Thus, in this bicentennial year, we may not all participate in the festivities with flag-waving fervor. Some may more quietly commemorate the suffering, struggle, and sacrifice that has triumphed over much of what was wrong with the original document, and observe the anniversary with hopes not realized and promises not fulfilled."[115]

The experience of the last one hundred years teaches us that racial progress in criminal justice is not inevitable, but it is possible, at least in some limited sense. Whether racial justice can be accomplished in a legal and political climate that rebuffs race discourse may still be an open question at the *Journal's* bicentennial in 2110. In the meantime, in 2010, nearly one million African Americans languish in prison, and millions more under some other form of criminal supervision.

---

115. Thurgood Marshall, Commentary, *Reflections on the Bicentennial of the United States Constitution*, 101 Harv. L. Rev. 1, 5 (1987).

Reading 3.2

Critical Race Perspectives

Explaining the Differential Treatment of Racial Minorities by the Criminal Justice System

Katharine Tellis, Nancy Rodriguez, and Cassia Spohn

In 2004, the United States celebrated the fiftieth anniversary of *Brown v. Board of Education,* the landmark Supreme Court case that ordered the desegregation of public schools. Also in 2004, the Sentencing Project issued a report entitled "Schools and Prisons: Fifty Years after *Brown v. Board of Education*" (Sentencing Project 2004). The report noted that, whereas many institutions in society had become more diverse and more responsive to the needs of people of color in the wake of the *Brown* decision, the American criminal justice system had taken "a giant step backward" (5). To illustrate this, the report pointed out that in 2004 there were *nine times* as many African Americans in prison or jail as on the day the *Brown* decision was handed down—the number had increased from 98,000 to 884,500. The report also noted that one of every three African American men and one of every 18 African American women born today could expect to be imprisoned at some point in his or her lifetime. The authors of the report concluded that "such an outcome should be shocking to all Americans" (5).

Differential treatment of racial minorities by the American criminal justice system is not confined to sentencing and corrections. Racial minorities are arrested, stopped and questioned, and shot and killed by the police out of all proportion to their representation in the population. Racial minorities, and particularly those suspected of crimes against whites, also are the victims of unequal justice in the courts. Although reforms mandated by the Supreme Court or adopted voluntarily by the states have eliminated much of the blatant racism directed against racial minorities who find themselves in the arms of the law, the race of the defendant continues to affect decisions regarding bail, charging, plea bargaining, and sentencing. The differences are particularly stark with respect to the death penalty. Study after study has demonstrated that those who murder whites are much more likely to be sentenced to death

Katharine Tellis, Nancy Rodriguez and Cassia Spohn, "Critical Race Perspectives: Explaining the Differential Treatment of Racial Minorities by the Criminal Justice System," *Criminology and Public Policy: Putting Theory to Work*, ed. Hugh Barlow and Scott H. Decker, pp. 233–253.

than those who murder African Americans; many of these studies also have shown that African Americans convicted of murdering whites receive the death penalty more often than whites who murder whites.

Criminologists and legal scholars use several complementary theoretical perspectives to explain differential treatment of whites and racial minorities. Critical race theorists (Crenshaw et al. 1995; Delgado and Stefancic 2001) contend that racism (and sexism) are ubiquitous and deeply embedded in laws and criminal justice policies and that the criminal justice system is an institution that reinforces hierarchies in society based on race, class, gender, and other socio-demographic characteristics. Similarly, conflict theorists argue that the administration of criminal justice reflects the unequal distribution of power in society and contend that the more powerful groups (i.e., whites) use the criminal justice system to maintain their dominant position and to repress groups or social movements that threaten it. Other theoretical perspectives focus on the role that race-linked stereotypes or attributions of dangerousness and threat play in criminal justice decision making.

The purpose of this [reading] is to provide an overview of three theoretical perspectives that attempt to account for the differential treatment of people of color in the criminal justice system. It begins with a discussion of critical race theory, followed by conflict theory and attribution theory. It concludes with a discussion of the relevance of these theories to public policy.

Critical Race Theory

Historical Development

Critical race theory emerged within the legal academy of the United States in the 1980s as an offshoot of critical legal studies, its predecessor of the 1970s. Critical legal studies spawned from a subsection of predominantly white, male, and left-wing legal scholars who challenged the neutrality and objectivity of American legal liberalism (Crenshaw 2002a, 2002b). Their skepticism was based on consideration of how history informs the current social reality; specifically, scholars within this tradition claim that the law is neither neutral nor objective when it oppresses the poor, women, and people of color, whether directly in terms of content or indirectly through its consequences (Valdes, Culp, and Harris 2002). A series of conferences dedicated to developing critical legal studies was held in the early 1980s. In 1985, scholars from the feminist wing of the critical legal studies movement articulated concern that, despite any reformist intentions, a meaningful analysis of race was missing from the critical legal studies framework, which viewed the law and its consequences through an elite, white, male lens (Crenshaw 2002a, 2002b). These concerns, in conjunction with the influential career and scholarship of Derrick Bell (1992), led to the development of critical race theory in the late 1980s (Valdes, Culp, and Harris 2002).

Critical race theory contends that the substance and procedures of American law, including antidiscrimination law, are structured to maintain white privilege (Valdes, Culp, and Harris 2002; see also McIntosh 2007). Further, it argues that neutrality and objectivity are not only unattainable ideals, but they are harmful fictions that obscure the normative supremacy of whiteness in American law and society (Valdes, Culp, and Harris 2002, 1). The following section examines the assumptions that underlie critical race theory and uses the theory to examine the issue of race and the criminal justice system.

Principal Assumptions of Critical Race Theory

Critical race theory begins with the rejection of three mainstream beliefs about racial injustice: (1) "blindness" to race will eliminate racism; (2) racism results from the behavior of individuals and is not systemic or institutional; and (3) one can fight racism without paying attention to sexism, heterosexism, economic exploitation, and other forms of oppression or injustice (Valdes, Culp, and Harris 2002). The first belief refers to the deeply entrenched individualism that influenced the development of the United States and the concomitant denial of group-based identities (Bell 1992). Critical race theorists reject the notion that ignoring race will eliminate racism. They maintain that racial identities have psychological benefits at the individual level in terms of pride and self-esteem and political benefits at the structural level in terms of influencing policy decisions (Crenshaw 2002a, 2002b). The second belief refers to the tendency of the courts to interpret antidiscrimination law by attempting to ascertain individual offenders and victims, as opposed to seeing racism and its everyday operation in the very structures within which the guilty and innocent are identified (Valdes, Culp, and Harris 2002, 3). The third belief, consistent with the assertions of critical race feminists, centers on the conception of race as socially constructed and emphasizes that race, class, and gender are interconnected. As a result, the particular configuration of these factors is critical to understanding a person's or group's experiences (Anderson and Collins 2007; see also Collins 2000). This intersectional perspective (see also Combahee River Collective 2001 [1972]; Crenshaw 1992), referred to as the "Matrix of Domination" by Patricia Hill Collins (2000), emphasizes that racial stratification is ordinary, ubiquitous, and reproduced in both mundane and extraordinary customs and experience (Brown 2003). In short, critical race theory assumes that race is a socially constructed and historically embedded phenomenon and that race is entrenched in U.S. laws and policies.

The following section considers the historical examples of sexual violence against slave women and the use of the death penalty against black men to examine the criminal justice system through a critical race perspective.

Slavery in the United States: Examining the Intersection of Race and Gender

Although the transatlantic slave trade began in the fifteenth century, the origins of chattel slavery—the process by which human beings of African descent were smuggled as property to be bought and sold—emerged in British colonies such as Bermuda in 1612 and in Jamestown, Virginia, in 1619 (Lerner 1972; Stevenson 1995). Whites in Virginia attempted to impose their authority on every aspect of slaves' lives, including the family, to subjugate and control their human chattel (Stevenson 1995, 39). For example, Virginia passed a law in 1662 requiring that a child born to a slave woman must take on the legal status of its mother (Stevenson 1995). Throughout the South, state legislatures followed suit, adopting *partus sequitur ventrem* statutes that served two purposes: first, to increase the slave population; and, second, to prevent any confusion as to citizenship status if a white man were to father a slave's child.

The process of dehumanization through objectification was advanced through laws that prohibited slaves from legally marrying, owning property, attending school, and testifying against whites in a courtroom and through forced segregation (Kennedy 1997). Importantly, traditional notions of gender as dictated by white patriarchal culture did not apply to male and female slaves as workers, as the primary focus was on economic exploitation of their labor (Collins 2004; Crenshaw 1992). Angela Davis (1981) argues that African American women were not perceived as women in the accepted (read, white) sense and that the slave system discouraged male supremacy among African Americans to affirm that fathers, mothers, and children were all equally subject to the slave master's power. Practically, this meant that slave women could not be treated as "weaker" and slave men could not be treated as "providers," as all worked alongside one another in the fields, including pregnant women (Collins 2004; Crenshaw 1992; Lerner 1972). Although in border states most slaves were house servants, the "slaveocracy" (Davis 1981) of the Deep South used Africans of both genders primarily for agricultural work. In characterizing the respective roles of female and male slaves, Davis comments:

> Work under threat of the whip in one sense undifferentiated their oppressions, yet sexual abuse was an issue unique to women.... Expediency characterized their [white slaveowners'] posture towards female slaves. When it was profitable to exploit them [laboriously] as men they did so, essentially making them genderless, but when deemed necessary to exploit them in ways suited only for women they were locked into exclusively female roles. (6)

In other words, male slaves dealt with whippings, beatings, floggings, mutilation, torture, and other forms of violent exploitation based solely on color, but the punishment inflicted on slave women exceeded in intensity the punishment suffered by the men, for women were not only whipped and mutilated but also raped (Collins 2000, 2004; hooks 1984; Kennedy 1997; Lerner 1972; Roberts 1997).

Randall Kennedy (1997) argues that the failure to protect female slaves from rape in antebellum America was formalized and deliberate, as illustrated in *George (a Slave) v. the State* (1859), a case that went through the High Court of Errors and Appeals in Mississippi.[1] In *George v. the State*, a male slave was convicted and sentenced to death for having had "carnal knowledge of a female slave under the age of ten." However, his conviction was overturned on appeal under the premise that because slaves had no rights under the common law, it was up to the legislature to decide what rights they might or might not have. Consequently, since no statutes specifically protected slave girls or women from rape, no law was violated by inflicting sexual violence on them (Kennedy 1997, 35).

In response to the *George* case, the Mississippi legislature passed a statute that offered at least some protection for a subsection of the female slave population (Kennedy 1997). It stated that the actual or attempted commission of a rape "by a negro or mulatto on a female negro or mulatto," *under twelve years of age*, is punishable with death or whipping, as the jury may decide.[2] Omitted from this legal conceptualization of victimhood are female slaves over the age of twelve and white male offenders. The fact that these omissions are not explicitly articulated in the statute illustrates the institutionalized nature of white male supremacy. This is further evident in their codified—albeit invisibly—impunity in regard to forced sexual access to women and in the power involved in defining both the victim and the offender. In other words, the criminal justice system served as a social control mechanism through which to maintain white hegemony through its enforcement of laws that disproportionately left African American women unprotected from sexual violence while simultaneously serving the economic needs particular to slavery (Crenshaw 2002a; Kennedy 1997). Consistent with the principles of critical race theory, the laws, which operated to preserve white supremacy, were neither racially neutral nor objective.

The history of lynching provides another example of how race and gender affected the experience of African Americans in the United States (Corzine, Creech, and Corzine 1983; Jacobs, Carmichael, and Kent 2005; Tolnay and Beck 1994). Historical analyses illustrate that during the period of Reconstruction after the Civil War, black men were particularly susceptible to this form of violence at the hands of white mobs (e.g., Kennedy 1997; Walker, Spohn, and DeLone 2007). Kennedy (1997, 45–46) notes that the lynching of black men was justified on several grounds. First, some contended that certain crimes were so heinous—for example,

1. 37 Miss. Rep. 316, 318 (1859).
2. 37 Miss. Rep. 320; emphasis added.

the rape of a white woman by a black man—that they demanded a punishment more swift and sure than the legal process could offer. Others, however, focused on the special threat posed by blacks. One theory suggested that blacks underwent a civilizing process through enslavement that tragically ended with emancipation. In other words, this theoretical perspective suggested that blacks who were freed from the discipline of enslavement would revert to their primitive and brutish ways. Other explanations view lynching and mob violence as part of a more comprehensive attempt by whites to maintain their social, economic, and political dominance. Whites, in other words, lynched blacks "in order to neutralize their threat to the political hegemony enjoyed by southern whites" (Tolnay and Beck 1994, 176).

The juxtaposition of the previously discussed leniency toward white men who raped black women is striking when one considers the public outrage engendered by an accusation of rape by a black man of a white woman. The belief was that black men lusted after white women with such powerful longing that ordinary means of control were insufficient (Kennedy 1997, 45). The assumption that sexual interaction between black men and white women was by default an act of rape illustrates the institutionalized nature of white male supremacy—that is, justifying violence via the goal of protecting white women from black men who were characterized as uncivilized savages. Importantly, this historical context retains significance in the political consciousness of African Americans in the present, particularly with regard to how crimes are processed in the criminal justice system (Kennedy 1997). For example, as Samuel Walker and his colleagues (2007, 299) point out in their discussion of differential treatment of interracial and intraracial sexual assault, 405 of the 453 men executed for rape in the United States from 1930 to 1972 (the death penalty for rape was ruled unconstitutional in 1977) were African American men convicted of raping white women. Research conducted in the past two decades demonstrates that this is not simply an historical fact. Although the results are not entirely consistent, studies continue to find that African American men accused of raping white women are treated more harshly than any other race-of-victim–race-of-offender combination (LaFree 1989).

In summary, critical race theory begins with the premise that race is completely embedded in U.S. laws and policies, which consequentially maintain a structural privilege for whites (white men in particular) to the detriment of people of color. Proponents of critical race theory attribute the paradoxical invisibility of race to the deep-seated individualism that underlies the legal liberalism and culture of the United States, which emphasizes issues of objectivity, neutrality, and color-blindness to promote civil justice. The answer, according to critical race theorists, is to incorporate a commitment to social justice not only in academic discussions but also in the formation of public policy to remedy the detrimental effects of institutionalized discrimination. By examining the policies and practices of the criminal justice system during slavery and beyond, critical race theory accounts for the failure to protect African American women from rape by white slave owners and for the overzealous prosecution of African American men labeled via unsubstantiated accusations of raping white women.

Conflict Theory

Like critical race theory, conflict theory emphasizes the salience of race and class in explanations of social control. In contrast to consensus theory, which views society as consisting of groups with common interests and the state as a means of protecting those interests, conflict theory posits that society is made up of groups with competing norms and values and contends that the authority of the state is used to protect the interests of those in power. Central to conflict theory is the premise that the law is applied to maintain the power of the dominant group to control the behavior of those who threaten that power; the law is applied, in other words, to protect the position and interests of elites from challenges by the powerless, especially racial minorities and the poor (Chambliss and Seidman 1971; Quinney 1970; Turk 1969). Related to this is the notion that the amount of social control imposed by those in power will depend on the degree to which they view the actions of individuals and groups challenging their power as a legitimate threat. As Richard Quinney (1970, 18) noted, "The probability that criminal definitions will be applied varies according to the extent to which the behaviors of the powerless conflict with the interests of the power segments."

The notion of "threat" is central to conflict theory, but the assessment of who or what is threatening varies. Original versions of the theory, reflecting its Marxist origins, emphasized the significance of social class and the importance of economic stratification. Quinney (1974), for example, argued that the dominant economic class used the legal system to protect its economic interests and to control the behavior of lower-class groups that otherwise would threaten the power and position of the economic elite. William Chambliss and Robert Seidman (1971) similarly proposed that legal sanctions are more likely to be imposed on offenders from lower social classes and suggested that the most severe sanctions will be imposed on people in the lowest social class. They also noted that the larger the gap in economic resources between dominant and subordinate groups, the greater the power exerted by the dominant group over subordinate groups. Thus, "the more economically stratified a society becomes, the more it becomes necessary for dominant groups to enforce through coercion the norms of conduct that guarantee supremacy" (Chambliss and Seidman 1982, 33).

Other theorists, while not discounting the importance of class, emphasize that those who threaten the status quo are likely to be members of what is variously referred to as the "surplus population" (Quinney 1977), the "rabble class" (Irwin 1985), or the "problem population" (Spitzer 1975). Conflict theorists also assert that these threatening groups are likely to be composed primarily of racial minorities (especially blacks), the unemployed, the poor, and the young (Box and Hale 1985; Liska and Chamlin 1984). For example, George Bridges and Robert Crutchfield (1988) indicate that criminal stereotypes of offenders as young black men result in more severe punishment for minorities and disadvantaged offenders. Echoing Quinney's (1977, 131) assertion that the criminal justice system "is the modern means of controlling surplus population," they emphasize that members of these groups "are more likely to be subjected to intensified social control—more criminalization, more formal processing by the criminal justice system, and increased incarceration" (Sampson and Laub 1993, 288).

Critical race theorists, and contemporary conflict theorists, contend that although offenders with various combinations of characteristics make up social dynamite, it is the combination of *race* and other characteristics linked to threat that is "its most explosive component" (Chiricos and Bales 1991, 719). Race, in other words, is the critical factor; it affects criminal justice decision making unilaterally *and* in combination with other factors. Studies of sentencing decisions provide compelling evidence in support of this. Darrell Steffensmeier and his colleagues (1998), for example, found that race, gender, and age had a significant direct effect on both the likelihood of incarceration and the length of the sentence. More important, they found that the three factors interacted to produce substantially harsher sentences for one category of offenders—young, black men—than for any other combination of age, race, and gender. Cassia Spohn and David Holleran (2000) similarly found that the offenders most likely to be sentenced to prison were young black and Hispanic men; their research also revealed that unemployed black and Hispanic men were more likely than employed white men to be incarcerated. The results of these studies highlight "the high cost of being black, young, and male" (Steffensmeier, Ulmer, and Kramer 1998, 789), as well as the fact that "offenders with other constellations of characteristics also pay a punishment penalty" (Spohn and Holleran 2000, 304).

Accounting for Anomalies or Inconsistencies

Although there is substantial evidence in support of conflict theory's premise that racial minorities—especially blacks—will be subjected to more formal social control than whites, there also is evidence that racial minorities either are treated no differently from whites or are treated more leniently than whites (for reviews, see Hawkins 1987; Spohn 2000; Zatz 1987). Darnell Hawkins (1987, 721) argues that many of these so-called anomalies or inconsistencies in research on racial bias in the administration of justice reflect "oversimplification" of conflict theory. This is reflected in the fact that many researchers simply test the hypothesis that racial minorities will be treated more harshly than whites, assuming, either explicitly or implicitly, that this will be so regardless of the nature of the crime, the race of the victim, or the relationship between the victim and the offender.

Hawkins (1987, 724) contends that the work of early conflict theorists such as Quinney (1970) and Chambliss and Seidman (1971) does not support the proposition that "blacks or other nonwhites will receive more severe punishment than whites for all crimes, under all conditions, and at similar levels of disproportion over time." Rather, conflict theorists argue that "the probability that criminal sanctions will be applied varies according to the extent to which the behaviors of the powerless conflict with the interests of the power segments" (Quinney 1970, 18). Crimes that threaten the power of the dominant class will therefore produce harsher penalties for blacks who commit those crimes, and crimes that pose relatively little threat to the system of white authority will not necessarily result in harsher sanctions for blacks.

According to this view, blacks who murder, rape, or rob whites will be treated more harshly than blacks who victimize members of their own race. As Ruth Peterson and John Hagan (1984, 54) note, "When black offenders assault or kill black victims, the devalued status of the black victims and the paternalistic attitudes of white authorities can justify lenient treatment.... When blacks violate white victims, the high sexual property value attached to the white victims and the racial fears of authorities can justify severe treatment." Gary LaFree makes a similar argument, maintaining that conflict theory is not disproved "if research demonstrates that sanctions are not particularly harsh when relatively powerless persons in society murder and rape each other" (1989, 48).

Conflict Theory and the Concept of Racial Threat

The amount of threat posed by racial minorities also has been linked to macro-level factors. A number of scholars contend that the degree to which the crime control apparatus of the state is used to protect the interests of wealthy and powerful citizens depends in part on the degree of threat that racial minorities *as a group* pose, which in turn depends on such things as the size, visibility, resources, and mobilization of the minority population (Blalock 1967; D'Alessio, Eitle, and Stolzenberg 2005; Eitle, D'Alessio, and Stolzenberg 2002; Stolzenberg, D'Alessio, and Eitle 2004). As their population grows and becomes more visible and their economic and political resources increase, in other words, the threat that minorities present to the dominant majority also increases, triggering increased levels of formal social control.

In the realm of criminal justice, most tests of the so-called racial threat hypothesis have focused on the relationship between the size of the minority population and the level of formal social control (cf. Chiricos, Hogan, and Gertz 1997; Jackson and Carroll 1981; Jacobs, Carmichael, and Kent 2005; Liska, Lawrence, and Benson 1981; Liska, Lawrence, and Sanchirico 1982; Petrocelli, Piquero, and Smith 2003). Researchers argue that whites view the percentage of non-whites in their community as an indicator of the seriousness of the crime problem, are more fearful of crime in communities with large minority populations, and perceive non-whites as more threatening and dangerous, and thus as more in need of formal social control, in communities where minorities make up a sizeable portion of the population. Thus, the larger the minority population, the greater the prejudice and discrimination that population faces. Hubert Blalock (1967), however, suggests that the relationship is not necessarily linear. Rather, there is a "tipping point," or threshold, beyond which further increases in the size of the minority population have little, if any, effect. Intensified social control due to racial threat may manifest in several ways, including discriminatory practices and the use of coercive force against racial and ethnic minorities (Stolzenberg, D'Alessio, and Eitle 2004). The racial threat hypothesis has been used to study the influence of the size of the black population on pretextual traffic stops, arrest rates, incarceration rates, executions, lynchings, hate crimes, and interracial killings.

Three threat-based hypotheses have been used to explain racial threat: the political threat hypothesis, the economic threat hypothesis, and the threat of black-on-white crime hypothesis (Blalock 1967; Eitle, D'Alessio, and Stolzenberg 2002; Stolzenberg, D'Alessio, and Eitle 2004). Each hypothesis predicts that there will be a positive relationship between the size of the black population and the amount of formal social control imposed on blacks, but the nature of the threat posed by the black population varies (Eitle, D'Alessio, and Stolzenberg 2002). Although all three hypotheses are concerned with group conflict, each of them focuses on a different social process. As Allen Liska asserts, "These differences are not just differences of terminology for similar concepts.... [T]here are real differences among these theories regarding who and what are threatening to whom" (1994, 63).

To date, studies have produced mixed results regarding the effect of racial threat on criminal justice outcomes. While some studies concluded that there was no direct evidence that blacks face a greater likelihood of arrest in cities with large black populations (Stolzenberg, D'Alessio, and Eitle 2004), others found that blacks are more likely to be arrested in areas where a high percentage of crimes involved a black offender and white victim (Eitle, D'Alessio, and Stolzenberg 2002). There also is little empirical support for the notion that political or economic competition between blacks and whites will lead to increased social control and higher arrest rates for blacks (Eitle, D'Alessio, and Stolzenberg 2002). Studies of criminal court sentencing processes and imprisonment rates have also produced mixed findings. Martha Myers and Susette Talarico (1987), for example, found no evidence that the black proportion of the population or the percentage of arrests involving blacks led to more severe sentences for blacks, but they did find that black offenders were treated more punitively in counties with high levels of unemployment. Other researchers have found that black concentration leads to increased risk of incarceration for all offenders, regardless of race (Britt 2000; Crawford, Chiricos, and Kleck 1998).

Empirical tests of the racial threat hypothesis have been subjected to various criticisms, including the lack of conceptual clarity that "threat" has received in previous studies. According to Liska (1987), because researchers have failed to define key constructs of the threat hypothesis theoretically and operationally, they have produced an array of studies with inconsistent and, in some cases, conflicting, findings. However, the different conceptualizations of threat and the inconsistent findings of research testing the racial threat hypothesis "does not mean that conflict theory is contradictory; it only means that the theory is complex and thus that the implications of both process [i.e., of both positive and negative relationships between racial threat and various types of social control] must be considered simultaneously in a multivariate causal model" (Liska 1994, 65).

Like critical race theory and conflict theory, then, the racial threat perspective posits that members of the dominant culture will use their power to control racial minorities who threaten them politically, economically, or socially. The amount of formal social control exerted by the dominant group, according to this perspective, will depend on the size, visibility, and resources of the racial minority population.

Attribution Theory

Critical race theory and conflict theory, both of which contend that law and the criminal justice system are used to maintain white privilege, focus on systemic factors and macro-level processes. In contrast, attribution theory (Heider 1958), which posits that race-linked perceptions and stereotypes shape decisions, focuses on the micro-level processes through which decision makers assess and evaluate offenders and their crimes. A number of scholars, for example, argue that the decisions made by judges, probation officers, and other criminal justice officials reflect their beliefs about an offender's potential for rehabilitation, which in turn rest on their perceptions of the causes of criminal behavior (cf. Bridges and Steen 1998; Hawkins 1980). According to this perspective, decision makers attribute causality either to *internal* factors (i.e., personal characteristics of the individual, such as an antisocial personality, lack of remorse, refusal to admit guilt, or refusal to cooperate with officials) or to *external* factors (i.e., factors within the environment, such as delinquent peers, a dysfunctional family, drug or alcohol use, or poverty). Individuals whose crimes are attributed to internal factors are viewed as more responsible, and thus as more blameworthy, than those whose crimes are viewed as stemming from external forces; more important, these attributions affect the decisions that criminal justice officials make about the appropriate outcome for the offender. Offenders whose crimes are attributed to internal factors are treated more harshly than are offenders whose crimes are attributed to environmental factors.

George Bridges and Sara Steen (1998, 555), who contend that most studies of racial bias fail to identify the *mechanisms by which* race affects criminal justice decision making, suggest that causal attribution theory can be used to explain "the race–punishment relationship." Building on theories of social cognition, which hold that racial and ethnic stereotypes affect officials' perceptions of minority offenders, Bridges and Steen propose that the harsher treatment of racial minorities may be due to the fact that criminal justice officials attribute their crimes to internal forces while attributing crimes committed by whites to external forces. They further argue that these "differential attributions about the causes of crime by minorities and whites may contribute directly to differential assessments of offender dangerousness" and, thus, to "racial differences in perceived risk and recommended punishment" (Bridges and Steen 1998, 557). John Wooldredge and Amy Thistlethwaite (2004) take this argument one step further, contending that perceptions of minority offenders as chronic and violent often intersect with notions of class, perpetuating stereotypes of "disadvantaged" minority offenders.

A second theory focusing on the linkages between officials' perceptions of offenders and their crimes and their decisions regarding the appropriate outcome in the case is the theory of bounded rationality/uncertainty avoidance (Albonetti 1991), which incorporates both organizational theory and causal attribution theory. Structural organizational theorists (Simon 1957), for example, contend that decision makers rarely have the information needed to make fully rational decisions; because they cannot identify all of the possible alternatives or the costs and benefits of each known alternative, they cannot always select the alternative that will provide the greatest benefit at the lowest cost. Instead, they use a decision-making process characterized by "bounded rationality" to search for a solution that will avoid, or at least, reduce, the uncertainty of obtaining a desirable outcome. According to Celesta Albonetti (1991, 249), "Decision makers seek to achieve a measure of rationality by developing 'patterned responses'" that reflect stereotypes, prejudices, and predictions regarding likely outcomes.

Applied to the criminal justice process, the theory of bounded rationality/uncertainty avoidance suggests that decisions of criminal justice officials—and, especially, prosecutors, judges, and probation and parole officials—hinge on their assessments of the offender's likelihood of recidivism. Because officials typically do not have the information they need to make accurate predictions regarding the odds of reoffending, they develop patterned responses based on case and offender characteristics that they believe will increase or decrease the risk of recidivism. They attempt to reduce the uncertainty of their predictions by using stereotypes of crime seriousness, offender blameworthiness, and offender dangerousness to classify or categorize offenders and their crimes. Offenders who commit crimes perceived to be more serious are treated more harshly, as are offenders who are deemed more blameworthy and dangerous. Thus, stereotypes linking race, gender, and social class to the risk of recidivism result in harsher treatment for racial minorities, men, and the poor.

Although attribution theory can be applied to any aspect of criminal justice decision making, it is most frequently used to explain sentencing decisions. Another theoretical perspective that has been used to explain differential sentencing of whites and non-whites is the focal concerns perspective, which incorporates and builds on the uncertainty avoidance perspective. As developed by Steffensmeier and his colleagues (1998), this theoretical perspective suggests that judges' sentencing decisions are guided by three "focal concerns": their assessment of the blameworthiness of the offender; their desire to protect the community by incapacitating dangerous offenders or deterring potential offenders; and their concerns about the practical consequences, or social costs, of sentencing decisions.

The first focal concern—offender blameworthiness—reflects judges' assessments of the seriousness of the crime, the offender's prior criminal record, and the offender's motivation and role in the offense. Thus, offenders convicted of more serious crimes or who have more serious criminal histories will be viewed as more blameworthy; consequently, they will be sentenced more harshly. Offenders who have suffered prior victimization at the hands of others or who played a minor role in the offense, by contrast, will be seen as less culpable and will therefore be sentenced more leniently. The second focal concern—protecting the community—rests on judges' perceptions of dangerousness and predictions of the likelihood of recidivism. Like judges' assessments of offender blameworthiness, these perceptions are predicated on the nature of the offense and the offender's criminal history. Thus, judges seek to protect the community by imposing harsher sentences on repeat violent offenders or offenders whose risk of re-offending is high. The third focal concern—the practical consequences or social costs of sentencing decisions—reflects judges' perceptions regarding such things as the offender's "ability to do time," the costs of incarcerating offenders with medical conditions or mental health problems, and the "social costs" of imprisoning offenders responsible for the care of dependent children. It also includes judges' concerns about maintaining relationships with other members of the courtroom workgroup and protecting the reputation of the court.

Like Albonetti's theory of bounded rationality, the focal concerns theory assumes that judges typically do not have the information they need to accurately determine an offender's culpability, dangerousness, or likelihood of recidivism. As a result, they develop a "perceptual shorthand" (Hawkins 1980, 280; see also Bridges and Steen 1998) based on stereotypes and attributions that are themselves linked to offender characteristics such as race, ethnicity, gender, and age. Thus, "race, age, and gender will interact to influence sentencing because of images or attributions relating these statuses to membership in social groups thought to be dangerous and crime prone" (Steffensmeier, Ulmer, and Kramer 1998, 768).

Testing Attribution Theory

The role that racial/ethnic stereotypes play in court processing has been primarily used to address the more severe treatment received by blacks relative to whites (Albonetti 1997; Bridges and Steen 1998; Crawford, Chiricos, and Kleck 1998; Leiber 1994; Leiber and Jamieson 1995; Leiber and Stairs 1999; Sampson and Laub 1993; Steffensmeier and Demuth 2000; Steffensmeier, Ulmer, and Kramer 1998). However, attributions of race and ethnicity that extend those of black offenders have been proposed in the sentencing research. For example, criminal court studies call attention to the attributions that link Latinos to gangs, drugs, and crime and American Indians as "outsiders" that result in more punitive treatment relative to whites (Levy, Kunitz, and Everett 1969; Robbins 1984; Spohn and Holleran 2000; Steffensmeier and Demuth 2000; Zatz, Lujan, and Snyder-Joy 1991).

Policy Implications of Critical Race Theory, Conflict Theory, and Attribution Theory

More than one hundred years ago, the great African American scholar W.E.B. Du Bois (1903, 13) asserted, "The problem of the twentieth century is the problem of the color line." Racism and racial discrimination, according to Du Bois, were the central problems facing modern society. These problems have not disappeared. The blatant, overt and widespread racism that Du Bois decried may be a thing of the past, but racial and ethnic disparity and discrimination have not been banished from the criminal justice system. Although criminal justice scholars and policymakers continue to debate the meaning of the disproportionately high arrest and incarceration rates for blacks and Hispanics—with some contending that they reflect higher offending rates and others that they signal differential enforcement of the law—there is no denying the fact that blacks and Hispanics are arrested and imprisoned at disproportionately high rates. In 2004, for example, 12.6 percent of African American men, 3.6 percent of Hispanic men, and 1.7 percent of white men in their late twenties were in jail or prison (U.S. Bureau of Justice Statistics 2005). There were similar racial disparities among women. Across all age groups, the incarceration rate for African American women was two and a half times greater than the rate for Hispanic women and four and a half times greater than the rate for white women.

As we have shown, critical race theory, conflict theory, and attribution theory offer complementary explanations for the disproportionate number of blacks and Hispanics under the control of the criminal justice system. The principles that form the foundation of these theoretical perspectives also have implications for policy and practice. In the sections that follow, we explore these policy implications, focusing on racial profiling and sentencing.

Racial Profiling

Critical race perspectives, which contend that criminal justice agencies wield their considerable power to control and subjugate those—especially racial minorities—who threaten the political and economic elite and which emphasize the role played by stereotypes linked to race, ethnicity, gender, and class, provide a cogent and convincing explanation of the ubiquitous practice of racial profiling. As used here, the term "racial profiling" has a broader and more comprehensive meaning than the use of race as a reason for pretextual traffic stops. Like Kennedy (1997, 137), we define racial profiling as the practice of using race "as a proxy for an increased likelihood of criminal misconduct." Racial profiling, according to this definition, is therefore not confined to law enforcement officials and traffic stops. All criminal justice officials may attempt to simplify and routinize decision making by using race (and ethnicity) as a sign of an increased likelihood of criminality, with the result that racial and ethnic minorities are subject to more formal social control than whites. The higher level of suspicion that attaches to race means that blacks and Latinos will be subjected not only to "a lifetime of numerous stops" by the police (Kennedy 1997, 157), but also to higher bail and more stringent bail conditions, more severe charges and less favorable plea bargains, harsher sentences and more restrictive conditions of probation, and so on. What this means in practice, according to Kennedy (1997, 157), is that Latinos and blacks are forced "to pay a racial tax for the purpose of more efficient law enforcement."

Viewed in this way, it is clear that racial profiling, whether on the streets or in the courtroom, does not result simply from the prejudice of individual police officers, prosecutors, or judges. Rather, it is an institutional practice that is deeply embedded in the agencies of the criminal justice system and that is widely regarded as a legitimate and effective weapon in the war on crime. It is a practice that labels members of the so-called problem population potential criminals and likely recidivists, without any regard for the presumption of innocence or for the notion that individuals should be judged on the basis of their own conduct and not on the basis of racial and ethnic stereotypes. It is a practice that "does great damage to individuals, to the social fabric of our country, to the rule of law, and to the entire legal and criminal justice system" (Harris 2002, 241).

The difficulties inherent in making informed, rational, and appropriate decisions about individuals who find themselves in the arms of the law, coupled with the pervasiveness of attributions of danger, threat, and criminality that are linked to race and ethnicity, suggest that eliminating racial profiling from the criminal justice system will not be easy. The situation is further complicated by state and federal court decisions that, rather than condemning the practice of racial profiling as a violation of the Equal Protection Clause of the Fourteenth Amendment, place a stamp of approval—albeit a limited one—on its use in the context of law enforcement. Courts have ruled, for example, that the Fourteenth Amendment is not violated if race is only one of several factors taken into account or if race is not the dominant factor used in determining suspiciousness.[3] These rulings, according to Kennedy (1997, 148) are "profoundly wrong ... even if race is only one of several factors behind a decision, tolerating it at all means tolerating it as potentially the *decisive* factor." David Harris's (2002, 242) critique is even more pointed. He argues that using skin color as evidence of criminal involvement "means, in clear and unequivocal terms, that *skin color itself has been criminalized.*"

Analyzed from a critical race perspective, racial profiling is institutional discrimination. While most visible in the context of law enforcement and traffic stops, it is a practice that affects all aspects of the criminal justice system. It stigmatizes all members of a racial or ethnic group and, the Equal Protection Clause notwithstanding, treats people differently—that is, more punitively—on the basis of the color of their skin. Like the failure to protect black women from rape during slavery or the use of lynching against black men suspected of crimes against whites, racial profiling reflects both a devaluation of the lives of racial minorities and a belief that increased levels of formal social control are required to protect white privilege from the "problem population."

Sentencing and Incarceration

Although truth-in-sentencing, mandatory minimums, and sentencing guidelines were created to eliminate unwarranted disparity and produce certainly, fairness, and proportionality in sentencing (U.S. Sentencing Commission 2004), the negative impact of sentencing reforms on racial and ethnic groups—especially drug offenders—has been well documented (Crawford, Chiricos, and Kleck 1998; Kramer and Steffensmeier 1993; Tonry 1996). The one-hundred-to-one disparity in the drug-quantity thresholds that triggered lengthy mandatory minimum sentences for offenders convicted of offenses involving crack and powder cocaine resulted in disproportionately longer sentences for black offenders, who were substantially more likely than either white or Hispanic offenders to be convicted of crack cocaine offenses. The crime control policies pursued during the war on drugs and habitual offender laws such as "three strikes" laws also contributed to an unprecedented number of racial and ethnic minorities in the nation's prisons.

After decades of sentencing research documenting the racial and ethnic biases in sentencing processes and outcomes, the U.S. Sentencing Commission, on December 11, 2007, amended the Federal Sentencing Guidelines to address the disparities between crack cocaine and powder cocaine offenses. The commission decided to apply the changes to the guidelines retroactively to deal with the more punitive treatment received by crack cocaine

3. *U.S. v. Martinez-Fuerte*, 428 U.S. 543 (1976); *State v. Dean*, 543 P.2d, 427 (Arizona 1975); *U.S. v. Weaver*, 966 F.2d 391 (CA 8 1992).

offenders. Although this represents a significant step toward addressing the racial biases of federal sentencing policy, the federal sentencing judge has discretion in deciding whether a crack cocaine offender is eligible for a lower sentence and for how much the sentence should be reduced. As of May 31, 2008, more than seven thousand crack cocaine offenders had been released since the amendment to the guidelines was implemented (U.S. Sentencing Commission 2008). While it is too early to assess the impact of these sentencing reductions, efforts aimed at correcting the biases produced by the federal sentencing guidelines are significant and noteworthy.

Prosecutors' discretion in charging and plea bargaining has also been linked to racial and ethnic disparities in court processes. Although minimal research has been conducted on prosecutorial practices such as charging and dismissal of offenses, researchers have concluded that racial and ethnic disparities are produced by plea bargaining (Kautt and Spohn 2002; Nagel 1990; Rhodes 1991; Roberts 1994; Tonry 1996). Eliminating biases during the prosecutorial phase requires resources and information. To make informed decisions about the appropriate sentences for offenders, especially drug offenders, mechanisms must be in place that reduce uncertainly about a perpetrator's risk of reoffending. Identifying the services that offenders need and implementing effective substance-abuse treatment programs hinges on comprehensive risk assessments and the willingness of court actors to seek alternatives to incarceration. This, of course, requires resources and the collaboration of prosecutors, defense attorneys, and probation services.

As previously discussed, racial and ethnic disparities can also be attributed to probation officers' assessments of offenders (Bridges and Steen 1998). Attributions of offender dangerousness and threat that are linked to race and ethnicity result in limited opportunities to receive services and treatment for the problems related to substance abuse and mental health that plague most offenders in the justice system. As sentencing policies continue to be monitored for racial biases, the examination of disparities that arise from pre-sentencing practices are often difficult to assess, given the few data sets that contain presentencing data (U.S. Sentencing Commission 2004). Whether it is racial and ethnic stereotypes, higher rates of involvement in crime, or incomplete information about offenders' risk, the impact of probation, prosecution, and sentencing practices on minorities will have a lasting, profound effect.

References

Albonetti, C. 1991. Integration of theories to explain judicial discretion. *Social Problems* 38: 47–266.

———. 1997. Sentencing under the Federal Sentencing Guidelines: Effects of defendant characteristics, guilty pleas, and departures on sentencing outcomes for drug offenses, 1991–1992. *Law and Society Review* 31:789–822.

Anderson, M., and P. H. Collins (Eds.). 2007. *Race, class, and gender: An anthology.* 7th ed. Wadsworth.

Bell, D. 1992. *Race, racism, and American law.* 3rd ed. Little, Brown.

Blalock, H. M. 1967. *Towards a theory of minority group relations.* Capricorn Books.

Box, S., and C. Hale. 1985. Unemployment, imprisonment, and prison overcrowding. *Contemporary Crises* 9:209–238.

Bridges, G. S., and R. H. Crutchfield. 1988. Law, social standing, and racial disparities in imprisonment. *Social Forces* 66:601–616.

Bridges, G. S., and S. Steen. 1998. Racial disparities in official assessments of juvenile offending: Attributional stereotypes as mediating mechanisms. *American Sociological Review* 65:554–570.

Britt, C. 2000. Social context and racial disparities in punishment decisions. *Justice Quarterly* 17:707–732.

Brown, T. 2003. Critical race theory speaks to the sociology of mental health. *Journal of Health and Social Behavior* 44:292–301.

Chambliss, W. J., and R. B. Seidman. 1971. *Law, order and power.* Addison-Wesley.

———. 1982. *Law, order, and power.* 2nd ed. Addison-Wesley.

Chiricos, T. G., and W. D. Bales. 1991. Unemployment and punishment: An empirical assessment. *Criminology* 29:701–724.

Chiricos, T. G., M. Hogan, and M. Gertz. 1997. Racial composition of neighborhoods and fear of crime. *Criminology* 35:107–131.

Collins, P. H. 2000. *Black feminist thought, knowledge, consciousness, and the politics of empowerment.* Routledge.

———. 2004. *Black sexual politics: African Americans, gender, and the new racism.* Routledge.

Combahee River Collective. 2001 (1972). A black feminist statement. In *Theorizing feminism: Parallel trends in the humanities and social sciences.* Ed. A. Herman and A Stewart, 29–37. Westview Press.

Corzine, J., J. Creech, and L. Corzine. 1983. Black concentration and lynchings in the South: Testing Blalock's power-threat hypothesis. *Social Forces* 61:774–796.

Crawford, C., T. D. Chiricos, and G. Kleck. 1998. Race, racial threat and the sentencing of habitual offenders. *Criminology* 36:481–511.

Crenshaw, K. 1992. Whose story is it anyway? Feminist and antiracist appropriations of Anita Hill. In *Race-ing justice, en-gendering power: Essays on Clarence Thomas, Anita Hill, and the social construction of social reality.* Ed. T. Morrison, 402–440. Pantheon Books.

———. 2002a. Mapping the margins: Intersectionality, identity politics, and violence against women of color. *Stanford Law Review* 43:1241–1299.

———. 2002b. The first decade: Critical reflections, or "a foot in the closing door." In *Crossroads, directions, and a new critical race theory.* Ed. F. Valdes, J. M. Culp, and A. P. Harris, 9–31. Temple University Press.

Crenshaw, K., N. Gotanda, G. Peller, and K. Thomas (Eds.). 1995. *Critical race theory: The key writings that formed the movement.* New Press.

D'Alessio, S. J., D. Eitle, and L. Stolzenberg. 2005. The impact of serious crime, racial and economic inequality on private police size. *Social Science Research* 34:267–282.

Davis, A. 1981. *Women, race, and class.* Random House.

Delgado, R., and J. Stefancic. 2001. *Critical race theory: An introduction.* New York University Press.

Du Bois, W.E.B. 1903. *The souls of black folk.* McClurg.

Eitle, D., S. J. D'Alessio, and L. Stolzenberg. 2002. Racial threat and social control: A test of the political, economic, and threat of black crime hypotheses. *Social Forces* 81: 557–576.

Harris, D. 2002. *Profiles in injustice: Why racial profiling cannot work.* New Press.

Hawkins, D. 1980. Perceptions of punishment for crime. *Deviant Behavior* 1:193–215.

———. 1987. Beyond anomalies: Rethinking the conflict perspective on race and criminal punishment. *Social Forces* 65:719–745.

Heider, F. 1958. *The psychology of interpersonal relations.* John Wiley and Sons.

hooks, b. 1984. *Feminist theory: From margin to center.* South End Press.

Irwin, J. 1985. *The jail: Managing the underclass in American society.* University of California Press.

Jackson, P. I., and L. Carroll. 1981. Race and the war on crime: The sociopolitical determinants of municipal police expenditures in 90 non-southern cities. *American Sociological Review* 46:390–405.

Jacobs, D., J. T. Carmichael, and S. L. Kent. 2005. Vigilantism, current racial threat, and death sentences. *American Sociological Review* 70:656–677.

Kautt, P., and C. Spohn. 2002. Crack-ing down on black drug offenders? Testing for interactions among offenders' race, drug type, and sentencing strategy in federal drug sentences. *Justice Quarterly* 19:1–36.

Kennedy, R. 1997. *Race, crime, and the law.* Random House.

Kramer, J. H., and D. Steffensmeier. 1993. Race and imprisonment decisions. *Sociological Quarterly* 34:357–376.

LaFree, G. 1989. *Rape and criminal justice: The social construction of sexual assault.* Wadsworth.

Leiber, M. J. 1994. Comparison of juvenile court outcomes for Native Americans, African Americans, and whites. *Justice Quarterly* 11:257–279.

Leiber, M. J., and K. M. Jamieson. 1995. Race and decision making within juvenile justice: The importance of context. *Journal of Quantitative Criminology* 11:363–388.

Leiber, M., and J. M. Stairs. 1999. Race, context, and the use of intake diversion. *Journal of Research in Crime and Delinquency* 36:56–86.

Lerner, G. (Ed.). 1972. *Black women in white America: A documentary history.* Pantheon.

Levy, J., S. Kunitz, and S. Everett. 1969. Navajo criminal homicide. *Southwestern Journal of Anthropology* 25:24–152.

Liska, A. E. 1987. A critical perspective on macro perspectives on crime control. *Annual Review of Sociology* 13:67–88.

———. 1994. Modeling the conflict perspective of social control. In *Inequality, crime and social control.* Ed. G. S. Bridges and M. A. Myers, 53–71. Westview Press.

Liska, A. E., and M. B. Chamlin. 1984. Social structure and crime control among macrosocial units. *American Journal of Sociology* 90:383–395.

Liska, A. E., J. J. Lawrence, and M. Benson. 1981. Perspectives on the legal order: Capacity for social control. *American Journal of Sociology* 87:413–426.

Liska, A. E., J. J. Lawrence, and S. Sanchirico. 1982. Fear of crime as a social fact. *Social Force* 60:760–770.

McIntosh, P. 2007. White privilege and male privilege: An account of coming to see correspondence through work in women's studies. In *Race, class, and gender: An anthology.* 7th ed. Ed. M. Anderson and P. H. Collins, 94–105. Wadsworth.

Myers, M. A., and S. M. Talarico. 1987. *Social contexts of criminal sentencing.* Springer-Verlag.

Nagel, I. H. 1990. Structuring sentencing discretion: The new Federal Sentencing Guidelines. *Journal of Criminal Law and Criminology* 80:883–943.

Peterson, R. D., and J. Hagan. 1984. Changing conceptions of race: Toward an account of anomalous findings of sentencing research. *American Sociological Review* 49:56–70.

Petrocelli, M., A. R. Piquero, and M. R. Smith. 2003. Conflict theory and racial profiling: An empirical analysis of police stop data. *Journal of Criminal Justice* 31:1–11.

Quinney, R. 1970. *The social reality of crime.* Little, Brown.

———. 1974. *Critique of legal order: Crime control in a capitalist society.* Boston: Little, Brown.

———. 1977. *Class, state and crime.* David McKay.

Rhodes, W. 1991. Federal criminal sentencing: Some measurement issues with application to pre-guideline sentencing disparity. *Journal of Criminal Law and Criminology* 81:1002–1033.

Robbins, S. P. 1984. Anglo concepts and Indian reality: A study of juvenile delinquency. *Journal of Contemporary Social Work* 85:235–241.

Roberts, D. 1997. *Policing the black body: Race, reproduction, and the meaning of liberty.* Random House.

Roberts, J. V. 1994. The role of criminal record in the Federal Sentencing Guidelines. *Criminal Justice Ethics* 13:21–30.

Sampson, R. J., and J. H. Laub. 1993. Structural variations in juvenile court processing: Inequality, the underclass, and social control. *Law and Society Review* 27:285–312.

Sentencing Project. 2004. Schools and prisons: Fifty years after *Brown v. the Board of Education.* Report. Sentencing Project, Washington, D.C.

Simon, H. 1957. *Administrative behavior: A study of decision making processes in administrative organization.* Free Press.

Spitzer, S. 1975. Toward a Marxian theory of deviance. *Social Problems* 22:638–651.

Spohn, C. 2000. Thirty years of sentencing reform: A quest for a racially neutral sentencing process. In *Policies, processes, and decisions of the criminal justice system*, Vol. 3, *Criminal Justice* 2000, 427–501. U.S. Department of Justice.

Spohn, C., and D. Holleran. 2000. The imprisonment penalty paid by young, unemployed black and Hispanic male offenders. *Criminology* 38:501–526.

Steffensmeier, D., and S. Demuth. 2000. Ethnicity and sentencing outcomes in U.S. federal courts: Who is punished more harshly? *American Sociological Review* 65:705–729.

Steffensmeier, D., J. Ulmer, and J. Kramer. 1998. The interaction of race, gender, and age in criminal sentencing: The punishment costs of being young, black, and male. *Criminology* 36:363–397.

Stevenson, B. 1995. Black family structure in colonial and antebellum Virginia. In *The decline in marriage among African Americans: Causes, consequences, and policy implications.* In B. Tucker and C. Mitchell-Kernan, 27–58. Russell Sage Foundation.

Stolzenberg, L., S. J. D'Alessio, and D. Eitle. 2004. A multilevel test of racial threat theory. *Criminology* 42:673–698.

Tolnay, S. E., and E. M. Beck. 1994. Lethal social control in the South: Lynchings and executions between 1880 and 1930. In *Inequality, crime and social control.* Ed. G. S. Bridges and M. A. Myers, 176–194. Westview Press.

Tonry, M. 1996. *Sentencing matters: Studies in crime and public policy.* Oxford University Press.

Turk, A. 1969. *Criminality and legal order.* Rand McNally.

U.S. Bureau of Justice Statistics. 2005. *Prison and jail inmates at midyear 2004.* Department of Justice.

U.S. Sentencing Commission. 2004. *Fifteen years of guidelines sentencing: An assessment of how well the federal criminal justice system is achieving the goals of sentencing reform.* U.S. Sentencing Commission.

———. 2008. *U.S. Sentencing Commission: Preliminary crack cocaine retroactivity data report.* U.S. Sentencing Commission.

Valdes, F., J. M. Culp, and A. P. Harris. 2002. Introduction: Battles waged, won, and lost: Critical race theory at the turn of the millennium. In *Crossroads, directions, and a new critical race Theory.* Ed. F. Valdes, J. M. Culp, and A. P. Harris, 1–8. Temple University Press.

Walker, S., C. Spohn, and M. DeLone. 2007. *The color of justice: Race, ethnicity and crime in America.* 4th ed. Thomson/Wadsworth.

Wooldredge, J., and A. Thistlethwaite. 2004. Bilevel disparities in court dispositions for intimate assault. *Criminology* 42:417–456.

Zatz, M. S. 1987. The changing forms of racial/ethnic biases in sentencing. *Journal of Research in Crime and Delinquency* 24:69–92.

Zatz, M. S., C. C. Lujan, and Z. K. Snyder-Joy. 1991. American Indians and criminal justice: Some conceptual and methodological considerations. In *Race and criminal justice.* Ed. M. J. Lynch and E. B. Patterson, 100–112. Harrow and Heston.

Reading 3.3

Meda Chesney-lind

Meda Chesney-Lind Fenstermaker

1. *Joanne Belknap (2004) describes you as "the mother of feminist criminology." At this point in your career, what does this title mean to you? Is it something you envisioned for yourself when you began your career? Is it something you ever imagined when you were on faculty at a community college early in your career?*

PHOTO 3.3.1

I'm a bit surprised and honored that someone would think of me in those terms. Certainly, when I began doing work on women and crime, I was well aware that there were risks doing the sort of work I was drawn to, particularly if one were looking for an academic job. Some of my closest friends were being denied tenure for doing what I considered to be outstanding work on gender. So, actually I went to the community colleges so that I could continue to study women and crime, even though it was a trifle hard, given the workload.

I also don't know that I can say that I thought much about my "career" as an academic. I backed into teaching in the community colleges to support my graduate studies. Then I got a job, and finally I was able to re-invent myself several times so that I could do the sort of research that blends my twin passions of gender and criminology. I know this sounds terribly accidental, but again, in the years that I was in college, there were so many doors that were effectively closed to us (law and medicine) and what was offered (traditional women's jobs), was poorly paid and dead end, that the academy seemed to offer those of us in my generation some semblance of opportunity. While much of this was, in retrospect, an illusion, we did not quite know that then. We had energy, youth, and the 60s at our backs, recall.

2. *One reason you may have that title is that your work has shaped discussions of sex, gender, and justice significantly, and in pioneering ways. What encourages you most about the development of feminist criminology over the course of your career? What troubles you the most?*

I never imagined that I would see so many young women in the field of criminology and criminal justice. This is just wonderful for the field. In a recent analysis I did of the program of the American Society of Criminology Meetings for 2009, I discovered exactly how powerful the focus on gender and crime has become. The meeting was organized into 137 area/sub-area groupings, with 1,419 submissions in total. The largest number of submissions to any one category on the program came with 52 panels submitted to the area/sub-area entitled "Gender, Crime and Justice: Gender and Offending." Two non-gender topics tied for second with 41 submissions each ("Corrections: Reentry" and "Juvenile Delinquency and Juvenile Justice Policy: Causes and Correlates of Delinquency"). These were followed by "Gender, Crime and Justice: Sexual and Physical Violence Against Women" with 38 submissions. Other areas of the field, even rather significant ones drew far fewer submissions; for example, "Theory and Research on Violence and Crime: Causes of Violence" (12) or "Organized, Organizational and White Collar Crime: White Collar Crime" (15). Essentially two of the top four areas in the entire field of criminology (as arrayed by the panels for the main academic body of the field) were feminist criminology topics. That said, this kind of success can sometimes be a challenge to manage; first, there's just the sheer work involved when we, the women, have to put together a huge chunk of the ASC program. I also suspect that some of our "success" is a function of the fact that these areas are seen as "add-ons" to the important (read "male") criminology, so despite our numbers, we still have a ways to go to be seen as a meaningful part of the field.

Christine Wenneras and Agnes Wold's work, published in the prestigious journal *Science* (1997), explored the awarding of postdoctoral fellowships in Sweden where because of a lawsuit, they were able to review actual applications as well as the score sheets. After a careful regression assessment of nine possible variables (including a number of "productivity" variables such as numbers of publications, citations, and journal prestige), they found that only two variables: "being male" and "knowing a reviewer" affected getting one of these awards. They concluded that a woman would need to be "on average 2.5 times as good" on their measures to be rated as highly as a male by reviewers. Sadly, this did not surprise me, and despite the age of the study, I fear things are not much better today.

Do you think that in some ways, the shift to the study of "gender and crime" has become disconnected from its feminist origins? Or is feminist criminology alive and well?

The Division on Women and Crime of the American Society of Criminology recently launched *Feminist Criminology* as their journal, so that is a good sign. However, the political backlash against feminism (and the word *feminism*) that was launched in the Reagan era has clearly taken its toll. The concept here is semantic derogation, where words attached to groups that are being vilified themselves become problematic (and people want to distance themselves from those words). Think of all the ways that African Americans have referred to themselves over the past centuries from "colored" to "Negro" to "Black" to African American. That said, we have to fight to avoid collusion with efforts to erase the word *feminist* from our lexicon. Being scholars who advocate feminism means that we understand that gender is a fundamental organizing principle of the social world, *and* we are committed to working to make that social world more equitable (Sprague 2005: 3). For feminist criminology, that means working to understand how both racism and sexism interact with (and are enmeshed within) the formal system of social control. That means researching and documenting not just gender, but also patriarchy; studying and explicating not just race but also institutional racism.

Gender has become a relatively "hot" topic in the academy (and this is reflected in the ASC program numbers), and I'm somewhat ambivalent about that "success." But I am greatly encouraged that instead of the "old" days when we had (and I remember those times) one panel on gender for the entire Pacific Sociological Association, we are a huge part of the program, and people want to be identified with this research (instead of fleeing it).

3. *You have written about your life as an academic "on the margins." Since so many feminist scholars speak of their careers that way, what "margins" do you find yourself on? Why is it so important to study the experiences of girls in the juvenile justice system* outside *of Criminal Justice or Criminology departments? What does a feminist analysis add to these conversations that is otherwise left out?*

Working within a vital Women's Studies Program means that I'm often challenged both theoretically and methodologically. Most recently, I have been teaching our feminist methods class, and I confess that I've learned as much as I've taught. Feminist scholars like Joey Sprague have urged critical scholars to re-think "methodology" with an eye toward epistemology, research methodology, and research methods (2005). More than that, feminists have called attention to the shortcomings of masculinist "science" which is generally unreflective of important issues of power and authority in research settings. Other good ideas that come from feminist methodology include "paying attention to what's missing," the importance of "studying up" instead of "studying down," and working from the standpoint of the disadvantaged.

Feminist theory has also a great deal to offer theoretical criminology. Right now, I'm very much interested in the importance of "theorizing patriarchy" to use Sylvia Walby's (1989) wonderful phrase. Those of us interested in the formal systems of social control obviously need to think about the ways that patriarchy interfaces with the criminal justice system. Much of my early work focused on this, and I'm very interested in returning to that project in my next book.

4. *The 21st century opened with a "mean girl" craze. It is said "mean girls" can be found everywhere. Even in the academy? If so, what does this dynamic say about feminism in general and feminist criminology in particular?*

We know that disempowered groups are always encouraged to engage in what Freire called "horizontal violence," often policing their own members. The social context for girls and women fighting is patriarchy, where men often are the reason women are fighting, the audience for the fight, and the winners at the end. I'm not a big fan of the "mean girl" stuff, because as Katherine Irwin and I said in *Beyond Bad Girls* (2007), the stereotype tracks too closely to the images of women as "manipulative bitches." We also know that covert aggression is not the exclusive province of girls (think Karl Rove). We certainly need to know about covert or indirect aggression so that when it is deployed against us, we know what is going on, and can deal with it effectively.

That said, not all feminists are women and not all women are feminists. Indeed, there are some women, including women in the academy, who pride themselves on being "one of the boys." So, sometimes you are blindsided if you think that you are speaking to a colleague, assuming like values and orientations, only to discover that you have been "played" by someone who is far more interested in male approval than you imagined. That's why I mentioned that *all* of us need to be aware of the possibility of covert aggression coming from a variety of possible sources. Some of the biggest perpetrators, I think, are men, but we can all recall times when a woman disappointed us. But again, there's plenty of reward for women to betray other women to please men, so we just go on. And what gets us through is the friendships between women. They listen to the tales, provide solace, and patch us up, so we can get back into the fray.

5. *You are an inspiration for both scholars and practitioners. Who are your intellectual inspirations? How do you maintain your energy and interests even as criminal and juvenile justice systems continue to expand their punitive reach into the lives of adolescent girls?*

Some of my greatest role models are visionary practitioners who have worked with girls and women in the criminal justice system. I'm thinking here of people like Marian Daniel, who was the author of one of my favorite assessments about delinquency programs. She famously noted that "For years, people assumed that all you have to do to make a program designed for boys work for girls is to paint the walls pink and take out the urinals" (Daniel, 1996: 34). Marian started a female-only probation program in Baltimore, Maryland; it didn't cost a penny more, and it got girls out of detention. Marian has a wonderful sense of humor, and she's a great role model to others in the field, particularly younger African American professionals. I'm profiling her in the work I'm currently doing for the National Institute of Justice. I think we need to forge more professional and person relationships across the professional divides, and that also has the effect of bringing us in touch with a far more diverse group of colleagues.

Of course, as a young scholar, I had my share of mentors and supporters. Here, a shout out to Lee Bowker, in particular, who helped both Joy Pollock and myself when we were students at Whitman College. Lee later went on to do pioneering work on violence against women, and also has served as an expert witness to get women out of prison who are doing time for killing their abusers. Lee was a fighter, not a button-down scholar, and when I first met him (and to this day) he was quite irreverent. I guess I learned from the best!

6. *What exactly does it mean to be a feminist criminologist during a time when many of our students are reluctant to even identify as feminists, since they are told that if they do they won't get a job. What advice do you give students who want to do what you do?*

Whenever I hear statements like this about feminism, I'm always tempted to open with one of my favorite quotes: "I myself have never been able to find out precisely what feminism is: I only know that people call me a feminist whenever I express sentiments that differentiate me from a doormat or a prostitute—Rebecca West, 1913." But seriously, the word *feminist* has been subjected to two decades of demonization by a relentless political backlash, so it is no mystery why younger women shrink from the label. In a misogynistic world, which has not receded despite the recent election, it's still bad to be a strong woman.

Of course, being in Women's Studies I am also aware that the word does not work for many who are seeking justice for girls and women. bell hooks famously noted that we have trouble coming to a consensus about "what feminism is" and she argues for a "shift in expression from 'I am a feminist' to 'I advocate feminism'" in recognition that the feminist struggle is really about ending sexism and all forms of group oppression (hooks 2000: 32).

As to what advice I'd give those starting out, that is a hard question to answer, but I would say that you need to follow your passion. I also think that you need to be committed to more than your "career" to make any lasting difference. Candidly, I didn't start out to have a career, it happened along the way as I was trying to make the world a better place. Fortunately, some folks thought that what I was finding was worth reading. Now, I just wish we could end mass incarceration in my lifetime. I feel as if it happened on "our" watch, and we need to be part of dismantling it.

> *A number of scholars now argue that the national investment in mass incarceration has undermined the investment in other important social institutions, including higher education. What implications might the nation's shifting priorities have on the critical research and writing conducted by scholars like you?*

We held a Teach In on the draconian budget cuts on our campus this fall, and my job was to talk about our Governor's choice to fund prison cells instead of classrooms. In the current great recession, I'm astonished that so little is being said about the enormous costs of our twin addictions to militarism and incarceration. Since I'm wearing my criminological hat, let me talk about the cost of imprisonment. If you look at the data over time, it's very clear that the nation pulled money out of higher education in particular; between 1987 and 2007 the amount of money the State has spent on corrections more than doubled (increasing 127%) while funding for higher education stayed essentially static increasing by an anemic 21% during the same time period (Pew Center on the States 2008). Since the cost of college soared during those decades, most of the increase was born by our students and their families as tuitions soared, and low income youth struggle to pay the new surging bills for even "public education."

Since most states are now struggling to pay the bills, you would think that the failed and demonstrably racist "war on drugs," which has fueled the prison boom, would be the subject of a vibrant discussion (at both the local and national level), and yet with the exception of Senator Jim Webb, most national leaders, including our first African American President, are curiously silent. We need to educate our students that they have been directly harmed by this cost-shifting so that they can put ending mass incarceration on their "to do" list.

7. *As a feminist criminologist, the voices of girls and women are central to your work. What challenges does this commitment pose in the more quantitatively oriented social sciences? What is the benefit of remaining committed to your approach?*

Well, to quote Lee Bowker about the publication bias in what he called "gatekeeper" journals when they received work that is feminist in content: "I think I have found the answer to the question, 'What is the correct methodology for carrying out feminist research?' It is 'Whatever methodology you didn't use'" (Bowker 1988: 171).

As someone seeking to use my research to better the lives of girls and women, I actually advocate a mixed methods approach. That way, the qualitative work we do can't be quite as easily dismissed. But of course, we have to talk to girls and women, and actually you learn an incredible amount when you do this. I also urge us to read the books that are increasingly being produced by the vibrant Convict Criminology crowd, though they lament having so few women in their ranks. But conversations, particularly if they are gathered in a more naturalistic setting where you can also see the context that produces the commentary is very, very important to understanding the "choices" that young people are being forced to make. It would be wonderful if we could all do this the way the "classic" anthropologists and ethnographers did their work, but that often is not realistic. Yet I know of outstanding work that is being done in feminist criminology by emerging scholars that mix advocacy for girls (and gender-responsive programming) with interviews/conversations with girls in those settings. It's hard listening to some of these stories, but very, very important. I also think increasingly about involving young women in participatory action research would be a good goal, so that everyone is engaged in changing and making the world better for young people.

8. *Much of your work—professional and personal—is committed to "truth telling." You've told the truth in your research about girls' experiences with victimization and their subsequent entrance into the criminal justice system. More recently, you've told the truth about girls' violence and the conditions of detention facilities for girls. On your own campus, you have told the truth about seemingly trivial yet insidious displays of sexism and misogyny. Telling the truth is an important feminist ideal but given the popular feminist backlash and increased opportunities for women to be "one of the boys," as you say, is it worth it?*

As you get older, you realize that you have warm and wonderful memories of people who are no longer here. That's very hard, but it also focuses the mind. Our lives are all we ultimately have as our legacy, and you want to look backwards and be proud of what you did and how you lived your life. I've told younger women who speak of the challenges they face as they quit jobs rather than do something demeaning (or put up with harassment), that they will look back on those moments as a badge of honor, even if it is quite stressful at the time. So, nope, no regrets—at least about the things you mention. If anything, I wish I'd done more or accomplished more, especially in my own home town, which runs terrible facilities for girls (and boys). My current project is to document those conditions to try to shame the polite judges that occasionally have to listen to me, to do far better for Hawaii's young people than they have. Of course, that's my beat, but every one of us needs to remember those under lock and key, and not get complacent about what's happening behind those doors. I learned this first teaching in prison, and I re-learn it every decade. The fact that during my "watch" the United States has become the world's largest incarcerator horrifies me. As many have noted, the criminal justice system has functioned really for the past 30 years or so as the "new Jim Crow." Think Henry Louis Gates who was arrested for breaking into his own home.

9. *Recently, your work has extended beyond girls' pathways to detention and incarceration to the conditions in which girls are confined. What do we need to know about the conditions in which girls are held?*

One of the things that struck me looking at the two sides of my town's detention center was the degree to which things have *not* changed in these facilities. Certainly, I'd given talks to workers about girls' needs, but when it came to the place where girls (and boys) are locked up, nothing had changed in the 40 years since I first saw the place. We still have way too much idleness, isolation, and the girls get far fewer programs than the boys. The boys fear the violent guards and other violent boys; the girls are over-policed and over-punished. The girls have far less space, and the boys have a basketball court, but many are in "lock-down" in their rooms. Too much isolation, too little school, and virtually no one visits. I gathered data in the room where the visitors were supposed to come, and almost no one ever showed up. The few parents I did see were visiting boys. I never saw a white girl in the facility, though there were a few white boys. Almost all were kids of color. I tried to tell these stories to the judges who put the kids there, but I was listened to politely and then ushered out. They were very busy in their committee meetings. Again, I feel so frustrated and guilty that I've not done more. We also need to look at ways to work around these issues that are more accessible to those who have the power to change things. I'm not sure academic articles are enough, though.

The Tenth Question

What was the worst (or most difficult, or most embarrassing) interview/field encounter you've had?

Well, I was teaching in the prison, and the course was Marriage and the Family. One of my worst attributes is that I often speak without thinking. In this case, one of the young women taking my class came up to ask me about a project she wanted to do for the course (the facility, at that time was a mixed facility holding both women and men). She said she'd like to study incest, and without thinking I said, "Why, that's a pretty boutique project." At which point she said, "Well most of the ladies in here have had that experience." I gulped, and said, you should definitely do the project, which she did. That's how I learned about the importance of studying sexual violence in the lives of women in prison. And it's also why I dedicated my first book to Michele Alvey, who taught me that and gave me permission to use her name. So, like I said, it's important to listen to the voices of girls and women; I know that first hand.

What did you really want to do for a living? What were you afraid you might end up doing?

Well, as a girl I never even got interviewed for the jobs we currently dismiss as paying too little (like working in a fast food place or in retail). I ended up not once, but twice, working as a nurse's aide. You can pretty much always get those jobs, because they are pretty grim and awful. So, since I don't have to give folks enemas and change sheets damp with urine, I figure I'm pretty lucky. Even there, I learned as Barbara Ehrenreich did, that there's plenty of unity among the women who work in those settings, so even that wasn't so bad. We were treated badly by just about everybody, but we found our ways to enjoy work and each other. As to what did I really want to do? Well, as a girl I really enjoyed the theater, and I especially liked comedy, so I think that was great training for what I'm doing now. Do I want to do theater now? Nope, too much night work and too much traveling.

What's the study you never pursued, but always wanted to?

I'm a collector of things, people, papers, ideas, etc. I have actually read a study of garage sales, and I'd love to do a study of thrift shops. They are incredibly rich sociologically; they are women's spaces (or were until recently), they are very mixed in terms of social class, and depending on the thrift store, there's a sort of camaraderie that develops among the shoppers, since it's really a treasure hunt as much as anything else. And people enjoy what they find. I did a very early paper on thrift shopping as a graduate student, and much more recently, I spoke at a criminology meeting about the "Thrill of the Gather." I'd like to do more with this idea at some point. Another unanticipated thing has happened to me here in Hawaii much more recently. About a year ago, I figured out that S. Ann Dunham Soetoro (Barack Obama's mother) did her BA, her MA, and her PhD here at the University of Hawaii at Manoa in Anthropology. In fact, she and I were getting our degrees at about the same time and in the same building. Last year, about this time I organized a colloquium on her wonderful dissertation on Indonesian crafts, featuring her dissertation chair, two friends and colleagues of hers that worked with her at different times in Indonesia, and her daughter, Maya Soetoro-Ng. I find myself thinking about her and the life she had here, which was cut tragically short by cancer. I've also been instrumental in helping her dissertation chair and one of those colleagues edit down her 1057-page dissertation into book length. I know that who her son and daughter are is very much tied up with who she was, and there is so much of her and her mother here in the Islands. I cannot do this work, I keep telling myself. I'm a criminologist, and I know nothing about biography, and yet as I told Maya recently in an e-mail, I find Ann popping up in my life in odd ways, so who knows?

Reading 3.4

Victor Rios

Victor Rios Fenstermaker

1. *Your book,* Punished: The Criminalization of Inner City Youth, *is drawn from the three years you spent shadowing African American and Latino youth in Oakland, California. What led you to consider a comparative analysis of youth experiences? What did you learn about punishment experienced by youth from different racial and ethnic backgrounds?*

PHOTO 3.4.1

Comparing the experiences of young Blacks and Latinos happened organically. I grew up in Oakland in a traditionally Black neighborhood that had recently experienced a large influx of Latinos. By the time I came of age, I noticed that Blacks and Latinos in my neighborhood encountered very similar experiences with domestic, street, and state violence. As I began my study I decided I wanted to understand how these young people made sense of these experiences. In my fieldwork I learned that race, of course, does matter, that Black youths often face more dire consequences and heavier criminalization. Moreover, Black and Latino youth respond in very similar ways to punishment, they resist it, they embrace it, or they find creative ways to survive it.

Scholars have written about the role that race or ethnicity plays in building relationships with respondents in the field, and in how our representations are received in the academy. In this volume, for example, Mary Pattillo writes, "While I think there is a certain authority attributed

Victor Rios Fenstermaker, "Victor Rios," *Sociologists Backstage: Answers to 10 Questions About What They Do,* ed. Sarah Fenstermaker and Nikki Jones, pp. 111–119. Copyright © 2011 by Taylor & Francis Group. Reprinted with permission.

to those of us who are Black and study Black people, there is also the kernel of skepticism that we are too close to our subjects (i.e., indigenous ethnographers) and thus not fully objective." How did sharing an ethnic background with one group in your study but not the other influence your fieldwork? Was it harder or easier to gain access or build trust with some boys? Do you feel as if your analysis of the experiences of Latino youth is given more "authority" than your analysis of the experiences of Black youth?

Although I brought my own biography to this study, that was not enough to give me the insights I needed to develop conceptualizations for understanding the conditions that marginalized young men from Oakland were facing. Based on my experience of reading theories of crime, delinquency, race, and punishment, I had my own ideas about youth and punishment in Oakland. However, these ideas only applied to me. I needed to go beyond my own experience and talk to people to see if they applied to others more widely. Experience alone did not guarantee entrée for me; I had to find other ways to tap into the world of these young people. Some Latino youth never gave me their trust, while some Black youth trusted me right away. The first questions in many youths' minds when they first met me were, "Is this guy a cop?" "Is he a probation officer?"

Colleagues have often wanted me to provide them with something like a "four food group" analysis of the boys. The expectation has been that I tell a racial story for each group. However, the boys I studied were more complex than this. Some racial differences did exist but their experiences and perspectives had more in common than I expected to find. It is important to accept the fact that many urban neighborhoods in the United States have become multi-ethnic and multi-racial. In my study, this meant that the boys shared a common sub-culture and understanding of social control that transcended racial common sense. However, I do realize that not being racialized as a Black person, I certainly missed some key insights from individuals who have grown up in the Black experience. I have to be the first to acknowledge that my observation and interviews with Black youth are different from what they would have been if a Black researcher who grew up in Oakland had conducted this study. I believe that after enough time in the field, any researcher, despite his or her background, could find the general patterns that I uncovered in the field: punitive social control, pervasive punishment, the youth control complex, and the need for a "public relations" approach to social control. However, access to certain interactions, more minute patterns, and specific community knowledge may only be grasped by those who are closest in social position to their participants.

2. *In your book, you reveal how your own experiences as a gang-involved youth motivated you to systematically study the punitive social control of inner city youth. You began your research project in 2002 at the age of 24, nearly a decade older than many of the youth in*

your study. What (if any) similarities and differences did you discover between your experiences and the experiences of your respondents?

During my time as an active gang member and juvenile delinquent in the streets of Oakland, 1991 to 1994, I witnessed and experienced punitive social control first-hand. However, by the time I conducted the study, I realized that this punitive social control had become formalized, ubiquitous, and systematic. The era of mass incarceration, beginning in the 1960s with law enforcement's repression of social movement activists, and later in the 1980s with disproportionate minority confinement—having increased the U.S. prison population from 700,000 in the 1970s to 2.2 million in 2002—brought about new forms of governance and laws that targeted crime committed by marginalized populations. By the new millennium, zero-tolerance policies in schools, juvenile justice, and criminal justice institutions had become even more punitive and had embedded themselves in the lives of children growing up in marginalized neighborhoods. In other words, my fieldwork taught me that by 2002, mass incarceration policies and practices had solidified themselves and become deeply embedded in the everyday lives of poor urban youths.

3. [...] *we've asked other field researchers to consider how our multiple identities influence the stories we tell, and how others receive them. This is something you write about as well. In what ways, if any, do your intersecting identities—Latino, male, highly educated, heterosexual—influence your ability to tell the stories of young Black and Latino men? What challenges do you confront in studying and telling stories about a population and a place that you know well, but are also trying to study systematically? What might you say to those scholars who would argue that you are "too close" to tell an "objective" sociological story? Do you see "objective" and "authentic" as fundamentally different?*

My work is inter-subjective. The stories of the youth in my study are told through my perspective. My personal background and academic training have an influence on what I choose to represent. However, my obligation is to report on patterns, recurring themes, and systematic findings that anyone who spends enough time in this context will uncover. I believe that acknowledging subjectivity and providing solid empirical evidence are not mutually exclusive. Knowing one's social position and shortfalls is the beginning of the knowledge production process. To conduct empirical work that is replicable, I recognize my multiple identities. I then utilize my subjective strengths and identify my objective weaknesses. I believe that being "too close" to my subjects provides me with an opportunity to reflect on my biases and to learn to separate my own experience from the objective reality of a new generation.

4. *In your current work, you explore patterns of surveillance among gang-associated Latino youth in Santa Barbara, California—a locale that is, at least on the surface, much different from the distressed urban neighborhoods of Oakland. What led you to this new research*

project? In what ways does this new project extend or complicate the field research you've completed in Northern California?

Santa Barbara serves as a great case study because of its race and class disparities. Approximately 30% of the population is Latino and working class and approximately 70% is white and middle or upper class. I was drawn to the Santa Barbara research project because I wanted to see if I could compare "delinquent" Latino youths living in relative deprivation with those living in concentrated poverty. In this way we can understand how punishment, race, class, and gender, are experienced and perceived in different contexts by similar populations.

5. [...] *Scott Brooks and Alford A. Young, Jr., among others, comment on the importance of mentoring—the mentoring they have received and the mentoring they give students. What role has mentoring played in the development of your career? What are the most important influences (or constraints) on who and how you mentor now?*

Without mentoring I wouldn't be here today. One of my academic mentors was Ronald Takaki, the great historian of multi-cultural America. He was there to hear me out when I felt that I did not belong and he always talked to me as if I did belong. I believe that the greatest challenge to mentors in academia is students' deep belief or disbelief in their own abilities. Many brilliant graduate students find it hard to believe in themselves. I have seen many amazing thinkers drop out of graduate school. How can we teach students to believe in themselves so that they can accomplish the unbelievable?

How do you teach students to believe that they have a place in the academic world? Are there particular practices, exercises, or conversations that you find most useful?

One of the strategies I have found useful with my students has been to provide them with a space of their own. Graduate students and I have organized Friday writing groups where we gather to work on our individual projects. We write for 45 minutes at a time and take 15 minute breaks where we catch up with each other. Another strategy that I have used to mentor graduate students is to involve undergraduates in the research process. This allows the graduate students to serve as mentors to undergraduates and in turn they receive mentoring from me. In the end, we all hold each other accountable for our work.

6. *You are married and the father of three, including twin girls. How has fathering twins, and twin girls, at that, influenced your sociological imagination? Has being a father encouraged new questions, new lines of research, or new ways of seeing the world?*

During my first week of graduate school at UC Berkeley I found out that my partner, Rebeca, was pregnant with twins. From that day on I realized that all my academic work had to be efficient. Being a father has taught me to let go of my ideas and questions, to allow myself to make my errors and mistakes public. This has produced a collective effect where colleagues, friends, and critics provide me with early feedback that then allows me to produce work already infused with communal feedback. Of course, I had to let go of my ego a long time ago.

Have your girls, now 10, made you see the women in the communities you studied—or their children—differently? If so, how?

Being a father of girls has given me even more drive to maintain a commitment to feminism. In particular, one of the areas I examine in my studies of boys is the ways in which their masculinity has a negative impact on girls in the community. I have also begun to study how some girls embrace masculinity as a self-defense mechanism. My goal is to identify gender practices in marginalized communities that work toward liberation and egalitarianism. In this way, program and policy recommendations can be shaped around strengthening these practices.

7. *You came of age in Oakland after the dramatic shift to mass incarceration. As Meda Chesney-Lind writes [...], this shift occurred on "our watch"—that is, it happened even as social scientists researched and published extensively on the consequences of these punitive turns. What hope do you have for the impact of your research in this context?*

I hope that my research enlightens the public, policymakers, schools, and police to change their perceptions, policies, and practices. That it informs us on how punitive social control has failed and how a new form of social control, one that is more egalitarian and productive can be developed.

You do a good deal of applied sociology in Santa Barbara, where you work and where your current research project is based. Can you explain how your field research informs policy and practice in Santa Barbara specifically?

I have made it my goal to become a public sociologist so that my research findings can influence policy and programs. In recent years, I have used my data to inform and advise local school districts and politicians. For example, in Santa Barbara, where I have conducted work on street-oriented youth, I have worked with the school district to devise a "gang prevention" program and to assess its effectiveness. In addition, I have advised private foundations and city and county offices on developing funding that addresses some of the dilemmas exposed by my research. I also conduct staff development with teachers to discuss "best practices" in motivating "at-promise" students to succeed.

8. *You are a faculty member in a department that includes several senior feminist scholars. What role does feminism play in your scholarship? Has engaging with your colleagues*

challenged or extended your understandings of gender inequality or intersections of race, gender, and class?

I feel honored to be part of a department that hosts so many groundbreaking and brilliant feminists. I learned about the liberatory power of theory through one of my undergraduate mentors and role models, Elizabeth "Betita" Martinez, a legend in the Chicana/o Movement. I remember reading bell hooks in her course. And the following line always follows me:

> ... I found a place of sanctuary in "theorizing," in making sense of what was happening. I found a place where I could imagine possible futures ... this "lived" experience of critical thinking, a place where I worked at explaining the hurt and making it go away. Fundamentally, I learned from this experience that theory could be a healing place. (1994: 61)

I believe that the feminists in my department, feminists I have studied under, feminists I have read, and feminists in the community, have taught me not just to heal my own personal wounds but to constantly make an effort to help others heal their wounds as well—intellectually, politically, programmatically, and in everyday interaction. My departmental colleagues have played a pivotal role in helping me develop my gender analysis when it comes to studying masculinity. I look forward to developing an even richer gender analysis with their support.

9. *You spent the first years of your career teaching in an institution different from the one you are in now. What advice might you have for young urban sociologists about where they can make the best institutional "home."*

At both institutions where I have taught I have said that I believe that I landed my dream job. The private liberal arts university, University of San Francisco, where I first taught, expected faculty to be committed to its students. I have always felt a deep passion for teaching and mentoring, so I fit in well at USF. My undergraduate students and I would march into marginalized neighborhoods and conduct "community development" programs supported by the university. This gave me an opportunity to teach my students about opportunity, privilege, and reflexivity, and to help young people with job skills, educational information, or youth violence prevention.

When I was offered the UC Santa Barbara job, I thought to myself, "Now I have to publish or perish. My teaching won't be taken into account." However, I have found that teaching at a Research I1 university has provided me with the opportunity to teach beyond the classroom. Being from a Research I university has opened up publication, speaking, and media opportunities that may not have been possible at a smaller university.

I would tell young urban sociologists to ask themselves, "What kind of teacher am I? Am I a one-on-one, quality time teacher, or do I want to teach at a more global scale?" Either way, I have enjoyed my time at both institutions. To graduate students who are headed for academic jobs, I say, "Whether you end up at a teaching university or a Research I university, you picked a great career."

The Tenth Question

What was the worst (or most difficult, or most embarrassing) interview/field encounter you've had?

There have been a few "difficult" field encounters. One of them happened in 2004 in Oakland. I was catching up with some of the boys in the study and I had not seen this group for a few weeks. The three boys I was catching up with, I knew well. A fourth boy—let's call him Tony—walked up to us. I had interviewed Tony once before but I did not know him well. He looked upset, huffing and puffing. He grabbed a CD case he was holding in his hand, lifted it high in the air, and slammed it with all his might on the ground. Dozens of clear plastic pieces scattered over an 8 feet radius. One of the other boys turned to me and said, "Tony is high man, don't even trip off him." Tony then looked at me in the eyes and said, "What is this snitch doing here?" At this point Tony reached towards his hip and over his XXL sized white t-shirt, sliding what appeared to be a gun to his opposite hip. "I don't like snitches. Snitches are bitches. I should put my thang [gun] down your throat." He reached down to his waist one more time, grabbed the pistol, flashed it in front of my face and put it away. At this point one of the other boys spotted a police car down the street and told Tony to put the gun away. The police car approached us and slowed down. Tony turned around and stared the officers down. Then he walked away. The officers got out of the car and asked the other three boys and I to turn around. Tony, meanwhile, continued to walk away. I was caught in a huge dilemma, "Do I tell the cops about Tony and confirm to him that I am a snitch?" I decided to fend for my life and did not say a word.

What did you really want to do for a living? What were you afraid you might end up doing?

I really wanted to become an auto mechanic. A few months before graduating from high school a teacher asked me what I was going to do after high school. I said, "Celebrate by drinking a forty [40 ounce malt liquor bottle] every day for the next 2 years and then go to school to become a mechanic." I was fortunate to have a teacher who connected with some college student mentors who convinced me that a mechanic could not have as much impact on society as a college educated person. With their support, I applied to college. The rest is history but I still love working on old cars. It helps me relieve my stress when I get anxious about tenure. During college, I feared that one day I would end up working for the "Man." Some might argue that my fears were certainly realized.

What's the study you never pursued, but always wanted to?

I have always wanted to study everyday acts of resilience among marginalized populations. How do everyday people navigate seemingliy insurmountable obstacles? What skills do those people who survive these obstacles hone? The study would be a comparative ethnography conducted in different parts of the globe where ordinary people are found to accomplish extraordinary acts. How does social efficacy operate in even the most marginalized communities?

Comprehension Questions for Unit III

Questions for Reading 3.1

1. If Butler were writing about race and crime in 1910, what crimes would he have focused on?
2. What other race and crime problems from 1910 would Butler have focused on?
3. What does Butler identify as "the fundamental paradox"?
4. Explain the "New Jim Crow" narrative of race and criminal justice.
5. Explain the "Celebration of Triumph" narrative.
6. Which narrative does Butler favor, and why does he favor it?

Questions for Reading 3.2

1. What are three theoretical perspectives that attempt to account for the differential treatment of people of color in the criminal justice system?
2. What are three principal assumptions of critical race theory?
3. How do race and gender intersect in slavery?
4. What notion is central to conflict theory?
5. Explain attribution theory.

Questions for Reading 3.3

1. What two things does it mean to be a scholar who advocates feminism?
2. For feminist criminology, being committed to those two things referred to in the previous question, means working to understand how ________________.
3. From Meda Chesney-Lind's perspective, what does it mean to be a feminist criminologist in a time when feminism in a "dirty" word in some quarters?

Questions for Reading 3.4

1. What did Victor Rios learn about punishment experienced by youth from different racial and ethnic backgrounds?
2. List one advantage and one disadvantage of sharing an ethnic background with a group of juveniles who you intend to interview and observe.
3. What similarities and differences did Rios discover between his own experiences as a gang-involved youth and the experiences of innercity youth in Oakland who Rios interviewed and observed?
4. How did Rios's intersecting identities—Latino, male, highly educated, heterosexual—influence his ability to tell the stories of young Black and Latino men? What would Rios say to those scholars who would argue that he was "too close" to tell an objective story about marginalized youth?

Unit IV

Do You Dare to Seek Justice?

Introduction to Unit IV

As a whole, the articles in this anthology speak to the importance of preparing readers to be good citizens and to support criminal justice reform. To accomplish this objective, we follow the lead of Paulo Freire's *Pedagogy of the Oppressed* (1970). Like Freire, we seek to create a dialogue between professors and students. Instead of following the banking model of education, where professors deposit knowledge into students' heads, we focus on striking up a conversation between professors and students as they mutually engage with the articles. Like Freire, the editors of this volume encourage students to take what they learn and use it to foster progressive change. The articles in Unit IV challenge students to consider taking action to confront some of the most vexing problems facing the criminal justice system.

In Reading 4.1, Charles R. Epp, Steven Maynard-Moody, and Donald P. Haider-Markel tackle the problem of racial injustice in police stops. Many of the deaths garnering media attention in recent years have resulted from armed police officers performing investigatory stops, often for traffic violations, even minor ones. The individual officers responsible for these harms must be held accountable. Then, too, police training must be improved so police can make better decisions. However, according to Epp, Maynard-Moody, and Haider-Markel, that will not get to the root of the problem. What is the root of the problem of racial injustice in police stops? What are the most plausible solutions? Reduce the types of violations for which police can stop cars? Get police out of the business of enforcing traffic laws? Limit police involvement to dangerous situations?

A debate breaks out in Reading 4.2. Dianna Post and Bishakha Datta argue about whether or not to legalize prostitution. Proponents of legalizing prostitution say it would reduce crime, improve public health, increase tax revenue, help people out of poverty, and allow consenting adults to make their own choices. They contend that prostitution is a victimless crime. Opponents say that legalizing prostitution would lead to increases in sexually transmitted diseases, human trafficking, and crimes such as rape and homicide. They maintain that prostitution is immoral, exploitative, and promotes the repression of women by men.

To provide an up close and personal perspective on one form of prostitution—human trafficking—we have included Reading 4.3 by Elizabeth Ringler-Jayanthan, Marni Barish, and Reynel Mirabal Tang. "Social Work Students Reflect on Learning About Sex Trafficking" presents narratives explaining what it takes to develop the necessary skills to work with women who have been trafficked. It allows readers to take an insider's view of human trafficking. It also shows you how someone like yourself can make a difference in responding to a serious problem pertaining to justice-involved people.

Convicting and imprisoning an innocent person is arguably the worst thing a government can do to one of its citizens, short of mistakenly executing them. Everyone agrees these are tragedies. What is less clear is what these cases say about America's justice system. Radley Balko considers this question from several angles in Reading 4.4, entitled "Wrongful Convictions."

In Reading 4.5, Anne Kim argues that it's time to abolish cash bail. Because cash bail involves the criminalization of poverty, it is a prime example of class bias in the criminal justice system. Under this system, a person experiencing poverty can be arrested for a nonviolent offense, such as drug possession or a traffic violation, and spend months (or longer) in jail waiting for a hearing or trial date. Cash bail perpetuates inequities in the justice system that are disproportionately felt by communities of color and those experiencing poverty. Spending even a few days in jail can result in people losing their job, housing, and even custody of their children. The other side of the cash bail story is that defenders of bail say bail protects society from dangerous criminals. Is this true? Do alternatives to bail protect the community just as well as bail?

Reading 4.6 plunges readers into the war on drugs, calling the question of whether or not it's time to end it. Future generations will look back on the war on drugs as a crude, barbaric, and inhumane response to the social and public health problem of drug addiction. And they will look back at how our "drug war" had ugly consequences. These monstrous consequences include racial inequities in both enforcement and punishment, the growth of government surveillance and erosion of privacy rights, and mass incarceration.

Reading 4.1

Toward Racial Justice in Police Stops

Charles R. Epp, Steven Maynard-Moody, and Donald P. Haider-Markel

> Say nothing and it just perpetuates it. And so I'm a minister, my whole thing is whatever you see say something about it. Even if it means that eventually that we have to start back to marching, sit-ins, whatever we need to do. You just have to start to put a stop to some of this stuff. Because if you say nothing or do nothing they ... you're helping the situation and not stopping it.[1]

On December 14, 2010, 21-year-old Marion Denmon was laid to rest, the victim of yet another apparent gang killing on Kansas City's troubled east side. During the funeral at the Macedonia Baptist Church several carfuls of young men drove up and fired more than seventy gunshots, apparently as a show of disrespect.[2] Pandemonium broke out and some mourners rushed to fire shots at the fleeing vehicles. The police had been told no violence was expected at the funeral and so they had stayed away. In a neighborhood all too familiar with shootings, nearly everybody agreed that this one, outside a church and during a funeral, had crossed the line. People were outraged. Nonetheless, witnesses stonewalled police efforts to identify the shooters. Nobody talked with the police, and no shooters were identified, much less caught. It was not the first time that Kansas City police faced thorough noncooperation in their investigations. As the

1. Mike, an African American driver commenting on police stops, in Charles R. Epp, Steven Maynard-Moody, and Donald P. Haider-Markel, "Driver Interview Archive," in *Reconstructing Law on the Street: Transcripts of Interviews and Focus Groups* (Lawrence, KS: KU ScholarWorks, 2011), 26–27, http://hdl.handle.net/1808/8544.
2. Najahe Sherman, "Pastors and Community Leaders Gather to Express Outrage over Church Shooting," 41 Action News, December 15, 2010, http://www.kshb.com/dpp/news/local_news/pastors-and-community-leaders-gather-to-express-outrage-over-church-shooting#ixzziyoKtT8AE.

mother of a young man shot only a few months before the funeral incident and only a short distance away observed, "In our community, people are quick to come and tell the family of the victim things, but they will not tell the police."[3]

If investigatory stops worked as claimed none of this should have happened. Advocates insist that investigatory stops get guns and drugs off the streets and make cities safer. They also claim that people and neighborhoods subjected to investigatory stops accept the stops and surveillance so long as officers are professional and courteous. East Kansas City is a testing ground for these claims. The Macedonia Baptist Church is in the heart of the area targeted by the Kansas City Gun Experiment, which, in the early 1990s, offered evidence that investigatory stops get guns off the street and dramatically reduce shootings.[4] Sixteen years later, these stops are everyday occurrences, yet guns abound and shootings continue. The Kansas City Police Department is among the more professionalized in the country and has first-rate systems for training and oversight over officers. But after a generation of investigatory stops, neighborhood residents in east Kansas City so distrust the police that they will not cooperate in investigations even when the crime is a gangland shooting at a church funeral.

This [reading] concluding message is simple: the benefits of investigatory stops are modest and greatly exaggerated, yet their costs are substantial and largely unrecognized. It is time to end this failed practice. Investigatory stops fail because they violate a widely shared norm of fair treatment.[5] This norm requires that people should be treated as equal, respected members of society and not as second-class outsiders, as participants in a common endeavor and not as objects to be controlled and manipulated. When police enforcement activities respect this fundamental norm, as they do in some collaborative, carefully targeted efforts that we will summarize below, members of the community are drawn into cooperation with the police and public safety is enhanced. When police enforcement activities violate this fundamental norm, as they do in investigatory stops, members of the community learn to distrust the police, putting public safety at risk.

Although police widely believe that investigatory stops help fight crime, the evidence supporting this belief is surprisingly thin. To be sure, officers sometimes seize guns and illegal drugs in these stops. But this occurs rarely; most people subjected to these stops are innocent and no weapon or contraband is seized. It is easier to remember the

---

3. Eric L. Wesson, "Unsolved Homicides: What Can Be Done?" *Call* (Kansas City) December 10–16, 2010.
4. Lawrence W. Sherman, James W. Shaw, and Dennis P. Rogan, "The Kansas City Gun Experiment," *Research in Brief*, January 1995, 1–11.
5. See Tom R. Tyler, *Why People Obey the Law?* (New Haven, CT: Yale University Press, 1990), [...].

successful stops: Jon Gould and Stephen Mastrofski found that officers unintentionally exaggerate how often they find drugs or guns.[6] In truth, it is extremely rare.

Nor is it clear that investigatory stops help to reduce the crime rate more generally, as the pioneering Kansas City Gun Experiment claimed. In that study, police targeted a neighborhood for widespread investigatory stops and were able to seize more guns than in other neighborhoods. Shootings declined in the targeted neighborhood for a brief period. Several attempts to replicate the experiment's findings in other cities, however, yielded unimpressive results. An attempt in Indianapolis compared two styles of proactive stops, employed in two different neighborhoods.[7] In one Indianapolis neighborhood the police made widespread investigatory stops of large numbers of drivers, as had been done in Kansas City; in the other, the police targeted a small number of especially suspicious drivers and pedestrians, and also made home visits to check up on violent criminal convicts who were on probation. Only in the second neighborhood, in which targeted enforcement was employed, was there a reduction in crime. In a second replication, in Pittsburgh, the study authors reported modest crime reduction effects from police stops, but, as a recent scientific review concluded, these effects were probably exaggerated and police stops in fact may have led to no significant decline in crime.[8]

But what about New York City? It is widely claimed that investigatory stops contributed to New York's much publicized success in reducing violent crime—but this, too, is dubious. The most careful analysis of what has worked in New York, by criminologist Franklin Zimring, concluded that widespread street stops of pedestrians do little to reduce crime.[9]

---

6. Jon B. Gould and Stephen D. Mastrofski, "Suspect Searches: Assessing Police Behavior under the Constitution," *Criminology and Public Policy* 3 (2004): 316–62.

7. Edmund F. McGarrell, Steven Chermak, and Alexander Weiss, "Reducing Firearms Violence Through Directed Patrol: Final Report on the Evaluation of the Indianapolis Police Department's Directed Patrol Project," *Report to the National Institute of Justice*, (Indianapolis, IN: Crime Control Policy Center, Hudson Institute, 2000); Edmund F. McGarrell, Steven Chermak, Alexander Weiss, and Jeremy Wilson, "Reducing Firearms Violence through Directed Police Patrol," *Criminology and Public Policy* 1 (2001): 119–48; Edmund F. McGarrell, Steven Chermak, and Alexander Weiss, "Reducing Gun Violence: Evaluation of the Indianapolis Police Department's Directed Patrol Project," NCJ-188740 (Washington DC: National Institute of Justice, United States Department of Justice, 2002).

8. The Pittsburgh study is reported in Jacqueline Cohen and Jens Ludwig, "Policing Crime Guns," in *Evaluating Gun Policy: Effects on Crime and Violence*, ed. Jens Ludwig and Phillip J. Cook, 217-50 (Washington DC: Brookings Institution Press, 2003); the evaluation is in Christopher S. Koper and Evan Mayo-Wilson, "Police Crackdowns on Illegal Gun Carrying: A Systematic Review of Their Impact on Gun Crime," *Journal of Experimental Criminology* 2 (2006): 227–61.

9. Franklin E. Zimring, *The City That Became Safe: New York's Lessons for Urban Crime and Its Control* (New York: Oxford University Press, 2011).

Instead, reductions in violent crime are due to other, less-publicized police enforcement efforts that carefully target the actual perpetrators of violent crime.

It is increasingly clear that the most effective kinds of police enforcement are efforts that respect procedural justice norms, as the research of David M. Kennedy on gang shootings has shown, and as careful meta-analyses have confirmed.[10] First, police enforcement is most effective when it carefully targets serious criminals rather than stopping large numbers of people, many of whom are innocent, in the hope of apprehending the few who are guilty. Targeting many to get the few is unjust and, as we will emphasize below, widely resented. Second, police effectiveness is enhanced when the police work closely with community members and groups to identify serious violators and to bring pressure on them to cease their predations. Even in low-income, high-crime neighborhoods only a small number of people commit the vast majority of the crime. Police and community members often know or can find out who these serious criminals are. Cooperation from community members is often crucial for identifying criminals and for bringing social pressure to bear on them in ways that ratify and amplify the efforts of the police. Community members are more likely to participate in efforts to control serious crime when police treat them as respected participants in a shared effort. Scattershot investigatory stops of people who merely look suspicious are at best a distraction from more focused police efforts. They are not effective.

Cascading Injustice

Scattershot investigatory stops also have serious costs. The most obvious of these is that investigatory stops, even if ostensibly focused on those who look suspicious, target innocent people for highly invasive intrusions aimed at catching the few who are serious criminals. And most of these innocent victims are racial minorities. While trying to prevent a gangland shooting or interdict a major drug shipment, officers day in and day out stop hundreds of innocent people like Deana and Lisa and Joe. As we have shown, African Americans are almost *three times* more likely than whites to be stopped in investigatory police stops. Dennis Rosenbaum observes, and we have confirmed, that "the vast majority of persons who are inconvenienced (if not offended) by these stops are innocent persons of color and limited

10. Anthony A. Braga et al., "Problem-Oriented Policing, Deterrence, and Youth Violence: An Evaluation of Boston's Operation Ceasefire," *Journal of Research in Crime and Delinquency* 38 (2001): 195–225; David M. Kennedy, *Don't Shoot: One Man, A Street Fellowship, and the End of Violence in Inner-City America* (New York: Bloomsbury, 2012); Anthony A. Braga and David L. Weisburd, "The Effects of Focused Deterrence Strategies on Crime: A Systematic Review and Meta-Analysis of the Empirical Evidence," *Journal of Research in Crime and Delinquency* 49, no. 3 (2012): 323–58.

means."[11] The investigatory stop sacrifices long-term engagement and effectiveness for a short-term "bust."

Racial disparities mar most aspects of U.S. social life from employment to lifespan—but few are as wide as the disparity in who is pulled over in investigatory stops. For example, African Americans suffering from heart disease are about 13 percent less likely than whites to be given angioplasties and about 33 percent less likely to be treated with bypass surgery, disparities that have caused widespread concern.[12] By comparison, African Americans are 270 percent more likely than whites to be subjected to an investigatory stop. This in itself is a deep racial injustice.

The racial disparity in who is stopped is compounded in what happens *during* the investigatory stop. During these stops the police act significantly more intrusively toward African Americans, and especially African American men, than whites. Officers may carry out a range of investigatory intrusions: they may ask drivers probing questions about where they are going and why they are in the neighborhood, may search the driver and the vehicle on the basis of visible evidence of criminality or consent of the driver, may handcuff the driver, may conduct tests for sobriety, and ultimately may arrest the driver. Typically officers proceed further with these intrusions as their suspicions grow after their initial contacts with the driver or passengers. Just as officers are vastly more likely to *stop* African American drivers than whites when carrying out investigatory stops, officers also proceed further with investigatory intrusions during stops of African American drivers. Thus, officers are *five times* more likely to search African Americans than whites, but they are much less likely to find a gun or contraband in searches of African Americans. These deeper intrusions, too, are a racial injustice.

Another cost is that widespread investigatory stops undermine trust in police and willingness to call the police for help. Even after taking into account other factors that contribute to lower levels of trust in the police, among them peoples' distrust of authority, lower levels of education, and higher rates of crime in their community, the experience of an investigatory police stop powerfully erodes peoples' trust in the police. Widespread stops, searches, questioning, and arrests, as Rosenbaum emphasizes, "drive a wedge between the police and the community, as the latter can begin to feel like targets rather than partners."[13] Like people everywhere, residents of low-income, high-crime communities appreciate police enforcement, but they also value freedom from intrusion and fair treatment; they resent being treated like criminals.

---

11. Dennis P. Rosenbaum, "The Limits of Hot Spots Policing," In *Police Innovation: Contrasting Perspectives*, edited by David Weisburd and A. A. Braga, 245–63 (Cambridge: Cambridge University Press, 2006), 255.
12. "Addressing Racial and Ethnic Disparities in Health Care: Fact Sheet," Agency for Healthcare Research and Quality, http://www.ahrq.gov/research/findings/factsheets/minority/disparit/.
13. Rosenbaum, "The Limits of Hot Spots Policing," 253.

Ultimately, as Dennis Rosenbaum concludes, these stops erode peoples' sense of empowerment and "run the risk of further undermining social control and a community's capacity for self-regulation."[14] Worse, they may so embitter neighborhood residents toward the police that people decline to cooperate in police investigations or even come to share a norm, like "no snitching," *against* cooperating with the police.[15] The basic observation of a generation of research is that neighborhood cooperation, both among residents and with the police, is a key condition for reducing the rate of crime. Crime is controlled primarily by communities working with the police, and not the police acting on their own.[16] Addressing persistent poverty and lack of opportunity is critical as well. But even among very poor areas, crime rates are considerably lower where residents share a sense of efficacy, work together to address disorder, call the police to help out with problems, and cooperate with police investigations.[17] Police depend on cooperation to solve crimes. When people are not willing to call the police or cooperate with police investigations the police have very little to go on. The Macedonia Baptist Church shooting remains unsolved simply because people were not willing to talk to the police. Investigatory stops thus rest on the professional illusion that policing can go it alone.

Strikingly, experiencing a traffic-safety stop does *not* erode peoples' trust in the police, and that difference tells us something important. It is simply not the case that every type of experience with the police or even every kind of police enforcement activity erodes trust in the police. *Investigatory* stops erode trust; other stops, which people recognize to be legitimate efforts to enforce the law, do not erode trust. Among African American drivers, in fact, when an officer gives the driver a lecture on driving safety, the driver is considerably more likely to evaluate the stop positively. Getting a driving-safety lecture confirms to the stopped driver that the stop's purpose was legitimate.

Drivers are well aware of the profound racial disparities in police stops, and this awareness shapes perceptions of the police and their own place in society. No one likes to be pulled over, but police stops teach different lessons to African Americans and whites. They teach African Americans that police stops are unpredictable, arbitrary, and a tool

---

14. Ibid., 257.

15. For general discussion of "stop snitching," see Delores Jones-Brown, "Forever the Symbolic Assailant: The More Things Change, the More they Remain the Same," *Criminology and Public Policy* 6, no. 1 (2007): 113–14.

16. David H. Bayley, *Police for the Future* (New York: Oxford University Press, 1994); Robert J. Sampson, Stephen W. Raudenbush, and Felton Earls. "Neighborhoods and Violent Crime: A Multilevel Study of Collective Efficacy," *Science* 277 (1997): 918–24; John E. Eck and William Spelman, "Problem-Solving: Problem-Oriented Policing in Newport News," (Washington DC: Police Executive Research Forum, 1987).

17. Robert J. Sampson and Stephen W. Raudenbush, "Systematic Social Observation of Public Spaces: A New Look at Disorder in Urban Neighborhoods," *American Journal of Sociology* 105, no. 3 (1999): 603–51.

of surveillance. They teach whites that police stops are predictable consequences of unsafe driving, and, remarkably, that even well-deserved stops may lead to being let off with a warning if the driver is respectful and polite to the officer. Police stops confirm whites' common assumption that they are full citizens deserving respect and leniency; they teach African Americans that they are targets of suspicion[18] Police stops tell African Americans that they are not free to travel in some areas and may decrease the likelihood of them voting.[19] They will learn to distrust the police and will be less likely to cooperate with the police. Distrust of the police is likely to be even deeper among undocumented immigrants, undermining willingness to call the police even when the need is great. Ethnic framing of records-requests will reproduce and deepen a growing "racialization" of Latino ethnicity. These processes are sadly predictable.

As new laws encourage police to hunt for illegal immigrants and the use of investigatory stops expands to target Latinos, these unjust and antidemocratic patterns, unless deliberately checked, are likely to only become more widespread. Police stops to check for immigration documents will be ethnically framed in the way investigatory stops have been racially framed. Persistent stereotypes that undocumented immigrants are mainly from Latin America will lead officers on the street to be more suspicious of people who appear to be Hispanic or Latino and to ask these people for proof of citizenship. The vast majority of the people asked for papers will be citizens or legal residents. These innocent targets of record requests will resent the question and the implication that they look like less than a full, respected member of society.

The Supreme Court's decision in *Arizona v. United States* (2012), upholding that state's requirement that local police officers check people's immigration status, is thus likely to cause real, palpable harm for many ordinary people.[20] To be sure, officers' authority to check for documentation is sharply restricted. Arizona law allows officers to check immigration documentation only in the context of a "lawful stop, detention, or arrest" or other "lawful contact," and so it does not authorize officers to stop people only in order to check for documentation. The court's decision adds further restrictions. It struck down a requirement that people carry documentation of their citizenship or immigration status, and it suggested that officers would be acting consistently with the Constitution only if they contacted federal authorities for documentation during an otherwise legal stop and only if they held the driver while waiting for documentation no longer than necessary to write a typical traffic ticket. These requirements will be difficult to follow in practice; police departments will need

18. This is the view reported in our survey by 20 percent of African American men under age 35.

19. Vesla M. Weaver and Amy E. Lerman, "Political Consequences of the Carceral State." *American Political Science Review* 104, no. 4 (November 2010): 817–33.

20. *Arizona v. United States* 567 U.S. 11–182 (2012).

to carefully train and oversee officers' activities.[21] It is widely expected that federal immigration authorities are unlikely to respond to requests for documentation within the short window allowed. Police errors, such as holding a driver too long, will expose local police agencies to considerable risk of liability, as rights advocacy groups stand ready to bring lawsuits challenging these stops.

Still, technically there are similar legal restrictions on investigatory stops, and these restrictions have not stopped the daily intrusions and violations documented throughout this [reading]. For example, the Supreme Court's decision in *Whren v. United States* authorizes investigatory vehicle stops only when the officer has a lawful justification for making the stop, precisely the Arizona law's requirement.[22] But Joe, the driver [...], described a stop in which the officer's stated justification was to conduct a "warrant check," which is not a lawful justification. Eighteen percent of black drivers in our survey reported that the officer gave them *no reason* for making the stop. In these stops officers proceeded to ask intrusive questions and often searched the vehicle. Conceivably the officers in these stops had observed the driver make some minor traffic violation but simply did not state it. It is not hard to find a lawful justification to make a stop. The point is that this technical requirement to have a lawful justification for a stop offers no meaningful limitation on officers' authority to make stops. Likewise, there is nothing in the Court's decision in *Arizona v. United States* that will keep officers from stopping drivers on some pretext, calling the federal immigration authorities for documentation, and then, after waiting without response for fifteen minutes, releasing these drivers. Such harassment will be perfectly legal, and many ordinary people will be harmed in the ways we have documented in this book.

Investigatory stops erode individual liberty, undermine democratic equality, and divide local communities by income, race, and ethnicity. They target those who are mainly racial or ethnic minorities for intrusive surveillance and leave others, who are mainly white, free from this intrusion. To be white is to be honored as an equal member of the community and treated fairly; to be African American or Latino is to be disrespected as less than an equal and subject to manipulation by arbitrary inquisitive power.

The core of the problem is not individual racism among a few officers. It is not simply officers' isolated discretionary choices to stop black people and, increasingly, Latinos and other minorities. It is, instead, an institutionally supported practice celebrated by police professional associations, leaders, and local departments. The practice of investigatory stops is itself the engine that racially frames police and public alike.

---

21. See, e.g., Margaret Stock, "Online Symposium: The Court Throws Arizona a Tough Bone to Chew," *SCOTUSblog*, June 27, 2012, http://www.scotusblog.com/2012/06/online-symposium-the-court-throws-arizona-a-tough-bone-to-chew/ (accessed November 15, 2012).

22. *Whren v. United States* 517 U.S. 806 (1996).

Our analysis has a broader implication. Racial disparities are widespread in American society, and we challenge scholars to examine whether institutionalized practices contribute to these disparities in areas other than policing. These disparities are well-known in education, health care, employment, and housing, to name but a few. In many of these areas the explanation for racial disparities is undoubtedly complex, and inequality by race in people's wealth is surely a major factor. But too little attention has been paid to the contribution of institutionalized practices, or, as we have described in this [reading], how accepted ways of carrying out a policy may be racially neutral on their face but racially framed in their deepest structure and implementation. Wherever racial disparities persist over decades, we challenge researchers and policy makers to assume that this is not simply a legacy of the past but an ongoing recreation of deliberate, if often hidden and unrecognized, practice. Studying these practices would require research carefully designed to get closer to the front-line workers who carry out policy and in the process remake it. This sort of research takes time and is not easily done—but there are some emerging models.[23] Importantly, this sort of research may help identify deliberate policy interventions that could make a real and immediate difference.

A Proposal

Our analysis suggests that the most prominent proposals for addressing racial disparities in police stops will not work. The Supreme Court's current solution is to accept investigatory stops, but prohibit officers from deliberately using a driver's race or ethnicity as the key reason for making a stop. Although an ever-present concern, deliberate racism is only a small part of the problem. The current solution of professional policing organizations with regard to racial disparities in stops is to better train officers to be polite and respectful. While professional courtesy is desirable, it is not nearly enough. Critical scholars like Michelle Alexander argue with considerable justification that no piecemeal reform short of ending the war on drugs and the entire punitive crime-control regime will be enough to address the problem.[24] We are sympathetic to this view. Still, emphasizing this overarching quest may lead too easily to a failure to take smaller steps that can make a real difference and which may become key parts of a comprehensive solution.

The immediate task is to change institutionalized practices that have become the taken-for-granted definitions of professionalism, of what it means to do good police work.

---

23. Brian D. Smedley, Adrienne Y. Stith, and Alan R. Nelson, eds. *Unequal Treatment: Confronting Racial and Ethnic Disparities in Health Care* (Washington DC: National Academy Press, 2003).

24. Michelle Alexander, *The New Jim Crow: Mass Incarceration in the Age of Colorblindness* (New York: New Press, 2010).

These practices embody norms and conceptions of good police work as well as particular rules and training protocols. Changing practice requires confronting the norms and ideas that undergird the prominence of investigatory stops in contemporary policing. It requires acknowledging that racial disparities are endemic to these stops and that current police practice contributes to an epidemic of injustice. As servants of state power, the police have an obligation to confront their role in contributing to and reducing this injustice. Bill Bratton, the former police chief of Los Angeles, New York, and Boston, observed, "If we don't solve the race issue, we'll never solve the other issues. The police have traditionally been the flash point for so many of America's racial problems."[25]

Changing norms and practice will also require the leadership of professional policing to frankly acknowledge and actively promote the message that investigatory stops cause harm. They cause harm even when the officer's street-wise hunch draws attention to a driver or pedestrian and when the officer remains courteous and professional throughout the encounter. The current message from leaders that these stops "work" is at best grossly imbalanced, at worst simply false. Every stop of an innocent person causes direct, palpable harm. Every stop justified by a minor violation, every inquisitive question, every light shined in a passenger compartment, every request for consent to search, every search, and every handcuffing of a person only to release them later causes harm. Investigatory stops *are counterproductive to the core crime-fighting mission of policing.* They also divide our communities by race and ethnicity.

To address these deeply entrenched problems, we propose modest pragmatic steps that can be made *tomorrow.* First, police leaders should promote the professional norm of not stopping drivers or pedestrians except when justified by clear evidence of criminal behavior. A new norm of avoiding car and pedestrian stops (except to sanction bad driving) should become a core part of shared professional knowledge within policing. Officers must have more than a pretextual reason for the vast majority of their stops. Professional associations should convey to their members that stops based on hunches or trivial violations is bad practice. Training academies should make it a core part of their curricula. Officers should be taught it in field training. Departments should remind officers of this lesson on an ongoing basis.

Second, to enforce this requirement, police departments should adopt internal guidelines and systems of oversight governing the decision to make a stop and conduct investigatory intrusions that are modeled on how departments regulate uses of force.[26] Thus, departments

---

25. Quoted in Tracey Meares, "The Legitimacy of Police among Young African-American Men," *Marquette Law Review* 92, no. 4 (2009): 562.

26. See, e.g., Samuel Walker, *The New World of Police Accountability* (Thousand Oaks, CA: Sage, 2005); Charles R. Epp, *Making Rights Real: Activists, Bureaucrats, and the Creation of the Legalistic State* (Chicago: University of Chicago Press, 2009).

should prohibit pretextual stops except when justified by an overriding public safety exigency. To oversee this guidance, departments should require officers in every stop to articulate and record their reason for the stop and departments should conduct internal reviews of these reasons. Departments should strive to make pretextual stops the rare exception rather than the common pattern. Further, a computerized search of the person's name in crime records should be allowed only after the legal basis for the stop is reported and recorded. These recording and oversight procedures would severely limit the use of pretext stops in the hunt for crime and deliberately so—but this is an essential step in limiting the racial bias now so evident in investigatory stops.

The essential third step is to prohibit searches unless based on probable cause to believe a crime has been committed. Consent searches authorize unfettered police discretion to search whoever they wish, even though a driver's consent cannot be considered freely given. Drivers told us that they felt they were "incarcerated" when pulled over and that they had no choice but to consent. Training police officers to solicit permission to search cars or persons takes undue advantage of individuals who are psychologically, if not legally, held by the police. Such consent relies on manipulation, as documented in Charles Remsberg's police training manual.[27] Searches should be conducted only after receiving specific authorization by a supervisor and should be allowed on an articulation of probable cause, or, in other words, particularized evidence to believe the person has committed a crime. This evidence should be recorded and evaluated by supervisors.

Although these three steps are far short of ending the war on drugs or punitive crime policy, they may still seem impractical and unlikely to be adopted. While changing well-established and widely accepted practices is difficult, it *is* possible and has precedent,[28] such as the great expansion of professional systems for limiting and regulating officers' uses of force. Forty years ago the police shot black people at dramatically higher rates than whites.[29] Careful study showed that the greatest disparities occurred in the shootings of people suspected of a felony who were fleeing arrest. Racial disparities were much lower in shootings of people who directly threatened the officer (or another person) with a gun or knife. Shooting at suspected felons who were running away was authorized by the "fleeing felon" shooting rule, an age-old, common-law practice. As controversy over the practice grew, police leaders defended the fleeing felon rule as necessary to help police fight crime. If police could not

27. Charles Remsberg, *Tactics for Criminal Patrol: Vehicle Stops, Drug Discovery and Officer Survival* (Northbrook, IL: Calibre Press, 1995), 214–16.

28. A useful catalog of possible reforms is found in David A. Harris, *Profiles in Injustice: Why Racial Profiling Cannot Work* (New York: New Press, 2002), 145–207.

29. On reform of racial disparities in police shootings see Samuel Walker, *Taming the System* (New York: Oxford University Press, 1993) and Epp, *Making Rights Real.*

shoot at people running away, it was said, *everybody* would run. Criminals would escape; crime would flourish.

Perhaps the "fleeing felon" shooting rule facilitated arrests. But resentment and controversy over the practice and studies demonstrating how it was a key source of racial disparities in who was shot underscored the practice's troubling costs. Many of the people shot were African American boys, killed when fleeing from the site of tragically minor crimes: a $10 burglary, a car taken for a joyride. Reform-oriented police leaders began forbidding their officers from shooting at anybody merely for running from a felony arrest; a shot was now justified only in order to defend a life from an imminent threat. This "defense of life" shooting rule spread among police departments and soon replaced the old "fleeing felon" rule. The Supreme Court endorsed the new approach and condemned the old as unconstitutional.[30] As departments trained their officers in the new approach and enforced it with careful oversight, racial disparities in shootings declined.

The parallels with the current situation are striking. Here, too, racial disparities are the product of a distinct practice, the investigatory stop. Here, too, police leaders defend this practice as an essential crime-fighting tool. Here, too, the human costs of the practice are becoming increasingly clear. And here, too, it is increasingly clear that professional policing can regulate and limit investigatory stops and can develop alternative crime-fighting strategies, strategies that may be *more* effective than an outmoded practice.

What is needed is motivation to change. Pressure from litigation, the public, media, and scholars may play a role. This helped to end the practice of shooting at fleeing felons.[31] It makes a difference in police stops, too. As Patricia Warren and Donald Tomaskovic-Devey have shown, police departments that have come under pressure from media attention over racial profiling have reduced the level of racial disparities in police stops in their jurisdictions.[32] It is certainly possible to carry out traffic stops without disproportionately stopping minorities, as demonstrated by our finding that traffic-safety stops are not biased.

Changes in law and court rulings, too, are necessary and could provide an enduring foundation for reforms. Although the Supreme Court's decision striking down the fleeing felon rule came late in the struggle to end that practice, it contributed to the widespread acceptance of restrictive shooting rules and aided in bringing laggard police departments into line with the new policy. Long before the Supreme Court's decision, litigation and decisions in lower courts had encouraged police departments to experiment with methods to control officers' uses of force. Especially as the courts have helped to legitimate the investigatory

30. *Tennessee v. Garner*, 471 U.S. 1 (1985).

31. Epp, *Making Rights Real*.

32. Patricia Y. Warren and Donald Tomaskovic-Devey, "Racial Profiling and Searches: Did the Politics of Racial Profiling Change Police Behavior?" *Criminology & Public Policy* 8, no. 2 (2009): 343–69.

stop, they have a responsibility to acknowledge its costs and help to end the practice. But, at a time when there is little sentiment for stepping back from the war on drugs and crime, waiting for changes in judicial rulings may condemn African Americans, Latinos, and others to several more generations of aggressive and intrusive policing. This is why we have asked police departments to take the lead. But they should know that unless they do, this problem and pressure for change will only grow.

Ultimately higher-court decisions ratifying a prohibition on pretextual stops will probably be necessary to bring recalcitrant departments into line. Even now, without any meaningful reform underway, our data suggest that smaller departments employ investigatory stops in more discriminatory ways than larger ones. If our proposal gains any traction, it is likely to be adopted more thoroughly by leading professionalized police departments than others. Some system for encouraging recalcitrant departments to stop the practice will be necessary. In the absence of a congressional act, something that seems unlikely, enforcement via judicial ruling may be the best that can be hoped for.

Perhaps a necessary step to encourage police reform is an effective alternative. It may be emerging. Some jurisdictions are restricting consent-based searches, and some are developing "targeted" or "focused" enforcement, in the words of David M. Kennedy and James Forman, to replace the "scattershot, stop-lots-of-people-in-the-hope-of-catching-a-few" practice of investigatory stops.[33] Targeted enforcement relies on close police collaboration with neighborhood groups to identify the individuals who engage in serious criminality. It eschews stopping large numbers of people in the hope that some stops will yield contraband or information leading to big busts. As a consequence, arrests are likely to become less numerous but more effective. At the same time, trust with communities is rebuilt, and the social cost of sweeping large numbers of people into the criminal justice system on low-level charges is reduced.

In the context of these changes in organizational norms, rules governing practice, and oversight procedures, improvements in training regarding implicit bias and stereotypes may be extremely valuable. None of us is free of the burden of implicit bias and stereotypes, but police, who carry out the coercive power of the state, have an added responsibility to confront the corrosive influence of implicit stereotypes. Training on implicit bias is likely to be most useful when tied to the implementation of particular rules. For example, training to reduce racial disparities in shootings was most successful when structured by concrete use-of-force rules that allowed shooting only when necessary to save the life of the officer or a third party. In the context of stops, likewise, training might focus on how justifications

33. See Kennedy, *Don't Shoot*; and Braga and Weisburg, "Focused Deterrence." James Forman Jr. and Trevor Stutz, "Beyond Stop and Frisk," *New York Times*, April 19, 2012, summarizes studies of several cities written under the auspices of the Innovations in Policing Clinic, Yale Law School.

for making stops should be similar across different racial groups. Unfortunately, the controversy over racial profiling has had the opposite effect: it has pushed any discussion of race and policing underground. Research and experience reiterate a discouraging observation: implicit bias resists change largely because it operates outside our conscious awareness. Recognizing the grip of our stereotypes of black criminality, violence, and lack of credibility helps bring the unconscious to awareness and may loosen their hold on our judgments.

In addition, any effort to complicate peoples' stereotypes by exposing police and the rest of us to alternative images of African Americans, especially young black men, erodes the foundations of peoples' bias. This may be one of the most positive aspects of community-engaged policing of the sort proposed by David M. Kennedy and James Forman, since even the most dangerous urban enclaves—areas seen by outsiders as a threatening wasteland—are full of honest, nonviolent, trustworthy people just trying to get by. Working directly with these law-abiding citizens may diminish the likelihood of seeing people like them as the obvious targets for a stop.

The proposed changes in police practice may in themselves reduce the hold of negative stereotypes of African Americans. Stereotypes and bias are not just cultural relics of our racist past; they are continually re-created by current policies and practices. All too often, the images of police officers pulling over black drivers or questioning black pedestrians reinforce the stereotype of black criminality. Deliberately changing police practice can, over time, weaken stereotypes by changing the complexion of who is stopped by the police. Changing who is stopped may lead to subtle changes in stereotypes of who is *deserving* of being stopped by the police.

But we also believe that no list of particular reforms will truly address the problem without a deep change in law, criminal justice policy, and police priorities. Deeper still, policies are needed to address the underlying conditions that give rise to high crime rates in some urban areas: concentrated poverty, poor housing, struggling schools, and lack of jobs. Without broader changes in public policy, and in *police* policy, officers on the street will continue to make biased choices. The discretionary choices of individual officers are not, and should not be, fully controllable. Even if the recommendations above are implemented, the officer on the street is likely to sometimes use minor traffic violations as justifications for making stops simply to carry out warrant checks, ask intrusive questions, or try to build a case for a full-blown search. But individual choices that deviate from policy are not at present the problem—the problem is police policy. If the leadership of American policing can be persuaded that investigatory stops, like shooting people simply for fleeing a felony arrest, are unprofessional, counterproductive, and morally repugnant, then investigatory stops, too, can be reformed, and we can move closer to racial justice in police stops.

Bibliography

"Addressing Racial and Ethnic Disparities in Health Care: Fact Sheet." Agency for Healthcare Research and Quality, U.S. Department of Health and Human Services. http://www.ahrq.gov/research/findings/factsheets/minority/disparit/.

Bayley, David F. *Police for the Future*. Oxford University Press, 1994.

Braga, Anthony A., David M. Kennedy, Elin J. Waring, and Anne Morrison Riehl. "Problem-Oriented Policing, Deterrence, and Youth Violence: An Evaluation of Boston's Operation Ceasefire." *Journal of Research in Crime and Delinquency* 38 (2001): 195–225.

Braga, Anthony A., and David Weisburd. "The Effects of Focused Deterrence Strategies on Crime: A Systematic Review and Meta-Analysis of the Empirical Evidence." *Journal of Research in Crime and Delinquency* 49, no. 3 (2012): 323–58.

Cohen, Jacqueline, and Jens Ludwig. "Policing Crime Guns." In *Evaluating Gun Policy: Effects on Crime and Violence*, edited by Jens Ludwig and Phillip J. Cook, 217–50. Brookings Institution Press, 2003.

Eck, John E., and William Spelman. *Problem-Solving: Problem-Oriented Policing in Newport News*. Police Executive Research Forum, 1987.

Epp, Charles R. *Making Rights Real: Activists, Bureaucrats, and the Creation of the Legalistic State*. University of Chicago Press, 2009.

Epp, Charles R., Steven Maynard-Moody, and Donald P. Haider-Markel. "Driver Interview Archive." In *Reconstructing Law on the Street: Transcripts of Interviews and Focus Groups*. KU ScholarWorks, 2011.

Gould, Jon B., and Stephen D. Mastrofski. "Suspect Searches: Assessing Police Behavior under the Constitution." *Criminology & Public Policy* 3 (2004): 316–62.

Harris, David A. *Profiles in Injustice: Why Racial Profiling Cannot Work*. The New Press, 2002.

Jones-Brown, Delores. "Forever the Symbolic Assailant: The More Things Change, the More They Stay the Same." *Criminology & Public Policy* 6, no. 1 (2007): 113–14.

Kennedy, David M. *Don't Shoot: One Man, a Street Fellowship, and the End of Violence in Inner-City America*. Bloomsbury, 2012.

Koper, Christopher S., and Evan Mayo-Wilson. "Police Crackdowns on Illegal Gun Carrying: A Systematic Review of the Impact on Gun Crime." *Journal of Experimental Criminology* 2 (2006): 227–61.

McGarrell, Edmund. "Reducing Firearms Violence through Directed Police Patrol." *Criminology & Public Policy* 1, no. 1 (2001): 119–48.

McGarrell, Edmund, Steven Chermak, and Alexander Weiss. "Reducing Firearms Violence through Directed Patrol: Final Report on the Evaluation of the Indianapolis Police Department's Directed Patrol Project." In *Report to the National Institute of Justice*. Crime Control Policy Center, Hudson Institute, 2000.

———. "Reducing Gun Violence: Evaluation of the Indianapolis Police Department's Directed Patrol Project, Ncj-188740." National Institute of Justice, United States Department of Justice, 2002.

Meares, Tracey. "The Legitimacy of Police among Young African-American Men." *Marquette Law Review* 92, no. 4 (Summer 2009): 651–66.

Remsberg, Charles. *Tactics for Criminal Patrol: Vehicle Stops, Drug Discovery and Officer Survival.* Calibre Press, 1995.

Rosenbaum, Dennis P. "The Limits of Hot Spots Policing." In *Police Innovation: Contrasting Perspectives*, edited by David Weisburd and Anthony A. Braga. 245–63. Cambridge University Press, 2006.

Sampson, Robert J., and Stephen W. Raudenbush. "Systematic Social Observation of Public Spaces: A New Look at Disorder in Urban Neighborhoods." *American Journal of Sociology* 105, no. 3 (Nov. 1999): 603–51.

Sampson, Robert J., Stephen W. Raudenbush, and Felton Earls. "Neighborhoods and Violent Crime." *Science* 277 (1997): 918–24.

Sherman, Lawrence W., James W. Shaw, and Dennis P. Rogan. "The Kansas City Gun Experiment." *Research in Brief*, January 1995, 1–11.

Smedley, Brian D., Adrienne Y. Stith, and Alan R. Nelson, eds. *Unequal Treatment: Confronting Racial and Ethnic Disparities in Health Care.* National Academy Press, 2003.

Stock, Margaret. "Online Symposium: The Court Throws Arizona a Tough Bone to Chew." *SCOTUSblog*, June 17, 2012. http://www.scotusblog.com/2012/06/online-symposium-the-court-throws-arizona-a-tough-bone-to-chew/.

———. *Why People Obey the Law.* Yale University Press, 1990.

———. *The New World of Police Accountability.* Sage, 2005.

———. *Taming the System: The Control of Discretion in Criminal Justice*, 1950–1990. Oxford University Press, 1993.

Warren, Patricia Y., and Donald Tomaskovic-Devey. "Racial Profiling and Searches: Did the Politics of Racial Profiling Change Police Behavior?" *Criminology & Public Policy* 8, no. 2 (May 2009): 343–69.

Weaver, Vesla M., and Amy E. Lerman. "Political Consequences of the Carceral State." *American Political Science Review* 104, no. 4 (November 2010): 817–33.

Zimring, Franklin E. *The City That Became Safe: New York's Lessons for Urban Crime and Its Control.* Oxford University Press, 2011.

Reading 4.2

Should Prostitution Be Legalized?

Human rights lawyer DIANNE POST and writer and filmmaker BISHAKHA DATTA go head-to-head.

Dianna Post and Datta Bishakha

NO

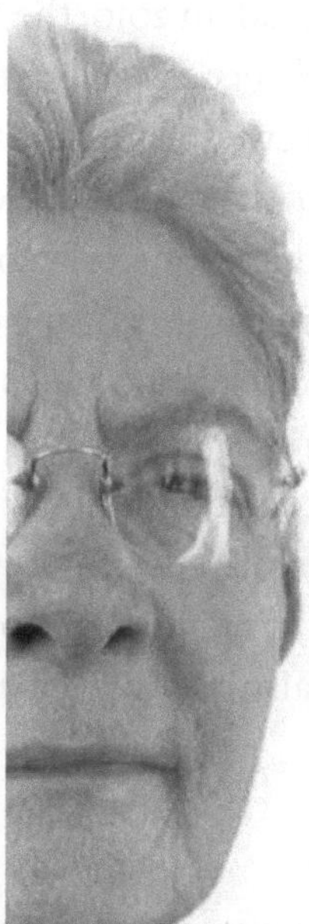

IMG 4.2.1 DIANNE POST is an international human rights attorney who spent 18 years representing battered women and children in family law, but since 1998 has been working internationally in 19 countries on gender-based violence. She is based in Phoenix, Arizona.

Dianne

Legalized prostitution cannot exist alongside the true equality of women. The idea that one group of women should be available for men's sexual access is founded on structural inequality by gender, class and race. Moreover, it is a violation of international law. In fact, failure to challenge legalized prostitution undermines every human rights norm mandating the dignity of the person and equality for all. As Melissa Farley says, 'Decriminalizing or legalizing prostitution would normalize and regulate practices which are human rights violations, and which in any other context would be legally actionable (sexual harassment, physical assault, rape, captivity, economic coercion or emotionally damaging verbal abuse).'

In Sweden, prostitution is officially acknowledged as violence against women and a tool of oppression. 'Legalization of prostitution means that the state imposes regulations with which they can control one class of women as prostituted' (Gunilla Ekberg). Prostitution is not only individual discrimination, exploitation or abuse by an individual man, but also a structure reflecting and maintaining inequality between men and women. It requires 'a devalued class of women ... Prostitution is colonization of women.' (Gunilla Ekberg) Legalization gives approval to violence, control and devaluation. When violence is directed at half the world's population—women—it undermines the entire structure of human rights. The Swedish model calls for no arrests of women, no blaming of the victim, no use of the criminal justice system to control women, but appropriate use of the state system to control violence against women.

Bishakha

I see it somewhat differently. Individuals have sex for a wide range of reasons—for fun and pleasure, to have children, to mark and deepen intimacy, out of duty, to earn a living or for other transactional purposes. It is wholly legitimate for adults to have sex for any, some or all of these reasons, which sometimes overlap.

This is particularly striking in the Indian context, where I come from and where poverty is widespread. In 2010, the World Bank stated that 68.7 per cent of people in India live on less than $2 per day.[1] We're talking about more than 600 million people struggling to find a way to eat two square meals a day.

Some of them turn to sex work just as others turn to other badly paid forms of informal labour—domestic work, construction work, farm labour and so on. All these livelihood options are based on using one or more parts of one's body. We legally accept individuals using their heads and hands and other body parts to earn a living and must do so in the case of sex workers too.

The International Labour Organization (ILO) accepted adult sex work as work in a ground-breaking 1998 report[2] and called for its global recognition as a legitimate form of work. All other forms of informal labour are legally recognized as 'work'—it is high time that adult sex work also got this legal recognition, which is long overdue.

Dianne

We need to listen to the voices of the women. In a five-country survey, over 90 per cent said they wanted to escape prostitution immediately. Nearly 70 per cent of prostituted women meet the criteria for a diagnosis of post-traumatic stress disorder and they constitute 15 per cent of all completed suicides. A Canadian report on prostitution and pornography concluded that girls and women in prostitution have a mortality rate 40 times higher than the national average. The average life span for a woman after entering prostitution is four years, with 50 per cent of the deaths due to murder.

---

1. en.wikipedia.org/wiki/Poverty_in_India
2. *The Sex Sector: The economic and social bases of prostitution in Southeast Asia* edited by Lin Lean Lim, International Labour Office, Geneva, 1998.

The average age of entry into prostitution is 13 or 14 years of age. Children learn very young that their body does not belong to them but to others with power and money. In Canada, 70 per cent of prostituted women are indigenous, despite those communities making up only seven per cent of the population. It's colonialism writ small on their bodies.

In dangerous jobs, we normally fight to eliminate harmful conditions so people can work in safety and with respect. The danger cannot be removed in prostitution because the act of prostitution is the harm. Women in prostitution tell us clearly they want the same options in life that others have: a decent job, safe housing, medical care and psychological counselling. We need exit strategies that include drug treatment, education, training, housing and other support. The answer is to demand equality and equitable distribution of resources.

Bishakha

I completely agree that we should listen to the voices of women in sex work. And here's what these voices are saying: in the first pan-India survey of 3,000 sex workers, about 71 per cent said they had entered sex work willingly. Many of these women, who are not organized, said they left other occupations because of low pay or the absence of regular work.[3]

The researchers say: 'For those coming to sex work from other labour markets, they have often experienced equally harsh (or worse) conditions of highly labour-intensive work for much lower incomes. It is from these background cases that the significance of sex work as a site of higher incomes or livelihoods emerges.'[4]

When adult women say sex work is a form of livelihood or commerce rather than coercion, we need to put aside our discomforts and listen to them. When these women say that the harm in sex work comes not from the act of selling sex, but from the stigma and violence surrounding it because of its illegal and hidden nature, we must hear them.

All over the world, women in sex work are demanding that adult sex work be decriminalized and that they be given rights, respect and recognition. That they be given the right to vote and access health services without stigma, that the cops do not harass them, that their complaints of violence be recorded. That they be given the right to be human, like anyone else.

---

3. Nivedita Menon, *Seeing Like A Feminist*, Zubaan, Penguin 2012.
4. Rohini Sahni and V Kalyan Shankar, *The First Pan-India Survey of Sex Workers: Preliminary Findings.*

Dianne

I believe that the answer to poor jobs, low pay and harsh working conditions for women is not to consign them to a lifetime of abuse, but to fight for all women to have adequate education for decent jobs and for all people to have decent working conditions.

Prostitution is a symptom of the problem, not the problem itself. The problem is patriarchy, inequality, discrimination, inequitable distribution of resources, religious control and fear of women. We need to turn our focus from the symptom to the underlying problem. We can and must do better for women. We need to join hands and together face the real enemy.

The focus on stopping demand is one method that is gaining traction and has been proven successful. Equalizing political power is another approach. In countries where women have a higher percentage of political power, violence against women is lower. Boys must be raised differently. The White Ribbon campaign in Canada and a similar campaign in Mexico are bringing the message to men worldwide. Child sexual abuse and incest in the family and institutions like the church, sports clubs and the Boy Scouts must be eradicated.

'Prostitution isn't like anything else. Rather, everything else is like prostitution because it is the model for women's condition' (Evelina Giobbe, 1992). If we believe in a world where human rights reign and women and men share equal power and dignity, we cannot legalize prostitution and maintain structural inequality founded on gender, class and race.

Bishakha

I fully agree that all human beings should be entitled to decent work, not in the sense of morality, but in the sense of decent working conditions. As Richard Howard of the ILO recently asked: 'Why is sex work not decent work?' His answer: 'I think criminalization is a key barrier that we face along with misinterpretation of religious doctrine and discrimination.'[5]

In Sweden, it is a crime to buy sex and this has adversely affected street sex workers. As one report says: 'Swedish street prostitutes experience a tougher time. They are more frequently exposed to dangerous clients, while the serious clients are afraid of being arrested ... They have less time to assess the client as the deal takes place very hurriedly due to fear on the part of the client ... If the client demands unprotected sex, many of the prostitutes

5. 'The Oldest Profession: Is Sex Work Work?' 26 July 2012 panel at International AIDS Conference, Washington DC.

cannot afford to say no. Harassment by the police has increased and the clients no longer provide tip-offs about pimps, for fear of being arrested themselves.'[6]

In New Zealand/Aotearoa on the other hand, adult sex work is decriminalized. Without making it sound too rosy, removing the 'criminal' label does make it possible for sex workers to access rights and services. Removing this label makes it possible for a sex worker to complain to the police if she is raped. It makes it possible to get health services, like any other citizen. It seems such an obvious—and just—course of action from a human rights perspective that I just can't understand why sex work has still not been decriminalized everywhere.

YES

IMG 4.2.2 BISHAKHA DATTA is a writer and filmmaker based in India. Her most recent book is *9 Degrees of Justice*, a collection of essays on struggles against violence on women in India. Her most recent documentaries include ***In The Flesh: Three Lives In Prostitution***. Bishakha is the executive director of Point of View, a Mumbai non-profit that promotes women's viewpoints through media, art and culture.

6. 'The Swedish Sex Purchase Act: Claimed Success and Documented Effect', by Susanne Dodillet and Petra Oestergren. Conference paper presented at the international workshop Decriminalizing Prostitution and Beyond: Practical Experiences and Challenges. The Hague, 3–4 March 2011.

Reading 4.3

Social Work Students Reflect on Learning about Sex Trafficking

Elizabeth Ringler-Jayanthan, Marni Barish, and Reynel Mirabal Tang

Elizabeth's Story

My journey in becoming an advocate for survivors of human trafficking, started during my time in the United States Peace Corps in Kyrgyzstan. During my service in the Peace Corps, I became aware of the problem of human trafficking in Central Asia. While human trafficking was a well-known problem in Eastern Europe, the problem was not well understood in the rest of the former Soviet states in Central Asia. As a result of the disintegration of the Soviet Union and the subsequent economic collapse, many of the Central Asian countries were left with few employment opportunities—despite having high levels of literacy and educational attainment. Those with means left, causing a major brain-drain in the region. In a state of desperation many individuals in Kyrgyzstan are lured by fraudulent means into sex trafficking in the Middle East, and labor trafficking in Russia and other countries. In neighboring Uzbekistan, every year the government forces the population to harvest cotton without paying them. Exploitation is rife in a region where few opportunities exist for the local population.

Upon my return to the United States, I attended the Graduate School of Public and International Affairs, focusing on Human Security. This gave me a greater understanding of the problem of human trafficking internationally. Later, I started working in refugee resettlement, in which I had the opportunity to work with T-Visa (trafficking visa) cases, providing them with direct services. This gave me a keen perspective on working with international labor trafficking cases. The refugee resettlement agency I worked for partnered with the Project to End Human Trafficking in Pittsburgh, as well as Homeland Security and the FBI for referrals for cases. I also joined the Western PA Human Trafficking Coalition and became more involved in this area. After joining the Western PA Human Trafficking Coalition, I became aware of other local efforts in the region to address human trafficking, and started volunteering with an agency called Living in Liberty. Through my involvement with Living in Liberty, I first heard of Domestic Minor Sex Trafficking and was introduced to the book *Renting Lacy: A Story of America's Prostituted Children*. I was stunned by this—I understood the lack of opportunities faced by those in Kyrgyzstan and how immigrants were tricked into a trafficking situation in United States, but I could not believe that people born in the United States were also trafficked. In 2015, I moved to Miami and started my master's in social work at Barry University. One of my key areas of interest was in working with human trafficking survivors. I began my field placement at the Life of Freedom Center, an anti-trafficking organization. This was my first opportunity to provide direct services to sex trafficking survivors or domestically trafficked individuals. I became aware of a common thread that ran through all of the stories of individuals I had worked with that had been trafficked—they were all vulnerable, lacked opportunities, and were tricked into a situation in which they were exploited. This was true of the people in Central Asia, the Central American labor trafficking cases I had worked with in Pittsburgh, and the domestic sex trafficking cases I worked with at the Life of Freedom Center.

At this time, I started working with Professor Zaoui. I had extensive experience in providing case management, but had no experience in providing therapy. I was offered the opportunity to work as her graduate assistant, in which I studied promising therapeutic techniques in working with trafficking survivors. Through this experience, I entered a deeper level of understanding in what happens in the brain of a trafficking survivor, the way they process trauma, and relate to the world. I have been able to implement the therapeutic techniques I have learned at Barry in working with trafficking survivors at my current field placement.

In October 2015, I had the opportunity to attend the Human Trafficking Summit in Tampa. Professor Zaoui organized Barry students to attend this conference and was able to secure scholarships for us. At this conference, I attended one talk in particular that was eye-opening for me—this talk focused on the vulnerability of transgender females in sex trafficking, as well as the vulnerability of the LGBT community and boys in general. This talk was given by Nathan Earl, the Director of the Ark of Freedom in Miami, an agency that focuses on this population. Again, the theme of vulnerability emerged as he spoke about the risk trans females endure as a result of rejection from their families, lack of employment opportunities related to discrimination, and struggles with homelessness that can ultimately lead to being trafficked.

That December 2015, I was fortunate to attend the Human Trafficking Academy held at St. Thomas Law School. This training focused on the legal efforts that have been made to address human trafficking. At this training, we learned about international, national, and state laws that have been adopted to combat trafficking, but also assessment tools to screen for human trafficking. As a social worker, I may be in a position to be the first person to identify and report trafficking, so these were important tools for me to implement into my practice as a professional.

With all of the education I have received on human trafficking, as well as the direct practice in administering services to trafficking survivors, I am now in a position to educate others on what I've learned. This fall, I was able to present with Professor Zaoui at the Inclusive Communities Mini-Conference at Barry University, where our audience was largely other Barry students. I was also able to present at the Council on Social Work Education conference in Atlanta with Professor Zaoui. The focus of this talk was on how to identify, assess, and treat human trafficking survivors, as well as how to integrate material on human trafficking into social work curriculum. I also had the opportunity to lead a group of Barry students to a conference on Human Trafficking at the University of Miami, in which the Human Trafficking Institute in Atlanta provided students with tools to organize efforts at their universities to raise awareness of this issue.

My passion for this population has been enhanced and cultivated by the opportunities that have been afforded to me during my time at Barry University. I hope to transform this passion into making a real difference for trafficking survivors through direct service, educating the community on this issue, and by influencing policy through advocacy and research. While it is an audacious goal, we must aspire to end human trafficking in our time. As abolitionist William Wilberforce is quoted as saying, "You may choose to look the other way but you can never say again that you did not know."

Marni's Story

My inspiration to become a social worker, and enroll as a social work student came after a series of introductions to the plight of those affected by the issue of sex trafficking. My first introduction to this issue happened while leaving the Former Soviet Union, when my path crossed with a mail order bride who shared her story with me. It was an introduction to a world that until that time, I had no idea existed; one where poverty, removal of protective factors, greed, and demand, created a context for others to be exploited. I had no idea at that time that this one meeting would change the course of my life forever.

An inability to ignore and proceed with life as usual grew within me and understanding came that there was a responsibility coupled with this knowledge. Working in outreach and awareness exposed me to first hand trauma stories that fueled a deeper desire for justice and restoration for victims. I knew my limited education was a barrier that hindered me from entering further arenas of healing with survivors of human trafficking. While my commitment to serve this population was solidified, next steps were unclear. In researching degrees, I came across the profession of social work and was struck by the many branches of reach and opportunity for impact on a micro, mezzo, and macro level. Equally striking, was the incredible core ethics and value for social justice and the dignity and worth of all peoples.

As a social work student, my internship afforded me an opportunity to work as a case manager with survivors of sex trafficking. Many of the principles and perspectives taught in my social work education assisted me in serving my clients. Survivors shared their stories that included profound injustices, exploitation of vulnerabilities, abuse and the breaking down of their humanity. Their needs ranged from case management, housing, legal, medical, education, mental health, and emotional support. Remembering a decade ago when awareness on human trafficking seemed sparse, I felt grateful for those offering service. Highlighted to me was the limited funding for long term residential programs, trauma counseling, and medical services, so often needed for survivors. I was inspired knowing that the social work profession is one that touches these various branches of need, educates and gathers together others in prospective fields to collaborate and advocate for change.

My social work education, offered me practical tools in working with those who have been affected by human trafficking. As a student, I was taught about the importance of empowerment and the awareness that power differentials exists. This was so valuable in working with a population whose experiences often included abuse of power and a sense of powerlessness. Yet, to look beneath the surface of a situation is to see the great resourcefulness, strength, and courage they possessed that caused them to survive. I am most thankful for the training in the strengths based perspective that deepened my belief that survivors cannot just heal but thrive. That lens had allowed me to witness and be inspired by some of the most courageous and resilient of people. Having had the opportunity to see them pull from the resources within and regain their voice is one of my greatest joys.

My social work education has not only broadened my understanding of the issues surrounding human trafficking, it has better equipped me to seek out solutions, and forever changed the way in which I view and experience the world.

Reynel's Story

I have been a Child Protective Investigator (CPI) for the State of Florida for 2 years. During my time as a CPI, I have seen numerous human trafficking cases, although many of them were not identified as human trafficking when the Abuse Hotline screened it in. However, due to my MSW and my knowledge on human trafficking, as a professional, I have been able to identify human trafficking cases, or signs of someone being trafficked.

Many of the cases which have been screened as human trafficking already come with a protocol on how to handle them, which can limit what a CPI is able to do. CPI's have a total of 60 days to build rapport with the child and seek appropriate services for the child. During the 60-day period the CPI has to confirm or deny the allegations.

However, if the case is not identified as human trafficking, once there is the possibility of human trafficking, a CPI is to call law enforcement as well as the Florida abuse hotline to make a report of human trafficking. By the time that CPI speaks to the child about the allegations, the child would have already spoken to a detective from their jurisdiction, as a CPI's job is to provide the appropriate services to the child and their family.

Having an MSW has given me the tools to identify a child who has been trafficked or is currently in the life. I have gained the insight and knowledge to not judge the child while gathering the information needed to confirm the allegations. Furthermore, being educated on human trafficking has given me the tools to be sensitive when addressing the issues of human trafficking and having the child open up without feeling judged. At times, a child will disclose to me but not to law enforcement, as they do not feel comfortable with law enforcement.

As a CPI, one must be certified prior to working on human trafficking cases; the certification consists of a 6-hour training on human trafficking and how to identify a child who has or is currently being trafficked. Such as, being on the lookout for tattoos, expensive jewelry, how the child is dressed, and areas where a child might hang out, that have been identified as areas where there is prostitution. Following the training, one is able to work human trafficking cases.

As a CPI, I have noticed how other people have very little education or knowledge on human trafficking, especially when it comes to interviewing the child. There have been CPI's that ask the child "Have you ever had sex for money?" Once the child says "No" the CPI will automatically close the case.

Learning about human trafficking while obtaining my bachelor's and master's in social work has given me the necessary tools to identify a trafficked child, as well as building rapport and speaking to them without judgment. I believe that without the extensive knowledge and experience, one will not be able to help the child.

Reading 4.4

Wrongful Convictions

How many innocent Americans are behind bars?

Radley Balko

When Paul House was finally released from prison in 2008, he was a specter of the man who had been sentenced to death more than 22 years earlier. When I visit his home in Crossville, Tennessee, in March, House's mother Joyce, who has cared for him since his release, points to a photo of House taken the day he was finally allowed to come home. In that photo and others from his last days in prison, House is all of 150 pounds, ashen and drawn, his fragile frame nearly consumed by his wheelchair. In most of the images he looks days away from death, although in one he wears the broad smile of a man finally escaping a long confinement.

PHOTO 4.4.1

When House's aunt called to congratulate him on his first day back, his mother handed him her cell phone so he could chat. He inspected the phone, gave her a frustrated look, and asked her to find him one that worked. That kind of Rip Van Winkle moment is common among people freed after a long stint in prison. Dennis Fritz, one of the two wrongly convicted men profiled in John Grisham's 2006 book *The Innocent Man,* talks about nearly calling the police upon seeing someone use an electronic key card the first time he found himself in a hotel after his release. He thought he'd witnessed a burglar use a credit card to jimmy open a door.

"Paul's first meal when he got home was chili verde," Joyce House says. "It's his favorite. And I had been waiting a long time to make it for him." And apparently quite a few meals after that.

House, now 49, has put on 75 pounds since his release. More important, he has been getting proper treatment for his advanced-stage multiple sclerosis, treatment the Tennessee prison system hadn't given him.

The years of inadequate care have taken a toll. House can't walk, and he needs help with such basic tasks as bathing, feeding himself, and maneuvering around in his wheelchair. His once distinctively deep voice (which had allegedly been heard by a witness at the crime scene) is now wispy and high-pitched. He spends his time playing computer games and watching game shows.

In the hour or so that I visit with House, his mental facilities fade in and out. Communicating with him can be like trying to listen to a baseball game broadcast by a distant radio station. He will give a slurred but lucid answer to one question, then answer the next one with silence, or with the answer to a previous question, or just with a random assortment of words. He frequently falls back on the resigned refrain, "Oh, well," delivered with a shrug. The gesture and phrasing are identical every time he uses them. It's what House says to kill the expectation that he will be able to deliver the words others in the room are waiting for. It's his signal to stop waiting for him and move on.

In 1986 House was convicted of murdering Carolyn Muncey in Union County, Tennessee, a rural part of the state that shoulders Appalachia. He was sentenced to death. His case is a textbook study in wrongful conviction. It includes mishandled evidence, prosecutorial misconduct, bad science, cops with tunnel vision, DNA testing, the near-execution of an innocent man, and an appellate court reluctant to reopen old cases even in the face of new evidence that strongly suggests the jury got it wrong.

House also embodies the tribulations and frustrations that the wrongly convicted encounter once they get out. According to the doctors treating him, his current condition is the direct result of the inadequate care he received in prison. If he is ever granted a formal exoneration—a process that can be as much political as it is judicial—he will be eligible for compensation for his years behind bars, but even then the money comes with vexing conditions and limitations.

Since 1989, DNA testing has freed 268 people who were convicted of crimes they did not commit. There are dozens of other cases, like House's, where DNA strongly suggests innocence but does not conclusively prove it. Convicting and imprisoning an innocent person is arguably the worst thing a government can do to one of its citizens, short of mistakenly executing him. (There's increasing evidence that this has happened too.) Just about everyone agrees that these are unfathomable tragedies. What is far less clear, and still hotly debated, is what these cases say about the way we administer justice in America, what we owe the wrongly convicted, and how the officials who send innocent people to prison should be held accountable.

How Many Are Innocent?

According to the Innocence Project, an advocacy group that provides legal aid to the wrongly convicted, the average DNA exoneree served 13 years in prison before he or she was freed. Seventeen had been sentenced to death. Remarkably, 67 percent of the exonerated were convicted after 2000, the year that marked the onset of modern DNA testing. Each new exoneration adds more urgency to the question that has hovered over these cases since the first convict was cleared by DNA in 1989: How many more innocent people are waiting to be freed?

Given the soundness of DNA testing, we can be nearly certain that the 268 cleared so far didn't commit the crimes for which they were convicted. There are hundreds of other cases where no DNA evidence exists to definitively establish guilt or innocence, but a prisoner has been freed due to lack of evidence, recantation of eyewitness testimony, or police or prosecutorial misconduct. Those convictions were overturned because there was insufficient evidence to overcome reasonable doubt; it does not necessarily mean the defendant didn't commit the crime. It's unclear whether and how those cases should be factored into any attempt to estimate the number of innocent people in prison.

In a country where there are 15,000 to 20,000 homicides each year, 268 exonerations over two decades may seem like an acceptable margin of error. But reform advocates point out that DNA testing is conclusive only in a small percentage of criminal cases. Testing is helpful only in solving crimes where exchange of DNA is common and significant, mostly rape and murder. (And most murder exonerations have come about because the murder was preceded by a rape that produced testable DNA.) Even within this subset of cases, DNA evidence is not always preserved, nor is it always dispositive to the identity of the perpetrator.

Death penalty cases add urgency to this debate. In a 2007 study published in the *Journal of Criminal Law and Criminology*, the Seton Hall law professor Michael Risinger looked at cases of exoneration for capital murder-rapes between 1982 and 1989, compared them to the total number of murder-rape cases over that period for which DNA would be a factor, and estimated from that data that 3 percent to 5 percent of the people convicted of capital crimes probably are innocent. If Risinger is right, it's still unclear how to extrapolate figures for the larger prison population. Some criminologists argue that there is more pressure on prosecutors and jurors to convict someone, *anyone,* in high-profile murder cases. That would suggest a higher wrongful conviction rate in death penalty cases. But defendants also tend to have better representation in capital cases, and media interest can also mean more scrutiny for police and prosecutors. That could lead to fewer wrongful convictions.

In a study published in the *Journal of Criminal Law and Criminology* in 2005, a team led by University of Michigan law professor Samuel Gross looked at 328 exonerations of people who had been convicted of rape, murder, and other felonies between 1989 and 2003. They found that while those who have been condemned to die make up just 1 percent of the prison population, they account for 22 percent of the exonerated. But does that mean capital cases are more likely to bring a wrongful conviction? Or does it mean the attention and scrutiny that death penalty cases get after conviction—particularly as an execution date nears—make it more likely that wrongful convictions in capital cases will be discovered?

Many states have special public defender offices that take over death penalty cases after a defendant has exhausted his appeals. These offices tend to be well-staffed, with enough funding to hire their own investigators and forensic specialists. That sometimes stands in stark contrast to the public defender offices that handled the same cases at trial. Perversely, this means that in some jurisdictions, a defendant wrongly convicted of murder may be better off with a death sentence than with life in prison.

Even if we were to drop below the floor set in the Risinger study and assume that 2 percent of the 2008 prison population was innocent, that would still mean about 46,000 people have been convicted and incarcerated for crimes they didn't commit. But some skeptics say even that figure is way too high.

Joshua Marquis, the district attorney for Clatsop County, Oregon, is an outspoken critic of the Innocence Project and of academics like Risinger and Gross. He is skeptical of the belief that wrongful convictions are common. "If I thought that 3 to 5 percent of people in prison right now were innocent, I'd quit my job," Marquis says. "I'd become a public defender or something. Maybe an activist. Look, nobody but a fool would say that wrongful convictions don't happen. As a prosecutor, my worst nightmare is not losing a case—I've lost cases; I'll lose cases in the future. My worst nightmare is convicting an innocent person, and I tell my staff that. But the question here is whether wrongful convictions are epidemic or episodic. And I just don't think it's possible that the number could be anywhere near 3 to 5 percent."

Marquis and Gross have been butting heads for several years. In a 2006 *New York Times* op-ed piece, Marquis took the 328 exonerations Gross and his colleagues found between 1989 and 2003, rounded it up to 340, then multiplied it by 10—a charitable act, he wrote, to "give the professor the benefit of the doubt." He then divided that number by 15 million, the total number of felony convictions during the same period, and came up with what he said was an error rate of just 0.027 percent. His column was later quoted in a concurring opinion by U.S. Supreme Court Justice Antonin Scalia in the 2006 case *Kansas v. Marsh,* the same opinion where Scalia made the notorious claim that nothing in the U.S. Constitution prevents the government from executing an innocent person.

Gross responded with a 2008 article in the *Annual Review of Law and Social Science*, pointing out that his original number was by no means comprehensive. Those were merely the cases in which a judicial or political process had exonerated someone. The figure suggested only that wrongful convictions *happen*. "By [Marquis'] logic we could estimate the proportion of baseball players who've used steroids by dividing the number of major league players who've been caught by the total of all baseball players at all levels: major league, minor league, semipro, college and Little League," Gross wrote, "and maybe throw in football and basketball players as well."

Whatever the total number of innocent convicts, there is good reason to believe that the 268 cases in which DNA evidence has proven innocence don't begin to scratch the surface. For one thing, the pace of these exonerations hasn't slowed down: There were 22 in 2009, making it the second busiest name-clearing year to date. Furthermore, exonerations are expensive in both time and resources. Merely discovering a possible case and requesting testing often isn't enough. With some commendable exceptions [...], prosecutors tend to fight requests for post-conviction DNA testing. (The U.S. Supreme Court held in 2009 that there is no constitutional right to such tests.) So for now, the pace of genetic exonerations appears to be limited primarily by the amount of money and staff that legal advocacy groups have to uncover these cases and argue them in court, the amount of evidence available for testing, and the willingness of courts to allow the process to happen, not by a lack of cases in need of further investigation.

The Guilt Market

Criminal snitching threatens the integrity of the justice system.

Alexandra Natapoff

Criminal snitches are a pervasive feature of the justice system that the public rarely sees. Every year thousands of offenders offer information to the government on street corners, in the back of police cruisers, in jails, and in courthouse offices. In exchange for the information, police and prosecutors tolerate those informants' crimes. Sometimes the informant avoids arrest altogether; in other cases, prosecutors reward cooperating defendants by filing lesser charges or seeking reduced sentences. Unlike traditional plea bargains, these deals often take place off the record, even as the information they generate is used to support warrants, arrests, and convictions.

(Continued)

The use of criminal informants is most common in drug enforcement, which relies on snitching at every stage of the legal process, from investigations to arrests to plea bargaining to sentencing. Since drug cases constitute about one-third of all state and federal dockets, informants are critical to the day-to-day operation of the justice system. But the snitching model is not limited to the war on drugs. It has spread to street crime, white collar crime, terrorism, and Internet investigations.

In short, the demand for helpful evidence has given rise to a massive underground marketplace in which government officials and suspects negotiate over criminal liability. These deals take place without the usual rules of record keeping, procedure, court oversight, and sometimes even defense counsel. All too often, the courts and the public never learn what offenses were committed or what deals were struck.

Informants can be powerful crime-fighting tools, providing inside information about gangs, drug distribution, organized crime, corporate fraud, and political corruption. But the evidence offered by informants is notoriously unreliable. According to a 2004 study by researchers at Northwestern University Law School, more than 45 percent of wrongful convictions in death penalty cases were due to false informant testimony, making snitches "the leading cause of wrongful convictions in U.S. capital cases."

A particularly pernicious form of snitching has taken root in prisons and jails. Jailhouse informants produce so many wrongful convictions that several states have concluded they can no longer be used without more stringent controls. The use of in-custody informants nevertheless remains widespread. The first public glimpse of the phenomenon was provided by the Los Angeles Grand Jury Report of 1990, which exposed a rampant culture of exchange and fabrication in the Los Angeles County Jail during the 1970s and '80s. Sheriffs, prosecutors, and inmates all understood that jailhouse snitches would be rewarded for coming up with information about other inmates, even when that information was clearly unreliable. Rewards ranged from dropped charges and shortened sentences to cash, jail privileges, even candy.

Federal law even has a special provision for jailhouse snitches. Rule 35 of the Federal Rules of Criminal Procedure offers sentence reductions to incarcerated offenders who provide information after they have started serving their sentences, a rule that Tucker Melancon, a U.S. district judge in Louisiana, has criticized as an invitation to fabrication. This rule created the conditions for the wrongful convictions of Ann Colomb and her three sons, Louisiana defendants who were found guilty of drug dealing in 2006 based on false information concocted by dozens of federal inmates trying to reduce their own sentences.

(Continued)

Drug informants constitute an even larger and arguably more troubling category than jailhouse snitches. In a highly publicized 2000 debacle, a federally funded drug task force made dozens of arrests in Hearne, Texas, based on information from a single informant—an addict with mental health problems who was trying to avoid new burglary charges. The resulting convictions were overturned after the informant was shown to have fabricated the evidence. The case triggered a lawsuit by the American Civil Liberties Union and inspired the 2009 movie *American Violet*. But law enforcement agencies still rely heavily on such witnesses, even though they have strong incentives to lie and even though the legal system is poorly equipped to verify their claims.

The good news is that there has been substantial movement toward reform. DNA exonerations and high-profile scandals like the ones in Los Angeles and Hearne have spurred legislators, journalists, and the public to question the shadowy practice of trading favors for evidence. California, Texas, Illinois, Florida, New York, and Washington state have considered or passed legislation restricting the use of informants, and several state commissions are studying the question. These efforts reflect the growing realization that widespread, unregulated informant deals are incompatible with a reliable, accountable, and transparent system of criminal justice.

Alexandra Natapoff, a professor at Loyola Law School in Los Angeles, is the author of Snitching: Criminal Informants and the Erosion of American Justice (NYU Press), which won the 2010 ABA Silver Gavel Award Honorable Mention for Books. She blogs at snitching.org.

It's notable that one of the few places in America where a district attorney has specifically dedicated staff and resources to seeking out bad convictions—Dallas County, Texas—has produced more exonerations than all but a handful of *states*. That's partly because Dallas County District Attorney Craig Watkins is more interested in reopening old cases than his counterparts elsewhere, and partly because of a historical quirk: Since the early 1980s the county has been sending biological crime scene evidence to a private crime lab for testing, and that lab has kept the evidence well preserved. Few states require such evidence be preserved once a defendant has exhausted his appeals, and in some jurisdictions the evidence is routinely destroyed at that point.

"I don't think there was anything unique about the way Dallas was prosecuting crimes," Watkins told me in 2008. "It's unfortunate that other places didn't preserve evidence too. We're just in a unique position where I can look at a case, test DNA evidence from that period, and say without a doubt that a person is innocent. ... But that doesn't mean other places don't have the same problems Dallas had."

If the rest of the country has an actual (but undetected) wrongful conviction rate as high as Dallas County's, the number of innocents in prison for felony crimes could be in the tens of thousands.

The Trial and Conviction of Paul House

As with many wrongful convictions, the case against Paul House once seemed watertight. House was an outsider, having only recently moved to Union County when Carolyn Muncey was murdered in 1985, and he was an ex-con, having served five years in a Utah prison for sexual assault. He got into scuffles with locals, although he considered Muncey and her husband, Hubert, friends. When Muncey turned up dead, House was a natural suspect.

House has claimed he was innocent of the Utah charge. His mother, Joyce, says it was a he said/she said case in which her son pleaded guilty on the advice of his attorney. "He could have been paroled earlier if he had shown some remorse," she says. "But he said, 'I pled guilty the one time, because that's what the lawyer told me I should do. I'm not going to say again that I did something I didn't do.' He said he'd rather serve more time than admit to the rape again." Joyce House and Mike Pemberton, Paul House's attorney, are hesitant to go into much detail about the Utah case, and public records aren't available due to the plea bargain. But while what happened in Utah certainly makes House less sympathetic, it has no bearing on whether House is the man who killed Carolyn Muncey.

House also didn't do himself any favors during the Muncey investigation. In initial questioning, he lied to the police about where he was the night of the murder, saying he was with his girlfriend all night. But he later admitted he had gone for a walk at one point and had come back without his shoes and with scratches on his arms. He initially lied to police about the scratches too, saying they were inflicted by his girlfriend's cats. House later said he'd been accosted by some locals while on his walk, scuffled with them, then fled through a field, where he lost his shoes. (House would learn years later that his shoes were found by police before his trial. There was no blood or other biological evidence on them, potentially exculpatory information that was never turned over to House's lawyers.)

"I think it was a situation where you're on parole, you're an outsider, and this woman has just been killed near where you live," says Pemberton, House's attorney. "It wasn't smart of him to lie to the police. But it was understandable."

Carolyn Muncey's husband, who House's attorneys would later suspect was her killer, also lied about where he was when she was killed. He would additionally claim, falsely, that he had never physically abused her. Still, House was clearly the early suspect.

The strongest evidence against House was semen found on Muncey's clothing, which an FBI agent testified at trial "could have" belonged to House. DNA testing didn't exist in

1986, but the agent said House was a secretor, meaning he produced blood type secretions in other body fluids, including semen, and that the type secreted in semen found on Muncey's nightgown was a match to House's type A blood. About 80 percent of people are secretors, and about 36 percent of Americans have type A blood. The agent also said the semen found on Muncey's panties included secretions that *didn't* match House's blood type, but added, inaccurately, that House's secretion could have "degraded" into a match. Muncey's husband was never tested.

The other strong evidence against House was some blood stains on his jeans that matched Muncey's blood type, but not his own. Those stains on House's jeans did turn out to have been Muncey's blood; the question is how they got there.

House was never charged with rape; there were no physical indications that Muncey had been sexually assaulted. But the semen was used to put him at the crime scene, and the state used the possibility of rape as an aggravating circumstance in arguing that House should receive the death penalty.

House was convicted in February 1986. The morning after his conviction, just hours before the sentencing portion of his trial, House slashed his wrists with a disposable razor. He left behind a suicide note in which he professed his innocence. Jail officials rushed him to a hospital in Knoxville, where doctors saved his life and stitched up his wounds. He was then sent back to the courthouse, where a jury sentenced him to death.

It wasn't until more than a decade later, in 1999, that the case against House began to erode. New witnesses came forward with accusations against Hubert Muncey, Carolyn's husband. Several said he was an alcoholic who frequently beat her. At an ensuing evidentiary hearing, two other women said Hubert had drunkenly confessed to killing his wife several months after the murder. When one went to the police with the information the next day, she said at the hearing, the sheriff brushed her off. Another witness testified that Hubert Muncey had asked her to lie to back up his alibi.

But it was the forensic evidence presented at that 1999 hearing that really unraveled the state's case. When House's attorneys were finally able to get DNA testing for the semen found on Carolyn Muncey's clothes, it showed that the semen was a match to Muncey's husband, not House. The state responded that rape was never part of their case against House (though it is why he was initially a suspect, it was the only conceivable motive, and it was presented as evidence in the sentencing portion of his trial). Besides, prosecutors argued, there was still the blood on House's jeans.

Except there were problems with that too. Cleland Blake, an assistant chief medical examiner for the state of Tennessee, testified that while the blood did belong to Muncey, its chemical composition indicated it was blood that had been taken *after* she had been autopsied. Worse still, three-quarters of a test tube of the blood taken during Muncey's autopsy went missing between the time of the autopsy and the time House's jeans arrived at the FBI crime lab for testing. The test tubes with Muncey's blood and House's jeans were transported in the same Styrofoam box. The blood on House's jeans, his attorneys argued, must have either been planted or spilled because of sloppy handling of the evidence.

It is extraordinarily difficult to win a new trial in a felony case, even in light of new evidence, and House's case was no exception. A federal circuit court judge denied his request for post-conviction relief, and the U.S. Court of Appeals for the 6th Circuit affirmed that decision. Somewhat surprisingly, the U.S. Supreme Court agreed to hear House's case, and in 2006 issued a rare, bitterly divided 5-to-3 ruling granting House a new trial.

The Supreme Court has occasionally thrown out death penalty convictions because of procedural errors or constitutional violations, but it's rare for the Court to methodically review the evidence in a capital case. Writing for the majority, Justice Anthony Kennedy did exactly that, finding in the end that "although the issue is close, we conclude that this is the rare case where—had the jury heard all the conflicting testimony—it is more likely than not that no reasonable juror viewing the record as a whole would lack reasonable doubt."

It was a surprising and significant victory for House. But it would be another three years before he would be released from prison.

How Do Wrongful Convictions Happen?

The most significant consequence of the spate of DNA exonerations has been a much-needed reassessment of what we thought we knew about how justice is administered in America. Consider the chief causes of wrongful convictions:

Bad forensic evidence. DNA technology was developed by scientists, and it has been thoroughly peer-reviewed by other scientists. Most of the forensic science used in the courtroom, on the other hand, was either invented in police stations and crime labs or has been refined and revised there to fight crime and obtain convictions. Most forensic evidence isn't peer-reviewed, isn't subject to blind testing, and is susceptible to corrupting bias, both intentional and unintentional. The most careful analysts can fall victim to cognitive bias creeping into their work, particularly when their lab falls under the auspices of a law enforcement agency. Even fingerprint analysis isn't as sound as is commonly believed.

A congressionally commissioned 2009 report by the National Academy of Sciences found that many other forensic specialties that are often presented in court with the gloss of science—hair and carpet fiber analysis, blood spatter analysis, shoe print identification, and especially bite mark analysis—lack the standards, peer review, and testing procedures of genuinely scientific research and analysis. Some are not supported by any scientific literature at all. Moreover, the report found, even the forensic specialties with some scientific support are often portrayed in court in ways that play down error rates and cognitive bias.

According to an Innocence Project analysis of the first 225; DNA exonerations, flawed or fraudulent forensic evidence factored into about half of the faulty convictions.

Eyewitness testimony. Social scientists have known about the inherent weakness of eyewitness testimony for decades. Yet it continues to be the leading cause of wrongful convictions in America; it was a factor in 77 percent of those first 225 cases. Simple steps, such as making sure police who administer lineups have no knowledge of the case (since they can give subtle clues to witnesses, even unintentionally) and that witnesses are told that the actual perpetrator may not be among the photos included in a lineup, can go a long way toward improving accuracy. But such reforms also make it more difficult to win convictions, so many jurisdictions, under pressure from police and prosecutor groups, have been hesitant to embrace them.

False confessions. Difficult as it may be to comprehend, people do confess to crimes they didn't commit. It happened in about one-quarter of the first 225 DNA exonerations. Confessions are more common among suspects who are minors or are mentally handicapped, but they can happen in other contexts as well, particularly after intense or abusive police interrogations.

In a candid 2008 op-ed piece for the *Los Angeles Times,* D.C. Police Detective Jim Trainum detailed how he unwittingly coaxed a false confession out of a 34-year-old woman he suspected of murder. She even revealed details about the crime that could only have been known to police investigators and the killer. But Trainum later discovered that the woman couldn't possibly have committed the crime. When he reviewed video of his interrogation, he realized that he had inadvertently provided the woman with those very specific details, which she then repeated back to him when she was ready to confess.

Trainum concluded that all police interrogations should be videotaped, a policy that would not just discourage abusive questioning but also provide an incontrovertible record of how a suspect's confession was obtained. Here too, however, there has been pushback from some police agencies, out of fear that jurors may be turned off even by legitimate forms of questioning.

Jailhouse informants. If you were to take every jailhouse informant at his word, you'd find that a remarkably high percentage of the people accused of felonies boast about their crimes to the complete strangers they meet in jail and prison cells. [...] Informants are particularly valuable in federal drug cases, where helping a prosecutor obtain more convictions is often the only way to get time cut from a mandatory minimum sentence. That gives them a pretty good incentive to lie.

There is some disagreement over a prosecutor's duty to verify the testimony he solicits from jailhouse informants. In the 2006, Church Point, Louisiana, case of Ann Colomb, for example, Brett Grayson, an assistant U.S. attorney in Louisiana, put on a parade of jailhouse informants whose claims about buying drugs from Colomb and her sons were rather improbable, especially when the sum of their testimony was considered as a whole. According to defense attorneys I spoke with, when one attorney asked him if he actually believed what his informants were telling the jury, Grayson replied that it doesn't matter if he believes his witnesses; it only matters if the jury does. He expressed a similar sentiment in his closing argument.

After indicating that he isn't familiar with the Colomb case and isn't commenting on Grayson specifically, Josh Marquis says that sentiment is wrong. "A prosecutor absolutely has a duty to only put on evidence he believes is truthful," Marquis says. "And that includes the testimony you put on from informants."

In a 2005 study, the Center on Wrongful Convictions in Chicago found that false or misleading informant testimony was responsible for 38 wrongful convictions in death penalty cases.

The professional culture of the criminal justice system. In addition to the more specific causes of wrongful convictions listed above, there is a problem with the institutional culture among prosecutors, police officers, forensic analysts, and other officials. Misplaced incentives value high conviction rates more than a fair and equal administration of justice. [...]

Prosecutors in particular enjoy absolute immunity from civil liability, even in cases where they manufacture evidence that leads to a wrongful conviction. The only time prosecutors can be sued is when they commit misconduct while acting as investigators—that is, while doing something police normally do. At that point they're subject to qualified immunity, which provides less protection than absolute immunity but still makes it difficult to recover damages.

Marquis says this isn't a problem. "Prosecutors are still subject to criminal liability," he says. "In fact, my predecessor here in Oregon was prosecuted for misconduct in criminal cases. State bars will also hold prosecutors accountable."

But criminal charges are few and far between, and prosecutors can make egregious mistakes that still don't rise to the level of criminal misconduct. Professional sanctions are also rare. A 2010 study by the Northern California Innocence Project found more than 700 examples between 1997 and 2009 in which a court had found misconduct on the part of a prosecutor in the state. Only six of those cases resulted in any disciplinary action by the state bar. A 2010 investigation of federal prosecutorial misconduct by *USA Today* produced similar results: Of 201 cases in which federal judges found that prosecutors had committed misconduct, just one resulted in discipline by a state bar association. Prosecutorial misconduct was a factor in about one-quarter of the first 225 DNA exonerations, but none of the prosecutors in those cases faced any significant discipline from the courts or the bar.

There is also a common misconception that appeals courts serve as a check on criminal justice abuse. It is actually rare for an appeals court to review the evidence in a criminal case. Appeals courts make sure trials abide by the state and federal constitutions and by state or federal rules of criminal procedure, but they almost never second-guess the conclusions of juries.

In a 2008 article published in the *Columbia Law Review*, the University of Virginia law professor Brandon L. Garrett looked at the procedural history of the first 200 cases of DNA exoneration. Of those, just 18 convictions were reversed by appellate courts. Another 67 defendants had their appeals denied with no written ruling at all. In 63 cases, the appellate court opinion described the defendant as guilty, and in 12 cases it referred to the "overwhelming" evidence of guilt. Keep in mind these were all cases in which DNA testing later proved actual innocence. In the remaining cases, the appeals courts either found the defendant's appeal without merit or found that the errors in the case were "harmless"—that is, there were problems with the case, but those problems were unlikely to have affected the jury's verdict due to the other overwhelming evidence of guilt.

"We've seen a lot of exoneration cases where, for example, the defendant raised a claim of ineffective assistance of counsel," says Peter Neufeld, co-founder of the Innocence Project of New York. "And in those cases, the appellate courts often found that the defense lawyer provided substandard representation. But they would then say that the poor lawyering didn't prejudice the case because the evidence of guilt was so overwhelming. Well, these people were later proven innocent! If you have a test that is frequently producing erroneous results, there's either something wrong with the test, or there's something wrong with the way it's being implemented."

Life on the Outside

Paul House was diagnosed with multiple sclerosis in 2000, a year after the evidentiary hearing that would eventually lead to his release. But while House was convicted of Carolyn Muncey's murder less than a year after it happened, it took a decade after his conviction was called into serious question for House to get back home to Crossville. During those 10 years, the state's case continued to fall apart. So did House's body.

After the U.S. Supreme Court overturned House's conviction in 2006, Paul Phillips, the district attorney for Tennessee's 8th Judicial District and the man who prosecuted House in 1986, pushed ahead with plans to retry him. In December 2007, after a series of delays, Harry S. Mattice Jr., a U.S. district court judge in Knoxville, finally ordered the state to try

House within 180 days or set him free. Those 180 days then came and went without House being freed, thanks to an extension granted by the 6th Circuit.

In another hearing held in May 2008, Phillips argued that House—who by that point couldn't walk or move his wheelchair without assistance—presented a flight risk. Later, Tennessee Associate Deputy Attorney General Jennifer Smith attempted to show that House presented a danger to the public because he was still capable of feeding himself with a fork, which apparently meant he was also capable of stabbing someone with one. House's bail was set at $500,000, later reduced to $100,000. In July 2008, an anonymous donor paid the bail, allowing House to finally leave prison.

That same month, Phillips told the Associated Press that he would send two additional pieces of biological evidence off for DNA testing: a hair found at the crime scene, and blood found under Carolyn Muncey's fingernails. House's defense team had asked to conduct its own testing of any untested biological evidence for years, but had been told that either there was no such evidence or, if there was, the state didn't know where it was. Philips told the A.P. that if the new tests didn't implicate House, he would drop the murder charge and allow House to go home. In February 2009 the results came back. They didn't implicate House, and in fact pointed to a third, unidentified man. In May of that year, Phillips finally dropped the charge. But he still wouldn't clear House's name, telling Knoxville's local TV station WATE, "There is very adequate proof that Mr. House was involved in this crime. We just don't know the degree of culpability beyond a reasonable doubt." (Phillips' office did not respond to my requests for comment.)

Culture of Misconduct

The misplaced priorities of prosecutors

Ken White

I began my term as a federal prosecutor on October 3, 1995, the day O.J. Simpson was acquitted. The approving roar of the crowd at Camp O.J. across the street from the Los Angeles federal courthouse interrupted my supervisor's earnest lecture on our obligations as prosecutors. It did not sound like an auspicious beginning.

After the tumult died down, my supervisor read us the famous passage from Supreme Court Justice George Sutherland's opinion in the 1935 case *Berger v. United States,* reminding us that our duty was not to win the case, but to see "that justice shall be done."

(Continued)

Veteran prosecutors across the country instruct neophytes with similar exhortations. They will commonly say, borrowing from Sutherland, that prosecutors may strike hard blows but not foul ones.

Yet state and federal prosecutors routinely fall short of this ideal. There are too many stories of convictions obtained through subornation of perjury, through suppression of exculpatory evidence, and through the willful use of unreliable, wrongfully obtained confessions.

It's difficult enough to detect misconduct, mostly due to inadequate funding for criminal defense. But if detection is rare, redress is even rarer. Prosecutors enjoy "absolute immunity" from lawsuits, a privilege no other profession in America enjoys save for judges. In theory, state bars should sanction misbehaving prosecutors, but that is also vanishingly rare. Last September, *USA Today* found 210 cases in which federal prosecutors had committed ethical breaches so egregious that a federal judge personally rebuked the prosecutor, overturned a conviction, or dismissed the criminal charges entirely. The prosecutor faced serious discipline from a state bar in just one of those 210 cases. Recent studies of misconduct among state prosecutors in California have produced similar results: disturbing examples of misconduct and an even more disturbing lack of accountability.

I've worked as both a prosecutor and a defense lawyer. In my experience, one primary problem drives all these issues: a professional culture that values winning above all else.

Defense lawyers, of course, do their absolute best for their clients in every case, but they tend to understand that the deck is stacked against them. They can't possibly win them all, in part because of the government's overwhelming resources, in part because of judges' and jurors' tendency to defer to law enforcement, and in part because many of our clients aren't particularly sympathetic. Defendants often actually did do *something,* even if it isn't quite what the government says.

By contrast, too many prosecutorial agencies develop a culture that treats victory as the only acceptable result; any defeat is a humiliating rebuke. They simply don't contemplate the possibility that a not-guilty verdict might be the just result. It isn't difficult to see how this culture of victory could pressure some prosecutors to go to extraordinary, sometimes unethical means to avoid the shame of defeat.

Willful ignorance is also a problem. It takes time, resources, and leadership to train young prosecutors on new developments in the constitutional and statutory rights of criminal defendants. Some offices just don't bother. They focus on the nuts and bolts

(Continued)

of trials and on the taxonomy of crime, but they don't seem as interested in keeping up to speed on the rights of the accused. Prosecutors, especially young ones, can't be expected to respect rights they don't understand. I'll never forget a prosecutor telling my partner—who had just won a motion to stop the prosecutor from bullying grand jury witnesses—that he'd have to "look into this whole Fifth Amendment thing." That prosecutor is now a judge. In a decision last March that will only make this problem worse, the U.S. Supreme Court ruled that municipalities can't be sued for failing to properly train prosecutors, even on basic ethical obligations such as the responsibility to turn over exculpatory evidence to defense attorneys.

Prosecutors grow up, go to law school, and practice law in the context of American culture. After 40 years of "law and order" rhetoric from politicians and public officials, that culture has grown explicitly hostile to the rights of criminal defendants. Movies, television shows, and pundits portray these rights not as a check against overreaching authority but as the mechanism by which gleeful murderers and rapists escape justice "on a technicality." (This is a canard: Federal prosecutors win 85 percent of cases that go to court, and state prosecutors win 60 percent to 85 percent. If you factor in plea bargains, conviction percentages can soar well into the 90s.)

Politicians decry judges as "soft on crime" or "black-robed tyrants" if they impose consequences on police and prosecutors who violate the rights of defendants. A vigorous defense is scorned as chicanery. We reward prosecutors with headlines and re-election for high-profile convictions but not for the cases they choose not to try for lack of evidence. Indeed, declining to bring charges in a high-profile case can be a career killer.

Fortunately, culture can cut both ways. Principled prosecutors can create a sense of professionalism that treats constitutional and statutory rights not as impediments or annoyances but as the only acceptable boundaries of conduct. I was privileged to serve under a U.S. attorney who made it clear that candor with the court and scrupulous regard for constitutional rights were essential elements of representing the United States. She set the tone for the office. The Department of justice has started a new Professional Misconduct Review Unit, which could serve to spread similar values to other U.S. attorneys' offices.

But ultimately, supervisors, district attorneys, and justice Department officials answer to the public. If we as a society continue to equate justice with conviction rates and mass incarceration, the culture of misconduct is not going to change.

Ken White, a former federal prosecutor, is a criminal defense attorney in Los Angeles.

By the time House was diagnosed with M.S. in 2000, his symptoms were already severe, although it took his mother, and not a prison doctor, to notice something was wrong. "I was visiting him, and I brought along some microwave popcorn," Joyce House recalls. "He asked me to heat it up, and I said, 'No, you heat it up.' When he got up, he had to prop himself up and drag along the wall to get to the microwave. He couldn't even stand up straight." According to Joyce House, her son's doctors today say that the Tennessee prison system's failure to diagnose House's M.S. earlier—then treat it properly after it was diagnosed—may have taken years off his life. (M.S. is also exacerbated by stress.) The disease has also significantly diminished the quality of the life House has left.

Under Tennessee's compensation law for the wrongly convicted, if House is formally exonerated—and that's still a big *if*—he will be eligible for $50,000 for each year he was in prison, up to $1 million. But there's a catch. The compensation is given in annual $50,000 installments over 20 years. If House dies before then, the payments stop.

Most of the 27 states with compensation laws similarly pay the money off in installments. Last October, A.P. ran a story about Victor Burnette, a 57-year-old Virginia man who served eight years for a 1979 rape before he was exonerated by DNA testing in 2006. Burnette actually turned down the $226,500 the state offered in compensation in 2010 because he was offended by the stipulation that it be paid out over 25 years. Even after the DNA test confirmed his innocence, it took another three years for Burnette to officially be pardoned, which finally made him eligible for the money. The installment plans make it unlikely that many exonerees—especially long-timers, who are arguably the most deserving—will ever see full compensation for their years in prison.

Only about half the people exonerated by DNA testing so far have been compensated at all. Most compensation laws require official findings of actual innocence, which eliminates just about any case that doesn't involve DNA. Some states also exclude anyone who played some role in their own conviction, which would disqualify a defendant who falsely confessed, even if the confession was coerced or beaten out of them.

Paul House has yet another predicament ahead of him. Even if he does win an official exoneration, and even if he somehow lives long enough to receive all of his compensation, he'll have to lose his health insurance to accept it. House's medical care is currently covered by TennCare, Tennessee's Medicare program. If he accepts compensation for his conviction, he will be ineligible. His $50,000 per year in compensation for nearly a quarter century on death row will then be offset by a steep increase in what he'll have to pay for his medical care.

These odd, sometimes absurd predicaments aren't intentionally cruel. They just work out that way. Paul House's attorney Mike Pemberton points out that the prosecutors in these cases aren't necessarily evil, either. "Paul Phillips is an honorable man, and an outstanding trial attorney," Pemberton says. "But on this case he was wrong." Pemberton, who was once a prosecutor himself, says the job can lend itself to tunnel vision, especially once a prosecutor has won a conviction. It can be hard to let go. We have a system with misplaced incentives and very little accountability for state actors who make mistakes. That's a system ripe for bad outcomes.

When I ask Paul House why he thinks it has taken so long to clear his name, he starts to answer, then stammers, looks away, and retreats again to *Oh well,* his cue to move on because he has no answer.

That may be an understandable response from a guy with advanced M.S. who just spent two decades on death row. But for too long our national response to the increasing evidence that our justice system is flawed has been the same sort of resignation. DNA has only begun to show us where some of those flaws lie. It will take a strong public will to see that policy-makers address them.

Reading 4.5

Time to Abolish Cash Bail

It Doesn't Keep Dangerous Criminals off the Streets. It Just Keeps the Poor in Jail—and Finance Companies Rolling in Profits.

Anne Kim

PHOTO 4.5.1 Innocent but not free: Baltimore resident Rafiq Shaw was acquitted on weapons charges after a mistaken arrest. But he still owes his bail bondsman $10,000.

THE ROW HOUSE ON CECIL AVENUE was just like any other in the rough-and-tumble East Baltimore neighborhood where Rafiq Shaw lives. But one chilly day in December 2015, he had the bad luck to be walking by right as the police were getting ready for a raid.

Anne Kim, "Time to Abolish Cash Bail," *The Washington Monthly*, vol. 49, no. 1, pp. 21–27.

"All out of the blue a bunch of police cars pulled up and grabbed me," Shaw told me in September. "They threw me to the wall and put cuffs on me." The officers insisted he had come out of the house, which Shaw just as vehemently denied. "They thought I was someone else," he said. "That's what they thought the whole time. They called a name out that wasn't me."

Shaw is a tall, heavyset thirty-one-year-old black man with a booming voice and an easy smile. He told his story almost cheerfully, emphasizing the absurdity of the harrowing situation he was describing.

Over his protests, Shaw continued, the police dragged him into the house, where a woman inside told the officers she had no idea who he was. The officers pushed him onto a couch and went through his pockets, finding the keys to his mother's car, parked nearby.

Later, at his trial, in August 2016, officers would testify that Shaw consented to a search of the car. (Shaw told me he didn't.) They also claimed to smell marijuana, although the doors were shut and the windows were up. Shaw's attorney, Maryland public defender Angela Oetting, said that's a claim Baltimore cops often use to justify searches of her clients.

The police did not, in fact, find marijuana in the car. But they did claim to find a gun, stashed in the glove compartment. It was a discovery that stunned Shaw, who said he has never owned a gun. "And this was my mom's car," he added. He was arrested and charged with two offenses: illegal possession of a handgun and possession of a handgun in a vehicle on a public road, punishable by up to three years in prison.

Police had no evidence, such as fingerprints, to prove the gun was Shaw's. He didn't even have a key to the glove compartment; the cops had to smash it open. After less than a half an hour of deliberation, the jury found Shaw innocent on both counts.

But Shaw is still paying for the crime he never committed. He's on the hook for the $10,000 his family agreed to pay the bail bondsman who got him out of jail two days after his arrest. In Maryland, as in the many other jurisdictions that rely on private bondsmen and a money bail system, bail arrangements are private contracts, unrelated to court outcomes. Innocent, guilty, or charges dropped—as often is the case—the bondsman still collects his fee. "It's crazy," Shaw said. But it's the inevitable result of a privatized pretrial system dependent on a commercial bail bond industry.

The stated purpose of cash bail is to ensure that defendants show up in court and that dangerous people stay off the streets. By requiring some amount of money up-front and threatening further cash penalties, defendants are motivated to comply. Or so the theory goes. But it's increasingly clear that cash bail doesn't accomplish these goals either fairly or efficiently, and that alternatives that don't require defendants to pay for their release are actually more effective. In the large swaths of the country that still rely on cash bail, it's all too often the poor—not the dangerous or delinquent—who remain behind bars when they can't afford to purchase their freedom. Those who do pay bail, like Shaw, often find themselves in another kind of prison: shackled for months or years to a debt that hobbles their opportunities to get ahead. And it's the government, prodded along by a powerful bail lobby, that enables the industry's privileged position by providing a steady stream of clients, by protecting the industry's right to collect, and by unthinkingly setting bail amounts that leave defendants little choice but to finance their freedom with a bondsman.

In Shaw's case, the district court commissioner who handled his arraignment set bail at $100,000. His fiancée and his mother scraped together what they had, and Shaw cleaned out his meager savings. They gave it all to their bail bondsman, who agreed to bail Shaw out—to be his "surety"—for a fee of 10 percent, or $10,000. Shaw and his family said they paid the bondsman about $2,000 up front, with a promise to pay $100 a week until the amount was paid in full. Shaw earns $10.15 an hour installing trailer hitches for U-Haul. "I'll be paying for a long time," he told me. "Like forever."

Baltimore Discount Bonds operates out of a storefront right next to the Baltimore Central Booking and Intake Center, on Eager Street downtown. It's one of more than 200 bail bondsmen advertising in the city's yellow pages and online.

One reason Baltimore's for-profit bail bond industry is thriving is the sheer number of arrests every day. From January 1 to September 30, 2016, Baltimore police made 19,905 arrests, including 2,136 in September alone—an average of seventy a day. Most of those arrested were young black men.

Nor is Baltimore an outlier in the zealousness—or overzealousness—of its police force. Thanks in part to "zero tolerance" policies and other crackdowns across the country, police made about 10.8 million arrests in 2015, according to the Federal Bureau of Investigation's Uniform Crime Reporting Statistics. Only a fraction of these arrests result in prosecutions, let alone in trials or convictions. Some of this has to do with the lack of capacity on the part of prosecutors to keep up with the flood of arrests. But in Baltimore, at least, many arrests are simply unwarranted to begin with. According to a 2016 investigation of the Baltimore Police Department by the U.S. Department of Justice, local prosecutors threw out more than 11,000 charges between 2010 and 2015 "because they lacked probable cause or otherwise did not merit prosecution." The Justice Department concluded that Baltimore police habitually engaged in unconstitutional stops, searches, and arrests, often disproportionately targeted at minorities. Justified or not, these arrests are a principal source of traffic at the Baltimore city jail.

Adding to the scrum at central booking is another peculiarity of Maryland law: the ability of any citizen to file a complaint with a district court commissioner if police or prosecutors don't investigate. According to a report by the state of Maryland, more than four in ten of the warrants issued by district court commissioners in 2012 were based on citizen complaints, which require no investigation beyond a sworn statement by the complainant.

All of these arrests are a great source of business for Baltimore's bail bondsmen, who are a fixture in the city's urban landscape. "Finding a bail bondsman is like finding a barber or a grocery store," said Greg Carpenter, the founder of 2AM Bakery, a Baltimore business that rehabilitates ex-offenders. "Where crime is really prevalent and people are going to jail every day, bail bondsmen are as common as anything else."

Competition is fierce. Despite a statutory prohibition on soliciting business near jails, bondsmen prowl the turf near central booking, looking for desperate loved ones of people in lockup. Shaw's fiancée, Destiny, told me she was approached by several bondsmen when she went to visit Shaw immediately after his arrest. "A lot of people come up to you and say, 'I'm a bail bondsman,'" she said. "It's a hustle for them."

Still, it pays to choose the right bondsman. Maryland law caps the fee a bondsman can charge at 10 percent of bail. Some bondsmen try to undercut the competition with "discounts" on their fees. Others offer financing with just 1 percent down. Shaw's fellow inmates recommended a bondsman who was reportedly cheap—but in Annapolis. Unable to make the trip, Shaw's mom and fiancée chose the option closest to the jail, the ironically named Baltimore Discount Bonds. The price they paid is like the price you get when you buy gas at the last station before the highway.

Bail bond contracts, like the one the Shaws signed, tend to follow a similar formula. They provide that the fee charged—the "premium"—is "fully earned" and "not refundable" once a person is released. They also often give bondsmen full access to all aspects of a bailee's personal life. At Lexington National, for example, one of the nation's largest bail bond companies, the standard contract available online gives the bail agent access to all "credit reports, Social Security Records, criminal records, civil records, driving records, tax records, telephone records, medical records, school records, worker compensation records, and employment records," as well as the right to "attach a location tracking device on any vehicle owned or driven" by the bailee.

Shaw's mother, Rosetta Wise, told me she is the principal guarantor on her son's bail contract. She said the bondsman calls her every few weeks, threatening garnishment if the debt isn't paid. Once, Shaw said, the bondsman came to offer a deal: $2,000 now to wipe out the debt. They couldn't afford it.

Wise has been covering the last several months of payments while Shaw and Destiny try to get back on their feet. Shaw continues to work at U-Haul, and Destiny works in the flower shop and the deli at a local supermarket, but her schedule is unpredictable and her hours have been cut back. Complicating matters further is that they have a new baby, Kay, who was four months old at the time I met Shaw.

In mid-September, I visited them at their home, a dilapidated Section 8 first-floor apartment in East Baltimore with a bodega in the basement. The living room had a couch against one wall, an armchair, and a baby swing, where Kay was napping in a fuzzy pink and purple polka dot sleeper. A flat-screen TV, tuned to Disney Junior, was the sole indulgence. There was one window, and no pictures hung on the beige-gray walls that may once have been cream. "There's no way I can pull it off," said Shaw of the $100 payments he owes each week.

But it bothered him that his mother is paying the bondsman, and it was a clear source of tension between his mother and Destiny. In a speakerphone call while I was there, Shaw's mother and his fiancée started disputing who paid what and how much. "You see what bail does to a family?" Shaw said.

Bail bondsmen call the fees they charge "premiums" in part to justify their non-refundability, but also because they argue that what they're providing is "insurance."

"Bail is similar to homeowners' or auto insurance," said Jeff Kirkpatrick, a bail bondsman in Jackson, Michigan, who is also executive vice president of the Professional Bail Agents of the United States, a trade association. "Say you went to jail for shoplifting or larceny and the judge set your bail at $10,000," Kirkpatrick told me. "In most states, you would pay 10 percent to 15 percent of that bond amount as a premium. In return, the bond agent is guaranteeing the court that should you fail to appear and the bail agent failed to produce you, they would pay the court that $10,000."

In truth, the "premiums" paid by defendants cover the fees that bail agents themselves pay to large insurance companies to guarantee payment on a bail bond. If somebody jumps bail, a bondsman calls on his insurer; he doesn't put up the cash himself or deed over his house. Bondsmen are essentially brokers for these bigger firms. In Rafiq Shaw's case, for example, his court files indicate that the surety of record is Crum & Forster Insurance, a subsidiary of a Toronto-based international conglomerate, Fairfax Financial Holdings Limited. Crum & Forster is one of fourteen national insurance companies and several regional insurance companies that specialize in cash bail. Many of them are members of the American Bail Coalition, another trade association for the bail industry.

The profit a bondsman makes is the difference between the premiums charged to a defendant and the premiums the bondsman has to pay the insurance company. That gives bondsmen an incentive to ensure that their clients show up in court: forfeiting a bond would have the same effect on their insurance as totaling a car. Kirkpatrick argued that this aspect of his business is a public service. "The bail agents do all the work they do at no cost to the taxpayer," he said. "It's one of those public-private partnerships that work really well. We've done a very good job of making sure that suspects appear."

But the biggest "risk" bondsmen seem to assess is whether defendants can pay their premiums. While shows like *Dog the Bounty Hunter* have popularized the idea of fearless bondsmen on the hunt for dangerous suspects, real-life bail bonding has more in common with the sketchier side of the financial services industry than with law enforcement. The website of the Professional Bail Agents of the United States includes a page titled "How to Become a Bail Agent." Half of the text is about choosing an insurance company to back your bail bonds; there is nothing about physical risk. "The bail profession is probably more about whom you know (or rather who knows you) than what you know," the site says.

Moreover, police officers are often the ones who end up doing the work of finding defendants who jump bail. "Of those that fail to appear, it's not bondsmen who bring them in," said Steve Chin, a pretrial services officer in Mesa County, Colorado, and spokesman for the Colorado Association of Pretrial Services. "Ninety percent of them are being arrested by law enforcement. The only ones I see bondsmen bring in are the ones who've made an agreement with a bondsman for a fee and didn't pay it back."

Nonetheless, the bail industry has worked hard to insulate its position by pursuing and winning favorable legislation in the states. For example, while some states, like Maryland, cap premiums at a fixed percentage, other states also set a *minimum* amount, eliminating room for price competition. In Virginia, for example, state law requires that bail bondsmen "shall not charge a bail bond premium less than 10 percent or more than 15 percent of the amount of the bond." Some states have also passed laws requiring judges to set money bail for certain kinds of offenses, such as domestic violence, thereby foreclosing judges from other options, such as release on personal recognizance. For example, until the recent passage of bail reform legislation that goes into effect next year, New Jersey required money bail for eighteen offenses, including murder and kidnapping but also resisting arrest, theft by extortion, and "corrupting or influencing a jury." Many jurisdictions also rely on "bail schedules" that require fixed amounts of bail for particular offenses with no discretion for judges. In Los Angeles County, for example, a charge of first-degree robbery carries a mandatory bail of $100,000. Other states grant bondsmen grace periods of up to two years before a bond is fully forfeited. In Florida, for example, bondsmen have up to two years to produce a no-show before they forfeit a bond. Even if the police happen to pick up a fugitive on a bench warrant, the bondsman still gets a refund if he "substantially attempt[ed]" to find a defendant.

Many of these industry-favorable laws were passed during the 1990s as the result of an extensive effort by the conservative American Legislative Exchange Council to promote the bail bond industry. The ALEC website still includes model legislation for a variety of pro-bail bills, including variants of the legislation recently passed by New Jersey to require bail for certain offenses (the Alternative Method of Court Appearances Act and the Crimes with Bail Restrictions Act); a replica of the Florida legislation providing a grace period for bondsmen to track down bail jumpers (the Bail Forfeiture Relief and Remissions Act); and a proposal requiring the expiration of bail bonds after thirty-six months (the Bail Bonds Expiration Act).

No one really knows how big the commercial bail bond industry is in the United States. Some of the nation's largest bail bond insurers are either foreign owned, such as Crum & Forster, or privately held, such as the American Surety Company, whose president is also chairman of the American Bail Coalition. A 2012 study by the Justice Policy Institute estimated that the industry writes roughly $14 billion in bail bonds per year, and the Professional Bail Agents of the United States says that there are about 14,000 bail agents nationwide.

"If I just wanted to make a lot of money, I'd get into the bonding business," said Cherise Fanno Burdeen, executive director of the Pretrial Justice Institute, a nonprofit research and advocacy group that opposes the use of cash bail. "It's high profit and almost zero risk."

Many defendants, however, can't afford a bail bondsman's services. Instead, they stay in jail until trial. It's the flip side of the damned-if-you-do, damned-if-you-don't nature of a criminal justice system that runs on money bail.

In fact, the majority of people currently in the nation's jails are defendants legally presumed innocent and awaiting trial. According to the U.S. Bureau of Justice Statistics, 467,500 of the nation's 744,592 jail inmates in mid-2014—or 63 percent—were "unconvicted" defendants in pretrial status, up from roughly 56 percent of the nation's 621,149 jail inmates in 2000. Most are unlikely to commit new crimes or fail to show up in court. According to a 2015 survey by the National Association of Counties, 69 percent of county jail administrators judged the majority of their inmates to be "low-risk" defendants.

One reason for the rise in pretrial inmates is a rise in the use of money bail. The Bureau of Justice Statistics reports that judges set money bail on two-thirds of felony defendants in 2004, compared to half in 1990. Much of the time, the bail amounts are too high for a defendant to afford, even with the help of a bondsman. According to the same Bureau of Justice Statistics report, just one in ten defendants with bail set at $100,000 or more was released, compared to seven in ten for defendants facing bail of $10,000 or less. One study of defendants in Harris County, Texas, found that 39 percent of felony defendants with bail of $2,000 or less couldn't afford to get out, as well as 22 percent of misdemeanor defendants with bail of $500 or less.

The inability to afford bail can have serious collateral consequences for defendants. For example, research by the Laura and John Arnold Foundation found that people detained pretrial were more than four times more likely to be sentenced to jail than people who were released, more likely to be given longer sentences, and more likely to be recidivists. People in jail are less able to meet with their lawyers, point them toward important witnesses, and put together the best defense. The disruptions resulting from staying in jail might mean the loss of a job or housing, which leads to economic instability or other consequences that could prompt a rearrest. People in pretrial detention are also more likely to plead guilty before the trial, because that might be the only way to avoid spending months or years in jail awaiting their time in court.

In Baltimore, defendants who can't make bail within twenty-four hours of their arrest are entitled to a bail review hearing, which takes place every morning at 11 at the district court on Wabash Avenue. At the hearing, a judge reviews the district court commissioner's initial bail determination to decide if the bail amount should be changed. Similar proceedings take place in many other jurisdictions around the country, and in Baltimore, at least, the result is yet one more level of capriciousness in the cash bail system.

While hearings take place in district court, the defendants are still in lockup at central booking. They appear in court via video on a screen at the left wall of the courtroom. This means that defendants who have questions for their attorneys can't confer with their counsel in private. The resolution is grainy, and what you see are about a dozen men in yellow jumpsuits, mostly black or Hispanic, seated four at a time in rows of folding chairs with one empty chair up front.

Individual faces are too difficult to make out—which is perhaps fitting, given the routinized nature of each hearing. Under Maryland law, the judges who hear bail reviews are

PHOTO 4.5.2 Open for business: Bail bonding storefronts line Eager Street in Baltimore, conveniently across the street from the city jail.

supposed to consider a variety of factors in deciding the conditions of a defendant's release. These factors include not just the nature of the crimes charged, but also the defendant's family ties in the area, work history, and prior record of appearances, as well as the recommendation of pretrial services, prosecutors, and the defendant's own attorney. But within this structure, judges have immense discretion.

"It matters so much who the judge is," Baltimore assistant public defender Nila Bala, one of the attorneys assigned to bail reviews, told me. "That matters more than anything else—more than the client, the charges, me, the state's attorney, or any other factor. And the judges vary widely in what they will do in certain cases."

To defend her clients, Bala drives to central booking at 7:30 every morning to interview the clients who are due for their hearings that day. She has about an hour to speak to her dozen clients before she jumps back in her car to get to the courthouse on time. If she's lucky, she has spent ten minutes with each of them—most of it spent shouting on a phone through a glass partition, surrounded by other lawyers and their clients all doing the same thing. Bala said her goal is to persuade the judge to reduce her clients' bail—or at least not increase it.

But on this day in September, her victories are few.

Judge Kent Boles, who is presiding today, calls a defendant on the screen, who shuffles toward the empty chair up front. Boles recites the charges and asks if the defendant understands the crimes he's been accused of committing. After a rapid-fire rundown of the defendant's address, education level, and prior record by a representative of pretrial services, the state's attorney argues to maintain the current bail or even increase it, based on statements provided by police and witnesses. The defendant's attorney then has a chance to respond. Much of what's presented at these hearings is hearsay evidence that would likely be inadmissible at trial, but no objections or cross-examinations are permitted. Each hearing takes about ten minutes.

First up is Michael Atkinson, who faces four charges of first-degree assault, second-degree assault, and conspiracy to commit assault. His bail was initially set at $50,000, and pretrial services notes a failure to appear from 2004. Bala points out that this occurred more than a decade ago and asks for a reduction in bail to $10,000. The request is denied.

Next up is Khourtney Woodard, charged with possession of drugs with intent to distribute and currently held without bail. Bala's colleague, public defender Elizabeth Whitman, argues that a defendant who is arrested for nonviolent drug violations, and who is a lifelong resident of Baltimore and unlikely to flee the city, should be allowed to bail himself out.

A few minutes after Whitman makes her case, the judge reduces Woodard's bail to $500,000—a meaningless reduction for an indigent defendant.

The cases quickly take on a numbing sameness.

Emmanuel Rose. Armed robbery, second-degree assault, and theft of less than $100. Initial bail: $100,000. No reduction.

Samuel Faust. Handgun on person. Initial bail: $200,000. No reduction.

In one case, Boles reduces bail from $50,000 to $25,000. The defendant is Amir Barnes, who is charged with possession with intent to distribute. Bala argues that Barnes has no prior record and was caught with only ten grams of marijuana.

Court records show that Barnes was later able to bail himself out. The surety of record: Lexington National, one of the nation's largest commercial bail companies.

Under a system of cash bail, a defendant's pretrial freedom is largely a function of his wealth—not about the risk of reoffending or failing to show up in court. Judges might set higher bail amounts for defendants they perceive as higher risk—on the theory that they won't get out—but demanding a cash ransom is a poor way to protect public safety. Indigent defendants who can't afford even token amounts of bail stay trapped in jail as if they were high-risk suspects likely to commit new crimes or flee. Meanwhile, a murderer with money could be out on the streets. The only ones who profit from this inefficiency and injustice are the bondsmen.

There is a simple solution to the myriad of problems caused by money bail: Abolish it.

What happens instead to defendants awaiting trial should depend on their actual risk to public safety and the odds of their being a no-show in court. Under a "risk-based" system such as this, judges first decide whether a defendant is safe enough to release pending trial. Dangerous defendants stay in, while lower-risk defendants get out. The conditions of release for these lower-risk defendants, however, would depend on the likelihood of their flight or rearrest. For example, some defendants might be required to check in weekly with a pretrial services officer, while others might simply be released on their own recognizance. Still others might be required to post a money bond, but the amount would depend on their ability to pay.

The states that have already moved or are moving to such a risk-based system are Kentucky, Colorado, Alaska, and New Jersey, all of which have recently passed or are implementing bail reform legislation that would dramatically reduce, if not end, the use of cash bail. In November, New Mexico voters approved a constitutional amendment prohibiting the detention of defendants solely because of their inability to pay bail.

(In the District of Columbia—which long ago effectively eliminated money bail—the pretrial justice system has come under fire for high-profile mistakes in releasing defendants due to what the *Washington Post* editorial board characterized as the lack of "a sound system that uses reliable data to assess risks.")

One factor driving this current wave of bail reform is new research finding that alternatives to up-front money bail work better to ensure that defendants show up in court.

A 2013 study by the Pretrial Justice Institute, funded by the Department of Justice, found that "unsecured" bonds, which require no money up-front but are due in full if someone skips town, are just as effective as traditional cash bail in ensuring court appearances and preventing rearrests. In a controlled experiment in Colorado, defendants released on an unsecured bond, regardless of their risk, were less likely to commit new crimes than defendants released on traditional money bail. And all but the highest-risk defendants were more likely to show up in court.

A 2011 study funded by the Justice Department also found that simply mailing defendants a reminder to show up in court significantly reduced the number of people who failed to appear. In an experiment involving more than 7,800 misdemeanor defendants in Nebraska, only 8.3 percent failed to show up after getting a mailed reminder about their court date, along with information about what would happen if they failed to show. By comparison, 12.6 percent of defendants who got no such reminder were no-shows.

A second factor driving bail reform is the emergence of new evidence-based tools—known as "risk assessment instruments"—to help judges decide whether a defendant should be released into the community and on what conditions. These instruments are helping to make a "risk-based" alternative to cash bail viable.

In Colorado, for example, which passed bail reform legislation in 2013, many judges now use the Colorado Pretrial Assessment Tool (CPAT), a twelve-question matrix that assesses a defendant's risk of flight and danger to the community using such variables as age of first arrest, prior failures to appear, and current mental health issues or alcohol and drug problems.

Although Colorado still has a commercial bail bond industry, it has shrunk dramatically since the passage of the new law, said Steve Chin of the Colorado Association of Pretrial Services. In Mesa County, where Chin works, the use of traditional money bail fell from 65 percent of cases in 2011 to 39 percent in 2014 without any increase in rates of failures to appear or new crimes committed by defendants released into the community.

A third factor driving reform is that states are realizing how expensive it is to house all these inmates awaiting trial, especially when so many of them are "low-risk." According to the Arnold Foundation, the cost of pretrial detention alone is at least $9 billion a year.

Alaska, for example, passed bail reform in the spring of 2016 as part of a sweeping criminal justice reform effort after legislators saw that the state's largest prison—the Goose Creek Correctional Center in Point MacKenzie—was already running out of room after its opening in 2012. According to a report by the Alaska Criminal Justice Commission, Alaska's jail population was growing at three times the rate of overall population growth in the state. Much of this growth was in the pretrial population, which grew 81 percent over the last decade. This growth, the commission found, was driven by reliance on cash bail.

"Our prison population trajectory was such that we'd have to build another prison within the next four years," said state senator John Coghill, the lead sponsor of Alaska's reforms. With the state already spending nearly 10 percent of its budget on corrections, building yet another prison was unpalatable to lawmakers.

As a result of all this activity, momentum is growing at the national level, too. Earlier this year, California Democratic Representative Ted Lieu introduced legislation that would require states to abolish cash bail as a condition of receiving federal grant support for state and local police. In December 2015, the White House convened a conference on excessive fines and fees in the criminal justice system that also included a look at cash bail.

Aspects of money bail are also under fresh judicial challenge. A pending class action suit in the Eleventh Circuit Court of Appeals, *Walker v. City of Calhoun,* is challenging the constitutionality of bail "schedules" like the one in Los Angeles County. In an amicus brief filed on behalf of the plaintiff, an indigent Georgia defendant named Maurice Walker, the U.S. Department of Justice argued that "bail practices that incarcerate indigent individuals before trial solely because of their inability to pay for their release violates the Fourteenth Amendment." And in Maryland, home to Rafiq Shaw, the state attorney general released an advisory opinion in October 2016 concluding that the state's current money bail system could be unconstitutional, on the grounds that imposing bail defendants can't afford may violate the Eighth Amendment's prohibition on "excessive bail" and the Fifth Amendment's guarantee of due process. In late November, the Standing Committee on Rules of Practice and Procedure of the Maryland Court of Appeals recommended overhauling the state's bail system, a significant first step toward reform and one that has taken advocates years to achieve.

By eliminating cash bail, states can ensure that poverty isn't the only reason a defendant stays behind bars, and they can end the predation of low-income defendants by a commercial bail bond industry motivated more by profit than by protecting public safety. Getting rid of money bail would also stop the absurdity of cases like Rafiq Shaw's—where an innocent man is paying for the mistakes of prosecutors and police.

"Bail is not fair," said Shaw, who is now working to get his arrest record expunged so he can find a better job. "I'm not guilty. The case is over."

The era of cash bail should end too.

Reading 4.6

Winding Down the War on Drugs

Reevaluating Global Drug Policy

Maria McFarland Sánchez-Moreno

PHOTO 4.6.1

ANY DISCUSSION ABOUT TRANSNATIONAL ORGANIZED CRIME almost inevitably includes the trade in illicit drugs. A 2011 analysis by the United Nations Office on Drugs and Crime (UNODC) found that illicit drugs constitute the largest income source for transnational crime, accounting for about half of transnational crime proceeds, and one-fifth of all crime proceeds. The UNODC has estimated the value of the 2003 global illicit drugs market to be US$322 billion—higher than the GDP that year of 88 percent of the world's countries.

Organized criminal groups from Mexico and Colombia to Guinea-Bissau, Russia, and Afghanistan obtain vast wealth from various facets of the illicit drug trade. They often use those resources to secure protection for their activities through corruption of state officials. Many of these groups have engaged in extreme violence to enforce their control and intimidate rivals.

Since the early 1960s, the primary international policy response to this trade has been prohibition, criminalization of drug use, possession, production, and distribution, and aggressive enforcement aimed at—as articulated in a 1988 UN General Assembly special session on drugs—creating a "family of nations free of drugs in the twenty-first century," and eliminating drug crops. Governments around the world have poured billions of dollars into combating drugs—some estimate at least US$100 billion a year—to pursue, conduct surveillance on, kill, prosecute, extradite, and imprison kingpins and low-level dealers, in source and destination countries alike. In countries like Colombia and Peru, governments—often with US backing—have fumigated crops, paid farmers to grow different crops, and interdicted shipments.

In their anti-drug zeal, many governments have criminalized even mere use and possession of drugs. As a result, in countries such as the United States, prisons and jails have become engorged with low-level participants in the drug trade, as well as many people who have done nothing more than possess drugs for personal consumption. Those arrested and imprisoned in the United States are disproportionately African American, even though African American and Caucasian persons consume illicit drugs at similar rates. In the United States and elsewhere, those imprisoned for drug offenses often face extremely harsh sentencing regimes. Many countries' drug policies have driven people who use drugs away from HIV testing and prevention services, or evidence-based drug dependency treatment and care, and often made controlled substances, such as morphine, inaccessible for medical use—all in an effort to control a business that supplies between an estiamted 162 million and 324 million consumers a year.

But this approach is now facing strong challenges from several sources. Uruguay and several US states have legalized marijuana, and countries as varied as Portugal and Jamaica have decriminalized some or all drug use. The Global Commission on Drug Policy, a panel of world leaders and prominent intellectuals, has asserted that "the global war on drugs has failed, with devastating consequences." Pressed by the governments of Mexico, Colombia, and Guatemala in 2012, which called for a global review of existing drug strategies, the United Nations has convened a special session of its General Assembly for 2016 to focus specifically on drug policy. There is increasing talk in international settings, including at the Organization of American States, about the need to review and reform drug laws and policies.

Even the US government—historically one of the strongest proponents of aggressive enforcement of criminal prohibitions on drug use, possession, production, and distribution—seems to be changing its tune. In August 2013, in response to state ballot initiatives that legalized marijuana in Washington and Colorado, Attorney General Eric Holder issued new guidance to prosecutors that gave the states some leeway to experiment with legalization. Three senators have recently introduced a bipartisan bill to reclassify marijuana as a drug with legitimate medical use, and to pursue a number of other federal changes to make it easier for states to explore alternative systems to regulate drugs. For the first time, the head of the Office of National Drug Control Policy, Michael Botticelli, has a background in public health, rather than law enforcement, and is himself in long-term substance abuse recovery.

On the foreign policy front, William Brownfield, the assistant secretary of state for international narcotics and law enforcement, has articulated a novel position for the United States: that the international community should accept a flexible interpretation of the UN drug conventions, and tolerate differing countries' drug control policies, so long as they "agree to combat and resist the criminal organizations ... those who market and traffic the product for economic gain." It is still far from clear what this means in practice. The United States has shown little inclination to change its traditional approaches to controlling the drug trade in Central and South America. Nonetheless, Brownfield's statement is a significant departure from past positions.

There are many reasons behind these shifts, including, within the United States, domestic concerns over the massive size and cost of the US system of prisons and jails, concerns over the racially disparate impact of harsh drug sentences on African Americans, the public health imperative of averting millions of new HIV infections among injecting drug users, and public pressure and movement at the state level toward alternate regulatory frameworks for marijuana.

Less discussed in the US context is the main argument being made by some countries at the epicenter of the so-called "drug war": the need to find alternative ways to deal with drug policy, so as not to continue fueling transnational organized crime and the devastation that it wreaks upon weak state institutions. This is a critical concern, and should be a key topic in global public debate around drugs.

Organized Crime and Drugs: Colombia and Beyond

If you talk to officials in US drug law enforcement, many will say that the United States has been tremendously successful in fighting drug-related organized crime. Their poster child is Colombia, where according to the latest UN World Drug Report, overall coca cultivation went down by 25 percent from 2011 to 2012 (more recent figures are not available, however the US estimates substantial reductions from 2007 to 2012 followed by a significant increase in 2014). Over the years, Colombia has extradited thousands of its citizens to the United States to face drug charges. Overall, homicide and kidnapping rates have declined from their peak over a decade ago.

But the Colombia story is not so simple. In the 1980s, Colombia was home to probably the most notorious drug syndicate in history, the Medellín Cartel. Under the ruthless leadership of cocaine kingpin Pablo Escobar—who, along with the brothers Jorge Luis, Fabio, and Juan David Ochoa, became so wealthy through drugs that *Forbes Magazine* included them in their 1987 World's Billionaire's List—the cartel engaged in a bloody "war" aimed in part at getting the Colombian government to ban extraditions to the United States. The car and airplane bombings, assassinations and kidnappings of prominent political figures, and widespread killings at that time led many to label Medellín the "murder capital of the world."

PHOTO 4.6.2 A woman posts flyers for missing women next to carboard figures. The figures honor female victims of Mexico's war on drugs as part of a 2011 peace tour of 12 Mexican states by human rights activists and families of victims of violence to protest drug-related violence.

Escobar, known for offering public officials a choice between *plata o plomo* ("silver or lead" or a bribe or a bullet), bought off or threatened vast sectors of law enforcement, making it extremely difficult to build criminal cases against him.

Colombian security forces, with US backing and covert assistance from the Cali cartel and disaffected former Escobar associates (which organized into a death squad known as the PEPES, or People Persecuted by Escobar), killed Escobar in 1993. The United States then turned its attention to Escobar's major rival, the Cali Cartel, which, with Escobar out of the picture, quickly became the world's most powerful cocaine trafficking organization. Colombian authorities arrested the cartel's leaders, the Rodríguez Orejuela brothers, in the mid-90s, and eventually extradited them to the United States, where they remain in prison after pleading guilty to drug trafficking charges in 2006.

That should have been the end of the "drug war" in Colombia. Instead, as the world turned its attention elsewhere in the mid-90s, others took the reins of the two cartels' operations.

In Medellin, brutal right-wing paramilitary groups descended from the PEPES and new criminal organizations quickly seized control of much of the business. In Cali, the Norte del Valle cartel quickly emerged as a major player. Other groups across the country, including to some extent the Marxist Revolutionary Armed Forces of Colombia (FARC) guerrillas, also took on new roles in a more fragmented but still enormously profitable drug trade.

The paramilitaries' rise was accompanied by yet another bloodbath. Claiming to be fighting the FARC and other left-wing guerrillas, paramilitary forces committed gruesome massacres—dismembering their victims alive, raping women in front of their families, and wiping out entire towns. They killed anyone who got in their way as they seized territory they wanted to control for various reasons—counterinsurgency goals, but also for coca production, or as drug transportation corridors. Illicit drug profits helped pay for their weapons and uniforms, wages for their "soldiers," and for bribes. More than 100 Colombian Congress members and countless other officials have been investigated in recent years for alleged collusion with paramilitaries.

The paramilitaries supposedly demobilized between 2004 and 2006, and Colombia extradited many of their leaders to the United States in 2008. But in the words of a young man I got to know in one of Medellin's low-income neighborhoods, "a dead king is a replaced king." No sooner does one organized crime leader or syndicate get toppled than another boss or group takes over.

As I documented in an extensive Human Rights Watch investigation in 2010, even as they demobilized, many of the paramilitaries' mid-level commanders were waiting in the wings to continue running their criminal organizations. The government calls the groups that are now in charge "criminal gangs" rather than paramilitaries, but the problem remains. The groups are engaged not only in drug trafficking, but also in serious abuses against communities to maintain their control. Violence fluctuates by region and over time, and in many cases the paramilitaries' successors have opted for more low-profile forms of control—such as threats and forced disappearances. But in other places the abuses are flagrant.

In the Afro-Colombian port town of Buenaventura, atrocities by paramilitary successor groups such as the Urabeños—known for the "chop houses" at which they have dismembered their victims—have caused the highest rate of forced displacement in Colombia, with tens of thousands of residents fleeing their homes every year. In some cases, government authorities have been known to tolerate or collude with the groups, impeding progress toward ending their control.

While coca cultivation seems to be down—reasons may include increased interdiction, fumigation, and eradication in source countries in South America, as well as decreased consumption in the United States—US efforts to shut down drug trafficking routes from Colombia to the United States have turned Mexico into a key transit point for cocaine. Mexico is also a major supplier of cannabis, and a transit point for opioids from Asia as well as methamphetamine.

Indeed in Mexico, an aggressive US-backed offensive against the country's drug syndicates started under the administration of Felipe Calderón, Mexico's president from 2006 to 2012. It resulted in large numbers of killings, arrests, and extraditions to the United States. Sinaloa cartel chief, Joaquín "El Chapo" Guzmán, who some portrayed as the world's most-wanted drug lord, was arrested in February 2014. But the offensive was accompanied by a dramatic escalation in violence by the cartels, which have become infamous for gruesome, highly visible crimes, as well as a disturbing increase in violence by security forces. And after all the death and destruction, it is far from clear whether the strategy has done much to fundamentally weaken the power of cartels in Mexico.

After decades of going along with US-backed tough enforcement approaches, in a 2012 letter to the United Nations, the presidents of Colombia, Mexico, and Guatemala expressed their frustration at this vicious cycle of organized crime, violence, and corruption. "Despite the efforts of the international community over decades," they said in a 2012 statement decrying the failure of prohibitionist strategies, "drug consumption keeps rising ... and generating substantial profits for criminal organizations worldwide [that] are capable of penetrating and corrupting state institutions." As long as current drug policies remain unchanged, they said, the flow of resources to organized crime from drugs and weapons "will continue to threaten our societies and governments."

Nor is this problem limited to Latin America. In many countries, illicit drug profits are a huge incentive for groups that commit atrocities and corrupt authorities, and undermine democracy and the rule of law.

A prime example is Afghanistan: since the Taliban government was overthrown in 2001, Afghanistan has experienced more than a decade of international military involvement and received hundreds of billions of dollars in aid, including substantial counternarcotics assistance. But it remains the world's largest opium producer, generating around 80 percent of the world supply. The illegal opium market and its billions in profits have dramatically distorted Afghanistan's power structure, bankrolling armed groups including the Taliban, as well as local warlords, government officials, militia forces responsible for numerous atrocities, and others. It also fuels rampant corruption, ultimately undermining the goals that the international community claims to be pursuing in the country.

Human Rights and Policy Implications

From a human rights perspective, the "war on drugs" is problematic on a number of levels: the criminalization of personal use and possession of drugs, for example, is itself inconsistent with international human rights standards on privacy and basic principles of autonomy on which all rights depend. Drug law enforcement has often been accompanied by serious rights abuses. These include thousands of extrajudicial killings and the militarization of drug treatment in Thailand's 2003 "war on drugs"; killings, torture, and enforced disappearances by security forces in Mexico; routine police brutality against people who use drugs in Canada, Kazakhstan, Bangladesh, Ukraine, and Tanzania; and the use of the death penalty against drug offenders in Indonesia, Singapore, Malaysia, Iran, and China.

The abuses also include disproportionately harsh sentencing and racially disparate treatment of drug offenders in the United States; mass incarceration in prisons that pose a high risk of HIV infection; death by overdose and other drug-related health conditions in Russia; denial of access to essential pain medicines to millions of people suffering from cancer and other illnesses; and detention in the name of treatment of people suspected of using drugs in abusive drug detention centers in Cambodia, Vietnam, China, and Laos.

Countries could arguably address these concerns without dramatically overhauling current drug policies such as by: decriminalizing personal use and possession of drugs; imposing stricter limits on security forces and holding them accountable for abuses; reforming criminal laws and practices that result in disproportionately harsh punishments; expanding voluntary, community-based drug dependence treatment; and eliminating regulatory or other obstacles that make pain medication or necessary medical care difficult to obtain. Indeed, these are critical steps, and it is encouraging to see some countries, primarily in Latin America and Western Europe, moving in this direction.

But none of those measures would deal with the basic problem the governments of Colombia, Mexico, and Guatemala have highlighted: that the illicit market in drugs by its nature generates massive profits for organized crime. As academics have observed, not all criminal organizations engage in high rates of violence at all times—the extent of violence may well vary according to the extent of their control, competition, and the protection schemes they are able to establish with state officials, among other factors. But far too often, they have committed atrocities. And in many countries, the enormous resources at these groups' disposal allow them to bribe or intimidate officials and escape justice, ultimately hollowing out the government institutions responsible for protecting all rights.

This is not to say that drugs are the only factor behind organized crime and violence in many of these societies—Colombia's five-decade war also has political and ideological underpinnings, and in Mexico, the country's crime syndicates are involved in many illicit businesses, not just drugs. Afghanistan's corruption problems go much deeper than the drug trade. Should the illicit drug trade disappear, criminal groups in these countries would no doubt seek other sources of illicit income. But it is far from clear that those sources of income would be as profitable and resilient as illicit drugs.

This is one reason why Human Rights Watch and an increasing number of other voices have called for a reexamination of existing drug policies—not only regarding drug use and possession, but also the drug trade.

Finding alternative ways to regulate production and distribution and cut into illicit drug profits would allow governments around the world to increase accountability in drug markets. That would ensure that profits go to legal entities, weaken the influence of organized crime, and reduce abuses—killings, torture, disproportionate sentencing, and barriers to access to health care—that governments often commit in the name of fighting drugs.

Potential alternatives to current policies are largely untested. It will also take a long time for the results of recent legalization efforts to become clear—and given the small sizes of the markets in Uruguay and the US states that have legalized marijuana, such results may not be that informative. Nonetheless, as noted in UNODC's World Drugs Report, at least one study conducted before the legalization in Washington and Colorado estimated that legalization of marijuana in one or two US states would have likely ripple effects in other states, lowering the price of marijuana nationwide and significantly cutting into Mexican cartel profits.

A shift in drug policy does not mean that illicit drugs like heroin or cocaine can or should be as freely available as alcohol or tobacco. But researchers have developed theoretical models for potential regulation, with both privatized and state-controlled supply, and with varying ways of handling licensing, taxation, treatment, public health education, marketing, and the protection of children. And new jurisdictions are beginning to put these models into practice.

Changing policies does, of course, carry risks of new problems or human rights concerns, and so governments around the world need to assess proposed solutions carefully. One key question will be how to effectively crowd out the black market in drugs, which requires addressing issues related to drug prices, safety, availability, and other factors. Governments will also have to examine how to protect children from illicit drug use, and expand access to appropriate drug dependency treatment and care.

Conclusion

Despite some of the changes US policymakers have recently adopted, the United States and the international community have a long way to go. The US call for flexibility in interpreting the drug conventions does not address the fact that some parts of those conventions simply need to be changed, if countries are to be allowed genuine experimentation with drug policy. And while the United States is looking at some domestic changes, it has said next to nothing about shifting its traditional approach to drug policy in countries like Colombia, Mexico, or Afghanistan.

But, with so many countries and prominent voices now questioning the status quo, this is a moment of opportunity. If carried out carefully and correctly, drug reform has the potential to bring substantial benefits for governments, the institutions that protect human rights and the daily lives of people around the world.

Comprehension Questions for Unit IV

Questions for Reading 4.1

1. What are the benefits of investigatory stops, according to advocates of these stops?
2. What is the position of Epp, Maynard-Moody, and Haider-Markel in regard to the benefits and costs of investigatory stops?
3. Based on David Kennedy's research on gang shootings, what are two conditions under which police enforcement is most effective?
4. What is meant by "cascading injustice"?
5. What predictions do the authors make about the impact of new laws that encourage police to hunt for illegal immigrants?
6. According to the authors, is the core of the problem of investigatory stops individual racism and poor exercise of discretion or is it institutional practices?
7. What is the authors' proposal for addressing racial disparities in police stops?

Questions for Reading 4.2

1. List Dianne Post's reasons for opposing the legalization of prostitution.
2. List Bishakha Datta's reasons for favoring the legalization of prostitution.

Questions for Reading 4.3

1. What is Elizabeth's story of how she became an advocate for survivors of human trafficking?
2. What is Marni's story of how she became involved in the issue of sex trafficking?
3. What is Reynel's story?
4. Did reading Reading 4.2 change your mind about the legalization of prostitution?

Questions for Reading 4.4

1. How is the Paul House case a textbook case in wrongful conviction?
2. How does the House case embody the tribulations and frustrations that the wrongly convicted encounter once they are released from prison?
3. According to Balko, why is there good reason to believe that the 268 cases in which DNA evidence has proven innocence (at the time Balko published his article in 2011) do not begin to scratch the surface?
4. How does criminal snitching threaten the integrity of the justice system?
5. What five causes of wrongful convictions does Balko cite?
6. What is a "culture of misconduct"?

Questions for Reading 4.5

1. What is the difference between the theoretical purpose of bail and how it actually works?
2. What are the reasons why Baltimore's for-profit bail bond industry is thriving?
3. Many defendants cannot afford a bail bondsman's services, so they remain in jail. What key facts does Kim reveal about those who go to jail?
4. What are the collateral consequences for defendants if they cannot afford bail?
5. What factors are driving the current wave of bail reform?

Questions for Reading 4.6

1. Do the authors frame the war on drugs as a white-collar crime problem, street crime problem, organized crime problem, or none of the above?
2. Describe the primary criminal justice policy response to the drug trade since the early 1960s.
3. From what sources is this policy response facing strong challenges?
4. What are the reasons behind shifts in state, national, and international drug policies?
5. From a human rights perspective, how is the war on drugs problematic?

Printed by Libri Plureos GmbH in Hamburg,
Germany

9 781793 544216